Richard Blower

LAURA THOMPSON is a writer and freelance journalist. She won the Somerset Maugham Award for her first book, *The Dogs*, and is also the author of the critically acclaimed biography of Nancy Mitford, *Life in a Cold Climate* (2003), *Agatha Christie: An English Mystery* (2007), and *A Different Class of Murder: The Story of Lord Lucan* (2014).

laurathompson.co.uk

Also by Laura Thompson

The Dogs: A Personal History of Greyhound Racing

Quest for Greatness

Newmarket

Life in a Cold Climate: A Biography of Nancy Mitford

Agatha Christie: An English Mystery

A Different Class of Murder: The Story of Lord Lucan

Additional Praise for *The Six*

"An engrossing group biography." —*The New York Times Book Review* (Editors' Choice)

"Meticulously researched, elegantly written . . . An artful history of a most enthralling family."
—*The Atlantic* ("Best Books We Missed in 2016")

"Riveting. *The Six* captures all the wayward magnetism and levity that have enchanted countless writers without neglecting the tragic darkness of many of the sisters' life choices and the savage sociopolitical currents that fueled them." —Tina Brown, *The New York Times Book Review*

"Lively, gossipy, and at times quite moving." —*The Boston Globe*

"Thompson's biography of some of the most infamous sisters of the twentieth century explores the answer to the question: How did one family produce such a remarkable range of [women]?" —*Time*

"Smart, jaunty, and wittily entertaining . . . Steeped in Mitford lore and mythmaking, the book offers sharply drawn portraits of each woman, teases out the complexities of their fraught, competitive relationships with one another, and sets their lives within the context of a radically changing world."
—*Kirkus Reviews* (starred review)

"I was enthralled and charmed by this group biography of all six Mitford sisters, which tells the intertwined stories of their stylish, scandalous lives in a fresh and admirably concise way—and with a striking contemporary sensibility, too."
—*Bookseller* (Editor's Choice)

"Engaging . . . Thompson's is an astute, highly readable and well-assembled book, and she writes with particular intelligence about the sisters' self-mythologizing and their ongoing hold on the public imagination."
—*The Observer* (UK)

"Thompson is marvellous at mapping and explicating the webs or skeins of sibling rivalry [in this] gripping and appalling family saga."
—*The Times* (UK)

"The first book to consider 'the whole six-pack' in the post-Mitford age. And what a remarkable story it is. . . . Thompson retells the story with great style and illuminating detail."
—*The Independent* (UK)

"Thompson has written this book with generosity and delicacy. It is amusing, poignant, and perceptive as a portrait of the sisters' long lives and changing times, and of their own apparent inability to change with them."
—Book Oxygen

"A breezy vigorous argument for the sisters' powerful, unrepeatable significance . . . Thompson combines a subtle understanding of history with enjoyably crisp, tart insights: This is an excellent place either to begin with the Mitfords or proceed with them."
—*Mail on Sunday* (UK)

"I was captivated by this group biography, which tells the story of the Mitfords' sensational lives in a fresh and concise way."
—*Sunday Express* (UK)

"A wonderful telling of an extraordinary family living in extraordinary times."
—*Gazette & Herald* (UK)

"This is a careful, realistic assessment of their virtues, follies, and charm."
—*Daily Mail* (UK)

THE SIX

The Lives of the Mitford Sisters

LAURA THOMPSON

Picador
St. Martin's Press
New York

picadorusa.com • picadorbookroom.tumblr.com
twitter.com/picadorusa • facebook.com/picadorusa

Picador® is a U.S. registered trademark and is used by Macmillan Publishing Group, LLC, under license from Pan Books Limited.

For book club information, please visit facebook.com/picadorbookclub or email marketing@picadorusa.com.

The Library of Congress has cataloged the St. Martin's Press edition as follows:

Names: Thompson, Laura, 1964– author.
Title: The six : the lives of the Mitford sisters / Laura Thompson.
Other titles: Take six sisters. | Lives of the Mitford sisters
Description: First U.S. edition. | New York : St. Martin's Press, [2016] | Previously published: Take Six Girls. London : Head of Zeus, 2015. | Includes bibliographical references and index.
Identifiers: LCCN 2016024061| ISBN 9781250099532 (hardcover) | ISBN 9781250099556 (ebook)
Subjects: LCSH: Mitford, Nancy, 1904–1973. | Mitford, Pamela, 1907–1994. | Mosley, Diana, 1910–2003. | Mitford, Unity, 1914–1948. | Mitford, Jessica, 1917–1996. | Devonshire, Deborah Vivien Freeman-Mitford Cavendish, Duchess of, 1920–2014. | Mitford family. | Women authors, English—20th century—Biography. | Authors, English—20th century—Biography. | Sisters—Great Britain—Biography. | Great Britain—Biography.
Classification: LCC DA566.9.A1 T62 2015 | DDC 920.72'0941—dc23
LC record available at https://lccn.loc.gov/2016024061

Picador Paperback ISBN 978-1-250-09954-9

Our books may be purchased in bulk for promotional, educational, or business use. Please contact your local bookseller or the Macmillan Corporate and Premium Sales Department at 1-800-221-7945, extension 5442, or by email at MacmillanSpecialMarkets@macmillan.com.

Originally published in Great Britain by Head of Zeus Ltd under the title *Take Six Girls*

First published in the United States by St. Martin's Press

First Picador Edition: October 2017

10 9 8 7 6 5 4 3

To Louis, the well-beloved

CONTENTS

THE MITFORD FAMILY TREE

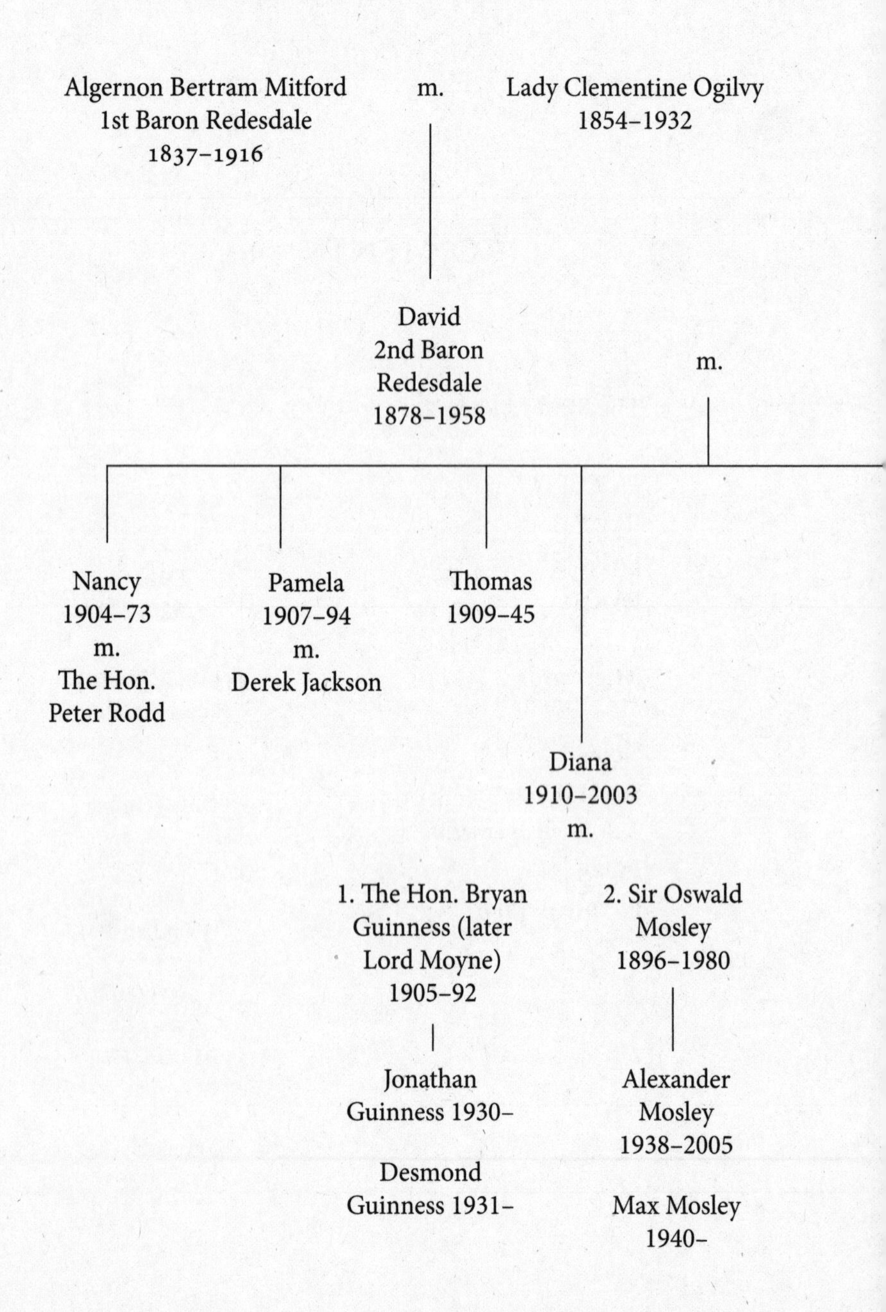

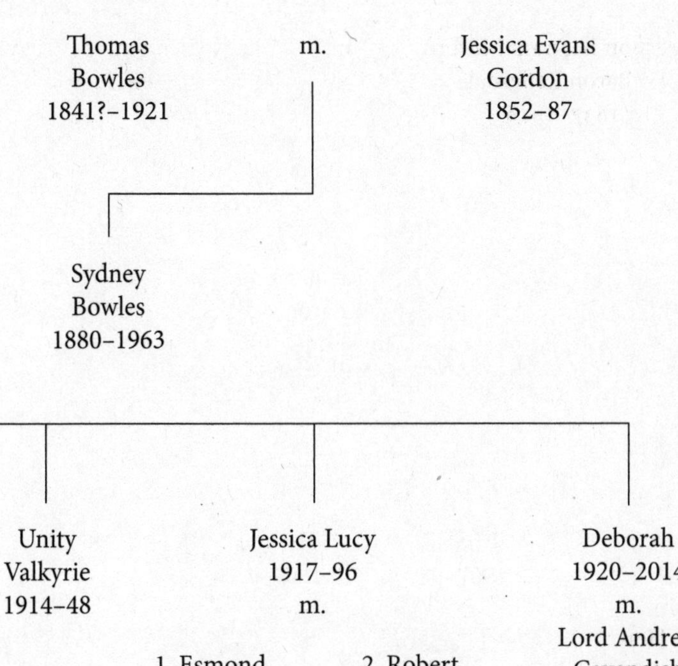

Lord Andrew Cavendish (11th Duke of Devonshire) 1920–2004

1. Esmond Romilly 1918–41

Julia Romilly 1937–38

Constancia Romilly 1941–

2. Robert Treuhaft 1912–2007

Nicholas Treuhaft 1944–55

Benjamin Treuhaft 1947–

Lady Emma Cavendish 1943–

Peregrine Cavendish, (12th Duke of Devonshire 1944–)

Lady Sophia Cavendish 1957–

THE MITFORD PHENOMENON

Take six girls, all of them rampant individualists, and let them loose upon one of the most politically explosive periods in history. That is the story of the Mitfords. It is like a social experiment, the results of which would have staggered even the most imaginative scientist, and no small part of its fascination lies in the fact that the experiment can never be repeated. Never again will there be six such girls, raised in such a way, at such a time.

The Mitford sisters were born in the heart of England, between 1904 and 1920, into a family of pre-Conquest antiquity. Daughters of the 2nd Lord and Lady Redesdale, they were expected to become wives, mothers, propagators of their class, the kind of women who appeared at state balls in slightly ill-fitting satin and tramped through Gloucestershire in good tweed. Something of this steadfast upbringing always remained with them: Nancy Mitford confessed on her deathbed that she would give anything for one more day's hunting. But a world beyond the Heythrop had long since claimed Nancy, and indeed all the girls except Pamela – the shadowy exception who threw the rest into even more powerful light.

One can chant the careers of the Mitford sisters in the manner of Henry VIII's wives, thus: Writer; Countrywoman; Fascist; Nazi; Communist; Duchess. One can recite the mini-biographies, pulling out extraordinary facts with the practised ease of a conjuror. Nancy, an auto-didact who never learned to punctuate (Evelyn Waugh: 'it is not your subject'), became a star author whose 1940s novels *The Pursuit of Love* and *Love in a Cold Climate* are deeply loved popular classics. Pamela, the bucolic chicken-breeder whose blue eyes matched her Rayburn, was adored by the young John Betjeman ('Gentle Pamela, most rural of them all'). Diana, the greatest beauty of her generation, calmly put herself beyond the social pale when she left her perfect husband for the leader of the British Union of Fascists, Sir Oswald Mosley. Unity, conceived in a Canadian town called Swastika, became a fervent Nazi and the close companion of Adolf Hitler. Jessica eloped with her fellow Communist, Esmond Romilly, the nephew (and rumoured son) of Winston Churchill, and proudly set up home among the working classes of Rotherhithe. Deborah became chatelaine of Chatsworth House, the magnificent seventeenth-century seat of the Devonshire family, where she filled her office with Elvis Presley memorabilia.

All this poured out in a great torrent of newsprint when Deborah – 'the Last Mitford Girl' – died in 2014, although the facts were already familiar. Some people may have thought that Nancy was the Fascist and Unity the Communist, but they pretty much had the basic idea. Equally familiar was the collective aspect of the sisters: their irrepressible aristocratic levity, their variations-on-a-theme faces, their idiom. The Mitfords inhabited a linguistic microclimate, whose almost nursery way of speech ('oh do be sorry for me') is famous above all for the nicknames they gave to everybody, especially to each other, which began as a private joke and were later displayed for public consumption. Again, people may have sometimes got things confused and thought that Woman was the Nazi and Honks the Writer, or that Stubby was the Countrywoman and Bobo the Duchess;[1] nevertheless there was an awareness that this was how the Mitfords went on. They all met Hitler and they all called him Hitty or Herr Housepainter. Or something like that.

Some years before she died I interviewed the then Duchess of Devonshire, or Debo, as she was always known (although Nancy –

have you heard this one? – called her 'Nine', after her alleged mental age). She admitted to a brisk bafflement with the whole Mitford industry. 'As for people being interested in all of us now – that's just amazing. But they seem to be, for some reason best known to themselves.' Her sister Diana Mosley (Honks, Bodley, Cord, Nardie), whom I also met, came more sharply to the point. 'The Mitford family has become a frightful bore,' she said, laughing her still-beautiful head off in a very Mitford way (almost silently, as if the mirth were too great for verbal expression). 'It bores us to death!'

Of course one might now say much the same about Henry VIII's wives. Oh God, no, not the one about Anne of Cleves's painting by Holbein. Who doesn't know that one?

Nonetheless, familiarity is undoubtedly an issue with the Mitford story. The life of Unity Mitford should be the subject of an opera, yet it has become more like the punchline to a sick joke – 'And then war was declared and she shot herself!'– than the astonishing, murky tragedy that it was. For familiarity does not merely induce boredom. It deadens significance. And the sisters *were* significant; still are, as a matter of fact. Those who long to rip apart the twee latticework of Mitfordiana – Farve, Muv, Hons' Cupboards[2] – may think otherwise, and I can quite see why, but at the same time I would say: look afresh at the familiar and consider. These girls are prize exhibits in a Museum of Englishness. What they represent is complex, although their image has a divine simplicity. And whatever one's opinion of what they represent, it is impossible, in truth, to find them boring.

As I say, the phenomenon of the Mitford sisters is unrepeatable. The nature of the girls, the nature of the world at that time: such a configuration can never happen again.

In the first place there is the simple fact that the Redesdales had so many children, seven in all (Tom, the only son, born in 1909, is generally overlooked, but his personality was at least as strong and intriguing as that of his sisters). Then there is their upbringing. Although Tom went to Eton, the girls were educated mostly at home, and the three large country houses that the family inhabited –

Batsford Park, Asthall Manor, Swinbrook House – became their imaginative playgrounds. The well-raised modern child has its every moment accounted for (oboe at 4, gluten allergy test at 4.30) and accompanies its parents into almost every adult arena, from saloon bar to Starbucks. The Mitford girls, conversely, lived in a world of their own. They had a freedom that today would seem almost feral. In a literal sense it was limited: they travelled nowhere beyond Scotland, nowhere without Nanny, and they talked to few people outside the family except grooms, governesses and gamekeepers. Their mother could be rigid in outlook, their father would create sudden violent storms about infringements of the behavioural code. Yet in a more profound sense the girls' freedom was near absolute, because nothing really prevented them from indulging their essential natures. How far this was a good thing is open to question, of course. But it made them the Mitfords.

They roamed around their homes, obsessing over books or love or animals (never a photograph without a wonderful dog in it), growing ever more beautiful and hungrier for life, experiencing the perverse stimulation of extreme boredom. They were not all together, all the time. They formed particular alliances: Diana and Tom, Jessica and Unity, Deborah and Jessica. Not least because of age differences, the sisters did not operate as a sextet (with Tom as semi-detached musical director). Nevertheless, and partly because there was nobody else freely available, they sparked off each other like tinder sticks. Competitive family hierarchies were set in place that would last all their lives. Right up to the end, when only Diana and Deborah were left, the Mitford girls remained intertwined in a network of rivalries and alliances.

And indeed, their startling – one might even say theatrical – individuality was all part of that complex, six-ply weave. It sounds facile in the extreme to say that Jessica became a rabid Communist because Unity, the sister to whom she was closest, became a rabid Nazi. It sounds equally glib to say that Unity became a Nazi because Diana – whom she admired and adored – became a Fascist. Yet to some extent these statements are true. Had these girls not grown up in such proximity, competing with or retreating from each other in a constant battling rhythm, they would not have become quite so singular. And had they not lived in such singular times, their individuality would – in some cases at least – have been expressed quite differently.

The Mitford girls came of age in a period of profound and, perhaps more importantly, highly *dramatic* change. Nancy made her society debut on 28 November 1922. The occasion was a ball at Asthall, reported in *The Times*'s court pages with the formal respect then given to the upper classes ('Among those who brought parties to the dance were Countess Bathurst...'), for all the world as if the Edwardian era had never come to an end. The dance for the youngest sister, Deborah, was held at the family's London home on 22 March 1938. Ten days previously, Adolf Hitler had instigated the *Anschluss*, the annexation of Austria by Nazi Germany.

In the sixteen years between the two coming-out balls, politics had become ever more openly polarized and extreme. Communism and Fascism stood at each end of the global chessboard like clumsy monoliths. Democracy seemed a feeble little beast by contrast, bleating of moderation in the face of the aftermath of war and the Russian Revolution, the Great Depression and mass unemployment. Of course Britain did not – as Italy, Spain and Germany did – turn to dictators, but there were many who craved those illusions and certainties, the politics of poster slogans. The British Communist Party was formed in 1920, followed three years later – almost inevitably – by the first, small Fascist Party.

Meanwhile a succession of governments, mostly very short-lived, grappled with the enduring economic crisis and the attendant fear of instability. The 'Zinoviev Letter' of 1924, purportedly an instruction from the president of the Communist International to unleash class war, was taken very seriously. Whatever the truth about the origins of the document, Bolshevik subsidies had indeed been paid to foment unrest; but there was cause enough anyway for real grievance. Unemployment was appallingly high, close to 3 million in 1933. The first of six National Hunger Marches took place a couple of weeks before Nancy's society debut. In 1926 came the General Strike; ten years later, the Jarrow Crusade. In 1929 the first Labour prime minister, Ramsay MacDonald, had appointed the dynamic young MP Sir Oswald Mosley to deal with the unemployment problem, but Mosley went his own way when his radical (though not unpopular) ideas were rejected. He formed the New Party in 1931 then, a year later, the British Union of Fascists.

In Germany, where 7 million were unemployed in 1933, where poverty was dire and a sense of post-war grievance primed to explode, a stark choice presented itself between Communism and Nazism. When Hitler became Chancellor he declared war on Marxism, and for this reason if no other was admired in some British quarters, as Mussolini had been when he took power in 1922. Certain members of the aristocracy were quite open in their desire to make common cause with Hitler: in 1936 the Anglo-German Fellowship held a dinner for Ambassador von Ribbentrop attended by, among others, the Duke of Wellington, Lord Londonderry, and Lord and Lady Redesdale. That same year Lord Redesdale praised Hitler almost unreservedly in the House of Lords, and attacked the press for 'the greatest exaggeration in such matters as the Nazi treatment of the Jews'. Then he came to the heart of the matter: 'Whatever might be said against certain details of his administration, it is certain that Herr Hitler saved Germany from going red.' This was the aristocrat's view. Yet it was shared in some measure by a good many normal, anxious Britons, in whom the terror of Communism ran deeper than can possibly be grasped today. On the other side, within a sizeable part of the intelligentsia – the kind of people whom Stalin was methodically liquidating – Communism represented a vision of alluring idealistic clarity; but it was also a bulwark against Fascism. The fact that these two wildly opposing creeds were, when one came down to it, remarkably similar was perceived by many, including Nancy and Deborah Mitford. But sanity of this sort was not altogether in tune with the 1930s. What was demanded were gesture politics, uncompromising affiliations, solutions based upon theory rather than the hesitant realities of human nature. Young people have always responded to the clarion call of extremism: Diana, Jessica and Unity did not resist.

Nevertheless what they did *was* extraordinary. Again, familiarity has dulled its significance; but again, consider. They were not the only bright young things who flirted with extremism at that time (a cousin, Clementine Mitford, got briefly carried away by the thrill of shiny jackboots), yet the point about the Mitford sisters is that they were *not* flirting, they carried their convictions through. As Deborah wrote of Jessica in 1952: 'Her blasted cause has become so much part of her that she can never forget it.' Can one imagine their equivalent today? A nineteen-year-old Jessica Mitford, absconding to a life with an Islamic fundamentalist? No: a girl of that class might dabble excitably in 'activism', in the sense of waving an anti-fracking banner in Sussex (where her parents have a house) or having a fling with a sexy anti-capitalist protester (who went to school with her brother). Jessica's fellow runaway Esmond Romilly *was* in fact a cousin of the family, an ex-Wellington boy; Jessica, as Nancy wrote in a fictionalized version of the situation, 'had been introduced to him and knew his surname'. Yet when she disappeared in 1937 – supposedly to meet friends in Dieppe, where she never arrived – the skies fell in for her parents. For a fortnight they did not know whether she was dead or alive, and simply sat beside the telephone, waiting for they did not know what. Lord Redesdale never saw Jessica again after seeing her off at Victoria Station. When news of her whereabouts finally arrived, her father is alleged to have said: 'Worse than I thought. Married to Esmond Romilly,' but if he did say this then he didn't mean it. The shock of what Jessica had done – the casual, callous finality with which she disowned her former life – was one from which her parents never recovered (although far worse was to come). 'I nearly went mad when it seemed you had quite disappeared,' Lady Redesdale wrote to her. And for Deborah: 'It was far the worst thing that happened to me.' Forty years after the event, Jessica wrote to Deborah that she was 'v astonished' to have caused her such distress, but the tone of this letter was defensive and not altogether convincing. The point is that back in 1937 Jessica hadn't much cared whom she hurt. Such was the power of the extremist cause, embodied in a man. The man alone might have led her to elope. It was the extremism that led to the swift absolutism with which all else was abandoned.

Usually it is disaffected men who embrace a dramatic ideology, although girls do it too. But the Mitford sisters? Those posh, protected creatures, who rode side-saddle to hounds, who were presented at court, who danced in and out of the great houses of London? Society tends to say of its young rebels: they have nothing to lose. This is not always true, but for sure they would have less to lose than the Mitfords. They had everything to lose. They were the smooth-skinned daughters of privilege. Nor were they too stupid to know what they were doing: Jessica was as sharp as a tack and Diana's idea of light reading was Goethe (her wedding present from Dr Goebbels was a complete set of Goethe's works, bound in pink calfskin). Jessica was also pretty, vital, by all accounts enchanting, while Diana, beautiful as a goddess, had a worshipping husband and two young sons, a life of picture-book perfection in Belgravia. Unity, as Deborah later put it, was 'always the odd one out'; nevertheless she was bright, handsome and popular despite her occasionally unnerving eccentricity.

Of course the sheer idiocy of youth played its part. 'The Führer got into quite a rage twice...it was wonderful,' is a typical phrase from Unity's letters, which sometimes give the impression that Hitler is Mick Jagger and she a favoured groupie circa 1966. But there was more. Something in these young women responded to the dark power of the times. Beneath the sunlit Mitford effervescence ran a deadlier, steadily determined tide. There was a strong sex element in it, in this willingness to embrace the aggressive and unyielding, and it was obviously connected to individual men – but it was still more mysterious than that: extremism calls upon the entire pre-civilized self.

Exactly why, and how, the girls took the paths that they did will be analysed more fully later. The starting point was Diana's deep, complex passion for Sir Oswald Mosley; although she had already been influenced by the intellectual Teutonic sympathies of her forebears. In the context of the period, and of the family dynamic, their behaviour does become just about comprehensible. It also remains almost incredible. 'What lives we do lead,' as Nancy wrote to her mother in 1940, her tone dry and disbelieving.

She had not hurled herself headlong into extremism. The family friend Violet Hammersley once wrote to Nancy, saying 'You Mitfords like dictators,' but this was only half true. Pamela married a Fascist sympathizer and met Hitler ('like an old farmer in a brown suit'), yet she stood quite apart from the behaviour of Diana and Unity. So too did Deborah, who spent the month before the Second World War at a house party for York races. Nancy helped Republican refugees in the Spanish Civil War, then went home to perform frenetic amounts of patriotic war work.

Nevertheless there *was* a characteristic aspect to the politicized girls. It wasn't simply what they did, it was the way they did it: with the smiles-over-steel quality that is definitively Mitford. They were naturally and comfortably shameless. Not necessarily flagrant, although Unity became so in her love of Nazism; more accurate to say that they were shame-free. Their confidence was blithe, adamantine. Whatever the subject matter, the idiom remained that of the nursery. There was a bizarre disconnect between their mode of expression (sweet Hitler, blissful Lenin) and what they were actually doing. The story of Jessica and Unity dividing a room in half, decorating one side with hammers and sickles, the other with swastikas, pretty much sums up the Mitford relationship with politics. Completely sincere, but also attention-seeking: showing off to Nanny.

They did not necessarily court publicity, of which they naturally received a large and damaging amount, but they were not afraid of it. Partly this was in the blood – they had two very showy grandfathers – but it was also *them*, their natures, the spectrum of beauty that they covered, the x 6 aspect that magnified them into something overwhelming. Looking as they did, the Mitford girls were never going to be ignored. Being what they were, they did not want to be. They had a feel for the limelight, a desire to prance in its glow. 'Whoever is going to look at you?' was their nanny's refrain, but that upper-class instinct towards self-effacement – the fear of being vulgar – was not really in them. Nancy was not just a writer, she was a 'celebrity' author (Evelyn Waugh: 'I saw Debo last week. I feel it my duty to tell you that she is spreading a very damaging story about you: that you have allowed yourself to be photographed by the Television.'[3]) She offered up her persona quite willingly, writing a highly opinionated column for the *Sunday Times*, co-operating with a slightly naff musical version of *The Pursuit of Love*[4] and, later, with a projected ITV comedy series based on the lives of the Mitford sisters.[5] Deborah gave numerous interviews as Duchess of Devonshire, and was possibly amused by the ease with which journalists could be coaxed to eat from her hand ('How could *anyone* resist her?'[6]). Diana, although she must have known it was asking for trouble, went on Radio 4's *Desert Island Discs* in 1989. The public reaction to her appearance was predictable outrage; but alongside the Mitford instinct for populism was a total lack of concern about what people thought of them. If they had ever used Twitter, which is not entirely impossible (one can certainly imagine Jessica), they would have roared with laughter at the #poshbitch abuse. They were tough, as well as airy. When Diana and her husband were placed under house arrest in 1943, they were besieged by a pack of pressmen and forced to sit tight with the curtains drawn: 'I would rather be *us* than them', wrote Diana, 'because it is the most frightful weather.' When Nancy wrote her 1955 treatise on class, 'The English Aristocracy',[7] with its famous division of vocabulary into 'U' (upper-class) and 'Non-U' – viz, writing paper versus notepaper – the enraged response left her essentially unshaken. 'Who *are* you anyway?' asked one reader. 'So difficult to answer, really!' was her reaction.

Snobbery, shallowness, stupidity, adultery, unpalatability – the

Mitfords were accused of all these things and rode out every criticism, smiling brightly, talking in that direct yet obtuse way that disarms attack. In Diana this 'never apologize, never explain' quality was intensified to an almost unparalleled degree. It is hard to think of anybody more truly indifferent to public opinion. 'Being hated means absolutely nothing to me as you know,' she wrote to Deborah in 2001. 'I admired him very much,' she said of Hitler on *Desert Island Discs*. 'My husband was a *very* clever man,' she remarked to me, in the same calm beatific way as she said almost everything. It has been suggested, surely rightly,[8] that she was incapable of telling anything other than the truth as she saw it. This made things simple for her, but also very difficult. She refused to defend or exonerate herself. She could have put the blame on circumstances, said that she had got carried away and now saw events differently: but no. Whatever one thinks of her, it has to be said that only a woman in a million would have stood as firm as she did. Instead she wrote articles that argued, with cool cogency, against unquestioned ideas such as the absolute rightness of war against Germany, or the absolute evil of the Vichy regime; she described Hitler as 'a terrible part' of history but refused retrospectively to edit her friendship with him; and her loyalty to Sir Oswald Mosley was so stalwart as to be almost beyond comprehension, like something from a legend. But Diana *did* have a mythic aspect, with her dynamic serenity, her sphinx smile. Even her sisters were confounded by her. Her political allegiances did not affect the remarkable, open-minded kindness that she displayed in every other area of her life. Her constant rippling urge to laughter did not prevent adherence to a creed that took itself insanely seriously. Far more than Jessica and Unity – both strongly influenced by her – Diana was an enigma. In fact she was quite possibly one of the most enigmatic women who ever lived. When people talk about the 'Mitford Girls', it is she and Nancy whom they really mean, because without the separate components of Diana and Nancy the spell of the whole would never have been created.

Diana defined the mysterious, implacable side of the sisters.

Nancy defined their wayward enchantment, their sublime silliness, their use of jokes as an act of defiance ('there is,' as Nancy wrote in a letter when she was dying of cancer, 'always something to laugh at.') This distinction is simplistic, however, because the dual nature of the Mitfords cannot be pulled apart: in its contradictions lie the very heart of their fascination.

There is no such word as 'Mitfordian', but – like Proustian, Dickensian or Gilbertian – it has a meaning. It is understood by people who may know little of the sisters' actual lives, yet who have absorbed their image.

The reason for this is ultimately very simple. The elements that make up the phenomenon of the Mitford sisters are various, complex and contradictory; but what *really* counts is the fact that this phenomenon was parcelled and wrapped and sold with a beautiful great bow on it: by Nancy. She is the begetter of 'the Mitfords'. In 1945 she wrote her family into life in *The Pursuit of Love*. Thereafter she – followed by Jessica in the autobiographical *Hons and Rebels* – nurtured and primed the Mitfordian image until it became the essence of aristocratic charm, accessible yet untouchable, and as dangerously irresistible as a drug.

Without Nancy, the sisters would have had their own separate significance, with Unity the most noteworthy. But their significance en masse – culturally, societally – came from the first Mitford girl. Not necessarily the cleverest of them – that was Diana – but by some measure the most intelligent, Nancy took an overview of her upbringing, gathered it up between her pretty little hands and remoulded it as art. By so doing – by writing *The Pursuit of Love*, that outbreath of familial memory, with its pinpoint accuracy shading into timeless haze – Nancy made of that world something definitive. So *felt* is her novel, it contains within it far more than she could possibly have intended during the three months of its creation. It contains the genesis of the Mitford myth. And the Mitford myth contains, first and foremost, an image of England.

To understand the sisters properly one must go to the Cotswolds, where they grew up, and to the adjacent villages of Asthall and Swinbrook, which was once their father's land. Four of them – Nancy, Unity, Diana and Pamela – are buried in the churchyard of St Mary's, Swinbrook. What strikes one most is how unassuming is this ending place, how embedded in the landscape, how secure in its acceptance of time and death, how unlike the bright frenetic span in which the sisters put their mark upon the world. 'Say not the struggle naught availeth' is the inscription on Unity's gravestone: a very moving thing to read, especially in this calm little square of green, where the silence is absolute except for the tentative bravura of birdsong and a hymn being sung inside an English church. Here, the struggle of Unity's short, misguided life drops away into irrelevance.

From the church – which houses a memorial to Tom Mitford and a set of oak pews paid for by Lord Redesdale's winning bet in the 1924 Grand National – one can walk a mile or so to Asthall Manor, where the greater part of the Mitford childhood was spent. This is where the imaginative lives of the girls were formed: in country the colour of hen pheasants, in a shallow flattened valley scooped from apparently limitless fields, amid drystone walls, fat healthy sheep and the constant rustle of the River Windrush. Asthall itself, dark brown and gabled, stands as rooted as a great tree, with beside it the church, whose graveyard was overlooked by the nursery windows.

Everything about Britain has changed since the Mitford girls lived in this small part of Oxfordshire, yet Asthall and Swinbrook seem not to have changed, and Asthall Manor is a peculiarly beautiful example of that unchanging ideal: the English country house. This magical constancy is the backdrop to *The Pursuit of Love.* Nancy reimagined Asthall as 'Alconleigh', peopled it with her family and described it, not with idealism, but with a ravishing lightness and clarity, like the sun spilling onto the fields at dawn.

It is a construct, of course. The Mitfords were not quite like Nancy's fictional 'Radletts'. Her father's rampaging eccentricity was rendered faithfully, as were his habits – such as writing down the names of people he disliked and putting the paper into a drawer, stuck with pins – but 'Uncle Matthew' was a simpler, more assured man than the real-life Lord Redesdale, and 'Aunt Sadie' a more benign woman than his real-life wife. Although the book covers the same timescale as the one that sent assorted Mitfords dashing towards political extremes, there is no reference to the fact that Lady Redesdale herself was an admirer of Hitler. The grimly naive remarks made by Lord Redesdale about pre-war Germany are also expunged. 'Good God, I never expected to harbour a full-blooded Hun in this house,' says Uncle Matthew, when the son of the Governor of the Bank of England (surname Kroesig) turns up at his daughter's coming-out ball. Nor does *The Pursuit of Love* allude to the dark passions of Unity and Diana, while Jessica's elopement is made light of: the fictional 'Jassy' absconds with a Hollywood film star, and the heroine Linda, who falls for a Communist, does so mainly because he is incredibly good-looking.

Then there is the emphasis that Nancy places upon continuum. The seasons come and go, as does the hunting and the lambing, the rhythms of country life; the Radlett children roam and flit like butterflies, searching for brightness; and Alconleigh itself stands immutable at the heart of it all, rooted in the land with which Uncle Matthew has an ineffable bond.

In fact the Mitfords had three main childhood homes, whose surrounding acres were disposed of in job lots. Lord Redesdale inherited considerable assets when he succeeded to the title in 1916, but he was unable to hold on to them. Batsford Park in Gloucestershire, a fairytale castle of old gold built by his father, was first to go in 1919, together with almost 10,000 acres. In 1926 Asthall Manor and more land was sold. The home that the family had grown to love was replaced with the self-built Swinbrook House, a chilly, over-symmetrical structure perched just outside the village. Nancy gave Alconleigh something of the appearance of Swinbrook – 'It was all as grim and as bare as a barracks, stuck upon the high hillside' – but little of its atmosphere. Only Deborah liked it there. Jessica, aged nine when the family moved to Swinbrook (or 'Swinebrook', as Nancy called it), longed to leave. She collected 'running-away money', and asked repeatedly to be sent to school, a request fulfilled only briefly. When she did escape, Lord Redesdale may have blamed himself for not giving her a happier home, but Jessica's teenage rebelliousness – which lasted well into middle age – was more complex than that. Nevertheless the move to Swinbrook was significant; it was the beginning of the end for the family as an entity. 'We never again had real family life after we left Asthall,'[9] Diana later wrote. Nancy devised a brittle tease about how their fortunes had descended from Batsford PARK to Asthall MANOR to Swinbrook HOUSE, but after Swinbrook was sold in 1938 there were no more country houses at all. That life was over.

The supreme irony about *The Pursuit of Love* is that, by the time it was published, pretty much everything that it represented was vanishing. Not just the world of feudal certainties and communion with the land; but that of the Mitfords themselves. Tragedy and dislocation comes to the fictional Radletts, yet the family remains essentially secure in itself, eternal despite the passage of time. In real life, the thunderous ideologies of the 1930s – so impersonal, so destructive of personal happiness – left the Mitfords bereft and broken.

For Nancy, there was creative glee in writing *The Pursuit of Love*, but it was also an act of poignant salvation. She was celebrating what had been lost: her own past, as well as that of her kind. And in doing so she triggered a public response that has never really faded.

After the war, and despite the election of the 1945 Labour government (for which Nancy herself voted), it seemed that people still craved what the 'Radletts' had: an ease, an unhurried confidence, a charm that made life a less exigent, more reassuring business, above all a rooted sense of Englishness. Certainly people liked reading about these things. As with *Brideshead Revisited*, also published in 1945, *The Pursuit of Love* was an instant, stunning success. It sold 200,000 copies within a year, 1 million copies by the time of Nancy's death in 1973, and even now – when the upper classes are about the only minority that can be attacked with impunity – it is as popular as it has ever been. So too is its 1949 successor, *Love in a Cold Climate*, in which the Radletts prance on the sidelines but the central drama exerts the same fundamental enchantment.

Nancy Mitford was an artist. Not major league, but nobody else could do quite what she did. She told her stories in such a way as to encapsulate – to *become* – the essence of what she was writing. As time went on she became the smiling gatekeeper to a particular image of England (rather than Britain), irresistible not just for its content but for the way in which this was presented. Nancy did not write about the upper classes as her friend Evelyn Waugh did, with an awed seriousness beneath the jokes: she treated them as if they were the most normal thing in the world – which, to her, they were. Nor did she satirize her characters, even the fabulously comedic ones. Her tone was innately good-natured and accepting. Yet her humour, which ran as deep and essential as the marrow in her bones, enabled her to see what she was, and to laugh at it; even though she believed in it.

Nancy offered up the aristocracy with a light touch, without self-consciousness. She exemplified the almost childlike lack of fear in the upper classes, their refusal to throw veils of half-embarrassed discretion over what they are or say. Take, for instance, the reaction of Linda Radlett to her new-born baby. 'It's really kinder not to look,' she says to her friend Fanny, who is equally appalled by the 'howling orange' in its swaddling. Now this is a reaction shared by many obliged to coo over cots, but few would dare to express it, and anybody who did would draw attention to their own daring. Nancy felt no such need. She said outrageous things with exactly the same polite, feminine precision as she said anything else. Linda, embarking on a train journey to Spain, tells Fanny that she dreads the journey alone. You may not be alone, says Fanny: 'Foreigners are greatly given, I believe, to rape.' 'Yes, that would be nice...' In *Love in a Cold Climate* another baby is born, this time to beautiful Polly and her creepy husband; it 'took one look, according to the Radletts, at its father, and quickly died again'. One's laughter at this is partly shock, but Nancy was never shocked, nor shockable. Her manners were impeccable, but she was delicately careless of the proprieties. And her refusal to be serious is the most subversive thing of all. When she arrived at Perpignan to work with Spanish Civil War refugees – a hard, distressing job that she performed with caring competence – she was nevertheless unable to resist saying that Unity was also on her way to help. Nothing quite that off-colour ever made it into her novels. They were not, as has been said, the whole truth: they turned the truth into a commodity.

What defines Nancy's writing – its Mitfordian quality – is the sincerity of her levity. All the sisters had this trait, as to an extent did their father. They brought it out in each other, and sometimes played to the gallery with it: as in Jessica's *Hons and Rebels*. But it *was* their natural idiom. A supreme example came from Diana, when she and Mosley were jailed in 1940 as suspected enemy sympathizers, and for three years in Holloway she endured unspeakable conditions and mental anguish. Nevertheless, as she put it to her husband, 'it was still lovely to wake up in the morning and feel that one was lovely *One*.' This remark, with its almost painful funniness born of pain, its lightness born of indomitability, above all its complete naturalness (Diana wasn't trying to be funny, she was simply saying what she meant) is wholly Mitfordian. So too is the private system of jokes, now so familiar that all those nicknames, all that Tuddemy (Tom[10]), Cake (the Queen Mother[11]), Boots (Cyril Connolly[12]), Joan Glover (von Ribbentrop[13]) and Bosomy (President Kennedy[14]), can become a bit of a crasher (bore) – although that is not the fault of the jokers themselves. In her novels Nancy modified it slightly. But the dominant voice of her characters[15] is her own, the Mitford voice, and thus that distinct, direct, wide-eyed, fantastical idiom has become a familiar mode of speech, unbearable to some, adorable to others, oddly impossible to imitate. It is part-childish, part-posh, part-1920s exaggeration – 'do admit', 'oh you are kind, the kindness of you', 'she ees *wondair*' – yet what makes it durable is the edge of perceptiveness, the nail on the head quality. 'You know, being a Conservative is much more restful,' says Linda Radlett, apropos the Communist Party, 'though one must remember that it is bad, not good. But it does take place within certain hours, and then finish...'

To be on the receiving end of the Mitford speech mode is an undoubtedly delightful experience. 'Oh now *aren't you clever*,' said Deborah to me, when I had done nothing more than recall the name of one of her husband's racehorses. 'Miss Thompson: *so* clever, and *so* nice,' said Diana, to an aged gentleman who joined us for tea in her Paris flat. I fell for it, but then so did pretty much everybody who met them (Diana could have had Karl Marx grovelling at her feet). The point, of course, was that the way the sisters spoke was an outward expression of charm. And here one comes down to it: after all the analysis, the identification of the elements that comprise the Mitford phenomenon – the x 6 power, the upbringing, the times in which they lived, the showmanship, the toughness, the humour – one is left with that single, fused element. Charm. A quality that can enrage, but whose mystery is brightly indestructible.

In itself there was nothing particularly remarkable about the fact of the Mitford sisters' charm. Many of their circle were charming, people like Lady Diana Cooper, Lord Berners, Sir Harold Acton and, in her lugubrious way, Violet Hammersley. It is a characteristic associated with the upper classes, who had the leisure to weave that ethereal web, and the confidence to override resistance. The 'creamy English charm' that Evelyn Waugh famously described in *Brideshead Revisited* poured its streams through society, soothing and poisoning as it went.

But the Mitford charm – which, for all its high-altitude chill, did the essential thing of making life seem better – was charm writ large. It had the quality of self-awareness, increasingly so after Nancy mythologized it. The Mitfords deployed their charm as a kind of tease, as part of a game in which the charmed were also invited to take part; and this knowingness, this self-ironizing, is the preservative that prevents decay.

The charm of the Mitfords en masse was very much Nancy's creation. But then there are the six individual girls, who in real life were charming all right, but were a lot of other things as well. When one thinks about Unity, in particular, the very notion of charm seems rather absurd. Indeed perhaps the most extraordinary aspect of the Mitfordian image is that it entrances and delights and at the same time contains so much that is not entrancing at all. Perhaps that is simply charm at work again, compelling people to overlook the lethal sympathies?

Without Nancy's mythologizing skills, the separate lives of the Mitford girls (except Pam) would be of interest, but because of her – because she marketed herself, her family and her class – interest still flourishes in the full six-pack. As current usage would have it, the sisters are 'iconic'. They are part Audrey Hepburn as Holly Golightly, part Patti Hearst in the Symbionese Liberation Army, part *Country Life* girls in pearls, part Malory Towers midnight feasters, part marble frieze of smiling young goddesses. Their significance has become detached from the realities of their own times, and is now a significance of image; as most things are today.

They are the stuff of themed fashion shoots (tweed, little hats, elegant brogues, shooting sticks) and mesmerized blogs ('The Divine Debo' is a fairly representative post title). A book was published recently entitled *The Mitford Girls' Guide to Life*. Who knows, there may be a guided tour to their widely varied habitat (Swinbrook, Chatsworth and Holloway jail). They are constantly referenced in popular culture. Caitlin Moran's fabled upbringing, with the eight auto-didact children running loose around a Wolverhampton council house, could be seen as a working-class take on the Mitfords. Meanwhile the sisters themselves have been satirized by razor-witted modern comedians: in BBC2's *Bellamy's People*,[16] two actresses dressed up as aged facsimiles of Jessica and Diana and sat in their drawing room beneath images of Stalin and Hitler. The Mitford idiom was magnificently conjured: 'Stalin – oh he was terribly *attrective*! With that wonderful peasant moustache – very *sixy*!!!' 'Fuffy – oh that's what I called the Führer – darling Fuffy, well, he was terribly misunderstood...' The joke was not exactly affectionate, but affection is not really what the Mitford girls inspire; one is always aware that they are not as cosy as they appear to be. The joke was also on us, incidentally, for turning these adherents to murderous ideologies into figures of fascination.

It *is* perverse. Society today seeks a nirvana of non-judgmentalism about everything, except the things that the Mitfords represented. Yet their image still seduces. Why?

Well: one might call it a variant strain of *Downton Abbey* Syndrome, in which people seek comfort by retreating to an age of hierarchies, prejudices and certainties. The posh past, in other words. Being upper class today can bring the wrath of God down upon one's head; attending public school can be, as Linda Radlett whispered of Oscar Wilde's unknown crimes, 'worse than murder'; possessing an RP accent, or a Labrador, can lead to fiery accusations of elitism: yet poshness retains its mystique, and this is a quality that the Mitfords embodied. In *The Pursuit of Love*, Nancy conjures her world with a cosy, companionable ease that still puts up invisible barriers. And her readers remain besotted: not just by her humour, charm and so on, but because we *like* what she is describing. We want the freedom to hate it yet we don't – most of us – want it to cease to exist (what would we do without class? We would be lost). As long as an upper-class person handles their social status in the right way – preferably with a larky wink to their own eccentricity – egalitarian Britain will forgive them for it.

And the Mitfords, with their populist streak and eye upon the gallery, were remarkably good at classless displays of class. Deborah would mock her own accent – 'Ridiculous. It's just silly, and up here [in Derbyshire] it sounds even sillier.'[17] 'Class is just too dull for words,' she would say, from the citadel of Chatsworth. Such broad-minded self-mockery is typical Mitford, although how deep it went is another story. In her letters Deborah expressed contempt for the left-wing politics of Jessica and family ('I'm afraid they'll find Chatsworth not very progressive'). A middle-class person would have suffered grievously for this kind of remark, but the 'thrillingly posh'[18] Deborah got away with it. Her autobiography *Wait for Me!* is full of brisk loathing for New Labour, and sends a lethal countrywoman's shot at Ivor Novello, a visitor to one of the Devonshires' homes, who called her coursing whippet 'an enchanting bit of beige' (a very Nancy phrase, but not to Deborah's taste). Meanwhile Diana, in person, seemed entirely devoid of snobbery, and was similarly amused by what she perceived as her outlandish voice when she saw herself on television.[19] But in her writings she could pull sudden, knowing rank: 'There is no such person as Lady Sybil Colefax,'[20] was a droll correction in a book review. In a published diary she quoted the peer Lord Strathmore saying that 'if he had a gun' he would shoot a fellow peer who had criticized the Queen. 'What are we coming to, when a Scotch landowner, in August, has not got a gun?'[21]

Note that 'Scotch', by the way. This is 'U' usage. The U and Non-U debate went a bit near the knuckle on the issue of class. In fact all the writing paper v. notepaper stuff is in *The Pursuit of Love*, but there, crucially, the reader is in on the joke: a subtle form of flattery is going on, as in *Four Weddings and a Funeral*, which offers viewers the comforting illusion that their own lives (including entrées to castles) are up on the screen. Conversely, the measured direct speech of 'The English Aristocracy' essay made it very plain that this was *Nancy's* joke. Not her invention – U and Non-U was the concept of the linguist Professor Alan Ross – but it was she who made it incendiary, because of who she was. Thousands of people were enthralled by her strictures, and never again in their lives said the word 'mantelpiece'. But she had annoyed them, all the same. ('We could do with something more interesting than listening to a snobbish woman airing her views on class distinction,' was the reaction of a viewer after Nancy appeared on the BBC.) Her followers were not *enchanted*, as they had been when, say, Aunt Sadie decreed Surrey a not-quite-appropriate location for a country house. So it was lucky that they did not see a letter written by Nancy in 1957, reassuring Jessica about her daughter, who was in Mexico at the time of an earthquake: 'People like us are *never killed in earthquakes* & furthermore only 29 people were, all non-U...' This was the brutish side of Nancy's 'teasing': the one that she softened for her public, but not for her friends, and especially not for her family. Today a remark of that kind would be almost as *mal vu* as a friendship with Hitler. But Nancy, were she alive to receive the criticism, would smile through it: just as she did the storm over 'U', in which accusations of snobbery and shallowness whirled around her elegant head like hailstones; just as Diana had sat, without a tremor, and faced down vilification that would have shaken most people into pieces.

This confidence of theirs – relaxed, diamond-hard – is fascinating. It particularly fascinates women. It is the confidence of the upper classes, embellished by femaleness: a kind of confidence that, for all their greater freedom, today's women do not find it easy to possess.

Women today ought to be high on self-assurance, given that men are obliged to behave around us with tiptoeing deference, the culture says that any way of life we choose should be ours for the taking, books tell us that we must celebrate our every last flaw, while at the same time urging us to be our best possible selves... but actually none of this is reassuring, quite the opposite. Women are in a metaphorical pressure cabin, on a state of high alert, chiefly about what other women are doing and whether it is better than what *One* is doing. Should one make cupcakes or become CEO of a multinational; should one strive to resemble an Oscar nominee or celebrate one's freedom from that particular tyranny; should one shave every inch of one's body or tweet pictures of one's statement armpits; should one be a domestic goddess, a yummy mummy, an alpha female, a pre-feminist, a post-feminist, a feminist, a feminist who nevertheless has a facelift... It is a shambolic state of affairs.

There is only one answer to all of this, which is to be oneself, but it seems extraordinarily hard to be sure of what that is. Hence the fascination of the Mitfords, who always had the confidence of their own choices, however mad these frequently were.

There is something essentially *unworried* about them. Again, today, this is almost impossible to achieve. It is not really to do with money – the Mitford girls grew up in a household that was lucky enough to have things to sell, but was nevertheless always selling them – although it is, of course, connected to privilege. Yet in truth this offered only a veil of protection against peculiarly cruel events. The trauma of Jessica's disappearance, the violent public excoriation of Unity and Diana, the disintegration of the family unit, the miscarriages and illnesses and shocking bereavements – the Mitford story was not unlike a soap opera in its constant assaulting dramas, and the sisters had all the resilience of soap opera matriarchs in the way that they weathered tragedy. Nevertheless, and in some mysterious way, their brows remained clear. As Nancy had it, there was always something to laugh at. This did not, as Diana once wrote,[22] mean that one was necessarily happy – only that something was funny – but it was a true philosophy, that yearning towards lightness, and it was as good a creed as any by which to live. It had the priceless quality of allowing one to rise above events and see them as transient, not quite as important as they thought they were, merely steps on the way to the churchyard at Swinbrook; therefore not worth worrying about.

It is frankly therapeutic to think of Diana, shaking helplessly with ill-suppressed laughter at the hey-nonny-nos of the folk singer 'who had so kindly come to Holloway to amuse the prisoners but had not meant to amuse them quite as much as that'. It is quite marvellous to read Nancy on her French lover, Gaston Palewski, who turned fifty '& *minds.* I've never minded being any of the terrible ages that have overtaken me and so don't quite understand.' Or indeed Nancy, sorting out her inheritance with Deborah while lying on her deathbed: 'We had screams over the Will.' Or Deborah, after losing her third baby, writing that the village nurse had called her Your Ladyship 'through the most undignified parts'. Or Diana, saying that sex, about which people made such a fuss, was no more difficult than eating a Mars bar.[23] All the things we take so seriously – suffering, ageing, dying, babies, love... The Mitfords took them seriously too, deep down. But what liberation there is, all the same, in pretending otherwise.

Fearless though they were, the Mitford girls nevertheless always operated within certain boundaries. They were a blend of formality and anarchy that is impossible now to achieve: revolutionaries who had been to the hairdresser, iconoclasts who put the milk in second, transgressors in tweeds. And this, too, fascinates women, this indestructibly feminine way of breaking the rules.

For sure they fascinate me. I remember Diana, moving gracefully about her airy apartment in the *septième*: a tall wraith, like a long exquisite wisp of grey-white smoke, entirely beautiful at the age of ninety. Her cheekbones retained the purity of a Canova, curving constantly as she dissolved into that almost silent Mitford laughter. I can still hear her saying, *en passant*: 'I've had a fantastic life.' Then Deborah, a vigorous and easeful figure with her dog at her side, sitting with her feet up on a stool in a casually grand anteroom at Chatsworth, instructing me firmly that a woman needs a 'proper husband, proper children' – advice totally contrary to my own ideas, but somehow I have never forgotten it. And then Nancy, beloved Nancy, architect of the Mitford myth, with her neat sharp brain, her romanticism, her cynicism, her felicitous heart-lifting turns of phrase; when I first read her, aged about thirteen, I could scarcely believe (so weighted down was I with Eliot and Hardy) that one was actually allowed this kind of pleasure, that literature could be soufflé-light as well as monolithic, and still tell memorable truths. Few are the women who do not relish Nancy (her sisters were among the exceptions, but that's another story). Her Dior silhouette, her French bulldogs, her spry energy, her sharp silliness, her love of Parisian smartness and seventeenth-century prettiness, her description of an ideal party as 'hours and hours of smiling politeness': all this satisfies female cravings for elegance in an inelegant world. But there is also a sense of real substance, of the daily courage in frivolity. As for her novels – like Jane Austen's they can be misunderstood in a way that flatters feminine fantasies. Linda Radlett meets a sexy French duke with a spare flat in the *seizième*; Lizzie Bennet meets a brooding Englishman with a magnificent estate; both women are loved for their Real Selves... Of course such interpretations turn a blind eye to the flickering shadows in these books. *The Pursuit of Love* is permeated with images of death – like the graveyard outside the nursery at Asthall – and, as does *Pride and Prejudice*, it reminds the reader constantly that love, the happy ending, is a matter of chance: that life is brief, and goes awry very easily. Yet what endures – not just in this book, but in everything that Nancy subsequently wrote – is the bright affirmativeness of her voice. It contains the sound of happiness, of sane good humour; it taught me that levity and seriousness are not incompatible, which was an important thing to learn.

So I am immensely grateful to the Mitfords, to the Mitfordian image that makes life quite simply more enjoyable, although naturally it is far from being the whole truth. To take just one example of what lay beneath: the appalling migraines that Diana suffered, which began after the war, affected neither her looks nor her calm demeanour, and can be seen as a metaphor for a mass of hidden tumult. There was a large price to pay for being one of six such girls. In 1972 Nancy told an interviewer that sisters were a protection against 'life's cruel circumstances', to which Jessica – who in 1944 praised her daughter by saying 'There's not a trace of Mitford in her' – replied that sisters *were* life's cruel circumstances ('particularly Nancy'). The family dynamic was a veritable morass of female rivalries, shifting and reconfiguring throughout their lives. Nancy was jealous of Pam then of Diana; Jessica was jealous of Deborah; Unity was in thrall to Diana; Jessica was in competition with Unity; Nancy and Jessica were wary allies; Diana was critical of Nancy; and so on, and on, until the end. Yet in the main, with one notable exception, the knotty ties remained in place. The sisters met quite frequently and corresponded for most of their lives; although when, from the 1980s onwards, what had previously been unseen was gradually revealed – for example what Nancy had written about one sister to another, thinking that the subject of the letter would never read it – the entire family structure rocked again.

And what of this? In a letter to Deborah, written in 1989 after she had been interviewed by a researcher for *Desert Island Discs*, Diana expressed the view that – contrary to the eager young Radio 4 girl's assumptions – there was nothing especially remarkable about any of the sisters, except Unity. 'Of course Birdie really *was* original to the last degree but the rest of us weren't a bit.' The whole phenomenon, she suggested, was invented by the newspapers.

A revisionist take on the Mitfords could indeed seek, thus, to rationalize their mystery. It could see them as nothing more than a typical upper-class family who happened to have a lot of daughters, half of whom happened to take an interest in extreme but fashionable ideologies. End of story? Yes, to the Mitford myth refuseniks. Although where that leaves Nancy's imperishable sliver of genius, Deborah's ability to secure the future of a national treasure like Chatsworth House while charming men like John F. Kennedy into rapt submission, the ruthless political fervour of Jessica, Diana and poor 'original' Unity, I am not sure. Even if one allows nothing more than the brimming variety of the Mitford sisters' contacts book – Winston Churchill, John F. Kennedy, Joseph Goebbels, Evelyn Waugh, Adolf Hitler, Lucian Freud, Lytton Strachey, Maya Angelou, Field Marshal Montgomery, one could go on – there is a level of engagement with their times that carries its own, powerful, unrepeatable significance.

Do admit.

PART I

'Familles! Je vous hais!'

From *Les Nourritures terrestres* by André Gide (1897)

I

Nancy's 'The English Aristocracy', published in 1955, is chiefly remembered for U and Non-U, but in fact the rest of the essay, a meditation on the nature of the aristocrat, is far more interesting and perceptive. She describes, for instance, an imaginary peer named Lord Fortinbras, of whom she writes that, owing to his cluelessness about land and money, 'he deserves to be ruined, and he is ruined.' She could very well have been talking about her own father, the 2nd Lord Redesdale.

'You were,' wrote Evelyn Waugh, in 'An Open Letter' responding to Nancy's essay, 'at the vital age of twelve when your father succeeded to his peerage, and until less than a year before there was little likelihood of his ever succeeding... If your uncle had not been killed in action, if your posthumous cousin had been a boy, all you enchanting children would have been whisked away to a ranch in Canada or a sheep-run in New Zealand. It is fascinating to speculate what your careers would then have been.'

This was a tease, of course, but quite true. Nancy's father David inherited his title in 1916 after the death the previous year of his older brother, Clement, whose wife was pregnant with what turned out to be a daughter. The Mitford girls acquired the prefix 'Honourable' only by default. In other words, as Waugh was suggesting, the unelected spokesperson upon class was not as grand as all that. Such was his own fascination with the subject, Waugh probably viewed his good friend Nancy's social status with a mixture of excitement, envy and narrow-eyed criticism. What he could not get away from, and it was the sort of thing that mattered to both of them, was the downright antiquity of the Mitford name. Poshness in mid-twentieth-century novels was often conveyed by the remark that 'so-and-so's people came over with the Conqueror, you know.' The Mitford people were here before that, teaching U and Non-U to the Anglo-Saxons.

Although Nancy does not mention it in her essay, doubtless she relished the knowledge that her family owned Mitford, near Morpeth, in the reign of Edward the Confessor, and that a daughter of Sir John de Mitford was given in marriage by William the Conqueror to a Norman knight. Sir John's motte-and-bailey castle, built in Northumberland in the eleventh century and reduced to ruins some three hundred years later, is now a scheduled ancient monument.

These Northumberland Mitfords were the main branch of the family; the sisters descended from a junior line, originating in Hampshire. Among their ancestors was a barrister, John, created the 1st Lord Redesdale in 1802. The previous year he had been a short-lived Speaker of the House of Commons, then became a rather unpopular Lord Chancellor of Ireland. In 1808 he inherited Batsford – an elegant, symmetrical Georgian house set in parkland – from an uncle by marriage, Thomas Freeman (the Mitford girls were sometimes given the surname Freeman-Mitford). There was a dearth of contiguous heirs in the family; Bertram Mitford, the sisters' grandfather, acquired Batsford as a cousin twice removed. He did not inherit the title, although it was re-created for him in 1902.

He was a remarkable man; more so really than the son, David, who was immortalized in *The Pursuit of Love*. Bertie Mitford had all the masculine energy of 'Uncle Matthew' and none of his lurking timidity (Uncle Matthew hates leaving his home). He was one of those vigorous Victorian types who go at life like a steam engine, running out of puff only when they die. Certain traits of the Mitford sisters can be perceived in him: good looks, a sophisticated morality, a knack for writing what people wanted to read and a deep affinity with Germany.

Born in 1837, he attended Eton and Christ Church before joining the Foreign Office, where he was posted to the embassies at St Petersburg, Peking and Tokyo. He spoke French, Russian, Chinese and German, translated Kant and Japanese literature. Again this talent was inherited: his son David had perfect French, Unity picked up German very quickly in order to chat to the Nazi high command, and Nancy and Diana both became translators.[1] As a writer, Bertie had a less singular gift than Nancy. The Mitfordian clarity of his prose is muffled by the near-inescapable orotundity of the age. Nevertheless his *Tales of Old Japan* was a raging success. He had been invited to watch the last officially decreed death by hara-kiri, and his account was described by a reviewer as 'one of the most horrific and unforgettable pieces of prose I have ever read'. He also wrote a book about his time in China, *An Attaché in Peking* (many years later one of Diana's sons found the unexpurgated Peking diary, 'full of dread SEX'). An autobiography, *Memories,* was published not long before his death in 1916. It was a 'Book of the Year', just as Nancy's later works usually were, and a reviewer remarked that it was loosely constructed but 'contains not a word of "twaddle"': the sort of thing that was customarily said about Nancy.

In 1874, Bertie was appointed by Disraeli to the post of Secretary of His Majesty's Office of Works. He worked on improvements to Hampton Court and supervised the restoration of the Chapel of St Peter ad Vincula at the Tower of London, where the remains of Anne Boleyn were interred. Almost in passing, he became MP for Stratford-on-Avon. He knew Dickens, Whistler, Browning – and as a close friend of the future King Edward VII he advised on the gardens at Buckingham Palace (described by his granddaughter Deborah, after a dinner with the Queen in 1961, as 'a literal vasty park' inhabited by field mice). On his own land at Batsford, where he moved in 1886, he grew bamboo and created a magnificent arboretum. He also spent fortunes on demolishing the old house and raising up the fairytale castle of rich dull gold – a successful Victorian's dream home – that today stands fantastical against the Cotswolds sky.

It was said of him that 'he has been everywhere and seen everything'. He was, literally, a man of the world, although there is the faintest sense of a Victorian gentleman doing the Grand Tour; not of great cultural works but of great 'experiences', such as meeting Garibaldi or hunting buffalo. As for his German friendships – what blend of naivety and empathy drew him to Houston Stewart Chamberlain, the son-in-law of Richard Wagner and an intellectual influence upon Hitler?

As a lover of music, it was natural that Bertie should attend the Bayreuth Festival and take pleasure in the company of the Wagner family. He became extremely close to the composer's son, Siegfried, who married the English-born Winifred Williams; when Nancy visited Bayreuth in 1968 she was 'summoned to the presence of Frau Winifred' and told that the only photograph in Siegfried's room had been of Bertie Mitford. Winifred, the festival's artistic director during the war, had been an admirer of Hitler. When Unity fell ill in Bayreuth in 1938, then collapsed after insisting upon attending a Nazi march-past in Breslau, it was Winifred who took care of her (at Hitler's request). Unity's middle name, Valkyrie, was in tribute to the composer. Bertie had suggested it; despite the fact that Unity was born just as war was declared on Germany.

His friendship with Houston Stewart Chamberlain was probably founded upon their shared love of Wagner. It went sufficiently deep, however, to lead Bertie to write an introduction to Chamberlain's *Die Grundlagen*, or *The Foundations of the Nineteenth Century*, published in translation in 1910. Chamberlain was English, but in 1916 became a naturalized German. When he died in 1927 (his funeral attended by Hitler and other Nazis), it was said that he had been the 'bitterest of anti-British renegades during the war'.

Yet before this, in *The Foundations*, he had set out theories that encompassed Britain in his conception of a pure 'Aryan' race. Such a race, he wrote, 'finally enables the most gifted individual to live for a super-individual purpose'. One can imagine this going down a storm with Hitler, and it is generally accepted that Chamberlain's theories supplied a philosophical foundation, or justification, of Nazi policy.

He was regarded in some quarters as the equal of Kant and Schopenhauer. Bertie Mitford was certainly an admirer, although a sceptical *Times* obituary of Chamberlain decreed that he had reduced history to a racial division of 'Teutonic and anti-Teutonic sheep and goats' – the anti-Teuton being the Jew. Of course the endgame of this kind of thinking was not yet apparent. And the grandiose ideal of a Teutonic alliance did find a response in Britain, which after all is deeply linked to Germany by early history, and by the ascension of King George I in 1714. It is not perhaps so surprising that Bertie Mitford should have fallen for Chamberlain's rhetoric, backed as it was by the stirring surges of Wagnerian opera. Nor is it beyond comprehension that certain aristocrats, including Bertie's son David, should in the 1930s have supported the Anglo-German Fellowship that sought to avoid another war between 'the Teutons'. Where the imagination does stumble is over the behaviour of Unity and, to a lesser extent, Diana. One merely notes that they were born into this mindset, the one that responded to the dark glories of *Lohengrin* and *Faustus* and saw Germany as a blood brother. Tom Mitford, to whom Diana was especially close, felt much the same way. Bertie's brother married a German girl, and in 1914 his son Jack had a lavish, highly publicized 'Anglo-German wedding' to an heiress named Marie von Friedlander Fuld.[2]

Cosmopolitan though he was, Bertie Mitford still tended his country person's roots. That was natural to him. He was, for instance, a president of the Shire Horse Society (David later used a gold goblet made from the melted-down medals won by his father's animals). His presence is still felt in Moreton-in-Marsh – the nearest town to Batsford and built of the same beautiful ochre stone, the colour of Gloucestershire – with its Redesdale Arms hotel, the market hall for which he paid. He may also be present in other surprising ways: in 1962 Deborah sent Nancy a photograph from the *Field* magazine of a keeper at Batsford who looked exactly like their father. 'Thanks for Uncle isn't he amazing!' Nancy replied.

Bertie – or, as Nancy called him, 'Naughty grandfather' – had form in this respect. So too had his mother. It has in fact been suggested that Bertie himself was born on the wrong side of the blanket, and that anybody who wanted to 'look up' a Mitford girl should bypass the entry for 'Redesdale' and move on to 'Sefton'. The rumour arose very simply. When Bertie was four, his mother Lady Georgina Ashburnham (another pre-Conquest family) ran off with a son of the Earl of Sefton. There is absolutely no proof that Bertie was the lover's child, but that did not stop people thinking it, just as they believed Lady Diana Manners – later Cooper – to be the natural daughter of the editor of the *Pall Mall Gazette*. 'I am cheered very much by *Tom Jones* on bastards,' was Diana's reaction. Bertie would probably have felt much the same. As his granddaughter wrote in 'The English Aristocracy': 'Shame is a bourgeois notion.' Certainly the hovering taint of scandal did not hold him back, either in his career or his private life. Soon after Edward VII took the throne in 1901, Bertie was reported to be 'dining with His Majesty' at Windsor, and his wife, Lady Clementine Ogilvy, was a daughter of the Earl of Airlie. This was a definite social leg-up – the Airlies had a proper castle, rather than a self-built one – which may have been the reason why Bertie's mother-in-law always addressed her daughter by her maiden name.

The Countess of Airlie, who died in 1921 aged ninety, belonged to the Stanley family whose letters Nancy would later edit. These two books, *The Ladies of Alderley* and *The Stanleys of Alderley*, were published in 1938–9 ('apart from a few rather irritating gibes about Munich, Miss Mitford has done her task in exemplary fashion', wrote a reviewer). An obituary of Nancy's father described him as carrying the 'redoubtable strain of the Stanleys of Alderley', which was certainly evident in Henrietta Blanche Airlie. When Nancy was four, Blanche instructed her – in the epigrammatic manner favoured in *Downton Abbey* – that 'there is nothing so inferior as a gentlewoman who has no French'. It was the sort of statement that made its mark on Nancy. She may also have been influenced by Blanche's admiration for Voltaire, with whom she herself became intensely fascinated (her historical biography *Voltaire in Love* was published in 1957). Blanche was not a joker like the Mitfords, but Nancy – whose *côté snob* was undeniable – would have relished her cultured grandeur, her friendships with Thomas Carlyle, Matthew Arnold and Gladstone. As a girl Blanche had attended salons at Holland House in Kensington, where the last grand ball was held before the outbreak of war in 1939. A century earlier the great house had been the social, artistic and political heart of London, visited by everybody from Disraeli to Byron. When Nancy was dying, she joked bravely about the importance of getting into the 'right set' in heaven – might the Holland House lot suit?

Blanche, like Nancy, took inordinate pleasure in the company of clever men. It has been suggested that these included Bertie Mitford, and that first-hand knowledge of his womanizing was the real reason for the objections to his marrying her daughter.

Again, who knows? What *is* almost certain is that Bertie had an affair with his sister-in-law Blanche Hozier, whose daughter Clementine bore a strong resemblance to David Mitford. Blanche, who was unhappily married, had several affairs, but apparently admitted to a friend that Clementine was Bertie's child.[3] This inter-familial bed-hopping may have continued in the next generation. Clementine's husband, Winston Churchill, was said to have had an affair with his sister-in-law Nellie Romilly, whose son Esmond – the future husband of Jessica Mitford – was rumoured to be Churchill's child. Esmond himself hinted at the truth of this (he did look like Churchill), but he may simply have got a kick out of doing so – the red-flag-waving scourge of the Establishment, son of the First Lord of the Admiralty! As Diana Mosley later quoted, in explanation of Esmond's provocative behaviour: 'He only does it to annoy, because he knows it teases…'[4]

Of course the Mitford sisters would not have batted an eyelid at any of this excitable misconduct. They were sophisticates, one and all. Their parents, David and Sydney, did not go in for adultery, but their maternal grandfather, Thomas Gibson Bowles, was made of similar stuff to Bertie Mitford. There was no doubt about *his* illegitimacy: he was the son of the MP Milner Gibson and his mistress Susan Bowles. Thomas's wife died young, after an abortion performed to save her from a fifth, life-threatening pregnancy (faint echoes here of the end of *The Pursuit of Love*), and he then took several mistresses. Among them was the family governess, Henrietta Shell, or 'Tello', with whom he had three sons. No attempt was made to shove this under the carpet. Sydney calmly acknowledged her half-brothers and Tello – who had another son, by a naval officer whom she met in Egypt – was friendly with the Mitford girls.[5] She often stayed at Asthall. In 1894 Thomas Bowles had appointed her editor of *The Lady*, the magazine that he founded: this capable, free-spirited woman held the position for twenty-five years. In 1930, when Thomas's son George was general manager, *The Lady* gave Nancy one of her first writing jobs, a weekly column on social events like point-to-points, satirical in tone but actually as mild as honey. This connection did not launch her career: she was already doing bits and bobs for *Vogue*, and her first novel *Highland Fling* – published in 1931 – caused family disapproval, if anything, for being 'awfully indecent'[6] and for drawing attention to its pretty young author (there was, for instance, a large photograph of Nancy in the *Sunday Dispatch*). Probably the Thomas Bowles and Bertie generation would have been broader-minded. Probably, too, their literary leanings gave Nancy the idea that she too might write, and that it would be easy to get published. ('I never had any trouble,' she later said. 'Luckily, because if I had it would have put me orf completely.'[7])

According to his obituary in *The Times*, Thomas Bowles – known as 'Tap' – was born in 1844, although he himself said 'I believe I was born in 1841.' Like his friend Bertie Mitford, he was a dynamic, hyper-industrious character. Like his daughter Sydney, he was eccentric rather than charming. The person in this story whom he also resembles is, oddly enough, Sir Oswald Mosley: both men made notable entries into Parliament, and both – either from principle or wilfulness – took isolated stands that effectively scuppered their governmental careers. Tap, wrote his obituarist, had 'a temperamental dislike of compromise, which was doubtless the chief reason why he never held office'. Similarly, Mosley moved from Conservative to Independent to Labour in the space of six years (1918–24) before, in 1931, forming the New Party then the British Union of Fascists. Tap was elected the Conservative member for King's Lynn in 1892, stood as a Free Trader in 1906, was returned as a Liberal in 1910 then rejoined the Conservatives in 1911. He was something of an attention-seeker: a trait that his granddaughters inherited, to varying degrees. He conducted his first campaign from his yacht and spoke in the local Norfolk dialect. He brought – and won – an action against the Bank of England, which he accused of having made tax deductions specified in the 1910 Finance Act before the law was actually passed. Impressive, of course. One can picture him today, telling everybody about it on *Newsnight.*

This almost aggressive desire to be *doing* may have been connected to Tap's uncertain upbringing (he was accepted into his father's household, but educated in France). Certainly he became a formidable achiever, founding *Vanity Fair* as well as *The Lady*, and he lived well. So too did Bertie, who – in addition to Batsford, with its arboretum, its lake and its deer park – had a splendid house on Kensington High Street; Nancy remembered sitting on 'Grandfather Redesdale's' balcony during the First World War, crocheting for the war effort 'like a *tricoteuse*'. The house did not long outlive its owner. A theme of Nancy's later novels was the destruction of London family residences – she describes how a particular mansion on Park Lane was replaced by a hotel 'the colour of old teeth'[8] – and indeed Bertie's home became part of the Milestone Hotel, whose 1926 advertising campaign stated, reverentially, that visitors would be treading the same floors as King Edward VII. The stable and courtyard had become the 'much admired restaurant', although still intact was an oak-panelled ballroom and, intriguingly, a private chapel. Quite a place, in other words; Bertie and his wife might have been living at the very edge of their means, but at the turn of the century the Mitford fortunes were high.

Tap Bowles, meanwhile, lived on Lowndes Square, which was even grander. And his housekeeper was Sydney; having lost her mother when she was aged just seven, she became inextricably wrapped up in her father's life and, despite the presence of Tello, acted something like a wife. She and her younger sister Dorothy ('Weenie') helped Tap canvass on his yacht and attended his dinner parties. From the age of fourteen, Sydney ran the huge Knightsbridge house. It is testament to her efficiency, but it was not much of a childhood. She never really had a mother and was treated like an adult by her father. This surely in part explains Sydney's mysterious, reserved character, which affected all her daughters in different ways.

Sydney, in turn, had been profoundly influenced by her father. She took on his rather bombastic quirks. He was a food bore, which she also became: she wrote frequently to newspapers about the importance of making one's own bread (a letter on this subject was published in November 1939, not long after Unity's attempted suicide), and about the value of unpasteurized milk (Deborah later claimed, quite unworriedly, that a lump in her neck – which remained all her life – developed after drinking the produce of her mother's TB-infected herd of Guernseys). 'Women should put their best brains to the study of food in relation to health (beginning with the Laws of Moses),' Sydney wrote to *The Times*. This was in line with Tap's belief that Jews did not get cancer. He also had a complete distrust of doctors; Sydney accordingly believed that the 'Good Body' would heal itself of pretty much anything. It was left to Jessica, aged around twelve, to telephone the doctor and inform him of her own case of appendicitis. Or so she wrote in *Hons and Rebels*: a book that was considered, by Diana, Deborah and Nancy, to be closer to fiction than fact. Jessica claimed, for instance, that after her appendix was removed she sold it to Deborah for £1. Years later Deborah would say that this was impossible, for the simple reason that she did not at that time have £1. A small instance of a theme that will recur: the question of truth and lies, multiplied and magnified within the charmed circle of the Mitford sisters.

II

Despite its oddity, it may be that life with the demanding, difficult but always invigorating Thomas Gibson Bowles was congenial to Sydney. She was intelligent – considered Girton material – and Tap associated with clever people. She loved his house in Wiltshire, whose eighteenth-century architecture was the style that she admired but would never again inhabit. She shared her father's pleasure in sailing, which he would do for months at a time, spending idyllic summers on his little yacht in the painters' paradises of Trouville and Deauville. 'My mother adored the sea, which she saw in terms of Tissot rather than Conrad,' wrote Nancy.[9] In her 1963 obituary, the family friend James Lees-Milne suggested that Sydney 'looked at life with the philosophic detachment of a mariner': an interesting *aperçu*. He also called her 'a woman out of the common. It would be strange indeed if a daughter of Thomas Gibson Bowles had been anything else.'

Her future husband, David Mitford – born two years before her, in 1878 – was also the child of a rare parent, although it was Bertie's heir, Clement, who showed most plainly his father's qualities. Clement was a paragon, kind and clever and popular. David was a slight problem. Clement went to Eton, David to Radley. Clement was a 2nd lieutenant with the glamorous 10th Royal Hussars. David was sent to Ceylon as a tea-planter after failing the written exam for Sandhurst.

But war is something of a leveller. Both young men fought in the Boer War, David in the Northumberland Fusiliers, and like his alter ego Uncle Matthew he was a brave fighter. Appointed orderly to his commanding officer, then (like his brother at last) a lieutenant, he saw a chance for the military career that he had wanted, and in 1901 wrote to his father, asking if Bertie would try to get him a commission. In March 1902, however, he was reported as 'severely wounded'. Then – according to the terse bulletins in *The Times* – he went from 'progressing very favourably' to 'gunshot wound, dangerously ill'. David had spent four days lying in a bullock wagon, his chest swarming with maggots and one of his lungs shot away (which did not stop him chain-smoking). He was invalided home, and at the age of twenty-four any hope of a life in the army was over.

It would have suited him: his casual gallantry, his relentless energy – he had all Bertie Mitford's vigour but few of the same outlets. ('The trouble with my father,' Nancy later said, 'is he simply hadn't got enough to *do*.'[10]) David was less cultured, but somehow more sensitive, than Bertie. He was full of bravura but lacking in confidence. His portrayal as Uncle Matthew captures this contradiction, although for comic purposes it emphasizes the bravura: the stock whips that he cracks on the lawn, the bloodhounds with which he hunts his children. True of David Mitford, and inevitably not the whole truth. Similarly Uncle Matthew is unquestioningly uxorious, indeed worshipping of the vague but astute Aunt Sadie, and their marriage is portrayed as a quietly happy constant. Again, real life was a little more complicated.

David Mitford and Sydney Bowles first met through their fathers: Tap visited his friend Bertie at Batsford in 1894 and took Sydney with him. It is not surprising that she should have been dazzled by David, who was astonishingly good-looking (no surprise either that this pair produced seven beautiful children). Ten years later they married at St Margaret's, Westminster. By then the scales had balanced, or even tipped the other way. David was still handsome, of course, but a slight crock with his missing lung, while Sydney was now hugely attractive. Having made her society debut she had, at last, some proper clothes (her father had previously supplied her mainly with sailor suits), as well as what James Lees-Milne described, in her eulogistic obituary, as a 'divinely formed, slightly drooping mouth which expressed worlds of humour and tragedy'. What she had, too, was a quality of control, of withholding, which can put a vulnerable man in a constant position of seeking to please. The fact that David proposed not long after a near-fatal injury, and the death of his hopes of an army career, might imply that he got married because he did not know what else to do with his life. Yet he had written a love letter to Sydney from hospital in South Africa, to be given to her in the event of his death. His feelings for her were real. The gunshot wound probably pushed him to act upon them.

She, meanwhile, was rumoured to have been in love with another man, and to have accepted David as a way of healing *that* particular injury. The reasons why people marry each other are not always straightforward, although the simplicity of physical attraction can make them seem so. It may be that David would have done better, in the end, with a warmer woman, and Sydney with a stronger man, one more like her father. Nevertheless the union between these two was contented, close enough to its representation in *The Pursuit of Love*, until the 1930s tested it to destruction. In 1937 David spoke out in the House of Lords against an amendment to the Marriage Bill, a clause stating that no petition for divorce could be made within five years of a wedding. He wanted the clause removed. Forcing couples to stay together would, he said, cause suffering.[11] For such a conservative man, this was an unusually liberal viewpoint. It is unlikely that he was thinking of himself – his relationship with Sydney was intact at this point – but the fragmentation of his world had begun with Diana's desertion of her first husband and Jessica's elopement. Every certainty, including that of marriage as a lifelong commitment, was now open to question.

Not so back in 1904, when people like David and Sydney Mitford could live behind Sloane Square with six servants on £1,000 a year, and the cataclysms of the next forty years were quite simply unimaginable. The young couple seemed ordinary representatives of their class. The most obviously exceptional thing about them was their looks. They were born to slightly unusual stock, but that in itself was quite usual. The fact is that one can trace back, discover creativity, musicality, brains, charm, eccentricity, love of Germany and so on within the Mitford pedigree – yet finding these traits after the event is something of a charlatan's art, like palmistry. There was nothing, when Nancy was born in November 1904, to say that she would grow up to be anything other than an upper-class wife and mother. Just before her third birthday, however, another baby arrived, and the first rivalry between the sisters began to shape the family. The birth of Pamela, Nancy later said, 'threw me into a permanent rage for about twenty years'. A joke; but not entirely. One day not long after her sister's arrival Nancy, walking with her parents along a London street, began to scream uncontrollably. Nothing would stop her until, quite suddenly, she said: 'The houses are all laughing at me.' Her mother was naturally embarrassed and displeased; years later she wrote to her daughter, saying 'you used to get into tremendous rages, often shaming us in the street.' Her father, who adored Nancy, may have been more indulgent. But an interesting thing for a child to say?

Those who know the Mitford childhood only through Nancy's mythmaking may be surprised by how urban it was, at least until the outbreak of the First World War. Her 'Radletts' are absolutely country people, steeped in the robust beauty of the rural seasons, with a love of hunting in their 'blood and bones' and a defining sense of freedom. Yet for the first ten years of Nancy's life – through the births of Pam, Tom in 1909, Diana the following year – the family's main home was in London. Upmarket London, naturally, with

Harrods and the Army and Navy stores on hand, but nevertheless with the attendant constraints of city streets, hansom-cab traffic jams, lack of space. The greenest thing the children saw was Kensington Gardens on their twice-daily outings with a nanny. David worked at *The Lady* (impossible to conceive of Uncle Matthew doing such a thing, or even to think of him walking through Covent Garden), dutifully supplementing his £400 a year from Bertie, and Sydney's allowance from Tap.

At first the Mitfords lived at 1 Graham Street, described by Diana as 'hardly more than a doll's house'; an exaggeration, of course, although with four young children it was certainly chock-full of prams and servants. There was a cook, three maids and two nannies: Laura Dicks – known as 'Blor', adored by the children – and a young girl called Ada Bowden. 'So what did my mother do all day?' Nancy later wrote. 'She says now, when cross-examined, that she lived for us. Perhaps she did, but nobody could say that she lived with us…' The 1911 census finds David and Sydney at Graham Street with the cook while the children, plus nannies, are named as 'boarders' at a house on the Undercliff at Bournemouth. This was April. That summer the family acquired a holiday home of its own, Old Mill Cottage in High Wycombe, leased by Tap and later bought by Sydney (a wise investment on her part: when retrenchment was required, as was often the case, the house could be a retreat or a source of rental income). The family travelled to it by train with their servants, a menagerie of dogs, mice, guinea pigs and grass snakes, plus – that first year – a Shetland pony that had taken David's fancy the previous day on his way home from *The Lady* (and that spent the night on a landing at Graham Street). The Shetland having been denied access to the guard's van, David took a third-class compartment in order to accommodate it. 'Of course it was most unusual for ANYONE to travel third class in those days,' Pamela later recalled, straight-faced, for a television documentary.[12] This vignette is reminiscent of a story recounted by Deborah, who during the Second World War travelled third class from Scotland to London with her goat, and in the middle of the night milked it in the first-class waiting room: 'which I should not have done'.[13] Very Mitford. Charming, eccentric, unselfconscious – except perhaps in the telling.

And so life continued, away from the Edwardian era (Nancy had a powerful memory, which she admitted was probably false, of her parents weeping into black-edged newspapers at the death of the king in 1910), into the sweetly unaware period in which things apparently stayed the same, but were in fact preparing for the great change of August 1914. Clement, heir to the Redesdale estates, married his cousin Lady Helen Ogilvy, and had a baby, Rosemary. Bertie Mitford was rich in sons – five (that we know of) plus three daughters – but his boys produced just three between them. David began prospecting for gold in Canada, travelling to Ontario for the first time with Sydney in 1913. They lived in a cabin in a small mining community in Swastika, where Unity was conceived. It was somehow typical of David, first that he should have tried such a bold and manly scheme, second that a property barely a mile away struck a rich seam of gold.[14] His own finances remained essentially unimproved. Nevertheless back in England he moved his family to a large house on Kensington's Victoria Road, where Unity was born four days after the outbreak of war.

War with Germany must have seemed particularly strange to Bertie Mitford, then aged seventy-seven. His son Jack had recently had a spectacular Berlin wedding (although the marriage to Fräulein Fuld was over within the year); his friend Houston Stewart Chamberlain was admired by the Kaiser. The conflict within Bertie would have been nothing like as strong as it was in Unity, who twenty-five years later was torn apart by the enmity between Britain and Germany, as to a lesser extent were Diana, Tom and Sydney. But Bertie may have felt some of this; especially when his son Clement was killed near Ypres in May 1915.

Nancy, never a friend to Germany, later wrote that she had 'prayed, as hard as I could, for war'.[15] What she had craved (aged nine) was the prospect of living in a tree, like Robin Hood, and killing an invader. In fact war *would* change her fortunes in a way that was ultimately favourable, but Clement's death caused her to feel intense guilt, as well as great sadness. Everybody had adored him. Pamela later recalled his death as the first time that she saw grown-ups cry. In February 1915 he had received the DSO, having been badly wounded when the 10th Hussars were attacked early in the war. He returned to active service as soon as possible, and died not long afterwards. His wife Helen was three months' pregnant; when she gave birth to a daughter, Clementine (who in 1937 would accompany Unity and Hitler to the Bayreuth Festival), David became heir to Lord Redesdale.

Aged thirty-six and with one lung, he had obviously been unsuited to active service, but he joined up anyway. Until the death of his brother he may have been glad of the war. Again it was a solution, of sorts, to the problem of what to do. Contented though he was in his family life, he undeniably burst forth when let loose, in the vast expanses of Ontario or upon the Oxfordshire land; one has the sense of a tame tiger padding back and forth to *The Lady* every day, longing to spring and flex its unused muscles. Small wonder, really, that David persuaded doctors to let him go to France as part of a group of officer reinforcements. He was not remotely fit enough, but in April 1915 he was made transport officer – in theory a less strenuous post, except that the appointment was instantly followed by the 2nd Battle of Ypres. David's efficient bravery in directing operations, leading wagons through the town at full gallop under heavy bombardment, sometimes twice nightly, surely proves that he should have had a military career; being robbed of it was part of what left him directionless. The battalion was never without supplies and did not lose a single man. It was David's finest hour. In a way he probably enjoyed it, but the strain was great, and horribly increased by grief for Clement. The middle years of the war were tough – Sydney was also struggling, living with five young children in a little house in Oxford, deprived of her husband's salary from *The Lady* – although on one of his leaves they managed to conceive Jessica, born in September 1917, not long after David was invalided home for good. By that time he was the 2nd Lord Redesdale. Dressed in his uniform, he took his seat in the Lords.

Bertie had died in August 1916. He had published his *Memories* a few months earlier, after the death of Clement: a final act of defiant vitality. He bequeathed to David around £17,000 and 36,000 acres. There should have been more money – Thomas Bowles left twice as much in 1921 – but the Redesdales had lived in that grand *fin-de-siècle* way that implied belief in an infinity of munificence; Bertie's widow Clementine, daughter of an earl, who moved to Northumberland and died in 1932 leaving £1,667 13s 8d, had probably never conceived such a thing as a day of financial reckoning. She had spent freely during her marriage, although the real expense had been the rebuilding of Batsford. As soon as he acquired the house, David knew that he would have to sell. There was simply not enough money to run such a place. Nevertheless the Mitford inheritance was considerable: relatively light on cash, but a treasure trove of land, furniture and paintings. A great deal of disposable wealth, in other words, which was extremely fortunate for a man like David. He began casting off in May 1917, when Batsford was first advertised for sale ('Tudor domestic reproduction in Bourton stone'... 'Park covers 350 acres'... 'part of villages and Moreton-in-Marsh, about 800 acres of woodland...'). Thereafter he never really stopped. He was like Nancy's fictional Lord Fortinbras, selling off everything in order to stave off want. In fact David was so blessed with possessions that he could hold on to many wonderfully civilized items, such as his father's collection of Chinese and Japanese screens. But the recital of what went to auction in just a couple of years – a Reynolds that made £14,800; a collection of Bertie's oriental porcelain that sold for £4,600; thousands of acres at Otterburn, Northumberland ('coal deposits possibly underground'); the Batsford Estate – leaves a slightly queasy impression of financial cluelessness.

In 1919, however, David still owned the heart of his inheritance: the village of Swinbrook, the trout fishing in the Windrush, the spreading acres in the shallow valley. 'All this belongs to you,' the kindly and dramatic Blanche Hozier said to her niece Nancy, then aged twelve, as they were standing on top of the hill at Batsford, overlooking the greater part of the Cotswolds. 'Oh, what utter rubbish,' was Sydney's reaction, when Nancy ran to tell her this tremendous news. '*Nothing* belongs to you.'

III

Then the life of 'the Mitfords' began. With part of the proceeds from his selling spree, David bought 1,000 acres adjoining Swinbrook, including Asthall Manor, the house where the family would remain for the next seven years. With the exception of Jessica (and Deborah, who never lived there at all), the children retained memories of Batsford. They had been given a home on the estate in early 1916, when they ceased to be Londoners. From 1917 they lived in the main house, congregated in a few rooms, like lodgers who happened to be in possession. Nancy in particular – almost fifteen when the house was sold – would have remembered the glorious golden grandeur hidden beneath the dustsheets, the great ballroom with its impossibly vaulted ceiling, the five staircases, the long window seats in dusky panelled rooms. This was aristocratic living: Nancy never had it again for herself (that was Deborah's lucky fate) but she always conjured it as an image of ineffable romance, about which she wrote with comfortable realism. For instance Hampton, the country house where the opening scenes of *Love in a Cold Climate* take place, is described in terms that approximate to Batsford, as a showy gothic castle built to replace a delightfully plain Adam house. ('"I suppose it is beautiful," people used to say, "but I don't admire it"...')

Diana, who was nine when Batsford was sold, remembered it chiefly as a place where one could always find an enormous room to read in, alone. This urgent passion for reading was shared by Nancy – later it would be a supreme solace for both sisters – and by Tom. When the Batsford contents were sold in 1919, David Mitford asked his son, then aged ten, to decide which books to keep; Tom was what his father called 'a literary cove'.

The cleverness of these three children was highly remarkable. And the fact that it developed into adulthood is an argument for a very simple educative plan: teach them to read, give them access to a marvellous library – like Bertie's – then let them get on with it. Of course this approach (which was really the opposite of a plan) left gaps in their knowledge, but it did the fundamental job of making them *want* to learn. They were also taken to nearby Stratford-upon-Avon three or four times a year, and became familiar with Shakespeare. There were two governesses, one French and one English, but the essential work the children did themselves. These sequestered Batsford years were thus formative for the older Mitfords; although Pamela did not progress in the same way. This was part-nature, part the nature of events. In 1911 Pam was stricken by infantile paralysis, which left her hesitant, with one leg slightly shorter than the other. And she suffered from Nancy's teasing, which she could not withstand (as when, during the General Strike, Nancy and Pamela ran a café supplying tea to the emergency services; Nancy disguised herself as a tramp and pretended to accost her sister. Most people would have seen through this ruse, but by all accounts Pam was completely terrorized by it). What Pamela really thought about Nancy thereafter is unknowable, because in a way Pam's façade was the most complete. She was passive, which was very non-Mitford. Yet she had her own slow, serene version of the family assurance, and a mode of expression that was perhaps the most natural of them all: viz, her description of Hitler as 'like a farmer in his old brown suit'. This really was somebody saying only and absolutely what they meant, the key to the Mitford idiom, and nobody did it better than Pamela. Some years later she bought an expensive Guernsey dairy cow only to find, as she put it, that 'the brute was bagless'. Not even Nancy was capable of this kind of direct phrase-making, although she stole it for her books.

Pam's role, laid down by character and circumstance at an early age, was probably a necessary one within the family. 'There'll never be any one remotely like her, will there?' wrote Deborah, when her sister died. Despite Nancy's taunts – calling Pam nicknames like 'Chunkie' (in youth she was rather fat, and all her life obsessed with food) – she was never exactly a butt. She had too much innate dignity for that. After her death she was described as remarkable for her goodness, but in fact she could be surprisingly tough – for example she did not really like children – and obtuse, as when she allowed her beloved dachshunds ('the Elles') to romp unchecked over the sofas at Chatsworth: 'She was herself with knobs on', wrote Deborah to Diana. This was a typical description. Pamela was the still centre of the Mitford girls – comforting in her oddity, untouched and untouchable – whose placid mad sayings would be relayed back and forth with intoxicated delight by the other, more mutable sisters, always with the postscript: 'She ees *wondair.*' John Betjeman, who proposed to her twice in 1932, saw an English magic in her countrywoman's demeanour. Compared with the rest of the family, she can seem like a vacuity. In fact she had the unignorable presence of one of her grandfather's shire horses, quiescent in the face of Nancy's jabbing little insect bites.

So at Batsford a substantial part of the Mitford dynamic was established. Nancy was black queen, dominating and dazzling. Pam was essentially withdrawn from the fight. Diana and Tom – close in age, cool and controlled – were soulmates, remaining steadfast in this even after the start of his schooling in 1918. Then at Asthall, where Deborah was born in 1920, a new dynamic was formed by the younger children. They talked in private languages, not just the 'do admit' stuff but actual, near-unintelligible variations on English, as if they were mini-tribes within the family. Unity and Jessica, who called each other 'Boud', spoke 'Boudledidge' (understood only by Deborah, who nevertheless did not presume to join in). This continued into adulthood: 'Jung va ja leddra,' wrote Unity to Jessica in 1937, meaning 'thanks for your letter', before going on to lecture 'my good Boud' about her elopement, and describing how Hitler had forbidden German newspapers to print the story, 'which was nice of him wasn't it'. The closeness between Unity and Jessica, which developed to the full in adolescence, was such that political polarization could not quite break it: the girls would discuss whether one would shoot the other under orders, yet they remained oddly allied.

Between Jessica and Deborah, there was an intense childhood bond. They called themselves the 'Hons' – this meant 'hen', rather than 'Honourable', and derived from the great brood of hens kept by their mother. They spoke 'Honnish'. In later life their letters were still full of this language: 'do write to yr old Hen,' and so on. Nevertheless, from Deborah's point of view, Jessica's elopement created a deeper rupture than her sister ever wanted to accept. Jessica herself later suggested that she had been jealous of Deborah.[16] Despite the constant enforced companionship that came with being the two youngest, the ceaseless skittish stream of Honnish, the relationship was probably more one-sided than that between Jessica and Unity; both of whom were misfits, although in childhood this was apparent only in Unity. Deborah, on the other hand, had a supremely well-adjusted nature, which may have been in some way inimical to Jessica.

In 1936, the three younger girls were taken on a Hellenic cruise by their mother. Perhaps Sydney scented trouble, and was trying to divert Unity and Jessica before too late. However Unity behaved in what was by then her usual way, arguing with a left-wing shipboard lecturer – the Duchess of Atholl, no less – and wearing her swastika badge in Spain, where she narrowly avoided attack. According to *Hons and Rebels*, Jessica then had a physical set-to with Unity about the Spanish Civil War. This is not mentioned in Deborah's account, which is determinedly normal in tone, and in which she and Jessica carry on in the sweet, irritating way of the younger sisters in Nancy's novels, calling a harmless academic 'the lecherous lecturer' (this made its way into *Love in a Cold Climate*) and staring mesmerized at a pair of eunuchs at the Topkapi Palace ('Children', said Sydney, 'you are not to mention those eunuchs at dinner'). The impression given by Deborah is of two silly and happy young girls. Jessica later wrote that she was all the while plotting her escape, which would be effected within a year.

The stories told by the sisters are versions of the Mitford childhood, just like *The Pursuit of Love.* Without Nancy's novel it is probable that no other account would have been written; as it was, the Mitfords became a commodity, and Jessica, Diana and Deborah all produced memoirs (Pamela also considered a book, but this did not happen).[17] Diana wrote in a clear, bare way that resisted fancifulness. Deborah – described by Diana as 'one of the truthful ones'[18] – relished her family's eccentricities, but refused to sensationalize. Jessica, on the other hand, produced in *Hons and Rebels* an autobiography so partial as to stray into the territory of fiction. 'Shameless but most diverting,' as one reviewer had it. It was also highly imitative of *The Pursuit of Love.* 'What I think is this,' wrote Nancy to Evelyn Waugh. 'In some respects she has seen the family, quite without knowing it herself, through the eyes of my books.' Yet there was a fundamental difference between the two accounts, and not simply that one was a novel, the other autobiography. Nancy's book was joyful, while her sister's was resentful. *Hons and Rebels* was full of vociferous complaints: about her parents' refusal to send Jessica to school, the blinkered conservatism of her upbringing, the prejudiced right-wingery that encased her early life. David Redesdale, wrote his daughter, regarded the entire world as 'outsiders': the only exceptions were certain family members and 'a very few tweeded, red-faced country neighbours to whom my father had for some reason taken a liking.' This was fairly predictable stuff, Nancy with the rogue element of genius removed. More grotesque, and deeply distressing to the other sisters, was an unfounded accusation made against their uncle Bertram (always known as Tommy): Jessica claimed that he got a kick out of his Justice of the Peace duty of being a witness at hangings. All of this was breezily relayed, but the reader was left in no doubt as to where his or her sympathies should lie.

Hons and Rebels is a very clever book, managing to have it both ways; attacking the reactionary eccentricities that nevertheless made such excellent copy. According to her sisters, it was also a very dishonest book. 'Silly old Hen,' was Deborah's characteristic killer judgment. Diana, meanwhile, was sufficiently roused by the review in the *Times Literary Supplement* to fire off a letter refuting some of its claims. What enraged her particularly was the suggestion that the Mitford household was devoid of culture (the Batsford library?) and her parents actively opposed to enlightenment: 'scorn of intellectual values was a matter of choice for the individual child, not of necessity.' The *Observer*, gulping down Jessica's tales like so many communion wafers, wrote a fierce attack on the Redesdales. Deborah remarked to Nancy that their mother could practically have sued for the implication that she had been unfit to bring up her children. When Sydney died, three years after the book's publication, her obituarist James Lees-Milne seized the chance to address its caricatured portrayal. Nothing, he wrote, 'is further from the truth than the popular conception of her, gleaned from *Hons and Rebels*, as a philistine mother with hidebound social standards'. According to Lees-Milne – a man of high culture himself – Sydney encouraged her children's interest in the arts, and 'probably inculcated the mental independence which has distinguished them'.

This, almost certainly, is right. For such a progressive, Jessica takes a very conventional view. It is quite possible that school would have enhanced her life with things that she otherwise lacked, but only somebody who did *not* spend their childhood years at school could see it in quite such an idealized light. As it happened, Jessica and Deborah did spend a term at a day establishment in High Wycombe, when they were aged about eleven and nine respectively. Clearly this wasn't enough for Jessica, but it was far too much for Deborah. 'I did not understand what the teachers wanted or why.'

Confronted with lunch, she said simply: 'No thank you.' When she was fourteen another attempt was made with her, and she became a weekly boarder in Oxford – 'no dog, no pony, no Nanny'[19] – where she lasted three days, during which time she fainted in geometry. After finishing the term as a day girl, she was allowed to give up, for which she was forever grateful to her mother (various interfering aunts had told Sydney that Deborah should be made to stick it out). The Mitford sister for whom school was tried most frequently was Unity, whose 'mental independence' was developing a little too freely at home. In 1929 she boarded at St Margaret's, Bushey, then two years later was a day girl at Queen's College in London, and was expelled from both establishments (or, as Sydney would faintly protest: 'no, no, *asked to leave*.') She had made no attempt to fit in. A fellow student recalled that she 'seemed not to get the point, on purpose'. Yet she was also said to have been saddened by this failure.[20] If formal education had been an attempt at 'socializing' Unity, then it did not succeed. Which rather implies that school or no school made little difference, in the end.

What made a difference to Jessica, almost certainly, was the fact that her close companion Unity had been sent to school, and she had not: the year 1929 was when her dissatisfaction with home really began. Nancy, who had attended Francis Holland aged five, shared Jessica's yearnings to escape, although this was perhaps more a show than a reality. At sixteen she was sent to a quasi-finishing school, Hatherop Castle. 'School, for her, was synonymous with paradise,' wrote Diana (who was terrified by the prospect, and was never sent). Naturally: to Nancy it represented something new, different, and above all sister-free. 'She prayed every night to be made, in some mysterious way she preferred not to think about, an only child.'[21] True, in a way, that Nancy longed to be alone and unassailably special, cut loose from that scurrying train of noisy little sisters. In another way she would have hated it – getting what one professes to want is rarely as enjoyable as wanting it – and her boredom would have been of a less productive quality.

IV

This, of course, is at the heart of the Mitford sisters' story: the collective life against which they chafed, to varying degrees, and which made them so singular. Exaggerated though it became, there is truth in the image of the family at Asthall, richly vital, running free yet rooted within the English countryside.

David – now Lord Redesdale – cherished a great dream of building a house of his own, on the hill just outside Swinbrook. Asthall was only ever meant to be a stopgap. Yet as soon as he moved there he began to use his fiery energy on DIY, building stables, kennels, bedrooms and 'cloisters' – a very successful addition, unorthodox yet of a piece with the house – leading to the library-cum-music room that he created from a large barn in the garden. This barn, a separate little house, allowed the privacy of Batsford to be replicated at Asthall. Tom, who had inherited his grandfather's passion for music, could play the piano undisturbed. Diana and Nancy could read and listen. Bach and Sir Walter Scott, Handel and Balzac, the creative heights of civilization were absorbed in an Oxfordshire barn while, all around, seethed the rural life of hunting, shooting and trapping, the Mitford life of dogs, mice, rats, guinea pigs, ponies, healthy blond children in jodhpurs jabbering away in Boudledidge and Honnish, Sydney with her hens, David with his stock whips, a beautiful life while it lasted.

Asthall itself, casual and handsome, had the precious quality of homeliness. Sydney had a great gift for interior design (inherited by Nancy), and Diana later described the natural flair with which her mother furnished the house. Bertie's Chinese screens were used to keep out the draughts in the long panelled hall, which had a fire at each end and windows on either side. The Japanese screens, painted with birds of prey, stood in the dining room. Outside the drawing-room windows was the church, so close as to form part of the same landscape; the children went there to evensong, and on one occasion heard the vicar preach a sermon attacking 'people who run shouting with their dogs across God's holy acre'. This referred to David, who habitually took his coursing dogs on a shortcut through the churchyard. From the age of fourteen Diana played the ancient organ in the church, into which a village boy pumped air: 'I used two stops, one for noise, one for pathos.' The Mitford sisters rode, hunted, went to tennis parties and dancing classes – 'we did everything badly,' wrote Diana[22] – but the spreading, teeming house was their life, with its nursery, its chilly schoolroom at the foot of the great oak staircase, its legendary poltergeist who was said to have pulled off the cook's bedclothes, its magical barn.

The Pursuit of Love has no equivalent of the Asthall barn. Instead, as the Radlett children's refuge, it has the 'Hons' Cupboard': in reality a large linen cupboard at Swinbrook House from which Jessica and Deborah ran the 'Hons' Society' (an alternative venue was an old bread oven at the High Wycombe cottage) and, with Unity, spoke their strange languages. Nancy was twenty-one by the time the family moved to Swinbrook, past the age of huddling in cupboards, but she used the image for her novel and it has become totemic, a kind of metaphorical HQ for the Mitford mythology. In *The Pursuit of Love* the cupboard is, more pragmatically, a retreat where the children go to be warm, exchange news and speculate upon subjects like childbirth and abortions ('Well, tremendous jumpings and hot baths anyway'). The heroine Linda, when she falls pregnant, lies in the cupboard with her dog and reads fairy stories.

So there is scant sense of any educational life, except as lived by the narrator Fanny, who attends what Uncle Matthew calls an 'awful middle-class establishment' where she learns to 'put the milk in first'. The novel *does* mention, as it were in passing, the fact that the Radlett children read extensively from the library – 'a good representative nineteenth-century library, which had been made by their grandfather, a most cultivated man' – although Nancy goes on to say, tellingly, that this reading in 'fits and starts', this autodidacticism, was no real substitute for a proper education. The Radletts/Mitfords had knowledge and 'gilded it with their own originality', but they were incapable of concentration and could not bear to be bored. The sense that they are thus improperly equipped for life – modern life, at any rate – permeates the book and infects Linda, certainly, who has an instinctive intelligence but very little sense.

This, then, is Nancy's oblique attack upon her own posh-feral upbringing, with its *laissez-faire* attitude to learning, its governesses and its anti-school snobbery ('my father thought one got thick calves from playing hockey,' she later said. 'Well, he was very much against these thick calves'[23]). In fact there was nothing odd about being home-taught, especially for girls of that class and time. Lady Diana Cooper once remarked upon the parental fear that if a girl went to school she would start wearing bangles (which, as Diana Mosley observed, would have been headline news if Nancy had said it).

Some of the Mitford governesses *were* inadequate, such as the one who taught Unity, Jessica and Deborah to shoplift ('jiggery-pokery') and another, small of stature, whom Unity would pick up and put on the sideboard. But the Batsford governesses were very good. Vanda Sereza, or 'Zella', who taught French and later married an Englishman, became a close friend of Nancy's (and visited Diana in Holloway). Miss Mirams, also at Batford, was described by Diana as 'rather severe' but nonetheless prepared Tom for his prep school (Lockers Park) where he excelled in the entrance exam. Miss Hussey, trained in the PNEU[24] programme of which Sydney approved, taught at Asthall in the early 1920s, then Swinbrook ten years on, thus catching all the girls except Nancy. She was entirely competent, despite the difficulty of adjusting lessons to such varied ages and abilities (Pam, she later recalled, 'had been kept rather behind.'[25]) And Miss Hussey did not, as *Hons and Rebels* had it, pass out when she saw Unity's snake, Enid, wrapped around a lavatory chain (the snake was Diana's, 'just a little grass snake', and nobody fainted at the sight of it). Jessica, again, was making merry with the facts. *The Pursuit of Love* had already started this particular hare when Nancy wrote that the Radlett governesses would scamper away after a couple of days, terrified of Uncle Matthew and his stock whips. Jessica – a highly gifted writer, but essentially a journalist rather than a creative – took hold of such flights of fancy and soared away with them; then called them autobiography.

Of course Nancy was also, beneath the flimsy disguise of fiction, writing what readers believed to be a true account of her childhood. It *was* true, in essence. The points where the truth bends are therefore not always easy to establish. Take the passage about the Radlett/Mitford education – Nancy *did* mean it in a way. She regretted the lack of a steady depth of knowledge such as her clever male friends possessed ('you must remember I am an *uneducated woman*', she wrote plaintively to Evelyn Waugh), and which she saw in her brother Tom. At the same time, *The Pursuit of Love* tells another story beneath the surface. The properly educated Fanny is a delightful person, but she has no vestige of the heady Radlett/Mitford charm, in which Nancy herself took barely concealed pride (and from which she made a very good living). Furthermore, when Uncle Matthew asks Fanny to tell him about George III, all she can come up with is 'He was King. He went mad,' whereas Linda ('you're uneducated, thank God') bursts forth with a scattering of disorganized but far more engaging facts. As for the idea that the children never learned the habit of concentrated endeavour – Nancy could write a book in three months, Jessica's journalistic research became formidable, Diana's articles are models of precision and, for Deborah, running Chatsworth would have been hugely demanding. These four were higher achievers than the average. If they were only interested in things that ignited their imagination, this is true of most people. What, then, would Roedean have added to the mix? The sisters were each other's influence and encouragement. Not always in a benign way, but it was Unity – the schoolgoer – who suffered most from this. As Aunt Sadie says in *The Pursuit of Love*, in a spasm of anxiety about her children's wayward upbringing, 'Do you honestly imagine it makes the smallest difference when they are grown-up?' Comes the reply: 'Probably not to your children, demons one and all...'

V

Nancy did not really want to be Fanny, although she took pleasure in her, and in her kindly, sensible aunt-guardian, Emily, who roundly defends the decision to send her to school. The connection between Fanny and Emily – perfectly done, and pretty much perfect – was wishful thinking on Nancy's part. It was also, in part, an attack upon her relationship with her mother.

As did Jessica, Nancy felt resentment about her early years, and this grew stronger with maturity: in later life she expressed the desire to write a straightforward autobiography. But whereas Jessica took aim at the whole Mitford clan and its conservative milieu, Nancy focussed ever more closely upon Sydney. This enigmatic woman was viewed quite differently by every one of her daughters; she was a symbol of their separate memories of a shared past and, although the least-known member of the Mitford family, she was the focal point for the rest.

When Nancy was near the end of her life and Jessica deep into middle age, the sisters formed an epistolary alliance against their mother. It is natural enough for people to look back, as it were, in search of a key that will unlock the mystery of their own selves. Nevertheless the back and forth of letters between these two sisters does put one in mind of the 'leagues' created by the Mitford children against whoever was considered an enemy, or 'Counter-Hon'. In this case, the Counter-Hon-in-Chief was Sydney.

In 1971, eight years after their mother's death, Nancy wrote to Jessica that she had never loved Sydney for the simple reason that Sydney had never loved her: had never hugged her as a child, was cold and 'sarky' with her, and had generally given an impression of having scant affection for her first daughter. 'I don't reproach her for it, people have a perfect right to dislike their children…' Jessica replied that she had loathed Sydney when growing up, especially as an adolescent, but in adulthood had become 'immensely fond of her'. However: 'The thing that *absolutely burned into my soul*', wrote Jessica, 'was the business of not being allowed to go to school.' The letter continued with a story of how, aged about eleven, Jessica had dreamed of becoming a scientist. Accordingly she had bicycled off to see the headmaster of a grammar school in Burford, near Swinbrook, where she learned that she could be admitted after passing a single exam. She returned home in triumph to ask her mother's formal permission: instantly refused, with no reason given. If true, this does indeed shine an unsympathetic light on Sydney's character as a mother. More likely it was exaggerated, or even invented – would Jessica really have stormed the citadel of a headmaster's study? Deborah certainly did not believe it, and anyway according to her recollection Jessica *was* attending a school at the age of eleven (when the pair of them were day girls in High Wycombe). But the point about the story is not so much the facts, as the fact of Jessica's enduring resentment.

Nancy, too, was honestly suffering, allowing her bright brain to brood over the past. She knew, of course, that she had been raised in an environment and class that did not encourage intense closeness between mother and child. Nancy would have ridiculed our infant-centric universe (although, in *The Pursuit of Love*, she created such a world); her problem with her mother was not quite of that nature. Nancy intuited an emotional disconnection between them and, being the proud, contained woman that she was – not unlike her image of Sydney, in fact – she behaved in a way that might have been designed to turn this feeling into reality. For example she wrote an essay, 'Blor', published in 1962: a homage to the Mitford nanny (Laura Dicks) that was also a critique of the Mitford mother. Nancy described how, before Blor's arrival in 1910, an 'Unkind Nanny' had been in charge of the children. This woman was sacked after 'unmistakable sounds of torture [had been] going on upstairs for a few months'. Was *that* true? Nancy's writing style is so light and ironic as to leave the necessary space for scepticism – yet that 'few months', with its suggestion of prolonged indifference, is a deliberate sharp stab, as is the description of the Unkind Nanny's dismissal by David Mitford. 'My mother retired to bed, as she often did when things became dramatic, leaving my father to perform the execution.' After this came Blor. She was then thirty-nine and regarded as possibly too old to look after four children, but she got the job in the very moment when she laid eyes upon Diana and said, in an exhalation of sincere delight: 'Oh! What a lovely baby!' (Diana, as Nancy later put it, was 'born beautiful, always beautiful'.[26])

The praise given to Blor is by implication an attack upon Sydney, who wrote to Nancy that she had given 'a charming account of the dearest Blor, though somehow she remains a shadowy figure'. (All right, *you* do it, Nancy might have been tempted to reply.) What comes across in Blor is warmth, which according to Nancy – and indeed to Jessica – is what their mother lacked. Blor also had a nanny-ish imperturbability, with her 'who's going to look at you, darling?' (to Diana, on her wedding morning) and her 'you'll be cold' (to Nancy, dressed for her coming-out ball). This quality was exaggerated to high comic effect in Nancy's 1951 novel *The Blessing*, in which the English nanny is transported to a great Provençal mansion, refuses a magnificent French lunch and asks if the chef can cook her a 'floury potato'. The real Blor could be funny in that way, but she also had depths of concealed wisdom. One wonders what she thought about some of what she saw in that household. 'I do wish you wouldn't keep going to Germany, darling,' she once said to Unity. 'All those men.' Which, as Nancy commented, was pretty close to the mark.

Blor died (aged nearly ninety) before the publication of this essay, but a few years earlier Nancy had sent her a copy of *The Blessing*, saying that the nanny in the novel is 'very much unlike you, darling'. Not entirely the case, and Blor probably recognized as much, but Nancy had sought to give reassurance.

She did so for her mother too, although not at all in the same way; for a start she did not warn Sydney beforehand that the 1962 article was being written. Having sent a typescript, to which Sydney reacted badly, Nancy responded in a muddle of guilt and irritation, semi-apologizing in the reluctant, furious way of a teenager (rather than a woman of fifty-seven). A couple of weeks later she wrote again, clearly very anxious although trying to glide over it with incidental gossip. As much as anything, she was upset by the fact that Sydney had been far less critical of *Hons and Rebels*, a really tough book. One's impression is that although Sydney was the person who had been hurt, Nancy's own distress had become the greater; nor was there anything that she could do to make it better, as she herself had created the entire situation. That was how it was between these two. It was a kind of emotional stalemate, and what made it worse for Nancy was the sense that her mother did not even much care, that she asked simply to be left alone ('I wish only one thing, that you would exclude me from your books') rather than prodded and niggled for attention. With the exception of Jessica, the surviving Mitford girls were wholly on Sydney's side.

'It is SUCH a shame to upset her & doesn't bear thinking of,' Diana wrote to Deborah about the 'Blor' essay. To Nancy, Deborah wrote in her usual way, with earthbound sense expressed in droll Mitfordese, making it clear that their mother was upset, and that this was not a good thing. Pamela, reported Diana, had been extremely distressed by the spectacle of Nancy and Jessica complaining about their childhoods at a dinner party: 'It's not TRUE,' Pam had wailed.

When Sydney died in 1963, and despite – or perhaps because of – the guilt that she felt about the relationship with her mother,

Nancy began to think more and more about writing her memoirs. These would be set mostly in adulthood, from the time of her success with *The Pursuit of Love*, but also flashing back to the past, using it to explain what she became. The book never happened, but by 1971 she was exchanging fervid thoughts about it with her partner in pain, Jessica.

Diana's contempt was excoriating for the two ageing ladies in the Hons' Cupboard. 'Decca and Naunce are a couple of bitter old creatures who can't forgive life for being so cruel & look for a scapegoat and find it in – Muv! Really rather rubbish.' This was to Deborah, who took a similar view but expressed it more merrily: it seemed to bother her less than it did Diana. Or perhaps, as a relatively young and extremely busy woman, she simply had a lot else to think about. She addressed a series of sharp, good-humoured correctives on the subject – for example, she gave Nancy her sceptical take on Jessica's urgent desire to be a child scientist – and basically, translated into modern parlance, suggested that they should both *get over themselves*. Which was good advice. At the same time Nancy was a writer, and writers see things differently. Everything is material; nothing, as Muriel Spark had it, is wasted. In that sense one must regret Nancy's lost autobiography, for herself as well as for her readers.

How true it would have been is another matter. Her dislike of Sydney was real, but that does not mean that it was wholly justified. There is no doubt that some of what Nancy wrote about her mother – in earlier letters, as it were *en passant* – does pull one up short. For example when Nancy's husband Peter Rodd joined up at the start of the Second World War, Sydney's immediate reaction was to say: 'I expect he'll be shot soon.' When Nancy was suffering fertility problems and was asked by a doctor whether she had ever come into contact with syphilis, Sydney confessed that, well, yes, her nursery maid had been infected with the disease. Of course this was all according to Nancy – were these things really said? The remark about Peter was probably at least part true, as it appears in two letters. As for the nursery-maid story – oddly enough, the usually sceptical Diana wrote that it made 'one's hair stand on end', so she had a degree of belief in it; or at least in *Nancy's* belief in it. Downright lying does seem unlikely. It is hard to think that even Nancy would have completely invented such a tale (unless she had been reading Ibsen). Given that she had no symptoms of syphilitic infection, it was clearly absurd that she should have thereafter blamed her mother for her struggle to have a baby. Nevertheless Sydney could be accused of lack of sympathy, or imagination, in her response to her daughter's darkest fears.

Then there is this, from Jessica. In a 1971 letter to Nancy she recounted how Sydney, aged around thirty – 'she must have been fairly horrid when young, too' – was staying in Dieppe, where she was confronted by a panic-stricken Nellie Romilly (Jessica's former mother-in-law). Nellie, very young at the time and not yet married, had lost £10 gambling, which she begged Sydney to lend to her. Instead Sydney 'informed': she marched off to Nellie's mother (Blanche Hozier) and told her exactly what had happened. According to Jessica, the story came from Sydney herself, who presumably – like many informers – still believed that she had done the right thing. In this instance what Jessica wrote has the ring of truth, and it does embody the cool, disapproving implacability that both she and Nancy disliked in their mother (interestingly their aunt Dorothy – 'Weenie' – displayed similar characteristics). Yet Nancy and Jessica could have chosen not to nurture resentment. Perhaps it was their nature – again, as writers – to cherish it instead. Doubtless Sydney and her sister could, in their turn, have decided to blame their father for everything. The odd, motherless, faintly stigmatized upbringing must have made them wary; so too being surrounded by their father's mistresses. Sydney was unsuited, perhaps, to the constant company of women. Amateur psychoanalysis can always find the sins of the parent in the child. What it can never quite do is allow for the fact that every influence is stimulated to different degrees.

It has to be said that, even allowing for Sydney's complex heredity, and her daughters' helpless habit of embroidery, the woman of Nancy and Jessica's collective memory is not easy to like. Cold, reserved, judgmental, miserly with praise: all the qualities one does not want in a mother. That said, they were highly demanding girls, and one cannot blame Sydney for withdrawing onto what *The Pursuit of Love* called 'her cloud'. Incidentally the portrait of Aunt Sadie was sympathetic – the character had the Mitford charm that Sydney lacked – and was used as a defence by Nancy after the 'Blor' essay: to little effect. Sydney had not especially liked being Aunt Sadie either.

Quite simply she had probably not wanted so many daughters (according to Deborah, she did not even bother to record her last child's birth in her 1920 engagement book; not that Deborah would have minded). As a younger woman she may have been jealous of them. She was twenty-four when Nancy was born, tremendously attractive, accustomed to that odd, diverting life with her father, full of flirtations and sailing and skating; the birth of her first child was difficult, so was the breastfeeding and so, in truth, was Nancy. For somebody who was not innately maternal, to find herself quite quickly surrounded by so many girls, screaming, showing off and competing for attention, must have required tremendous inward adjustments and sacrifices. It is not so difficult to see why she gave an impression of chilliness, nor to understand this from both Sydney's and Nancy's points of view. Jessica is slightly more problematical, as it is generally accepted by the sisters that Sydney mellowed after Deborah's birth when she was forty (this too is echoed in *The Pursuit of Love*). She went to immense efforts to keep her younger daughters amused; this in an era where one could not simply plonk them in front of a screen. In the face of Jessica's and Unity's sulking and discontentment she arranged holidays, trips, cruises – too much perhaps. Later she may have wondered whether it had been worth it.

How affected they all were by her, nonetheless! – still discussing her influence, her character, right up to the end. Even Diana –

'I adored my mother'[27] – confessed in late life to being 'horrified' by how strict Sydney had been during the Asthall years. She had been reading some of Pamela's letters and was left with this impression. One suspects that if the letters had been written by Nancy or Jessica, she would have dismissed them as exaggeration; even though she herself, in youth, 'had been distant, resentful and rather scornful of Sydney'[28] and on more than one occasion fell victim to her lethal disapproval. When, for instance, Diana left her first husband for Sir Oswald Mosley, her mother refused to allow Jessica and Deborah to see her – at the time Diana was as resentful and bitter as Nancy would have been but, as she wrote many years later, she had chosen to forget such displays of 'cruelty'. What changed things was Sydney's behaviour during the war, the loyalty that she showed when her daughter was imprisoned in Holloway, and her fondness for Mosley. Diana's husband massively affected her feelings towards her family. He adored Sydney and could scarcely tolerate Nancy (who saw through him: the worst thing with a man of that kind). And then Sydney, like the Mosleys, was very much against war with Germany. She met Hitler and liked him; nor did she renege on her belief in appeasement. In the first week of the war she threatened to turf Nancy out of a car because her daughter had said something rude about Hitler. Or so Nancy wrote, to Jessica, who thirty years later recounted this story during a BBC documentary.[29] So unfair, raged Diana. People won't realize how nasty and 'needling' Nancy could be to their mother. In other words, Sydney had been at the end of her tether, rather than roused to defend the Führer. 'Muv was so much more marvellous than Nancy,' concluded Diana, rather pathetically.

As ever, Deborah was emollient. She really was the only Mitford girl to retain good relations with all the others and to receive, and deftly juggle, all their confidences. Despite the Hitler nonsense, which she largely ignored, Deborah adored Diana and respected her sister's passionate desire to defend Sydney. Jessica, in Deborah's view, was inevitably prepared to attack their mother as a reactionary, a right-winger, all the rest of it – but 'the old hen has a heart'. Nancy was – as Deborah conceded – a tricky one, who had been unable to mature sufficiently to accept her mother as a person in her own right, but whose life had perhaps required the creation of a familial scapegoat? Deborah was easier on Nancy than Diana was. But this youngest daughter had also been unequivocally fond of Sydney, able to see that her Mrs Bennet life was enough to drive a clever woman round the twist and that, rather than become obsessively wrapped up in her daughters, she had deployed a mixture of detachment and rigidity that had frustrated Nancy, angered Jessica and left Unity, just possibly, fatally derailed. Deborah, in contrast, was perfectly suited by her upbringing, or perhaps she was unaffected by it. She conveyed her mother's withdrawn air by prefixing her every utterance with the evocation of a languid drawl: 'Orrnnnhh'. By this simple device – typically Deborah in its dry, perceptive absurdity – any sense of Sydney's coldness and abstraction is neutralized. 'Telling Muv something thrilling or frightening seldom evoked more than "Orrnnnhh, Stubby, fancy"...' In Deborah's account, all her other sisters periodically complained about Sydney; she freely admitted that being the youngest made it easier for her. For example she went hunting alone from the age of twelve. 'It's all right for Lady Redesdale,' said another mother, 'she's got five more girls so it doesn't matter if anything happens to Debo...'

VI

The complex influence of Sydney extended to the family friend James Lees-Milne, who wrote in her 1963 obituary that she presided over the Mitfords with 'imperturbable serenity, pride and sweetness'. Far from being off-putting, her 'patrician reserve' was 'one of her chief charms'. Looking back upon his stays at Asthall and Swinbrook, he concluded: 'The source of those cloudless days was – I now realise it with pangs of sadness – that enigmatical, generous, great-minded matriarchal figure...'

What may or may not be relevant here is that Lees-Milne worshipped Diana – a couple of years her senior, he thought her a perfect girl and remained steadfast throughout her problematical adulthood – and did not entirely like Nancy. They were friends, but in his writings he was often critical of her. 'I did not much enjoy [dinner] for Nancy's scintillations dry me up,' was a typical diary entry. Her teasing, he wrote, had a 'sharp little barb barely concealed like the hook of an angler's fly beneath a riot of gay feathers'. Many people saw Nancy as barbed, including Diana. John Betjeman, on the other hand, who knew the family well, thought that 'Nancy was the warmest'. With his poetic perception, he might have seen her relationship with Sydney as a dense, sad, accumulation of stubbornness that not even death could break down. To those inclined to criticize, however, Nancy's relationship with her mother showed her in a poor light. Lees-Milne celebrated the very qualities in Sydney that left Nancy feeling guilty and misunderstood; one wonders what she made of his obituary. Jessica, who liked it, was large-minded enough not to object to the criticisms of *Hons and Rebels*, although she was droll about the notion of Sydney's 'mariner' soul. 'All very well for J. Lees-Milne, thought I, but who wants to be brought up by a mariner?'[30]

Lees-Milne had, by his own account, been one of the first people to observe the phenomenon of the 'Mitford girls' in action. In his autobiography he recalled a dinner at Swinbrook in 1926, in the course of which – so the story went – David had thrown a gigantic tantrum. He had reacted furiously to Lees-Milne's suggestion that England should be making friends with Germany (something of a recurring theme, this), and shouted: 'You don't know what the bloody Huns are like. They are worse than all the devils in hell.' The sainted Sydney had calmed her husband down ('with a pained expression on her dear face') but the situation had gone too far for retrieval. According to Lees-Milne, all the girls – from Nancy, aged twenty-one, to Deborah aged six – 'looked at one another and then chanted in unison: '"We don't want to lose you/ But we think you ought to go."'

As it happened, the girls did no such thing. For somebody who did not admire Nancy's writing – as he later admitted was the case – Lees-Milne had bought in completely to her myth-making. His recollection of the evening was published in 1970, twenty-five years after *The Pursuit of Love*, and what it offers is tantamount to an omitted and rediscovered scene from the novel: raging Uncle Matthew, tranquil Aunt Sadie, the x 6 entity of the beautiful, buoyant sisters. The Mitford girls of Lees-Milne's description were a literary construct rather than a memory. In fact the dinner party in question took place in 1928, and there was no merry singing at the end of it; it is doubtful whether the younger sisters were even there. The evening disintegrated into extreme and unusual discomfiture. This was made clear in a letter written by Nancy at the time, to Tom Mitford. Many years later Diana remembered it as an exceptional occasion at which 'everybody' lost their tempers.

It was through Tom that Lees-Milne met the Mitfords; the two boys attended the same prep school and at Eton had a love affair. In another volume of autobiography Lees-Milne described his relationship with Tom with remarkable touching openness: how, outside the school chapel on Sunday evenings, 'he and I would… passionately embrace, lips to lips, body pressed to body, each feeling the opposite fibre of the other…' After Eton, as Lees-Milne recalled, Tom became exclusively heterosexual, although he had had several affairs at school, including a fling with Hamish St Clair-Erskine, whom Nancy later dreamed of marrying. On one occasion he had a friend to stay at Swinbrook and his mother asked whether they would mind sharing his bedroom, whereupon his sisters collapsed in hysteria. In other words they knew perfectly well what Tom got up to – he probably simply told them – which makes it all the more perverse that Nancy later refused to accept Hamish's obvious homosexuality.

Tom, like Diana, was a perfect distillation of the Mitford looks and cleverness. The qualities of the family collected themselves together in him, breeding a man who did not, in worldly terms, achieve all that he might have done, but who left a mark simply by what he was. He was a refined product, with an impassive countenance and a fastidious mind: 'with him,' wrote Lees-Milne, 'the second best simply did not pass muster'.[31] His rarefied tastes – Milton, Schopenhauer, Bach – communicated themselves to his sisters, Diana in particular. At Batsford, when Tom was prepared for his prep school, Nancy had been spurred to academic rivalry with him. Later, Jessica's sense of stultification was alleviated by the literature that Tom inspired her to read.

After Eton – which he left in 1927, not long after the Mitford move to Swinbrook House – rather than go to university he travelled to Europe, where he studied music, and stayed for a time in Austria at the ancient Schloss Bernstein belonging to the Hungarian count, Janos von Almasy. It has been suggested[32] that Tom had an affair with Almasy (later this would also be said of Unity). There is no evidence for this, other than Tom's youthful predilections. Nancy did tease her brother that Sydney thought his 'Austrian friends' were 'getting hold of' him – nudge nudge – but in fact he had fallen for a girl, Francesca Erdody. Subsequently he spent time in Berlin. As with his grandfather and two of his sisters, something in that thunderous, uncompromising culture spoke to him.

Tom had dreamed of a musician's career, but in 1929 began studying for the law at Inner Temple. He needed to earn; although David gave him an allowance there was no real financial safety net. He entered the chambers of Norman Birkett, an esteemed KC, and in 1935 was part of the defence team for Alma Rattenbury, who was accused of conspiring with her much younger lover to murder her husband.[33] This was one of the most sensational criminal trials of the decade; in her debutante year Jessica sneaked in to watch proceedings at the Old Bailey, to which her father reacted rather as Uncle Matthew did when his children mentioned Oscar Wilde.

Meanwhile Tom was a sleek social animal. His close friends included his second cousin Randolph Churchill – despite an age difference of thirty-five years, he was also friendly with Winston – and he had lots of girlfriends. It was thought that he might marry pretty young Penelope Dudley Ward, but (in the style of the then Prince of Wales) he preferred women of the world like the Countess Erdody, the married Princesse de Faucigny-Lucinge, or the Austrian dancer Tilly Losch. Perhaps their extreme sophistication was the best antidote to all those clamorous sisters – Losch, for instance, was a professional at playing hard to get, and that was one quality that the Mitford girls did not really possess.

But certainly Tom was not frightened of women. This is what was impressive about him: surrounded by so many girls, so strong in personality, so energetic even in their boredom, so relentlessly competitive – including for his attention – he could have gone down the Branwell Brontë route and decided to be overwhelmed. He could have been embarrassed by the girls, taking the side of his male friends against them. Instead he was extraordinarily good to Nancy when she was trapped in her futile passion for Hamish St Clair-Erskine; on one occasion in 1929 he rescued her from the Café de Paris, where she had gone with Hamish with 7½d between them (this was typical). 'We were panicking rather,' she wrote to a friend, 'when the sallow & disapproving countenance of old Mit was observed...' Tom lent Nancy £1 and swept her away to another nightclub: perfect brotherly behaviour, as was taking Jessica as his escort to the Inner Temple ball in 1935 (her debutante season). Tom could have become petulant, demanding, anything he chose really, given that he was – like Alexei, the heir to Tsar Nicholas II – the sole prized boy. Instead he went the other way, and dealt with it all as if it was the easiest thing in the world. He was the embodiment of an overused concept: cool. True cool does not exclude warmth, but Tom always had the ability to keep himself at a slight distance, to make others want to please him. If this was a natural consequence of growing up with the Mitford girls then it was a good ploy, the best possible way of coping with them. The sisters to whom he was closest – Nancy and Diana – both ended up with men who were always at a remove, who made the women come to them.

It was later suggested, by Unity's biographer, that there was something faintly decadent in the relationship between brother and sisters: incest was said to be a 'beloved Mitford topic' and Tom 'had more than his share of this joke'.[34] Certainly one can imagine Unity making excitable cracks along these lines. Possibly Nancy might have done so, in a would-be daring spirit. But this is the kind of thing that can be made to sound a little warped, if one wishes to express a generalized disapproval; it would have been amazing if Tom *hadn't* been teased in some way.

Despite the mutual affection, which really does seem to have been cloudless, he was quite different from his sisters. For instance he suffered from depression, whereas they had that iron will to happiness. He enjoyed their rippling flurry of constant jokes but did not have that same instinct to make absolutely everything funny. In 1930, however, he disguised himself as 'Bruno Hat', an avant-garde German painter, confined by ill-health to a wheelchair in which he made an appearance at a private view, staged by Diana and her first husband (the catalogue for the event was written by Evelyn Waugh). Poor Lytton Strachey actually bought one of Bruno Hat's paintings. He may have done so to please Diana, whose friend he was; by this time the older Mitford girls had joined the outside world that Tom had, for some ten years, symbolized to them.

Rather like Pamela, but in a more dynamic way, Tom was necessary to the family. Otherwise the jagged composite of Nancy, Diana, Unity and Jessica would have overbalanced it completely. Tom was the person whom everybody both respected *and* liked. To achieve that, all he really had to do was be male and keep relatively quiet, but he did more – the imprint of his personality was enduring. Nevertheless he remained a mystery. Later his sisters would tear themselves to pieces over whether he had or had not been a Fascist sympathizer. Nobody knew quite what he felt about anything. Unlike the Radletts in *The Pursuit of Love,* who 'tell' everything, Tom was the male equivalent of exquisite Polly Hampton in *Love in a Cold Climate,* who burns with emotions but keeps them entirely to herself. Polly is to some degree based upon Diana; yet even she, enigmatic though she was, did at least 'explain' herself in letters and writings – very few of Tom's letters survive. They are friendly and perceptive but most decidedly not in the Mitford idiom. In 1930, for example, Tom describes to his mother a flight along the English coast in a '7 man unit' whose passengers included Churchill and T. E. Lawrence: 'It was very amusing flying *very* low over the edge of the sea and jumping the piers at Brighton and Littlehampton, to the astonishment of the people there . . .' That year Tom, who had joined the Auxiliary Air Force, was in a flying accident when his plane crashed into a tree while taking off from Swinbrook. He was taken to Burford hospital and suffered concussion only, but one may imagine – in the days before misfortune began to come at the Mitfords from every direction – the carefully concealed terror of his parents.

Also in 1930, Tom holidayed with his parents and assorted sisters at St Moritz, where they skated constantly. This was a family obsession. As a girl Sydney had loved skating, and had a passion for her instructor: 'I would even let him kiss me,' she wrote in her diary. David, still with that excess of energy in his early fifties, often visited the skating rink in Oxford with his brother Jack, where both men flirted gallantly with the Austrian instructresses. Unity won a medal for skating (although on one occasion she fell on her face, having failed to put out her hands in time: 'I was waiting to see if nature would prompt me'). Tom was talented enough to partner the Olympic champion Sonja Henie (who skated through several Hollywood films), while Deborah, who at St Moritz partnered the Conservative statesman Sir Samuel Hoare, was actually invited to join the British junior team, although her mother turned this down without telling her of the offer (the regret that Deborah admitted to in her autobiography was quite strong, by her standards). Jack Mitford was also on the St Moritz trip, preparing to do the Cresta run. With him was a glamorous chorus girl named Sheilah Graham, who later became a hugely successful Hollywood columnist (one of the first iconoclast celebrity journalists) and the last love of F. Scott Fitzgerald. One of those clever young creatures who instinctively recognize how to find advantage in every situation, Graham relished mixing with the Mitfords – although at that point they had no fame – and aspired to what she saw as their cultured conversation, as well as their aristocratic ease. Perhaps it was her nature to do this, but she became – almost uniquely – fascinated by the Mitford men rather than the women. Tom, whom she described as 'one of the handsomest men I had ever seen', was naturally the focus of her fantasies. 'Perhaps I could found an aristocracy of my own. And I would choose Tom Mitford to be the father, and my sons would look like Saxon kings.'[35]

VII

David, too, was compared with a Saxon king. Sheilah Graham may have known about the antiquity of the Mitford family, but really she was judging David by his physicality and demeanour: his 'great shoulders', his 'finely chiselled head', the undiminished air of the aristocrat who had dominated through strength, who had ascended to power because he looked as though it naturally belonged to him.

The impression is of a man who would have thrived in those simpler times. Nancy, too, portrayed her father in this way. 'Such men as... Uncle Matthew would not have been themselves had they not always been kings in their own little castles,' she wrote in the valedictory 1960 novel *Don't Tell Alfred*. 'Their kind is vanishing as surely as the peasants, the horses and the [Parisian] avenues, to be replaced, like them, by something less picturesque, more utilitarian.' By then David was dead, and had long ceased to be Uncle Matthew, but in Nancy's literary imagination he had become a symbol of something irrecoverable, grander and wilder than the age to which they both belonged.

The other Mitford girls essentially concurred in the representation of David as Uncle Matthew. Diana protested a little – 'he wasn't as mad as that'[36] – and both she and Deborah corrected Nancy's repeated suggestion that he was violent. But David did not, as his wife did, arouse deep divisions of opinion within the sisters. He was warmer than Sydney, more vulnerable, easier to know; and weaker, despite the confidence of his breed. Overlooked as a boy, overshadowed by a charismatic father and paragon brother, thwarted in his desired army career, he naturally gravitated towards the calm divinity that was the young Sydney, and in the early years of their marriage he wrote of his great happiness. Like Tom he was comfortable with a house full of women. When Deborah was born in 1920, the parlourmaid Mabel said: 'I knew it was a girl by the look on his Lordship's face,' but the disappointment would have been superficial. If the honeymoon gloss of his London family life had worn away a little, the seven years at Asthall were surely still the most contented period that David would know: when he could stretch his limbs across his pheasant-coloured land, prowl in his coverts, fish for trout in his three miles of the Windrush, occupy his space in the world with his own people. Deborah would later recall how, as a child, her father would pick her up and carry her lightly as he went about his countryman's business: 'the comforting feel of his velveteen waistcoat is inseparable from my memories of him.'[37]

Like Uncle Matthew, David was an indulgent father. Although – unlike a modern parent – he was most definitely a father rather than a friend, he enjoyed entering his children's world, they entranced him with their spirited, fantastical, sometimes bad-tempered behaviour, and he sought to encourage them (albeit not intellectually). The pony that he took to High Wycombe in a third-class carriage was bought (under Blackfriars Bridge) because he suddenly thought that his children would like it. At Asthall he made a pool in the river where they could learn to swim, together with a diving board. Walking back home after bathing, in his dark-blue serge suit plus what he called his 'crinoline' – a bizarre little skirt worn for modesty – he would amuse them by picking up sticks and stones with his feet, saying: 'Look what my prehensile extremities can do.' His turn of phrase, which was his own, was a mixture of deliberate droll pedantry, surreal adjectives ('take your degraded elbows off the table') and straightforward statements whose very plainness created a kind of poetry ('he's a meaningless piece of meat/ a literary cove/ a putrid sort of fella'). Like the Mitford girl idiom, this mode of speech was completely natural to him, although one has the sense that he knew it amused his daughters and deployed it accordingly. Thanks to Nancy, it gave him a kind of immortality.

Uncle Matthew was a more accurate portrait than Nancy's first shot at portraying her father, as the blustering, blimpish General Murgatroyd in *Highland Fling*. But both creations had his wilful, unaccountable temper. As Deborah put it, 'reason was not part of his make-up.' In youth he was prone to appalling tantrums and was once locked in a room by his father, where he heated a poker with which to launch a revenge attack. *The Pursuit of Love* describes how his children could push him, inch by inch, in what Nancy called a game of 'Tom Tiddler's ground', teasing and badgering and measuring his head to see whether he was a 'subhuman'; all of which he would take in high good humour, until suddenly the explosion would come.

This was close to real life, although David's rages had an irritable oddity that his alter ego lacked. Uncle Matthew would flare up over all sorts of things – punctuality ('in precisely six and three-quarter minutes the damned fella will be late'), his neighbour Lady Montdore ('the hell-bag'), his daughters' young men ('sewers'),[38] Slavs ('so that's a Serb, is it? Well, just what one would expect, needs a shave'), any foreigner ('they're all the same, and they all make me sick') – and so on. Yet so widespread is this hatred that it creates a perversely benign effect: it is token, almost meaningless. David was milder in the general way of things, but his anger was more disconcerting. It may have sprung from frustration – as if he were constantly fighting against the missing lung, the broken pelvis that put an end to riding – rather than bombast. David had no vices (unless one counts smoking). He did not drink, gambled only occasionally, almost certainly never womanized and, despite memberships of the usual places – the House of Lords, the Carlton and Marlborough Clubs – he did not really indulge in the wallowing relaxation of masculine company. So he had no outlets for emotional steam: except these sudden manifestations of temper. He could be rude, as to James Lees-Milne. He was obsessively fastidious, and had a horror of untidy eating, of spills on the 'good tablecloth', of stickiness anywhere (his stated idea of hell was honey on his bowler hat). He was also provoked by Unity's habit of eating vast quantities of mashed potatoes while staring at him with her giant baleful eyes. Sometimes she would slide down from her chair and simply sit beneath the table. This is where David's raging and Sydney's detachment failed, quite seriously, to meet the case; but who knows what would have worked better?

Jessica picked up and ran with the image of her father as Uncle Matthew (she even bought into him as General Murgatroyd), most particularly in his ideas relating to literacy. She promoted the Nancy-created myths that he loathed education for girls (sort of true), loathed reading (not really true), and loathed girls reading. The claim was that if he found one of his daughters with a book, he would come up with some sort of errand: 'Go and tell Hooper' – the groom – to thwart them. Perhaps it might have happened that way if the girl in question had been seen lounging with a book in the house, but as most of the books were in the Asthall barn the dread activity of reading could take place in peace.

Anyway he did not want ignorant daughters (like his grandmother, Lady Airlie, he was insistent upon proficiency in French). He simply had the ideas of his class about what was desirable. A country-living aristocrat born in the mid-Victorian era *would* think that girls should be educated chiefly at home, should acquire charm and accomplishments and a good seat on a horse, with a view to a successful debut in society. David was more liberal than most fathers; in no real way did he clamp down upon his daughters' behaviour. This reactionary-cum-liberal attitude, this potent mixture of restraint and freedom, has been held responsible – in part at least – for the excesses of certain Mitford girls. And probably quite rightly. But it was more complicated than that: there were more factors at work. It was not David's fault that he had so many daughters, that they were bright and mischievous and competitive, that they fought for the attention of a distant mother, that they came of age when the world went mad.

What certainly influenced the sisters was the sheer scale of David's personality, the theatricality that blossomed when he acquired his inheritance. He was a big man, in every sense. And the girls were most attracted, on the whole, to highly masculine types; the New Man would have done very little for them. It was not until later that they realized the inadequacies that lay within their father's splendid exterior.

He was, for instance, truly hopeless with money. 'Poor Dowdie, *so unlucky*,' was the sweet, demeaning judgment of his mother Clementine (no home economist either: having got through thousands of her own, in old age she moved from a house in Earl's Court to Redesdale Cottage in Northumberland, where she kept a pig on a lead). Again David could not be blamed for his lack of financial sense, although he may have blamed himself. After selling Batsford and a proportion of its contents, as well as disposing of the Kensington house and the Northumberland estate, he should have been comfortably set up for life (not least because only Tom's education would have cost real money). In 1921 Sydney received a financial shot in the arm, when her father died leaving her just under a quarter of his £60,000 estate; this was her own money, but it all helped. Meanwhile David added to the Swinbrook acres, a perfectly reasonable investment. However, as Nancy wrote crisply of her imaginary Lord Fortinbras, 'he and his forebears have always regarded their estates with the eyes of sportsmen rather than cultivators.'

David, like Fortinbras, planted woods for game and regarded his land as a vast outdoor playground. At Asthall Manor, he made plenty of sensible changes – in addition to the new outbuildings he installed water-powered electric light, and created a lovely beech avenue leading to the house – but all for a place that he wanted to get rid of. 'Oh how mad to have done all that & then sold it at a loss to build Swinbrook,' Diana lamented to Deborah, sixty years after the event. Mad indeed. Had he not determined upon moving to Swinbrook House, 'he could have hung on' – meaning financially – but there was a sort of stubbornness, and again a frustration, that compelled David to do these things.

Although Asthall Manor was not sold until 1926, it was advertised for sale – together with 2,140 acres – as early as 1922, and to let the following year. Either there were no takers, or David changed his mind for a while. Then came the dreaded Swinbrook, eighteen bedrooms' worth of it, built on the site of an old house called South Lawn. Of course there was nothing really wrong with the place (although over-symmetry gave it an institutional air), but homeliness is not a quality that can be fabricated, and after Asthall it seemed bare and shivery (hence the lure of the Hons' Cupboard, and the childish cries of 'the knives and forks are so cold we can't eat with them'). The interior doors were elm, which warps easily. Nancy, who teased atrociously about Swinebrook, contended that one could put a head around a locked bathroom door and see what was going on behind it. The beautiful furniture was arranged with Sydney's usual flair but never looked as though it belonged to the rooms. Although Deborah loved the house, being too young (six) to know much of the sprawling easy charm of Asthall, to everybody else it was a dull disappointment. For this, too, David may have blamed himself. 'At Swinbrook,' wrote Diana, 'his gaiety seemed to diminish, and he became almost, if never quite, grown up.'

The move did fragment the family. With unconscious poetry Sydney evoked the sense of loss by saying that she remembered life at Asthall as 'all summers'. Yet by 1926 there were other changes, coincidental and inevitable. Nancy and Pam were now out in society. Tom was in his last year at Eton. Diana was being readied for her debutante season. The family was splitting in two, in the nature of things. The older children could not really regret the fact that their grandfather's library was now housed in David's study, nor that the piano stood on public display in the long white drawing room, where nobody felt very inclined to play it. But Jessica, certainly, must have felt the lack of the Asthall barn, that wonderful retreat. One does have the impression that the world of the younger Mitford girls was sillier, more facile, than that of Nancy and Diana. If this is partly because of the way that Jassy and Victoria behave in *Love in a Cold Climate* – squawking constantly about sex ('blissikins') and chanting headlines from the *Daily Express* – then one also assumes that Nancy caught their mood from life. It was fine for Deborah, with her beautifully healthy character and love of country pursuits; there were no ill-effects from this introverted life among extrovert people. She was totally absorbed in the long Oxfordshire days, the pretty village with its small green square of cricket ground, the little church where she would lick the pew[39] and arrange primroses for the Easter decorations, the woods with the Gibbet Oak that had once been a hanging tree, the blacksmith doing his rough, dextrous work with hooves and shoes, the adored groom Hooper whose mare – a war horse – dropped dead during the Armistice silence in 1927, the marvellous abundance of dogs, the hens that gossiped around her feet and whose eggs she sold to her mother for extra pocket money – it all formed an indestructible bedrock of security against the storms to come. But Jessica and Unity suffered more, at

Swinbrook, from the sense of being cut off and mutually reliant; even though Unity need not have been either, had she managed to stay at school.

In autumn 1926, before the move to Swinbrook, Sydney travelled with her daughters (and Blor) to Paris, where they spent several months at a family hotel in the Avenue Victor-Hugo – quite a normal practice in those days, far cheaper than it would be today – and Diana was enrolled at the Cours Fénelon finishing school (where she admitted learning more in six months than she had in six years at Asthall). A governess was found for the three youngest girls. Nancy, whose good friend Mary O'Neill was then staying in Paris with her grandfather, the British ambassador, had a glorious time judging from an excitable letter to Tom. She went with Pam to stay with Baron Robert de Rothschild, dined at the embassy with Mary and began to steep herself in the eighteenth century French history that would later become her passion ('they were all exactly like *One*, that's the truth!' she wrote of the Versailles court in the age of Louis XV).

Nancy had visited Paris for the first time in 1922 – with girls from Hatherop Castle school – and experienced something of a premonitory *coup de foudre*, encountering that dusk-and-honey-colour city where she would later be so happy. Waiting for a bus in the Avenue Henri-Martin she had, she wrote, found herself in tears at the sheer loveliness. Her worship of Paris, of France, of almost every French person both past and present, may have been nurtured during the Second World War in reaction to the Teutonic sympathies of certain family members; but it was also real. Nancy's light, formal, discriminating spirit found its counterpart in Fragonard and Sèvres. After the blissful 1926 Paris sojourn it was therefore especially ghastly to return to the new house at Swinbrook. To Tom, again, she expressed her feelings: 'Deep depression has the Mitford family in its clutches...' Rather like children – but with the wryness of young adults – the brother and sister invented an imaginary land, 'Kr', that was the opposite of Swinbrook.

Some relief came from the fact that David had by this time acquired another London house, 26 Rutland Gate, with a mews behind. It had cost almost £28,000, an enormous sum. This was not a particularly beautiful place either – a tall, stand-alone building, which like Asthall had a graveyard beside it (for the Russian Orthodox church). But it was also rather splendid, with a balcony overlooking Hyde Park, a lift installed by David, a charming grey and gold drawing room and an odd internal communication system, whereby one blew down a mouthpiece to alert another floor and then talked into it. This makes the house sound extremely large, which it was: a real giant old London home, with nine servants. It was close to what Sydney called 'wicked old Harrod' (Harrods) which delivered food, to the Albert Hall where the family had permanent seats, and (which Deborah adored) to the Tattersalls auction house that in those days sold thoroughbred horses on Knightsbridge Green.

It was, however, rented out much of the time from 1929 onwards: the point at which the Mitford finances went truly awry. Rutland Gate was let first to the Earl of Elgin, while Sir Charles Hambro took Swinbrook. The Daimler was sold. The girls hunkered down in the mews and at Sydney's cottage in High Wycombe. David went gold prospecting again in Canada. (Evelyn Waugh, then at a loose end, mused: 'I might go and dig in Lord Redesdale's bogus gold mine if he would let me.'[40])

As poverty went, it was relative – and relatively intermittent, in that the family returned to Swinbrook in 1931 – and could in part be attributed to the Wall Street Crash that took so much down with it. But David had sold and built, sold and bought for the past ten years, always doing too much of everything, living as if the future would mysteriously resolve itself, while at the same time warning his daughters that they would have no funds (which they did not: 'Oh, I never had any *money*!' shrieked Nancy in a television interview,[41] claiming that she had written *Highland Fling* for the simple reason that she wanted to 'earn £100'.) Interestingly, none of the Mitford girls seems to have minded about their father's financial incompetence. The impression is that they just accepted it, or did not take it very seriously. 'We lived under the shadow, so to speak, of two hammers,' Nancy would later say in her airy way, 'the builder's and the auctioneer's.'[42] But there *had* been a fine inheritance. Once Batsford was sold – and many aristocratic families at the time got rid of those vast houses – there should have been no more problems. Quite simply, the problem was David. He was married to a woman who kept immaculate accounts, who prudently paid her children's governesses from the eggs that she sold to London clubs, who attempted to teach economy by asking them to plan how to spend a household budget of £500 ('Flowers: £490', was Nancy's first entry), yet who seems to have been incapable of guiding her husband away from his worst instincts. One might say that she was essentially a Victorian, born into an era in which wives did not question their husbands – but in fact any woman not married to a monster could always shove her man gently towards the path of good sense. Perhaps Diana, who later said that her mother had a dreadful time with so much selling and moving, was right when she suggested that her father had 'paid no heed to Muv'.

He had sold Asthall at a loss – typical 'poor Dowdie' behaviour – nor had he received a particularly good price for Batsford. Having been advertised for auction, the estate was instead sold privately; as was the Otterburn land in Northumberland, some 12,000-plus acres, which the buyer then sold on immediately. This transaction was cited in a Parliamentary debate, expressing concern about 'cases of disturbance of tenants by reason of speculation in land values'. The strong implication here is that David had offloaded something that he should have tried harder to keep. Money goes; land does not.

So then David sought to make money, through business ventures. He went at it like somebody in a *Boy's Own* comic, dashing off to gold mines, investing in a scheme to raise gold bullion from a sunken galleon. Most unfortunately of all, he was persuaded by his brother-in-law, Geoffrey Bowles, to put money into a business run by a mysterious South American, the 'Marquis of Andia'. This man had devised ways to hide what was then called a wireless, that is to say a radio, which in those days – the late 1920s – was an ugly great thing. The marquis had created a whole series of decorative plastic containers that could, as Diana put it in her delicately mirthful way, 'take an honoured place among the old Famille Rose'. At the time this may have seemed a good idea, although it now sounds tremendously bogus (reminiscent of the woman in Patrick Hamilton's *Mr Stimpson and Mr Gorse* who conceals her telephone beneath the skirts of a Marie Antoinette doll). And indeed David, having become a director of the 'Artandia Ltd' company, took fright fairly quickly. He warned his friend Lord Dulverton (to whom he had sold Batsford) against investing; by a succession of Chinese whispers this led to a slander case at the High Court in 1930, in which David was accused of saying that the marquis was a conman with no right to his title, and that his wife was 'no better than she ought to be'. Of course he had said these things. But he stood up firmly to cross-examination, the judge was very much on his side, and the case was dismissed.

Although the marquis repaid £13,000 to David, how much he actually put into similar schemes is unclear. 'That's where the millions [sic] he got for Batsford disappeared,' wrote Diana to Deborah many years later. 'Farve was an innocent.' His judgment was almost perfectly the inverse of what it should have been. He turned down an opportunity to invest in the first ice-making machines, which were eventually installed in pretty much every British pub. It was said that he decided against putting money into his old friend William Morris's car business, despite taking a great interest in motoring: in 1929 he attended a House of Lords debate about the proposed introduction of the driving test, which he unsurprisingly opposed, citing an examination that he had passed in order to drive in France: 'It was a most unutterable farce and proved nothing.' After the sale of the chauffeur-driven Daimler, David bought a Morris, happily drove it himself and spent hours at his friend's car factory in Cowley, just outside Oxford. 'As he had nothing much to do,' wrote Diana, 'it seems a pity, looking back, that he didn't earn his living by joining this immensely successful firm.'[43]

But then, as Nancy put it in 'The English Aristocracy', 'Does it occur to either Lord or Lady Fortinbras to get a job and retrieve the family fortunes? It does not.'

VIII

Uncle Matthew is described as having rather a lot of money, so much so that the subject is never spoken of by the family. It is mostly tied up in land, which is sacred to him. It is impossible to imagine him selling any part of it, and it is nearly impossible to imagine him away from it. As he says to Fanny, 'you know I never go inside other people's houses if I can help it.'

So it is something of a surprise to read the court pages of *The Times*, that fragrant daily burst of Georgette Heyer, and see just how often the names of Lord and Lady Redesdale appear. Of 'Aunt Sadie' it is said that she has 'known the world' – a lovely phrase – and that she rather enjoys parties, although as a wife she naturally, and contentedly, humours her husband's preference (later Diana would concur with this, suggesting that her mother should have perhaps married somebody more social, but had not minded about it.) Nevertheless the impression from the court pages is of an outgoing couple, rather than the opposite. It is easy to forget that David was a scion of illustrious families, that he would in the nature of things attend state balls, royal weddings and, in 1928, a garden party held by 'Mrs Baldwin' at 10 Downing Street (although the aristocracy did not greatly care for the bourgeois Stanley Baldwin). Uncle Matthew goes to a grand ball in *Love in a Cold Climate*, squeezed into knee breeches so tight that he dare not sit down, but this is very much a one-off. He attends the House of Lords, voting unaccountably and according to conscience, making a speech against the admission of peeresses in their own right as they would use the peers' lavatory. (According to his daughter Linda, this was what all the lords were thinking but only her father dared to say.)

As usual, this magnificent, free-spirited portrait is about half true of David. He *was* a somewhat maverick member of the Lords, but he was also frequently in attendance – it was not quite true to write, as he later did, 'I never come to London if I can avoid it.' To him the Lords was a necessity, an honourable place. His dream was to return the second chamber to the days before Lloyd George's 1911 Parliament Act, which had curtailed its veto and removed its role in financial legislation. 'Does it never occur to anybody,' he wrote to *The Times* in 1926, 'that this present Gargantuan orgy of extravagance in which this country is indulging, which is ruining it, not inch by inch, but league by league, is directly attributable to Single Chamber government in finance? This view, though naturally not popular with politicians, is well understood by the people as a whole...' Whatever one thinks of this, it is not the argument of a raging illiterate; which Nancy – or more precisely Jessica, *après* Nancy – sometimes showed their father to be.

David was a true conservative, a tendency inherited only by Deborah (and possibly Pam). And one senses fear in him, an emotion that his daughters seem never to have felt. In 1922 his reaction to the 'very grave crisis in the country' – the dire post-war slump, the first national hunger march – was to join a new movement called 'the Diehards', along with the Lords Salisbury and Londonderry. As much as anything they were motivated by terror of what Salisbury called 'the Bolshevist bogy'. This nervousness about the spread of Communism was absolutely real, and by no means as irrational as it now seems. The Diehards were formed during a Conservative administration, but they felt let down by its broken promise to repeal the Parliament Act; and now Ramsay MacDonald was around the corner. 'We trust Labour,' said Salisbury bravely. Nevertheless in 1934 – ten years after MacDonald formed his first administration – Salisbury would put forward a reform bill that proposed the election of 150 peers, on the grounds that a future Labour government might destroy the second chamber if it remained wholly unelected.

David, who passionately disagreed with the bill, put forward a motion for rejecting it. He would have done sterling battle against Tony Blair (described by Deborah as 'a stranger to common sense'), who in 1999 removed all but ninety-two of the hereditary peers. Denying the hereditary principle, said David, 'was a direct blow to the Crown, and to the very foundation of the Christian faith'. Who knows whether he was genuinely religious – church every Sunday was about one's position rather than one's soul – but there were ideals in which he absolutely believed: *noblesse oblige* and England.

However much he really longed to be lurking in coverts with his beloved gamekeeper, Steele, he spent much of his time in public service (like Lord Fortinbras, who is 'on the go' all the time, although 'it is a go that does not bring in one penny'). He served on the local bench and county council – that was in the nature of things – but he was also in London, doing all sorts of jobs that one would imagine to have bored Uncle Matthew to death. He sat dutifully on select committees, often at the head, considering such *recherché* questions as the boundaries of Brighton. In 1931 he became Chairman of the Charity Organization Society, and wrote regular letters to the newspapers, pleading with the public not to cut its donations. He was genuinely concerned about unemployment – by then rising to appalling levels, more than 20 per cent of the working population in 1933 – but he believed equally in the need to cut state dependency, as with the introduction of means testing in 1931. To David, solutions lay in reviving 'the family ideal', as opposed to 'the mass-charity of the State'. He would probably have liked the concept of the Big Society, although he might have ground his dentures at the career politicians (smarmy sort of fellas) who so smoothly propounded it.

Social responsibility was natural to him – he had a genuine bond of trust with his estate workers, just as Deborah would later have at Chatsworth – but he believed that it could best be achieved by direct and personal means. This, of course, was soon to become very unfashionable.

A subliminal yet major theme of *The Pursuit of Love* is Nancy's elegiac homage to the feudalism of men like her father, which in theory is so easy to attack, but in practice sort of worked, and which by the time she wrote the book – 1945 – had been almost completely eradicated. What Nancy called her 'vague' Socialism (and Diana called 'synthetic cochineal') probably derived from an attempt to translate the principles implicit within her upbringing – paternalistic, non-capitalist – into a modern political idiom. The same was true of her later Gaullism, and of Deborah's old-style Conservatism. But Unity, Diana and Jessica reacted against the essential stability of their world: how consciously, who can say. They placed their faith in change, in systems and in men who had scant awareness of their own fallibility. Beneath his aristocrat's confidence David was only too aware of being fallible. That is why he – and Uncle Matthew – remain likeable *malgré tout*.

But David was weaker than his fictional counterpart, and nothing made this clearer than the way in which he transmuted his love for England into a hapless, hopeful belief in Hitler's Germany. Uncle Matthew has only contempt for the Hun; this emotion remains as steadfast as the aim of his shotgun, so much so that one senses Nancy willing it to have been true of her father also. David wavered, for which he paid a high price. He seems genuinely to have thought, for a time, that the Anglo-German Fellowship was a worthy enterprise, that alliance with Germany would be the saviour of his own country.

Whether he would have thought this, or wanted to think it, had two of his daughters behaved differently in the 1930s, is another story.

IX

On 7 February 1928, a dance was held at the Astor family's London house on St James's Square. 'The Duke and Duchess of York honoured the Viscountess Astor with their presence last night,' read the court report, which then went on to name those who attended. Among the guests were members of the Devonshire family, David's uncle the 11th Earl of Airlie, David and Sydney themselves, and three of their daughters: Nancy, Pamela and Diana. This was Diana's first London event, although she had already attended a ball in Oxford. She was not yet eighteen (her birthday fell on 10 June), nor formally launched upon her debutante season.

There was nothing noteworthy about the Astor dance. It was simply a high-end example of a typical 1920s society occasion, although what makes it interesting is that it contained within the guest list – the smiling, dancing, chit-chatting throng – a number of people whose lives would later collide spectacularly. For example Lady Dorothy Macmillan – sister of the Duke of Devonshire – was there with her husband Harold, the future prime minister; as was the Conservative MP, Bob Boothby, whom she would seduce the following year, starting an affair that lasted until her death (in between his forays for rough trade in the company of Ron Kray[44]). Also present was another brilliant young politician, this one a Labour MP, accompanied by his wife, the former Lady Cynthia Curzon. Did Oswald Mosley notice the seventeen-year-old Diana Mitford, or she him?

Mosley was fourteen years older than Diana, and perhaps at their respective ages the gap was too great to be bridged – she would have looked to him like a lovely schoolgirl, not a potential paramour. He had both hands full anyway, as another guest of the Astors was his sister-in-law and mistress Lady Ravensdale ('Vote Labour, sleep Tory' was then his motto). However Diana had already received the tribute of devotion from several other men, both younger and older than Mosley. 'Why are you so amazingly sympathique as well as charming?' asked James Lees-Milne, as if in bewilderment at the completeness of her charm (Lees-Milne – who retained homosexual tendencies despite his later marriage to Alvilde Chaplin – in *Brideshead*-style loved both Tom and Diana Mitford). 'I dare say you are very vain,' he wrote in 1926, when Diana was staying in Paris, 'and indeed you have cause to be.' Around the same time her second cousin Randolph Churchill became besotted, and raged sulkily against Diana's 'extraordinarily cruel and callous behaviour' when she turned him down. (In fact he never really forgave her, and when she became engaged to another man in 1928 spread rumours about her flirtatious character. Not that he didn't chase other girls; for example in 1932 Nancy wrote to a friend: 'Randolph C tried to rape me. It was very funny.')

In Easter 1927 Diana's education at the Cours Fénelon in Paris came to a sudden end when her mother read a diary containing the inevitable girlish indiscretions. Although ensconced in ultra-respectable lodgings on the Avenue Victor-Hugo, Diana had – after the departure of her family – been free for the first time. She was allowed to walk short distances alone: no chaperone (in London she would have needed one to walk to Harrods). Looking as she did, in a city where natural appreciation of the female is so heightened and relentless, it would have been fairly astonishing if she had not tested her power over men. Sydney should certainly have foreseen as much, but it is hard to know what she really felt about her girls and their development.

Diana's diary contained references to cinema dates and tea dances with young men, the innocence of which – by today's standards – is almost painful, although at the time she was obliged to cover by inventing music lessons and so on. The diary also mentioned sittings for the painter Paul César Helleu, whose family lived nearby. Sydney had known Helleu for years, which meant that Diana could spend time with him. Helleu could hardly believe his luck. This young girl, who looked like a living Canova (a Raphael, according to Lees-Milne, but that did not evoke her marmoreal quality), was hungry to learn – she was clever, as well as beautiful and enchanting – and here was he, with all the credentials for imparting artistic knowledge and, at the age of sixty-seven, a perfectly avuncular aspect, able to escort her to the Louvre and Versailles, to show her off to painter friends (one can imagine) and, above all, to draw and paint her in his studio. Although his fame had waned somewhat, Helleu had been a hugely fashionable portrait artist, and had had what Diana called 'an amazing *vie amoureuse*'. Nevertheless, as she told Lees-Milne: 'He called me "*beauté divine*" always, and said, "*Tu es la femme la plus voluptueuse que je n'ai jamais connu.*"' Lees-Milne replied: 'How I would adore to have a picture of you by M. Helleu. You must be like Emma Lady Hamilton sitting to Romsey.' Helleu became ill in early 1927, and his daughter refused to let Diana visit him; clearly his ageing passion had been visible to the family. 'A man whom I have almost worshipped, and who has worshipped me for three months, is going to die,' wrote Diana, again to Lees-Milne. 'How can I bear it?' And then, after his death: 'Nobody will ever admire me as he did.' ('What a horrifying little beast I must have been,' she later commented.)

It is unlikely that Diana wrote in her diary the things that Helleu said to her, all that 'Sweetheart, *comme tu es belle*' and the like. The cinema dates would have been enough to spark her father's rage (as when Uncle Matthew goes berserk at Linda and Fanny, after they slope off to lunch in undergraduate rooms in Oxford: 'if you were married women, your husbands could divorce you for doing this.') The cold disapproval of her mother would have ostensibly sprung from the same source. 'Nobody,' she informed her daughter, 'would ask you to their houses if they knew *half* of what you had done.' Yet one does wonder whether the real issue, for Sydney, was Diana's straightforward desirability – especially to Helleu (however circumspect the diary entries, it would not have been hard to read between the lines.) As a girl Sydney had also been painted by Helleu. His summer studio had been a yacht moored at Deauville, where

Thomas Bowles had sailed with his daughters; Helleu had admired Sydney for her noble, sensuous looks; it is no easy thing for a woman to realize that the qualities she once possessed are now in the grasp of another – in fact it is the most difficult thing of all, even when that other is one's daughter. A maternal woman can cope with it but Sydney, for all her virtues of strength and sense, was not maternal. Time mellowed her towards Jessica and Deborah; by then their prettiness was no longer something to be intensely coveted. But the relationship with her two most spectacular daughters, Diana and Nancy, was complex, and perhaps understandably so. Straightforward pride in one's children is assumed to be an instinct, but it is not always that simple. Diana later took her mother's part staunchly, but back in 1927 – when she was removed summarily from the Cours Fénelon and exiled to a great-aunt's house in Devon with her three youngest sisters – this affection for Sydney was a long way in the future.

Of course by today's standards Diana had done nothing wrong, and the furore seems laughable. Nevertheless there is a quality to the relationship with Helleu (which reads rather like something from a French arthouse film) that hints at the Diana to come. She must have known that the poor man was going crazy about her. At just sixteen, an age when most girls would have been either giggly or uninterested, she instead allowed something to flourish: something both innocent and not innocent. Helleu's worship of her played out against a backdrop of painting and sculpture, and thus, in an ineffable yet powerful way, the amorality of great art became conflated with the amorality of beauty: what this brief sentimental education taught Diana was that a girl who looked as she did, that is to say like one of the white marble sculptures in the Louvre, created her own laws of behaviour. 'You have no fundamental moral sense,' wrote Randolph Churchill in 1928, in a fit of pique that achieved a degree of perceptiveness. 'In other words, though you rarely do wrong, you do not actually see anything WRONG in sin. With all of which you will, I am sure, agree.' She may have been flattered by this; she may or may not have agreed. Churchill's words were not quite accurate – Diana was not, in the sense that he meant, a sinner; in the ordinary way she was kinder, straighter and more generous than most. But in some way he had divined in her a peculiar quality of *will.* It was as if the world was different for somebody like her, who fitted the exigent demand of Dr Astrov in *The Seagull,* that 'everything about a person should be beautiful'.

This was emphasized in Diana because she did not behave like a 'stock' beauty. Except in the early years of her first marriage, her clothes were nothing special; she had the grace of a ballerina, but none of the usual mannerisms of a good-looking woman. She seemed to be without vanity, devoid of coquetry. At the same time she was wholly aware of her looks and, for all her apparent sphinx-like quiescence, she abounded in sensuality. It absolutely rippled through her. How confounding she must have been, both to men and to women, in her dynamic serenity, her warmth and her coolness, her superior brains and her physical perfection – how could she not, in truth, have felt that she could do *whatever she wanted* and it would be all right? Helleu was just the start of a career in conquest; she surely realized that.

Her parents may have realized it too, dimly, which is why they stashed her away in Devon through the summer of 1927. It was a stupid thing to have done, like putting a young lioness in a playpen, guaranteed to create the urge to flee. She 'ached', as the Mitford girls put it, during three months of atrocious boredom, which finally ended with a visit to the Churchill house at Chartwell (Winston's daughter Diana was a good friend). There she re-encountered the scientist Frederick Lindemann, who advised her to study German – which her parents refused – and fell down before her like a ninepin, just as Helleu had done. After her unofficial debut that autumn, at the Radcliffe Infirmary ball in Oxford, Lindemann rang to ask how many proposals she had received. He was, quite incidentally, the first person Diana ever met who abused somebody (Nancy's close friend Brian Howard) purely on the grounds that they were a Jew.

Then came the Astor dance; where among the guests, mingling with Mosley and co., was a comely young man – neat-featured, soulful of expression, not overly tall – named Bryan Guinness. He knew Nancy and Pam slightly, and therefore would have spoken to Diana that night. It was not until May, however, that the pair sat next to each other at a dinner party – again arranged for one of the Astor daughters – in Carlton House Terrace, and Bryan in his turn succumbed to that vision of pale perfection. In July he and Diana both attended a ball in Grosvenor Square, and later that month another at Grosvenor House on Park Lane. On that occasion Bryan asked Diana to marry him. She did not say yes immediately, but wrote a note when she got home to accept his proposal. His reply was touching, open, wholly characteristic. 'I still don't know how much you love me, nor really understand what you felt last night. But I am glad. I am glad that you are glad. I am glad that I love you. I am altogether glad again.'

Bryan, then aged twenty-two and not long down from Oxford, belonged to one of the richest families in the country, awash with money from its brewery business. His father, Colonel Walter Guinness, later Lord Moyne, was a Conservative MP, his mother Lady Evelyn an enchanting – one might even say Mitfordian – eccentric. (When Bryan informed Lady Evelyn that his intended bride could cook, she responded in her characteristic whisper: 'I've never *heard* of such a thing, it's *too* clever.'). The Guinnesses owned two giant houses in London – one at Grosvenor Place (numbers 10 and 11 knocked together, oligarch-style); the other in Hampstead – as well as a chunk of the Sussex coast, an estate in Hampshire, land in Dublin, a flat in Paris and so on. This was the kind of wealth that shrugs off slumps and depressions, like coats falling from one's shoulders. Bryan himself was a beneficiary of the Guinness Trust, founded by his grandfather, from which he received the then vast sum of £20,000 a year. He was also handsome, kind, clever, artistic, a poet and would-be novelist – the perfect counterpart to Diana, but also entirely in thrall to her. He was, in fact, overqualified as an escape route from Swinbrook. Nevertheless, that is essentially what he was. When he exclaimed that their love would last for ever, she replied in a delicate murmur: 'Well, for a long time, anyway.'

What finally ensured Bryan's success was the attitude of the Redesdales, who yet again went in for laying down the law, telling Diana that she was too young to marry and that a year must pass before her engagement could be announced. This time they had a point. Yet their former severity meant that Diana, as was her way, had become obdurate. Bryan, who of course wanted to capture his bride as soon as possible, tried to arrange a meeting with her father. 'I never come to London if I can avoid it,' wrote David, on the verge of rudeness, 'and as I can avoid it at the moment I am not likely to be there for some time...' But having used this tone he was on the back foot; he lacked the confidence to carry it through, particularly as by now even Sydney saw the marriage as a fait accompli. Not long afterwards he had a manly talk with Bryan in the billiard room of the Marlborough Club, and an agreement was made to a wedding the following Easter. It was what David called 'the thin end of the wedge'. The couple married at St Margaret's, Westminster on 30 January 1929. Diana, dressed with the help of Nanny Blor in a parchment-tinted satin picture gown and Lady Evelyn's veil, walked down the aisle in front of eleven bridesmaids including Nancy and Unity. Jessica and Deborah were ill and unable to attend, which according to Diana ruined the day.

In a final attempt to assert themselves, the Redesdales had objected to a religious wedding. Diana, they said, was not a believer. This was quite true – she was a staunch atheist – but Bryan was shocked nonetheless. In his naive young voice (so contrary to that of the determinedly ironic age) he wrote to Diana, explaining his desire to be married in church. 'Just as painters embody ideas of spring, summer, autumn or winter allegorically in human shape, so we realize this idea of beauty, which includes Christian kindness (which is beauty of deed) has been embodied in a personal deity. My worship of this ideal beauty is directed towards its most perfect manifestation, which is yourself...' It was an interesting take on the philosophy of Helleu.

Looking back at the behaviour of the Mitford parents, their haphazard attempts to harness girls who were naturally kicking up their heels, one has the impression that they asked for some of what they got, when the rebellions began in earnest. In Dorothy L. Sayers' *Gaudy Night*, Lord Peter Wimsey says of his wayward nephew that 'he is not amenable to a discipline of alternate indulgence and severity; and indeed I do not know who is.' Yet as with the Mitford childhood, who can say whether what the Redesdales did, or did not do, made much difference in the end? There is a limit to the effects of parental control, whether it is wielded wisely or without much logic.

Of course it was not easy for Sydney Redesdale, bringing out all those daughters, knowing that some of them had the potential to be loose cannons, hoping that following the rules would get her – and them – through. The worry and the work of it took over her life for sixteen years. Unlike Mrs Bennet, she could not simply take her girls everywhere en masse and hurl them at young men. There were six court presentations, six coming-out balls, six lots of clothes, six sets of debutante lunch parties and suppers (at which Sydney used a porcelain set that had belonged to Warren Hastings; an earlier Mitford had bought it at a sale to raise funds for Hastings's trial – 'Heaven knows,' wrote Deborah, who took the remains of the set to Chatsworth, 'how much of this priceless china was smashed in the hurried washing-up after midnight'). For any mother, let alone Sydney, it was a huge palaver – not least because so much depended upon it: this was where one found out if a girl would sink or swim. Poor Lady Montdore in *Love in a Cold Climate*, whose daughter Polly is the most beautiful of the season but who is nonetheless a flop ('isn't she lovely,' the eldest sons would say, before going off with 'some chinless little creature from Cadogan Square'), is in a rage of fatigue and frustration at the whole process. Probably some of the mothers – the younger, flightier ones – had a rather marvellous time themselves, taking a house in London and scurrying hither and thither with a perfect alibi for who knows what. On the other hand they were very much in the company of women, sitting on gilt chairs with the other mothers, pushing a piece of salmon around a Goode's plate as they sussed out the competition and agonized over who would nab the Prince of Wales: debs' lunches were a sort of school gate in pearls. Lady Montdore is particularly exercised about the way in which Aunt Sadie's daughters are 'snapped up' the moment they show their faces outside the schoolroom. This was not entirely true of the Mitford girls, but one can imagine all that bright beauty causing a shudder of fury nonetheless. There must have been a collective relief (suppressed beneath the well-bred smiles) when Diana was swept from the stage almost before she had stepped on to it.

Typically of the family, the Mitford debuts were a mixture of the homespun and the grand. Nancy, like the oldest daughter Louisa in *The Pursuit of Love*, came out at her family's country house, surrounded by relatively old men – the Airlies, her uncles Jack and Tommy – wearing a home-made dress and with very little idea of how to dance. The novel has Uncle Matthew importing twenty oil-stoves to alleviate the pervasive cold, which has a ring of terrible truth. So too does the description of the band – 'Clifford Essex's third string' – resting up before the dance at a local cottage. Clifford Essex's Band (first string) was much in demand at London balls; its name, together with that of Pilbeam's, Jack Harris's and the 400 Club, recurred as phrases in the strange echoing poetry of *The Times* social pages ('The Clifford Essex band played...'). Nancy was a constant presence at these parties. In April 1923 Sydney took a house at Gloucester Square – not particularly smart, but on the mysterious radar of the upper classes – and so it began: Nancy at a dance held by 'Mrs Lamb' at 47 Grosvenor Square, Nancy at Bathurst House on Belgrave Square, Nancy with her parents at Londonderry House, the great Park Lane mansion inhabited by the political hostess Lady

Londonderry (tamely adored by Ramsay MacDonald) and her wildly adulterous husband. Nancy was presented in May: that bizarre ceremony in which a girl curtseyed to the King and Queen and then became, miraculously, 'out'. She sat in the long queue of Daimlers and Rolls-Royces that inched its way down the Mall to Buckingham Palace, watched by the same sort of crowds as would today line a red carpet with smartphones to hand – in those days debutantes were news. Their dresses were described in *The Times* with the hunger for detail (more decorously expressed) now accorded to those of Oscar-nominated actresses. Nancy's was 'of white and gold brocade with a train of old lace'; no mention of a shop or designer, so again it must have been home-made (probably by her mother's maid Gladys, with material bought at John Lewis) and set off by wonderfully white doeskin gloves. She would have looked marvellous. Her slim and buoyant figure, the body of a patrician athlete (like Katherine Hepburn in *The Philadelphia Story*), was perfect for the 1920s and perfect for clothes – Dior came later, but she got away with even the scratchy unyielding tweeds described in *Love in a Cold Climate*. Although not strictly a beauty, with her mournful Pierrot eyes and a neat little mouth made for mockery, the eighteen-year-old Nancy was a lovely thing to behold. Probably all the debutantes were, even the plain ones, in their white and their youth.

As her friend Evelyn Waugh later wrote in *Brideshead Revisited*, the year of Nancy's debut was perhaps the 'most brilliant season since the war' – death had finally fled the scene, money and frivolity were back – although the rhapsodic haze through which Waugh portrayed the summer of 1923 bore little relation to the reality experienced by Nancy. She enjoyed herself, no question. She swam rather than sank. She was extremely popular, especially with other girls such as Mary O'Neill, Mary Milnes-Gaskell, the Countess of Seafield (Nina) and Waugh's future wife Evelyn Gardner. And then – as with Diana – there was the straightforward ecstasy of being away from home: from the sisters among whom she strode like an elegant virago, making up jokes (informing the three youngest that the middle syllables of their names were 'nit', 'sick' and 'bore') that were increasingly arcane and idiotic; from the parents who had begun to seem like Victorian monoliths in an Art Deco age. Of course, even as she longed to get away so she was drawn to the world of her upbringing, absorbing it, letting every aspect of it sink in; albeit with no thought yet of how it would be re-created as literature.

Nancy was not as naturally daring as Diana. Far from it. Although an agitator, she always instinctively understood that she operated best in the milieu that she knew. She would never have formed that friendship with Helleu, for instance – he would not have seen in her what he saw in Diana, and she would not have wanted him to. On her school trip abroad in 1922 she met a man in a hotel in Florence with whom she had long conversations about John Ruskin – 'my old man' as she called him ('he is really, quite 45'), was clearly amazed that this pretty giggler had actually heard of Ruskin – but the innocence of the episode, as she described it, is overpowering. Nancy's most significant acts of youthful rebellion were cosmetic only: shingling her hair, for instance, although these alone caused tremors on the Mitford–Richter scale. Nancy, wrote Jessica in *Hons and Rebels*, 'had broken ground for all of us but only at terrific cost in violent scenes followed by silence and tears'. This sounds exaggerated, as usual with Jessica, and there is a minor inaccuracy in that Nancy is described as cutting her hair at the age of twenty, whereas in fact she did so almost two years later. Nevertheless her various actions – not just the hair-shingling but wearing lipstick, smoking a cigarette, wearing trousers – do seem to have caused a ruckus, not quite on the Diana diary scale but sizeable enough. In late 1926 Nancy wrote to Tom from Paris, begging him to praise her hair as her parents had been so 'nasty' about it; true to form, or at least to Nancy's version of form, Sydney had remarked to her daughter that 'nobody would look at you twice now.' Around the same time David wrote to Diana, when she too shingled her hair: 'Have you or have you not recovered your hair which was cut off. You must not leave it in Paris' – these words, joking as they were, confirmed that shingling was indeed regarded as a transgression. But Nancy was twenty-two; even by the standards of the time it was extraordinary that the Redesdales should have made such an unholy fuss about something that almost every girl in the Western world was doing. Again one has the sense of them taking silly stands against behaviour that was natural and harmless, because in some indefinable way they feared that these quick shows of lightning were the herald of greater storms. And they were right, although not at all in the way that they imagined.

For Nancy, to put it bluntly, the problem was that she did not get married. This worried her mother, as did the fact that Diana found a husband before her two older sisters; again Sydney was no Mrs Bennet. Actually Pamela, then aged twenty-one, had been due to marry around the same time as Diana. *The Times* had announced that Pam's wedding to Oliver Watney would 'take place quietly' in Oxfordshire on 22 January 1929, but it was later reported that this had been 'postponed owing to illness'. Watney – who lived near Swinbrook and, like Bryan, was from a brewing family – suffered from chronic TB. He had been obliged to miss his father's funeral, in September 1928, because he was in a nursing home; as his family had urged the marriage to Pam, the death of Watney senior now eased that particular obligation. The postponement of the wedding became, almost inevitably, a cancellation. Although this was officially described as a mutual decision, it was probably Watney's. In May 1929 Nancy wrote to Tom that she was 'simply furious' about it, but that Pam was behaving very calmly: '& anyway what a let off in the way of brother-in-laws'. Pam was left with who knows what emotions – sadness? embarrassment? relief? – and an engagement ring that she passed on to Unity, who gave it to Hitler. Tom meanwhile drove around London in his little car, returning wedding presents.

Whether Nancy was *really* simply furious about Pam being dumped is another story. Her teasing of 'Chunkie' was not quite over – for instance she would find out which young men her sister fancied, and report seeing them with other girls – but far more to the point was that she, Nancy, had not come within even a mile of an altar.

The Hon. Mr Right had not emerged from the pack. And when that did not happen, a girl – however attractive – was left mysteriously high and dry. For Nancy it was an odd prospect: returning for season after season, moving into the danger years of her mid-twenties, like an over-bright flapper in a short story by Fitzgerald; showing up at balls in dresses that grew a little more raggedy every year, dyeing her Ascot outfit so that it could be worn for another Gold Cup day; and in between times the retreat to Swinbrook, with its drawing room filled with girls, always girls. In early 1927 Nancy enrolled at the Slade School of Fine Art – after another fight with her parents – and wrote to Tom, rather poignantly, that if she could exhibit her paintings in Paris 'the family would have no more hold over me at all'. She was already far too old to be talking that way. But without money or a husband she had no real notion of how to escape: a job, in the modern sense of the word, was simply not an option. During her unsuccessful studies at the Slade she took a bedsit in a boarding house in South Kensington; this lasted about a month. Not only did Nancy have no clue as to how to look after herself, she did not actually much like it. Again, her desire for freedom was kept within very particular limits.

It is possible that what Nancy craved, during her protracted girlhood – she did three debutante seasons proper, but was roaming around 'society' for eleven years – was the tension between rebellion and restraint: a writerly attitude, although she would not yet have known that. Sometimes her letters read like a child trying to shock, as when she writes that she is very drunk and must give up cocktails or she will end up running around Swinbrook with delirium tremens. One has the impression that this image is not unappealing to her, and that being drunk would be far less fun if there was nobody there to object to it. At the same time, and rather more nebulously, there is the sense that she is putting on an act altogether; that dashing about on semi-hysterical japes is not really her thing – that she was quite good at being young, but that being older would be infinitely better. Her last two novels, *The Blessing* and *Don't Tell Alfred*, are underpinned by a belief that civilized middle age is far superior to silly youth, something that Nancy absolutely believed and may have intuited early on.

This was especially the case with regard to men. Naturally she had suitors, looking as she did – her letters allude to a soldier named Archer Clive; a friend of Tom's, Nigel Birch; a well-to-do landowner named Roger Fleetwood Hesketh – but she seems to have taken none of them truly seriously. In her late twenties, however, she was courted by a different kind of man, a Grenadier Guard named Sir Hugh Smiley who was nothing if not serious, and who, as she put it, 'laid his ginger bread mansion at my feet'. He proposed on three occasions, in fact. The first time Nancy answered that she was in the middle of writing her novel, *Highland Fling*, and could not think properly about anything else. This was a reasonable excuse, so Sir Hugh tried again, twice: the second time with orchids at the Café Royal. By 1932 one might have thought that Nancy would be more than glad to accept. Here was a man who could effect a Bryan Guinness-type transformation on her life, who offered wealth and escape, the things that Diana had. Yet she could not quite do it. She was simply not that kind of girl, the kind that makes a marriage with a hard head. She admitted that Sir Hugh was nice, she knew that he was rich, but she feared that their children would be 'blond & stupid'. There were elements of *The Pursuit of Love*'s Tony Kroesig in Sir Hugh – the heroine Linda marries him in a state of romantic agitation, but quickly finds him to be hopelessly pompous. With Sir Hugh, Nancy did not even have the illusion of being in love. Nevertheless he was the best offer that she had in ten years.

There were two things going on here: first, Nancy was simply not as attractive to men as she should have been, given her entrancing appearance. She was not especially *good* at men. It is a gift like any other, and she did not have it – she laughed when she should have sympathized, she gave way when she should have held off, and so on – it took an extremely confident suitor to see past this and appreciate her, and he was still some way in the future. In truth all her sisters (but especially Diana and Deborah) were better at handling men than Nancy. When the men in question include Adolf Hitler, one might justifiably say that this was not a gift worth having. Nevertheless it is fascinating that Unity *could* talk to Hitler, then a demi-god in his homeland, and talk to him as a man; partly this was the Mitford confidence in action, but it was also some feminine instinct at work.

Nancy's problem was her intelligence, of course, which at some point or another riled most of the men she knew (honourable exceptions included her brother and Evelyn Waugh). This would probably be true today – feminism notwithstanding, female cleverness is still most acceptable when it spouts orthodoxies, or in some way conforms to a type. Nancy, with her spry chic and lethal tongue, was a one-off. As such she was certainly never going to flower fully among the men of her youth. They could accept Diana's brain because it came within the packaging of a goddess, and because – crucially – she knew how and when to show off or shut up. With Nancy, if a witticism came to mind then it also came out of her mouth, and damn the consequences. Her cleverness was rooted in her humour; indeed the two were completely intertwined, both deriving from the childlike clarity of vision that enabled her to perceive what most people leave unseen and unsaid. This, too, is not a quality made for the enhancement of love affairs.

The second, related point is that deep down she probably did not *want* to get married, although she thought that she did. In one way, yes, she wanted a husband – there was never a less bohemian iconoclast than Nancy, her *côté convenable* always required fulfilment – and she probably felt the need to dispel the memory of being Diana's bridesmaid. However, and despite her liking for Bryan Guinness, Nancy was not entirely convinced by that particular coupling. As Randolph Churchill did, she saw a mismatch. And her novels, from the first, were essentially engaged with the question of what constitutes a successful marriage: the question that plagues most thinking people, in fact, of whether it is possible for love and reality to coexist.

One of Nancy's most sharply-realized characters was created for the little-known 1932 novel *Christmas Pudding*: Amabelle Fortescue, a sleek and worldly former prostitute ('in her young days a woman either had a good reputation or an international reputation'). At forty-five she is rather wise, the first example of Nancy's belief that the middle-aged had more to offer than the young. She says: 'The trouble is that people seem to expect happiness in life. I can't imagine why, but they do. They are unhappy before they marry, and they imagine to themselves that the reason of their unhappiness will be removed when they are married. When it isn't they blame the other person, which is clearly absurd...' Like most writers Nancy understood life better on the page, and at the age of twenty-seven, when she wrote those words, she knew little of that kind of truth. Nevertheless it shows that she had, even in relative youth, a degree of healthy scepticism about 'happy ever after'. At the same time she was intensely romantic. These two qualities could embrace each other, without being exactly reconciled, in a novel like *The Pursuit of Love*. In life, not so much.

Diana, writing later about this limbo period of her sister's twenties, saw it as a veritable hell in which Nancy was trapped, penniless, disliking her parents but unable to leave them – 'Why was she so utterly stuck, poor Naunce.' The answer was that she did not get married. But Diana's view was partial, seen through the prism of her own ideas of happiness, seen also – perhaps – through an odd desire to *believe* that Nancy had been unhappy. The truth was more complicated than that, as it usually is with creative people. Nancy was not, in her own head, stuck. How could she be, when her writing career began at this time? From 1929 she was writing her social columns for *Vogue* and *The Lady*. Aged just twenty-five, without benefit of a degree in creative writing, or even an A level in English literature, she produced a callow, derivative but supremely accomplished novel – *Highland Fling* – followed almost immediately by another – *Christmas Pudding*: books that were not a patch on what would follow, but which sold respectably, were well received, turned her into a minor celebrity and were, in truth, a phenomenal achievement.

And anyway: if Nancy had truly wanted to be married, if that had been her dearest deepest wish, then why – at around the same time as she started to write – did she decide to be in love with Hamish St Clair-Erskine?

XI

Of course she told everybody, not least herself, that she and Hamish (a second son of the Earl of Rosslyn) would be married any time soon. When Hamish came down from Oxford, when they had money, when family opposition dissolved, when Hamish stopped being homosexual… this last was never spelled out. Nevertheless the signs were pretty glaring. Tom Mitford had had a fling with Hamish at Eton, and although Tom now chased girls – which might have encouraged hope – Hamish told Nancy that 'he didn't think he would ever feel up to sleeping with a woman'.

It is not uncommon for girls to fall for homosexuals, but it is extraordinary that somebody as intelligent as Nancy would delude herself that she could marry one. Yet in a way it was precisely *because* she was intelligent that she embarked upon this relationship, which worked in the sphere of imagination: as clever girls sometimes do, she was living in her own mind, which was exceptionally interesting to her, and distancing herself from the rather more banal reality. The only problem was that her emotions, based though they were upon illusion, did become real. She suffered terribly over Hamish St Clair-Erskine, which was not worth doing – described by James Lees-Milne as 'shallowly sophisticated', he was a smart social animal and very much a snob. Although he undoubtedly strung Nancy along, she herself chose to let this unofficial engagement go on for more than four years. In 1931 she actually tried to gas herself, such was her unhappiness with the situation, although the sincerity of the attempt is doubtful. As for Hamish himself, his motives are mysterious. He may have enjoyed playing the lover – perhaps deluding himself as well as Nancy – and he would certainly have liked the power that she handed him: 'He was flattered, he was four years younger than she, and she was waiting on him hand and foot,'[45] said a friend who observed them. Meanwhile Sir Hugh Smiley, who at the Café Royal offered his orchids, together with what a good many girls would have considered a life worth having, was chucked as Hamish giggled knowingly at a nearby table. One can hardly blame Sir Hugh for his somewhat bitter parting shot at Nancy, that she was on her way to becoming an old maid. In 1929 she had written to Diana that she wanted to marry money but had, most unfortunately, fallen in love with a poor man. This was perverse in the extreme; again, however, it was Nancy's choice.

Hamish – who could not have been more different from Hugh – was a slightly tarnished example of the Bright Young Thing, whose day had coincided with much of Nancy's extended adolescence. She herself was a semi-detached member of the clan: her first novel was spiked and gilded with its ironies. A character in *Highland Fling* suggests calling his new baby Morris in order to get a free car, while another declares that English society has 'no sex or brain left, only nerves and the herd instinct'. *Christmas Pudding* – a much better book, really very funny at times, because closer to Nancy's natural idiom – is steeped in jibes against Cotswolds manor houses and rural living: 'Nobody knows how horrible it is to live in the country always, you might just as well be in prison.' Both books suffer from having a fictionalized Hamish at their centre. Nevertheless one has to thank him in a way for their existence, as Nancy began writing *Highland Fling* – which is dedicated to Hamish – in order to earn money that she would spend in his company (or on him). She made £90 from it, ten short of the hundred she had wanted.

The book, with its modernist aspect and self-conscious cynicism, was very much in the spirit of Evelyn Waugh. Nancy did not imitate *Vile Bodies*, which was published after her own novel was finished (and which she did not admire), but said that she had had to make changes to *Highland Fling* to avoid that accusation. In fact Sydney had suggested calling the novel *Our Vile Age*, which also had to be ditched because of Waugh – although it is worth noting that this apparently critical mother had taken the trouble to come up with a pun. David, conversely, seems to have reacted to the book not unlike his caricatured portrait, General Murgatroyd. It is rather odd: he adored Nancy as a child, and was proud of her as a woman, but the interim period saw them absolutely on each other's nerves. He hated the publicity that naturally went to an attractive young author. More than anything, however, both Redesdales objected to the dedication, which according to the *Sunday Dispatch* was to Nancy's 'fiancé'. They could hardly be blamed, in this instance, for their misgivings. One would almost suspect Nancy of formulating a passion for a gay Roman Catholic with the sole aim of irritating the 'revereds', as she called them, were it not that her letters are suffused with the feelings that she misdirected at him. David recognized that Hamish was homosexual, and one assumes that Sydney did also. In 1929, during a visit to Northumberland, Nancy wrote that her grandmother was 'divine' about Hamish, despite hating all his forebears (they were both Scottish aristocrats); but the seventy-five year old Clementine would probably *not* have known that he was gay, and on paper, after all, he was a good match.

In her letter to Diana about the publication of *Highland Fling*, which ought to have been celebratory, Nancy wrote instead about the great row that it had precipitated with the Redesdales, as if the book had become a symbol of everything that agitated them about their daughter. They accused her of mixing with 'drunkards', of ruining her health and her character. She should not, they said, go to London for the summer. In fact, given her advanced age (twenty-six!) she should stop going out altogether and simply live in the country.

Allowing for the usual exaggeration, one can again imagine that her parents were genuinely concerned. David had cut Nancy's £125 a year allowance, partly because of his own money troubles, partly out of exasperation. What they really feared, who can say – given Hamish's proclivities loss of virtue was unlikely – although, later, Nancy's future sister-in-law would call her 'shop-soiled', implying that she had had love affairs (with whom? Sir Hugh Smiley?) There is absolutely no evidence for this. It sounds like bitchiness – a snide aside about the overlong stay on the social stage – and it almost certainly was. The fact is that Nancy's failure to marry, in a world where girls did not have careers and could not wave feminist literature at their critics, made her vulnerable. Nor did she have the Diana-like assurance to carry it off. Despite her class confidence Nancy was a nervous filly. She had, she wrote to Diana, more or less agreed to her parents' demands that she stay in Oxfordshire for the summer.

What a paradox she was – this mulish child, this sophisticated talent. But then she had had the escape route – Sir Hugh – and did not take it. How fortunate for her therefore that she had friends (her gift for friendship was lifelong), and that some of them happened to be the most amusing men of their generation.

Hamish, as in her deepest soul Nancy probably knew, was really the least important man in her circle. The people who mattered were a collection of sublimely clever aesthetes – for convenience's sake one calls them Bright Young Things, although with the odd exception they had more staying power than that – whom she had begun to meet in her early debutante years, and who by the end of the 1920s had become a group of enduring friends. She saw them in London and in Oxford, where, like Hamish (who was sent down), they had mostly been undergraduates. Again like Hamish, they were mostly homosexual; and they were completely unfazed by Nancy's cleverness. On occasion they would visit Swinbrook, where they would droop about in their giant trousers, craving a *cachet faivre* while being offered instead what David referred to as 'thinkers' (pigs' brains), and generally staggering him with their otherness. 'At weekends they would swoop down from Oxford or London in merry hordes', wrote Jessica in *Hons and Rebels*. 'Boud [Unity], Debo and I were on the whole carefully insulated from Nancy's friends, as my mother considered them a totally bad influence. "*What* a set!" she always said... They talked in the jargon of the day: "Darling, too, too divine, too utterly sickmaking, how shamemaking!"'

And how dull they sound, in that description, like actors in an amateur production of *The Vortex*; except that they weren't. They must have been marvellous, suited to their time and to each other in a way that happens rarely. Of course they didn't have *television*, or indeed the internet. This is so obvious that it should hardly need saying – yet it is a central factor to the whole Mitford story, this absolute need to amuse, to push one's personality outwards for the benefit of society, to fill the hours with efforts of one's own: the possibility of turning on a screen and letting it take the strain simply did not exist. Which would have made the days more tiring, sometimes more boring, but in the end much more fun; and *real*.

Nevertheless Nancy's friends were peculiarly well equipped to deal with the *longueurs* of life without Instagram. They included Brian Howard (an inspiration for Anthony Blanche in *Brideshead Revisited*), Harold Acton (also part-Blanche, and according to Diana 'the cleverest of our friends'), his painter brother William Acton (who famously sketched the Mitford girls), the designer Oliver Messel, the future film producer John Sutro, the writer Robert Byron (another homosexual to whom Nancy was attracted) and Mark Ogilvie-Grant, who illustrated *Highland Fling*. Diana described Mark as 'almost like a brother to Nancy'[46] and he received most of her outpourings about Hamish. Probably Nancy knew that Mark was too kind to say the unsayable. Robert Byron, she told Mark, had laughed himself sick over the suicide attempt.

Mark was a cousin of Nancy's close friend Nina Seafield (despite being gay he had thought of marrying Nina; one does see in a way why Nancy thought homosexuality was a state to be entered and left at will). So it was mainly through Mark that all these connections began, although there were other felicitous links: for instance Acton knew Tom Mitford from Eton. Then there were other friends, who did not visit Swinbrook but became very important to Nancy: John Betjeman and, especially, Evelyn Waugh, whose first wife – 'She-Evelyn' – had been a fellow deb. In 1929 the Waughs were living in Canonbury Square and offered Nancy their spare room; this would have probably worked rather well, but the arrangement lasted just a month. That summer the marriage broke down – 'Evelyn has been pleased to make a cuckold of me with [John] Heygate,' Waugh wrote tersely to Acton. After the separation Nancy took Waugh's part, and their friendship – luckily for posterity, kept up chiefly through some of the funniest letters ever written – later developed into one of the most significant of her life.

With these young men Nancy began to bloom in her true colours, which were not those of the Cotswolds, nor of London, but something more cosmopolitan and rococo. The frivolity described by Jessica was only a part of the picture. Men like Messel and Sutro were not dilettantes. True, Brian Howard was the kind of person who flowers early and withers fast:[47] gifted in a vague way, he painted the pictures for the spoof 'Bruno Hat' exhibition staged in 1930. He was intensely camp – 'now dear, you're not *putting out a fire*', he once remonstrated with a boyfriend, who was spraying scent on himself at Guerlain – and self-consciously eccentric, as when, in Nancy's company, he used a small Picasso wrapped in pyjamas as protection against a snowstorm (hats were 'so expensive'). But he was also sharp, sensitive and rigorously intelligent. When he informed Harold Acton that his new friend Nancy was 'a delicious creature, quite pyrotechnical my dear, and sometimes even profound', Acton knew that his judgment could be respected.

As for Acton himself, socially speaking he was the leader of the pack. He too specialized in effeteness: when a fellow dinner-party guest, a brusque female whose car had broken down nearby, snapped 'you're not the kind of young man one can imagine doing things under a car', he answered smoothly: 'Well, it depends who with.' (His brother William was even more *recherché*: Diana saw him in 1940 and asked what he was doing in the war, to which he replied: 'Learning Urdu.') Harold Acton was a gloriously stylish figure, a magnet to his friends, a champion of the new (as referenced when Anthony Blanche recites *The Waste Land* to a bunch of Oxford oarsmen), and personally a great influence upon Waugh: 'What, I think, we had in common was *gusto* in the English use of the word; a zest for the variety and absurdity of the life opening to us...'[48] Waugh was the talent – Acton published a novel, *Hum Drum*, at the same time as *Decline and Fall*, and suffered by comparison – but Acton's genius was in his life, in what Diana called 'the brilliance and charm of his personality, unequalled in his generation'. He had Anthony Blanche's refined critical faculty, and he appreciated Nancy. Years later he wrote her first biography, full of delicate yet tough-minded perception. Among his *aperçus* was this: that Nancy's non-judgmental portrayal of homosexuals – especially the wildly camp Cedric Hampton in *Love in a Cold Climate* – contributed to the removal of 'social stigma' around sexual orientation. Homosexuality was still then illegal, but one would certainly never have known it from Nancy's joyful Cedric. ('I shall never write about normal love again,' she wrote to Mark Ogilvie-Grant, 'as I see there is a far larger and more enthusiastic public for the *other sort*.')

Nancy's ability to hold her own with people of this kind drew her, to a degree, into the *Vile Bodies* world that now seems to typify 1920s high society: 'Oh, Nina, *what a lot of parties*,' as the central character says. Or, as Nancy later put it: 'We hardly ever saw the light of day, except at dawn.' The novel contains a scene in which the older generation sit together at a formal London dance, speculating as to the behaviour of the young: 'I mean, *do* they...?' 'My dear, from all I hear, I think they do.' So perhaps that is what the Redesdales thought about Nancy.

Yet the sense is that their concern centred upon Hamish, and the madness of their daughter's association with him. *Vile Bodies* was a fantastical satire on the era, which like a Vorticist painting captured a splintered, uncertain mood. The fact is that Nancy may have attended nightclubs and the odd dubious party enlivened by 'naughty salt', but she was also at society weddings, a dance in Belgrave Square, all the usual things that kept *The Tatler* trading and comprised the world of her class. Nor were her clever friends truly threatening to the Redesdales. Of course they could, as and when, be used as a weapon to attack Nancy. Nevertheless they were invited often enough to Swinbrook; despite appearances they were the kind of people who wrote thank-you letters and knew how to ride to hounds. David was appalled when a comb fell out of the pocket of one particular young man, and to another, who proved incompetent with a gun, he said: 'I'd rather take a housemaid shooting than you.' But the incident at which he lost his temper with James Lees-Milne was unusual; his manners, in the main, were better than that. He had a great liking for Mark Ogilvie-Grant, who – as Nancy later told Sydney – during his time as a POW dreamed of the layer-cake with jam served at Swinbrook. 'The Mitford family are very amusing,' wrote Robert Byron to his mother about a stay with the Redesdales, 'and I enjoy being here.' Not much sense there of a fight to the death between Uncle Matthew and the modernist tendency.

These men were also friends of Diana and Bryan Guinness. Indeed from the time of Diana's marriage, in January 1929, they began to congregate at the Guinnesses' lovely Lutyens home in Buckingham Street. Diana later disclaimed any real connection with the Bright Young Things – such as they were – but she was, as it were by divine right, placed instantly at the centre of London's artistic life. Acton, Byron, Howard; Henry Yorke, who wrote novels under the name Henry Green; Lytton Strachey and the painter Dora Carrington; the magnificently eccentric musician Gerald Berners; the Sitwells; Lotte Lenya – they all headed for Diana's drawing room and, in one way or another, paid homage to the young woman who looked like a dream yet was in such admiration of their talent. 'Writers and painters and composers seemed to me then the princes of mankind,' she would later write. Bryan was an artistic type himself, who had courted Diana by taking her to the theatre almost every night. Although a qualified barrister he wrote good, rather tortured poetry and, in 1930, an unsuccessful novel called *Desires and Discoveries*.[49] He enjoyed the company of his guests. Nevertheless his idea of marriage had been to have Diana to himself, rather than to watch her poised at the epicentre of fashionable London. 'I too could be arty, I too could get on/With Sickert, the Guinnesses, Gertler and John,' as John Betjeman wrote, in acknowledgment of the Buckingham Street salon. The Guinnesses also owned Biddesden, a wonderful Queen Anne house in Wiltshire whose interior design was described fulsomely in January 1932 by the *Daily Telegraph*: 'Mrs Guinness during the last six months has taken enormous trouble to bring out the exquisite grace of the rooms by the use of clear pastel colours used in a simple youthful way.' This house, too, was filled with people and parties. At twenty-one Diana was 'already something of a legend', wrote her future stepson Nicholas Mosley, astutely noting her very Mitfordian 'ability to seem both conventional and unconventional at the same time'.[50]

Nancy, naturally, was a frequent visitor to Diana and Bryan, not least because she could see her friends at their house. After the breakdown of Evelyn Waugh's marriage, which deprived Nancy of her room in Canonbury Square, she was offered an alternative bolthole at Buckingham Street. She lived there on and off, and was visited by Waugh, who soon started coming to the house most days.

'Do you… share my admiration for Diana?' he wrote to Henry Yorke in September 1929. 'She seems to me the one encouraging figure in this generation.'

In fact Waugh, who dedicated *Vile Bodies* to the Guinnesses, had fallen head over heels for Diana. She had not, she said, realized this at the time; but given her history, the way in which she cast a trance-like spell over almost every man she met, it is difficult to believe that she had no inkling when, during her first pregnancy (with Jonathan, born in 1930), the brilliant young novelist chose to sit on her bed every morning like a prospective doula.

And Nancy, for all her obtuseness about her own affairs, would have seen this very clearly. She would have also noted Diana's gilded life, the money, the Paris clothes, the babies (Desmond was born in 1931), the adoring husband: the more obviously enviable things. Yet what may well have been harder to take was watching Evelyn Waugh behave like a suddenly bewitched Lysander in *A Midsummer Night's Dream*. Not that she wanted him for herself, at least not as a lovestruck admirer. But it was a symbolic shift of allegiance, like Robert Byron's (whom Waugh, pierced by his own shaft of jealousy, would accuse Diana of preferring to himself). After all the years that Nancy had spent collecting friends, those people who would lighten the burden of parental pressure and unrequited love, to find that in the blink of an eye they had placed Diana at the centre of their lives... This was the first major move in the relationship between these two Mitford sisters, the white and black queens who dominated the rest, and who each would have dominated outright had it not been for the other.

PART II

'We'll have a crack
At Captain Jack
Because we think
His heart is black.'

From *Wigs on the Green* by Nancy Mitford (1935)

I

On 7 July 1932, Diana gave a London ball for Unity, who was then almost eighteen. A couple of months earlier the Guinnesses had moved to 96 Cheyne Walk, formerly the home of Whistler. The magnificent riverside house had a giant ballroom that could accommodate 300 guests. Among them, and the real reason why the party was being held, was Sir Oswald Mosley.

'You were dazzling as the presiding goddess,' wrote the society hostess Emerald Cunard to Diana, 'fresh and dewy from Olympus.' Robert Byron said: 'It was the best party ever given, even by you. I feel as if I had been raised from the dead by it.' Many years later, the artist Osbert Lancaster[1] – another guest – gave a slightly different view. He recalled arriving at the party with James Lees-Milne. It was the time of a famous murder trial, in which a young society woman, Mrs Elvira Barney, was accused of shooting her lover in a Knightsbridge mews, and acquitted thanks to her extremely expensive defence. 'It was also the slump,' said Lancaster, 'and there was a nasty feeling about the upper classes. The crowd outside the dance was not in a pleasant mood, their remarks were all about Mrs Barney...'

As with the parade of debutantes along the Mall, people at the time would congregate outside society parties to observe the guests arriving (or, in the case of the Cheyne Walk ball, to watch Augustus

John being carried out raging drunk by two footmen). Lancaster's remarks about the mood of this particular crowd were telling. The contrast between a Guinness and an average Londoner enduring the Great Depression was dangerously glaring, in a way not unfamiliar to us today. Diana, one might say, led the life of a non-dom bride. It was more refined – wealth was not expressed by heating empty houses or by throwing children's parties on Necker – but it was still, somehow, almost vulgar in its relentless gratifications. The worshipping husband, the worshipping friends, the articles in *Tatler* and *Bystander* cooing over her every move (a new hairstyle, her habit of wearing trousers in the garden), the offer of the part of Perdita in C. B. Cochran's new production of *The Winter's Tale* (refused: Diana never did that kind of thing). How easy it was, to have the world at one's feet at the age of twenty-two! And then the summers in the Mediterranean, the magnificent Stanley Spencer given by Bryan for the birth of Jonathan, the Aubussons in the children's nursery ('so good for them to see pretty things when they're crawling about'), the two bathrooms deemed necessary to civilized life by her father-in-law (this at a time when a tin bath and an outside privy were quite normal), the Biddesden gazebo lined with mosaics by Boris Anrep, including Diana as Erato . . . The only rugged thing in her dreamlike world was her great Irish wolfhound, Pilgrim, who ate raw meat from her hands.

Yet from the time of the first hunger marches Diana had been politically aware; at least as much as Jessica, who made more noise about it. Many years later she reviewed a book about the Labour movement and wrote with astringent compassion of '[Stanley] Baldwin's wicked deflation in 1926, the starving of the miners into submission after the General Strike collapsed . . . the grinding poverty, the bitterness of unemployment, the frightful conditions of those days'. And there was no doubt in Diana's mind where the blame lay for all this post-war suffering. 'The Tories were in power and they did nothing.' To Deborah she later wrote that she had been 'violently anti-Tory' since the age of sixteen. Nor did the Labour leader, Ramsay MacDonald, commend himself to her: the emergency National Government that he led between 1931 and 1935 was 'Tory in all but name'. In young adulthood, and in so far as she had any allegiance – she voted only once in her life – Diana described herself as a 'Lloyd George Liberal'. Later Lloyd George would speak in favour of Sir Oswald Mosley, and against war with Germany: both causes dear to Diana. Nevertheless he had previously dedicated himself to removing power from a body, the House of Lords, that gave protection and status to the Mitford family. This may seem like a pretty substantial irony; as does the disconnect between the succession of mansions in which Diana lived, the priceless possessions that glided easily into her hands, and her robust antipathy to the party of wealth. But she was not a champagne socialist – that particular breed would have aroused her contempt also. She was, more particularly, an instinctive radical; perhaps one that lived in the wrong time.

'In 1932 we all – everyone with the slightest intelligence – thought about politics,' she later wrote. 'We believed that our parents' generation had made the war, that by *will* plus *cleverness* its horrible legacy could be cancelled out, and the world could be changed...' Ah: the belief in change. So seductive, especially to the young. So unaccountable, in that the changes are rarely the ones that were intended.

The boredom that Diana had begun to feel with Bryan Guinness – which came to a head at Unity's dance – was in some way allied to this radicalism. The complacency that she saw in the British political system was linked to that of her feather-bedded marriage. The perfection was simply *too great* – 'dead perfection, nothing more', as Tennyson writes in *Maud,* whose heroine bore such a resemblance to the Diana of this time: 'You have but fed on the roses and lain in the lilies of life.' Of course she did not want to be down and out, sharing the miseries of poverty like Gordon Comstock in *Keep the Aspidistra Flying.* But she wanted *more.* After the birth of her first son, in March 1930, she was champing at the bit. Not against the fact of motherhood, which she adored – Deborah later described her sister as a 'specially maternal sort of bloke' – but simply to be back in the world, feeding off new experiences. Evelyn Waugh had been so upset by this ('pure jealousy', he later admitted) that their friendship foundered. 'After Jonathan's birth you began to enlarge your circle. I felt lower in your affections than Harold Acton and Robert Byron and I couldn't compete or take a humbler place.'[2] He refused an invitation that summer to Knockmaroon, the family house just outside Dublin. Bryan had probably hoped to have his wife to himself, but Diana invited a house party including Nancy, Hamish and Lytton Strachey: 'there is nothing to do,' she wrote to Strachey, 'but go to the Abbey Theatre and see sickening Irish plays.' During their courtship she had relished Bryan's theatregoing habit as a totem of civilization. Now, on one particular evening, she swept out of the Abbey during a performance with the rest of the party scurrying behind her like supplicant pages.

Diana fell pregnant again at the end of 1930, which she had not intended. 'Of course we'd have had you one day, darling,' she later told her son Desmond, 'but not *just* then'. Would they, though? By this time, when the marriage was barely two years old, the constant presence of Diana's husband was becoming oppressive. Bryan had been called to the Bar, but had pretty much given it up ('Mr Guinness doesn't need three guineas,' said his clerk, as he gave out briefs to other junior barristers.) He was at Buckingham Street continually. After a life spent surrounded by other people, in which privacy had been the most valuable commodity of all, it was alarming for Diana to find that Bryan was just as demanding of her company as her chattering, attention-seeking sisters had been. Freedom, for which she had longed, now became a desperate craving. Bryan did leave her to visit Austria with Tom Mitford – he liked Tom, as did everybody – but wrote a forty-page letter saying: 'I lie awake thinking and worrying about you.' *Why?* she would have longed to ask (Mitfords did not do that kind of sentiment). His manner with Diana, an uneasy mixture of pleading and insistence, was as wrong-headed as

Nancy's with Hamish St Clair-Erskine: like Nancy, Bryan handed over all the power in the relationship and expected the other person (*l'un qui se laisse aimer*) to handle it with care. This is not, sad to say, what people do. A woman such as Diana, whose extraordinary strength was tensile and vibrating beneath the Madonna smiles, would have felt only a kind of contempt, all the more so because she knew that Bryan did not remotely deserve it. But he was on her nerves, and there is no answer to that other than a serious change of tactics. Worship was what she had in spades; she needed something more bracing; a man as intelligent as Bryan should have realized this.

It was to Diana's credit, really, that a near-infinite supply of money and adoration was not enough for her. She had not wanted Bryan because he was so rich (as she exclaimed, with some glee, 'I became terribly poor when I left him!'[3] – although this was the relative poverty of Eaton Square). Like Nancy, in fact like all the Mitford girls, she lacked that particular hard-headed quality. She had married because Bryan represented a new world, and perhaps because her parents' opposition had pushed her into it. They had been right to say that she was too young, but it probably would have made no difference. Straightforward contentment was always going to be too easy for such a woman, who had been given every blessing without the obligation of payment.

II

In February 1932, the *Sunday Graphic* reported: 'A young writer who will shortly be back in London is Miss Nancy Mitford who in a week or two's time will have completed her new novel [*Christmas Pudding*]. She tells me that she finds it easier to write in the country, and probably more amusing, since her mother, Lady Redesdale, gave a ball last week for her youngest sister [sic], who rejoices in the name of Unity Valkyrie. Lady Redesdale does not share her daughter's talent for writing, but she is an excellent baker...'

The first dance for Unity was held at Swinbrook, just over five months before the Cheyne Walk ball. She made her debut at the start of what would be a tumultuous year, the one that set everything off for the Mitfords: the calamities, the tragedies, the fame, the myth. But it all seemed normal enough when the next daughter in line made her expected emergence into society. If this particular girl was a little different – lacking the attractions of Nancy, the placidity of Pam, the beauty of Diana – that was just the way it was. The debutante mothers may have whispered over the teacups about Sydney Redesdale's difficulties – four girls 'out', only one married, Nancy *almost thirty* my dear and now this giant daughter like something out of Norse mythology – but nothing, as yet, had gone cataclysmically wrong.

Descriptions of Unity as a girl differ. Jessica recalled her as sulky and moody; John Betjeman as lively and humorous; a fellow schoolgirl as 'really a suicide, she was so self-destructive'. The family parlourmaid, Mabel, said that she was 'awful to Miss Hussey', one of the Mitford governesses; yet Miss Hussey remembered Unity with compassionate affection: 'she had a look of a little St Joan of Arc which I've never forgotten.' As Deborah – who admitted to her own bewilderment – wrote many years later: 'Perhaps it is too easy to say that she was inexplicable, but it is a fact.' There is a certain amount of wisdom after the event in some memories of Unity, exaggeration or over-analysis of her oddities. As with a murderer who is subsequently described as 'a loner... a bit of an obsessive' – traits that would probably not be remarked upon in a law-abiding person – so one can look at Unity's bizarre pets, her double expulsion from school, and see therein the seeds of lunacy; notwithstanding the facts that Deborah owned a pet goat, she too was unable to cope with formal education, and nobody was ever more sane than she.

Certainly Unity could be a disruptive presence at home (as indicated by the persistent attempts to send her to school). She was not necessarily loud – in fact she had a predilection for 'dumb insolence', particularly when under the watch of her father's critical and fastidious eye. David's tendency to flare up over small things would have been exacerbated, in turn, by Unity's habits (such as sliding under the table at mealtimes). And even in those large houses she was as inescapable as a piece of garden statuary cluttering up the hallway. Her sullenness had a funny side; on one occasion her mother, taking on teaching duties, read out a passage and asked Unity to recount it for her, which for some reason she refused to do. Did she not remember a *single word* of the passage, coaxed Sydney? Just one word? All right, said Unity: 'The.' And her letters give off an extraordinary vivacity, almost as if trying to contain the Mitfordian excess of personality. An interesting side issue is Miss Hussey's recollection of Unity's talent for art. 'She did drawings and paintings rather like Blake. Such imagination.' The Mitford girls were gifted to varying degrees, in various ways, and Unity later attended art college in London (at Sickert's old school). Yet the outlet this offered, the putative channel for her frustrations, was insufficient; or possibly it came at the wrong time. In the end she made one of her clever collages for that other painter manqué, Adolf Hitler.

From the age of twelve or so, Jessica could be similarly difficult, although this was not really recognized in the same way, perhaps because her neat entrancing prettiness – she was the smallest of the sisters – made her less overwhelming. Unity was a huge girl, nearly six feet tall, handsome but with bad teeth from her mashed-potatoes diet: she had two grey fillings at the front. She was like Diana's gawky, slightly misshapen twin: 'shy, farouche, the features exaggerated by a bigger face, more chin'.[4] was a contemporary judgment. But the newspapers, which handed out judgments on the debs in a prim variant of the *Daily Mail*'s 'sidebar of shame', were complimentary. 'I thought that the prettiest girl at Epsom was Hon Unity Mitford,' the *Daily Express* pronounced after the 1932

Derby. This was almost certainly not the case. There was, in fact, already a sense in which Unity had been singled out for notice because she was a Mitford sister.

It was in 1932 that John Betjeman wrote his oddly touching little ditty, 'The Mitford Girls! the Mitford Girls, I love them for their sins…' He was like the young poet in Muriel Spark's *The Girls of Slender Means*, whose imagination is struck by the configurative aspect of a group of young women in a genteel London boarding house; and by one in particular, who symbolizes the whole. For Betjeman the one was Pamela ('most rural of them all'). She was then living at Biddesden, where Betjeman was a frequent visitor. The end of her engagement to Oliver Watney had seen her at a loose end, rather subdued, carted about abroad with her parents as an obviously unmarried daughter. She went to Canada with her father (more prospecting) and to St Moritz with the family. At home she bred Border terriers and advertised them for sale in *The Times.* In some ways she was the most satisfactory of the sisters, in that she gave no trouble, but – as with Nancy – she still embodied the dread question: what does a girl do if she fails to marry? It was terrible, really, how little had changed in the hundred-plus years since Charlotte Lucas was obliged to thank God for Mr Collins.

But Pam solved the problem herself, for a while, by suggesting to Bryan Guinness that she manage his 350 acres of dairy farm. He instantly agreed – he was fond of Diana's sisters; perhaps, like his fellow poet Betjeman, he responded to the collective picture that they presented[5] – and provided her with a cottage on the estate. 'Miss Pam', as the dairy workers called her, presented to the susceptible Betjeman an image of timeless countrified calm. She was attractive – again a version of Diana, but mixed with something passive and ovine; she had little of the Mitford spark but, in her unaware way, all its mysterious charm. 'Woman', the sisters' nickname, was an apt joke. 'My thoughts are still with Miss Pam,' Betjeman told Diana in February 1932. 'I have been seeing whether a little absence makes the heart grow fonder and, my God, it does.

Does Miss Pam's heart still warm towards that ghastly Czechoslovakian Count?' This was in fact a Russian named Serge Orloff, no more than a friend according to Pam, although Nancy (typically) claimed that Pam 'didn't play her cards very well' with him. Betjeman harped on Orloff a little and gave up his pursuit. He had proposed to Pam twice. She later said that she had been very fond of him, but not in love; so 'I rather declined'. In 1932 he wrote to Nancy, whom he liked enormously: 'If Pamela Mitford refuses me finally, you might marry me – I'm rich, handsome and aristocratic.' Almost forty years later, when he received his knighthood, Nancy sent cheerful congratulations, saying: 'If I had accepted your invitation – "Since Miss Pam won't marry me I think you had better" – I should now be a lady. Alas too late.'[6] She liked him too. His love of Victoriana, an eccentricity in the 1920s, was one of the running jokes in *Highland Fling*, and the hesitant young writer in *Christmas Pudding* was based on him. Their relationship was light, generous and a significant counterbalance to the evidence suggesting that Nancy was a repository of spite. 'How nice and clever we all are,' she wrote to him, in reply to his letter praising *The Pursuit of Love*. ('I am proud to know you', he had said.)

Betjeman's description of Biddesden is a veritable heaven. 'It was a sort of Oxford set, we used to see things as an endless party.' The three-storey building, formal and exquisite as its chatelaine, was the backdrop to what might have been a series of tableaux from an antique home movie: Bryan Guinness doing conjuring tricks, Unity and Betjeman singing evangelical hymns, Diana sitting for a portrait by Henry Lamb, Pamela in riding breeches with her herd of cows.

Lytton Strachey was also part of the Biddesden scene. Although homosexual, he too had fallen under Diana's spell. Their first meeting came at a post-opera supper held by Emerald Cunard, who had offered him a seat next to the renowned beauty Lady Diana Cooper. 'I want to sit next to the other Diana,' he had said, perhaps in a spirit of perversity, but as she later wrote 'we flew together like iron filings & magnet.' Her hunger for learning, which her childhood had stimulated but not fulfilled, made Strachey a perfect companion at this stage in life. 'Partly because of him I grew up quickly.' In fact she gracefully gave the impression that she was his acolyte. Diana was never arrogant about her own ability to attract.

Strachey had a house near to Biddesden – Ham Spray – that was home to a typically Bloomsbury set-up comprising Dora Carrington, her husband and her husband's lover. Although entirely broad-minded Diana had nothing Bloomsbury about her. She would never, as they did, equate free-spiritedness with grubby living: 'The poorest peasant in central Europe would refuse to put up with such discomfort as they did.' Carrington (as she was always called) was hopelessly in love with Strachey, but rather than competing with Diana became a good friend. She was a frequent visitor to Biddesden, where she created a surprise painting on a window for the birth of Diana's son Desmond. After a visit in 1931 she wrote to Strachey that she had met '3 sisters and Mama Redesdale. The little sisters [Jessica and Deborah] were ravishingly beautiful, and another of sixteen [Unity] very marvellous, and grecian. I thought the mother was rather remarkable, very sensible and no upper-class graces...'

'I imagined I knew her intimately,' Diana later wrote of Carrington, 'but this was mere illusion.' She had not realized the strength of Carrington's feelings for Strachey – 'Only Lytton counted' – and regretted that her friend's considerable talent as a painter was subsumed into that strange and overriding passion, which was soon to enter its last act. By 1931 Strachey had become very ill, with typhoid on top of an inoperable cancer. He died in January 1932, after which Carrington tried to gas herself. She then asked Bryan whether she could borrow a gun, to which he agreed only reluctantly, although he was reassured when she visited him for a picnic in March and wrote a happy thank-you letter: 'You never realize how much I love my visits to Biddesden.' A few days later she shot herself. Bryan, who felt immense if irrational guilt, was consoled by Diana, who in turn was devastated. She had been in London when it happened. On 21 February she had attended a lunch party, where she had been placed between one of the Rothschild family and Sir Oswald Mosley, whom she knew by sight but now spoke to properly for the first time. Years later, writing about the Ham Spray ménage, she said that the strains within it had been palpable: 'Yet to me there was also a feeling of permanence, perhaps only because to the young the idea that the present is transient seldom occurs.'[7] With the death of Strachey and Carrington, the transience of the idyll at Biddesden was soon to be apparent.

For Unity, too, it was an enchanted place, one that revealed her own capacity for happiness. Betjeman – who always called her 'Unity Valkyrie' – remembered her as 'a joyful version of Miss Pam', with the idiosyncratic Mitford way of speaking. She loved communal games like Grandmother's Footsteps – Betjeman recalled playing Statues on the lawn at Ham Spray – and had a fascination with film stars (she would watch entire programmes at the Empire Leicester Square, two or three times in a row). 'Unity Valkyrie *was* funny,' he said, wholly unembarrassed by the affection in which he had held her, 'she had a lot of humour which doesn't come out in the accounts of her.'

In May 1932 Unity was presented at Buckingham Palace, and wrote happily about it to Diana – 'it was great fun waiting in the Mall'. Diana had given her a grey and white dress by Norman Hartnell (a far cry from Gladys the maid) as well as a fur coat, gloves, the lot. 'I was entirely dressed by you.' There is no real sense of Unity as an uneasy or reluctant debutante. She would have known – girls do – that she was not physically equipped to be a great favourite with nervous young Englishmen, who would inevitably prefer something smaller and more conventional, but she had a few partners nonetheless. In *Hons and Rebels*, Jessica portrayed an image of 'rather alarming' oddity, causing ripples of shock to pass through the staid landscape of aristocratic ballrooms: Unity would put her rat, Ratular, in her handbag and sit stroking him at dances; she would wind her snake, Enid, around her throat in lieu of a necklace.

'Legend has it that she sometimes took her rat, but legends cannot be relied upon,' was Deborah's oblique but caustic comment on this. As so often with the Mitford sisters, memories clashed according to agenda. It was in character with the Unity of myth (and Jessica was a great one for mythmaking) that she should have wished to *épate* society by accessorizing Hartnell with a serpent. It was in character with the pragmatic Deborah to suggest that Unity did nothing of the kind. A family photograph does show her wearing Ratular on her shoulder, but in the faintly feral, semi-surreal world of the Mitfords this was hardly remarkable behaviour. Other stories, that she stole writing paper from Buckingham Palace during the wait to be presented, that she went to Blackfriars to watch all-in-wrestling before a ball at the Hurlingham Club, are not exactly shocking. They are the sort of thing that any girl might do if, fearing a lack of the usual kind of attention, she sought to be noticed. And Unity was, above all, an attention-seeker, but she was not any girl.

III

Her fate was bound up with Diana's, although Diana disclaimed any responsibility. 'Unity was a revolutionary,' she later said. 'The end would have been the same whether I had taken her to Germany or not.'

There was, too, the question of what the end would have been had Diana not met Sir Oswald Mosley at a lunch party in February 1932.

On that occasion she took so little notice in the great seducer that Bryan, who watched his wife with a sad relentless constancy that must have driven her mad, saw no cause for concern. Soon afterwards, however, Mosley began his pursuit; and all changed. He had been observing Diana since a ball the previous summer, given at the Park Lane house owned by her brother's friend, Sir Philip Sassoon. He had an eye on her, naturally. Pre-publicity is a great aid to desire, and no woman in London had more of that than Diana. Afterwards he wrote that she had the 'ineffable expression of a Gothic madonna'; it is interesting that whereas romantics like James Lees-Milne saw her in Italianate form, as a Raphael, for Mosley her beauty was that of the older, northern European kind.

The Mosley of 1931 – that is to say, before history did its work upon him – was not exactly the male counterpart to Diana, but he was a figure of similar note in society. He had already been the coming man, a star from the very first, when he entered Parliament after the First World War. Now he was taking a breather – *reculer pour mieux sauter*, as he would have seen it – and planning to launch himself on the political stage: this time on his own terms. He was also famous within upper-class London circles as a formidable philanderer, despite his marriage to Lady Cynthia Curzon. Using the phraseology of the field sportsman, he called his pursuit of married women 'flushing the covers'. He was, in modern parlance, a textbook alpha male: the first that Diana had encountered as a potential mate, although she had grown up regarding such men as the norm – her two grandfathers in particular and, to an extent, her father.

Born in 1896 into the Staffordshire squirearchy, Mosley came from a family of considerable wealth, who had owned part of the land on which central Manchester was built. Named after his father, he was generally known as Tom, although Diana called him Kit (and Nancy called him Sir Ogre). He was brought up in the main by his grandfather, his parents having separated when he was five. 'It was,' he said, 'a Corinthian childhood':[8] deliberately tough and manly. His grandfather (whom he remembered with fondness) had been a boxer, and one day knocked him out with a single punch. Mosley was always remarkably keen on fitness, a fine rider and fencer, although at Winchester he disliked team games. His high-toned physical presence – standing braced, as if for action of who knew what kind – was central to his extraordinary confidence, to his political dynamism and sexual allure.

Having served in the army and the Royal Flying Corps, he won the safe seat of Harrow for the Conservatives in 1918 and, in 1920, made an alliance with the Curzon family that was, in career terms, quasi-dynastic. Lord Curzon was Foreign Secretary and former Viceroy of India. He was viewed as heir apparent to Andrew Bonar Law as prime minister, although it was (tellingly) middle-class Baldwin who got the job. He had three daughters, Cynthia being the second; always known as 'Cimmie', she was a good-looking girl and a prize by any standards. Her wedding to Mosley, the build-up to which was reported for days in the newspapers, was at the Chapel Royal, St James's Palace – by permission of George V, who attended along with a spectacular guest list including the Dowager Countess of Airlie, Diana's great-grandmother. The reception was at Lord Curzon's superb house on Carlton House Terrace.

Curzon's money, which was in the Guinness league, came mostly from America; like a lot of peers he had shored up the family with commercial wealth. His first wife Mary was the daughter of a Jewish millionaire from Chicago. His second, Grace, was the widow of a hugely rich American. In between times he had an affair with the novelist Elinor Glyn, creator of the 'It' girl phenomenon. He had something in common with his son-in-law, in fact, although Mosley outstripped the competition by some distance. At one point after their marriage he confessed all his liaisons to Cimmie: 'Well', he remarked to Bob Boothby, 'all except her stepmother and her sister.' The sister referred to was Irene, Lady Ravensdale (a title she inherited in her own right). In the Mosley variation on a Chekhovian theme he later conducted an additional relationship with the other, married sister, Alexandra 'Baba' Metcalfe.

Infidelity is perfectly normal, of course, as is recreational sex. In Mosley's circles it was almost expected for a man to pursue a pretty married woman (the uxorious Bryan Guinness was probably more unusual in his behaviour). Certainly nobody would have been shocked by it – everybody knew that people crept about country houses at night, looking for the desired nameplate on the bedroom door. Nevertheless there was a peculiar wilfulness about Mosley's approach. He took lovers even though he much preferred the primary women in his life – Cimmie, then Diana – to any alternative; he did so to ridiculous excess; and one senses that he did it, as much as anything, to show off. Along with his sisters-in-law his conquests in the 1920s included Sylvia, Lady Ashley (a former chorus girl who later married Clark Gable) and Sacheverell Sitwell's wife, Georgia. During a summer weekend at the Mosleys' country house, Savehay, in Buckinghamshire, Georgia Sitwell wrote: 'Tom evidently fancies himself very much in bathing shorts.' How one can picture it. In the twelve years between his marriage and his meeting with Diana, Mosley had some three dozen affairs. This secondary career was facilitated when he acquired a 'bachelor flat' in Ebury Street in 1929; he also used 'fencing practice' as an alibi. Cimmie, in the main, was deceived. A kind and popular woman, an extremely supportive (and rich) wife, the mother of three children, she thought the best of Mosley and assuredly deserved better from him.

He quickly made a name for himself in politics, but again in that slightly deviant show-off way, almost as if he sought to put himself outside a situation that was comfortable and promising. In this, as in much else, he resembled Diana. By 1922 he was standing as an 'Independent Conservative' – railing against the government's 'failure to check excessive expenditure' and the use of the Black and Tans in Ireland – and in 1924 he crossed the floor to join Ramsay MacDonald's Labour Party. Needless to say this was highly remarkable, given his class background, and much deplored by Lord Curzon. It was probably motivated less by conviction than by a desire to extricate himself from the Conservatives, with whom he had become rather unpopular; although, again like Diana, he was a staunch supporter of the miners in the General Strike, and genuinely exercised by the shameful levels of unemployment. At any rate, more than seventy local Labour constituencies invited him to stand as their candidate in the 1924 election. It was characteristic of Mosley that he chose to stand against Neville Chamberlain, a future prime minister whose family had held the Ladywood seat for fifty years. He nearly won. Two years later he took Smethwick for Labour in a by-election, and in 1927 he spoke at a meeting that was broken up by a pesky little group calling itself the British National Fascists. Cimmie, loyal to Mosley's defection and a political animal herself, decided to stand as a Labour candidate: she won Stoke-on-Trent in 1929. Mosley gave her a brooch with the figures of her majority spelled out in rubies. The previous year his father had died, leaving him a baronetcy – 'not worth renouncing', Mosley airily decreed – and some £250,000. The couple's massive combined wealth and continued presence in high society was, inevitably, repellent and baffling to many in the party. 'It was truly an amazing and saddening spectacle,' wrote a commentator upon the way in which Mosley was embraced by Labour, 'to see these working men … literally prostrate themselves in their worship of the Golden Calf.' But the British relationship with class is complex, antagonistic yet underpinned by mysterious yearnings. The conjunction in Mosley of old-style paternalism and modern dynamism created an astonishing force that some, for sure, found irresistible.

A young German journalist described Mosley's appearance at a Labour Party meeting in London in 1924:

> Suddenly there was a movement in the crowd and a young man with the face of the ruling class of Great Britain but with the gait of a Douglas Fairbanks thrust himself forward through the throng to the platform followed by a lady [Cimmie] in heavy, costly furs. There stood Oswald Mosley, whose later ascent was to be one of the strangest phenomena of the working class movement of the world …
>
> The new man spoke … It was a hymn, an emotional appeal directed not to the intellect, but to the Socialist idea.

Here, then, was the great orator in action. At the end of speech, the crowd was described as beside itself, 'in uproar; as at a boxing match, or a fair'.

Given this mass appeal, which reads uncomfortably like a Nuremberg *en petit*, it was unsurprising that there were those in Parliament who distrusted the dashing young Labour baronet. Mosley would look around at his fellow MPs with an air of disdain and pronounce: 'A dead fish rots from the head down.' Nevertheless, as Bob Boothby wrote to Cimmie: 'I think your husband (damned Socialist though he is By God) will be Prime Minister for a very very long time, because he has the Divine Spark which is almost lost nowadays...' He was indeed spoken of in these terms. Stanley Baldwin growled that 'Tom Mosley is a cad and a wrong 'un', but in 1929, when he was promoted to Chancellor of the Duchy of Lancaster with the brief of tackling unemployment, it was Baldwin – and wary Labour men like Herbert Morrison – who seemed out of step.

The following year came the 'Mosley Memorandum': a manifesto for recovery that was subsequently described as both a generation ahead of its time and an alarming hint of tendencies to come. It combined Keynesian-style economics (for instance, unemployment to be dealt with in the short term by expensive road-building) with a plan for much stronger, indeed authoritarian executive powers. A large section of the Labour Party supported the Memorandum – although others thought it far too bold – and it was only narrowly defeated at the party conference in 1930. Typically, this spurred Mosley into irreversible action. He resigned from Labour, and in 1931 MacDonald formed a National Government. Effectively the party had been split, not exactly because of the Memorandum, but because of the divergent views that it exposed. Mosley, had he held on, would almost certainly have become Labour leader. His belief, however, was that he could bring his followers – who included Aneurin Bevan – to the New Party that he then formed. These events almost certainly explain the contempt that Diana later expressed for Ramsay MacDonald, and for the 'Tory in all but name' government that he led until 1935. (She often used her writings to settle old scores: for example Lady Diana Cooper's husband Duff, who in 1923 described Mosley as a 'canting, sliming, slobbering Bolshie [sic]', was ripped to shreds thirty years on.[9]) Mosley was surely right in one thing: that more radical solutions were needed to the problem of unemployment, which stood at 2 million when he wrote the Memorandum, and would rise to 3 million by 1933. By then the New Party had evolved into the British Union of Fascists.

At the time of his first proper meeting with Diana, Mosley was in a limbo stage: out of Parliament, preparing for his next move, fatally available to pursue the goddess. The New Party had come and gone. In the 1931 election, all twenty-four of its candidates lost. James Lees-Milne had campaigned briefly for Mosley, although he was not really a convert. Years later he would recall his impressions of that time, and what he wrote is a fascinating indicator of the direction in which Mosley's oratorical skills, his rock-star-like power to command an audience, were taking him. 'He was in those days a man of overweening egotism... The posturing, the grimacing, the switching on and off of those gleaming teeth and the overall swashbuckling so purposeful and so calculated, were more likely to appeal to Mayfair flappers than to sway indigent workers in the Potteries.' A previous supporter, Harold Nicolson, accompanied Mosley on a visit to Mussolini. He wrote: 'He believes in fascism. I don't.' Yet Diana, who despite appearances was no Mayfair flapper, became convinced over the course of 1932 that Mosley was the man who could rescue Britain. 'Occasionally we argued,' she wrote. 'But on the whole I was completely converted.' She believed in his belief. And, as Mitfords did, she gave him a nickname: 'The Leader'.

IV

On the evening of Unity's dance at Cheyne Walk, at which Diana wore a grey tulle dress of surpassing beauty and quantities of diamonds, she and Mosley finally pledged themselves to each other. At the same time he told her that he would never leave Cimmie. What Diana thought about this, who knows, but she accepted it to the extent that she did not give him up. This arrogant, errant lover weighed heavier in the balance than her husband (who wrote her a letter, poignant in its formal understatement, asking her to stop 'lunching' with Mosley), her two sons, her remarkable perfect life. The following morning Mosley rang the house and, heedless of who had answered the phone, said to the maid: 'Darling, when can I see you again?'

During this same key period – between the ball in July and the launch of the BUF in October – the Guinnesses held a *fête champêtre* at Biddesden. Diana was crowned with a silver wig made by Robert Byron, Mosley was all in black (no surprise there), and according to a guest at the party: 'Diana was telling everyone how thrilling she found him, like having a crush on a film star.' She was, of course, only twenty-two. To the painter Henry Lamb, whom she caught looking at Mosley askance, she said in her smiling, self-mocking way: 'You're thinking what a frightful bounder he is.' Her own behaviour was careless. She and Mosley spent much of the evening upstairs inside the house. Cimmie, dressed meekly as a shepherdess, was apparently aware of what was happening: the loyal wife, who followed her husband's politics like one of her imaginary lambs and had painstakingly made a banner for the BUF, was being cheated on by her hostess while most of those present pretended not to notice. What Bryan thought can only be imagined. But he cannot have been wholly amazed when, in November 1932, Diana told him that she wanted to leave. Whether he believed that she meant it is another story. On New Year's Eve she walked calmly into a party held by Mosley and Cimmie, at which the two other Curzon sisters, spitting blood on behalf of all three of them, were also present. It was a quite extraordinary thing to do, possible only if one is young, indifferent and high on conviction. The following day she took a lease on a little house in Eaton Square, cut-price because of its poor condition but close to Mosley's flat – 'Bloody damnable cursed Ebury,' said Cimmie, who for all her saintliness was a woman of passion, 'how often does she come there?' Diana set up home with her sons and four servants; she had, at a stroke, become a highly public and unabashed Other Woman.

From that moment the Mitford family began to fall apart. Unity and Jessica's actions would be influenced by Diana's nonpareil act of rebellion; the Redesdales would succumb to anger, shame and despair; Diana's own life would be set on a course that led to vilification, pariah status and Holloway jail. The days when Nancy was a cause of concern for her daring novels and silly unrequited passion, when David fretted over money lost in a scheme to make plastic wireless covers – they would seem halcyon, unclouded. In 1935 a photographer would take the last in a long series of Mitford family portraits, but the people that it represented in it would go their separate ways the moment after the shutter had clicked. 'I often think,' wrote Nancy in *The Pursuit of Love*, 'that there is nothing quite so poignantly sad as old family groups.'

The Mitfords did not let Diana go without a fight. Knowing how much it would hurt, Sydney refused to allow Unity, Jessica and Deborah anywhere near their sister. David made common cause with Bryan's father, now Lord Moyne, and together they visited Mosley at Ebury Street. Diana and Mosley were two of a kind, all right – the meeting would have led most men to cave in. Instead he merely told Randolph Churchill that he would wear a 'balls protector', and shrugged the whole thing off, saying: 'Diana must be allowed to do what she wants.' Even today Diana's act would be viewed as calamitous, setting up alone as *maîtresse en titre* to London's worst philanderer; an act of madness, walking out on a man who adored her, who had given her everything, to face a future of absolute uncertainty. In 1932, when even divorce was a stigma (worse yet, a bar to the Royal Enclosure at Ascot), open adultery of this kind was scandalous beyond comprehension. It was not the way things were done. One had affairs and kept the family show on the road. But Diana's radicalism and refusal to tell lies extended, as it were instinctively, into the private sphere.

'You are SO young to be getting in wrong with the world, if that's what's going to happen,' wrote Nancy, sounding genuinely concerned for Diana and adding that she would always be on her sister's side. Tom Mitford, whose opinion would ordinarily have counted most, also expressed horror: not least because Bryan was his good friend. Later he and his parents blamed Nancy for supporting Diana's decision to leave her marriage. Tom also astutely remarked that £2,500 annual maintenance, which Bryan offered for life, would seem like nothing. It wasn't a small sum, by any means, although after the near-infinite largesse of the past four years it was relative poverty. But Diana rather liked that idea, its purity and newness.

Cheyne Walk, so recently acquired, furnished with such care for every detail, was sold. 'The servants are resenting you going so much,' wrote Bryan, in a pathetic burst of ill-directed anger. It was typical of Diana that, having caused such incalculable unhappiness to her husband, she should then find him a flat in Chelsea and decorate it for him. 'Darling, I really do think you are kind', he wrote. 'I do love you for it. I mean, I would if you wanted me to.' In return he gave her the Cheyne Walk contents – including the two Aubusson carpets, a gift from her now enraged father-in-law – although she refused the Stanley Spencer, which was hung at Biddesden. She also returned the Guinness jewels. Lord Moyne urged his son to behave more like a man (Mosley?) and *do something*. Bryan's response was to write more hopeless letters. 'Are you positive that you love Tom more than me… You were my ewe lamb.' This abject attitude hints, oh-so faintly, at a desire to induce guilt or regret. How could it not? Nobody could really have been as disinterestedly generous as Bryan, it was beyond nature, as Nancy suggested in a letter to Diana. Having seen Bryan in London, she wrote: 'He was pretty spiky I thought, kept saying I suppose it's my *duty* to take her back & balls of that sort.' This was Nancy, of course, and therefore not entirely to be trusted. But it would be reassuring, really, to think that Bryan was insanely cross beneath all that decency.

Sydney Redesdale, wise beneath her detachment, wrote fine counsel to her daughter: 'I was so glad I was able to see you the other night and to realize what I did think was the case: the affection you have for Bryan through and beyond everything. His worst fault seems to be a too great fondness for you and perhaps you on your side are too impatient. Do, I beg you, think well before you throw away what is worth while and good for what is nothing and bad.'

If anything could have stopped Diana, it was that letter. But the obduracy she had shown when she wanted to marry Bryan now returned, to the power of a hundred, and being told not to leave him made her all the more determined. Later she wrote: 'In a strange way I think Kit and I both knew it was "pour la vie" and that we should always love each other.'

She was right: they did stay together. And is it so hard to understand why she fell for this man, who erupted into her life with the bounding force of Pilgrim the wolfhound?

Perhaps as much as anything she wanted freedom. Bryan was both perfect and entirely wrong for her. Devotion was something that she could command with too much ease to value it. Mosley represented the first real challenge she had ever encountered; he pursued her but he did not fall at her feet; he continued to live with his wife, to sleep with his sisters-in-law; in trying to prise him away from all this Diana had something to get her teeth into. Rather as rich aristocrats, for whom the world lay on a Sèvres plate, have historically hurled vast quantities of time and money at the thoroughbred racehorses that never quite did their bidding, so Diana remained intrigued by the mystery of her lover. And he would have been a proper lover. Our old friend sex played a huge part in all of this. Bryan was a very good-looking man, but the diffident young upper-classes are not noted for their Casanova qualities. Mosley brimmed with the particular confidence of the sexually successful; probably Diana had never met such a creature before he turned the full blast of his masculinity upon her. And a relationship that begins with irresistible physical attraction – unless this turns to repulsion – always retains something of that memory. One only has to look at photographs of the Mosleys in later life to understand that Diana fancied him until the day he died.

Again, the weight of history makes this seem barely comprehensible. Mosley became a demonized figure, a terrible symbol of authoritarianism, up to and beyond his death in 1980. Even pop culture used him as a kind of shorthand for all that must be resisted in politics: Elvis Costello's first album in 1977 contained an attack on him – 'calling Mr Oswald with the swastika tattoo'[10] – that was not entirely accurate (Mosley was never a Nazi) but showed how, almost forty years after the threat he represented had been contained, he remained a uniquely powerful totem. 'He loved Britain and has been waiting for its call,' wrote Clive James in 1976, 'all unawares that the best reason for loving Britain has always [to date] been its reluctance to call him, or anybody like him.'

In 1932, when Fascism meant Mussolini – with whom the British were quite comfortable, and who later helped fund the BUF[11] – Mosley symbolized something different. Although the days were gone when he had been seen as a future prime minister (for the Conservatives, at first, as well as for Labour), he was not a political leper. He did not have the vast following that he wanted, but he could command serious support. 'The origin of the BUF,' he wrote, 'was the formation of an emergency group of men and women to advocate a practical policy capable of being put into immediate operation in order to meet a specific plan for the crisis in Britain.' And there *was* a crisis – financial panic, mass unemployment, the Communist threat: it was not as unreasonable as it now seems to portray democracy as too weak to cope. In the ten months between its inception and August 1933 the BUF expanded so quickly that it had to move to large premises on the King's Road in Chelsea – the 'Black House' – which was said to be 'filled with students eager to learn about this new, exciting crusade'.[12] The party gathered together the various little strands of Fascism (such as the body that had abused Mosley back in 1927) that had been waving alluringly since the early 1920s. Even today it is apparent that Britain, for all its innate and healthy scepticism, has a weakness for people who spout solutions that they will never be called upon to enact: the mainstream is muddy with compromise, while those outside it can stand clean and clear, dangling the great glittering hypnotist's tool that is 'change'. This is the word that still holds its magic, and nobody promised it more than Mosley. Lord Rothermere's *Daily Mail* was behind the BUF until as late as 1934: 'Hurrah for the Blackshirts!' was a headline in January that year. The BUF was perceived as the party of 'youth'. In other words, it embodied that other political shibboleth, the need to inspire young people, which always sounds so good and can lead to such extremes of idiocy. Lloyd George declared that 'Sir Oswald Mosley is a very able man and he is making considerable headway.' To the members of the Fabian Society, of all people, George Bernard Shaw made a speech, saying that Mosley 'is a very interesting man to read just now… you instinctively hate him because you do not know where he will land you, and he evidently means to uproot some of you'.

The radicalism implied therein appealed to an agitator like Shaw, and to Diana. This is the unfathomable paradox within her: that she was a woman of the most intensely civilized values, a woman of profound humour, a woman who craved personal freedom, a woman who enjoyed without apology all the beauty that life could offer and that she herself embodied; and that she was, in her deepest soul, attracted to something dark, harsh, dictatorial and violent, something that above all took itself absolutely seriously. How, one wonders, did the Mitford love of laughter not cause her to fall about at the sight of Mosley in his black and his boots? Similarly – how could she have watched Hitler, screaming his nonsense at full volume, without the family sense of the ridiculous kicking in? Well: it didn't.

Diana was not, like Miss Jean Brodie, 'a born Fascist'. But that quality of *will* in her, the strong reverberating rod of steel inside her, responded to the same thing in Mosley. Over dinner, his son Nicholas recalled, he would offer his variation on the theories of Nietzsche. 'And then he would do his trick of flashing his eyes on and off as if they were a lighthouse.'[13] It is easy to think how incredibly silly this would have looked. Perhaps, as they say, one had to be there. Or one had to be receptive, to feel a quasi-religious faith in what Mosley called 'the will to achievement'.

In her later writings, which are taut, rigorous and full of cogent arguments against ideas such as the rightfulness of going to war against Germany, Diana shows quite clearly the unyielding nature that would have responded to Mosley's certainties. Reviewing a book about British politics in the years leading up to the Second World War, she wrote crisply: 'For members of Parliament, to declare war on Germany was the answer to many things. All the great neglected problems of the day, unemployment, housing, poverty, were solved at a stroke... Oswald Mosley is denounced for predicting "collapse", but he has unfortunately been proved right in the event.'[14]

This was the thing: Diana believed in Mosley. 'It was this,' she said, 'which gave me the courage to survive ostracism, the anger of my parents... the disapproval of absolutely everyone.' She fell in love with the man, not the ideology, but it was *because* he brought with him that unparalleled force of conviction, that charge of aggression with its sexual undertow, that she fell so heavily. It is not unknown: the response of pale protected girls to a mysterious male force is the stuff of the vampire myth, of romantic poetry, of laser-lit rock concerts. And Diana was, it must be reiterated, extremely young. Of course she stayed loyal to Mosley all her life but, had she been ten years older when she met him, she might have found him easier to resist. 'You only do great things in a great way,' he later said; to a girl who saw democracy as an innately compromised system, incapable of making things better, this would have sounded like a magnificent creed. And the kind of man who could say it was magnificent, also.

So she went off to 'the Eatonry', as she called her little house in Eaton Square, and sat there in all her goddess splendour to wait for Mosley, who fitted her in between his wife, the two Curzon sisters and plans for political dominance. He probably felt rather pleased with himself. What further proof of his fabulousness could he want, than the willingness of the most beautiful girl in London to chuck everything on his behalf? If Diana ever felt a qualm, nobody ever knew it. It had been clear to her from the days in Paris with Paul César Helleu that somebody who looked as she did could make her own rules of life. Beauty annihilated convention. So far, she had got away with anything she chose to do, had been handed everything that she ever wanted. It may have interested her, to see what happened when she loaded the dice against herself as heavily as she knew how.

V

Nancy, whose unconventionality remained within the barriers that Diana had just dismantled, stuck by her sister. She visited the Eatonry as often as she could; so too did all Diana's friends, although she was completely cut by the more established members of society, and rumours (such as the one spread by Henry Lamb – how gallant – that she had had an affair with Randolph Churchill) naturally circulated.

It was at Eaton Square, in June 1933, that Nancy received a phone call from Hamish St Clair-Erskine, telling her that he had become engaged to another woman. He had warned Diana of what he planned to say; there was no truth in it but it was, he thought, the only way to put their increasingly ludicrous association to an end. 'You must be very careful,' Diana said to him. 'She might do herself an injury.'

In fact Nancy responded as women of her kind sometimes do: by getting angry, then blaming herself. 'I can't sleep without saying I am so sorry & miserable that I was unkind to you just now,' she wrote, in her last letter to Hamish. 'I knew you weren't *in love* with me...' It was not until many years had elapsed that she had her revenge, the kind of which chucked people dream: Hamish would creep round to her flat in Paris – where she lived in supremely elegant munificence – and make a nuisance of himself ('*very* poor and rather pathetic', as Nancy described him to Evelyn Waugh in 1951). Towards the end of her life he ventured that they might, now, have been married for years. 'Help!' Nancy wrote to Deborah.

But back in 1933 her unhappiness, shame, and doubtless excruciating embarrassment were overwhelming. She was now twenty-eight: what to do? The answer seemed like a miracle. A handsome, clever man named Peter Rodd proposed marriage, and within little more than a month Nancy was engaged. 'Well the happiness,' she wrote to Mark Ogilvie-Grant in August. 'Oh goodness gracious I am happy.'

For once she had the advantage over Diana, who was recently divorced. Hamish's phone call had come through when Nancy, Pam and Unity were giving support to their sister the day before her court appearance, at which, in an undefended suit, 'Mrs Diana Guinness of Eaton Square prayed for the dissolution of her marriage with Mr Bryan Walter Guinness on the grounds of his adultery with Isolde Field at an hotel at Brighton in March last.' In the lead-up to the hearing Lord Moyne ('may he burn in hell') had put a firm of private detectives onto Diana, although – perhaps at Bryan's insistence –

any evidence against her went unused. The unknown Ms Field was, of course, one of the girls who in return for payment would pretend to sleep with a man willing to give his wife an easy way out. Like Tony Last in Evelyn Waugh's *A Handful of Dust*, who endures a peculiarly ghastly comedic version of this charade, Bryan was through and through a gentleman (with the masochistic tendencies that sometimes attend the breed). His novel, *Singing out of Tune*, which was published in 1933, also describes the Brighton scenario, and a marriage that founders because the beautiful wife 'seemed to be converted to some worldly heresy of lovelessness'. Please, he begged Diana, make it clear to everybody that this is not our story. It wasn't, as it happened; their story was *sui generis*.

For in another twist that fiction would have rejected as absurdly fanciful, in May 1933 Cimmie Mosley died of peritonitis at the age of thirty-four. She had begun to feel ill during a stay at Savehay – the family home in Buckinghamshire – and had an almighty quarrel with Mosley about his behaviour. His response was to drive off to Diana. In a sombre echo of Nancy's letter to Hamish – which for all its sincerity was based upon a relationship devised in her own head – Cimmie wrote the next morning to her husband: 'Darling heart, I want to apologize for last night but I was feeling already pretty rotten and I suppose that made me silly.' That night she was taken to hospital with a burst appendix. Mosley visited her, then skipped off to lunch with Diana, where he met Unity for the first time. A few days later Cimmie was dead. 'Oh God what a terrible doom for Tom [Mosley]!' wrote Irene Ravensdale, 'and to think that Cim is gone and that Guinness is free and alive and oh! where is there any balance or justice!' Irene was at rapacious war with her sister Baba for Mosley's affections, but no sense of this irony seems to have touched her. And she may have been right to think that Cimmie had failed to fight for life, on account of Diana.

Mosley's grief was great. He was described as 'like a man demented'.[15] After his first, typically selfish reaction to her illness, he had stayed at Cimmie's bedside throughout the last few days of her life. He had never intended to leave her; what Diana chose to do was her business, in the end. Nor had Diana asked Mosley to break up his marriage; she had simply set herself up like Mrs Jordan to his William IV. Nevertheless only a sociopath would have failed to feel appalling guilt, and both Mosley and Diana did feel it. She kept up the façade, attended dinner parties with a face white as chalk, but her position as outcast became more solid, immutable. No wonder she would say, in her old age: 'Being hated means absolutely nothing to me as you know.' She had had years of practice. Cimmie dead, eulogized in the newspapers, sanctified within society, was a far darker shadow between her and Mosley than she had been alive. Yet the intrusion of reality into what may, until then, have been something of a social and sexual game, albeit one with high stakes, made Diana's commitment to Mosley itself more real. As things went wrong for them, so it became ever more necessary for Diana to justify her decision to throw in her lot with this man.

He grieved, but he did not change. Although deeply attached to Diana, he continued to dally with the Curzon sisters. Rivals though they were, they united against 'Guinness'. Mosley took Baba on holiday to France; this, he told Diana, was an excellent way of diverting attention from their own relationship, but in fact the affair with Baba was quite genuine (as Diana surely knew). Irene wrote: 'I pray this obsession with her [Baba] will utterly oust Diana Guinness.' In an attempt to boost her own credentials, and impelled by the urge to protect Cimmie's offspring, Irene moved into Savehay and took charge of the Mosley children. Diana, who had time on her hands while Mosley played away, briefly visited Swinbrook, where her father refused to speak to her. Later that year – and again in 1935 – she was obliged to terminate a pregnancy; a dodgy business, even for women with the means to avoid a backstreet abortionist; but it was impossible in the circumstances to have Mosley's baby.

The sordidness of the whole thing is overwhelming, so too the temptation to travel back in time and say to Diana, what in hell do you think you are doing? Even more so when, in July 1933, she attended a Communist rally and held up her arm in a Fascist salute. Only when one of Mosley's boys stepped in was she saved from attack. By now the BUF's 'youth' appeal had translated into something rather less innocent. Mosley had a de facto bodyguard of young Blackshirts trained, military style, at the Black House in Chelsea. It was becoming clear that young men, full of rampant energy in search of a direction, were attaching themselves to Fascism because it gave them what is now called an 'identity'. Some of them would have been simply harmless and excitable;[16] quite a lot were looking for a full-scale punch-up. They were not much different to football hooligans, the seriously tough kind who organize themselves into 'firms' and travel to matches in straightforward pursuit of aggro. Who the opposition was did not much matter, so long as it existed, and in this case it was Communism. And, of course, Jews.

'For years Red hooliganism has reigned unchecked at political gatherings,' wrote a correspondent to *The Times*, defending (as many did) Mosley's claim that any aggression by his men was merely retaliatory. Again, the idea was that Communism was the real threat. Fascism was patriotic, Communism was alien. Another letter, printed after the 1934 Olympia rally that degenerated into mass violence, described 'young men, mostly Jews', who 'were clearly in a fighting mood – and they got what they wanted!' The anti-Semitism issue is central, although oddly confused. Mosley, who had asked Diana's Jewish friend John Sutro to stand as a candidate for the New Party, stated in 1933: 'Hitler has made his greatest mistake with attacks on the Jews.' Yet if he had sought to disassociate himself from this particular German policy, he did so in the same year that the BUF sent a delegation to Nuremberg. To his sister-in-law Irene, Mosley admitted that the Jews were useful to him, in that every movement needs a scapegoat (quite true). Given that Irene clung so to Mosley, it is interesting that she should have turned up at a 1934 charity première in aid of German Jews. Perhaps this was intended as a snub, and if so it was probably connected to Mosley's relationship with Diana.

In the same year, meanwhile, he denounced the Conservatives because they 'worshipped at the shrine of an Italian Jew' – meaning Disraeli – and made a ghastly speech at a rally in Manchester, in which he referred to the 'sweepings of the Continental ghettoes, hired by Jewish financiers'. This was the argument, that the Jews backed high finance, and that therein lay corruption. 'One felt that the City was feathering its nest while 3 million unemployed were starved,' as Diana later wrote. Yet at the same time Jews were also identified with Communism: the concept of 'Judeo-Bolshevism' was a prevalent nonsense, propagated in Germany during the 1920s, not just in *Mein Kampf* but in an influential pamphlet[17] that identified Moses as a Communist. A conspiracy theory can flourish only if enough people want to believe in it, and certainly Mosley touched a nerve when he claimed that the Jews were attacking his blameless patriotic movement. An uneasy comparison exists with today: the pervasive loathing of 'bankers', identified as the guilty party in our national sufferings; the revival of an anti-Semitism that does not quite know what it is saying, only that it means it.

Many years later Mosley still held to the argument that any attacks by his followers upon Jews had been made in self-defence: 'you will never catch Sir Oswald admitting to anti-Semitism', wrote Clive James. 'All he does is embody it.'[18] As for Diana: her heritage had given her a natural affinity with German culture and philosophy. Her grandfather had believed in Teutonic supremacy; her brother had a profound adoration of Wagner and Goethe; it was instinct in her to be gladdened by the image of an Aryan Europe, pale and pure, warlike and noble. Fascism touched something deep, almost subliminal, in a woman who also revered the civilizations of France, Rome, Greece. The Nazis drew up a 'Black Book', a list of people to be taken into 'protective custody' after a successful invasion of Britain; along with Churchill, Eden and the like, one of the names listed was that of Lytton Strachey – dead since 1932 – on account of his dangerous aestheticism, his intellectual iconoclasm, his Bloomsbury politics, probably his homosexuality. This was a man whom Diana had loved. Yet in some way she responded to the Nazi creed that sought his destruction. A few years after the war she wrote that one of her greatest delights was to read the memoirs of St-Simon, those *petit-point* samplers of life at the court of Louis XIV. Yet she had sat at the BUF rallies, surrounded by uproar and aggression, like the Mona Lisa at Upton Park: her thoughts an irreducible mystery.

Clashes between Fascists and Communists took place regularly throughout 1934, but the Olympia meeting in June was climactic. It was described in *The Times* in measured terms that nonetheless read like utter madness. The Communist presence was highly organized, with Jessica Mitford's future husband, the seventeen-year-old Esmond Romilly, among its number. Hecklers were systematically 'seized ju-jitsu fashion and dragged out' by Mosley's stewards. Fighting broke out, including between young women; knives and knuckledusters were wielded. Meanwhile much of the 12,000-strong crowd, poor and middle-aged, looked on in bewilderment. Afterwards Lord Rothermere withdrew *Daily Mail* backing from the BUF. There was a genuine fear, or for some a hope, that the 1935 election could lead to 'rule by dictatorship'.

Before Olympia, Diana gave a dinner party at Eaton Square, where the guests included the fantastical aesthete Lord Berners, a man who filled his mini-stately home with doves dyed like confetti: again, how was it possible? Also present was Nancy, who went on to the rally with her brother Tom. This was not her sole experience of the BUF: in November 1933 she had attended a meeting in Oxford with her new fiancé, Peter Rodd. Her motives are unclear, but curiosity was probably top of the list. Peter, who was described by Jessica as 'on the left, which suited my thinking',[19] was briefly convinced by the notion that the BUF held a solution to Britain's social problems. He looked, as Nancy later wrote to Evelyn Waugh, 'very pretty in a black shirt. But we were young & high spirited then and didn't know about Buchenwald.' Nancy wrote an account of the meeting to Diana, saying that Mosley had 'brought along a few

Sydney and David, 2nd Lord and Lady Redesdale, the Mitford parents.

Bertie Mitford, 1st Lord Redesdale, paternal grandfather to the Mitford girls.

Thomas Bowles, founder of *The Lady*, the girls' maternal grandfather.

The Mitford Girls

Nancy

Pamela

Diana

Unity

Deborah

Jessica

Batsford Park, first home to the Mitford family, built by Bertie and sold in 1919.

Asthall Manor, where life was 'all summers'.

Swinbrook House, built by David, hated by all his children except Deborah.

Unity Mitford, aged eight, and her younger sister Jessica, at Asthall.

Diana in 1930, photographed in Hyde Park with her first husband, Bryan Guinness. Her wolfhound, Pilgrim, ate raw meat straight from her hands.

Diana and Nancy, white and black queen of the Mitford girls, in 1932.

The TATLER

Vol. CXXIX. No. 1675. London, August 2, 1933 POSTAGE: Inland 1½d.; Canada and Newfoundland, 1½d.; Foreign, 3d. Price One Shilling

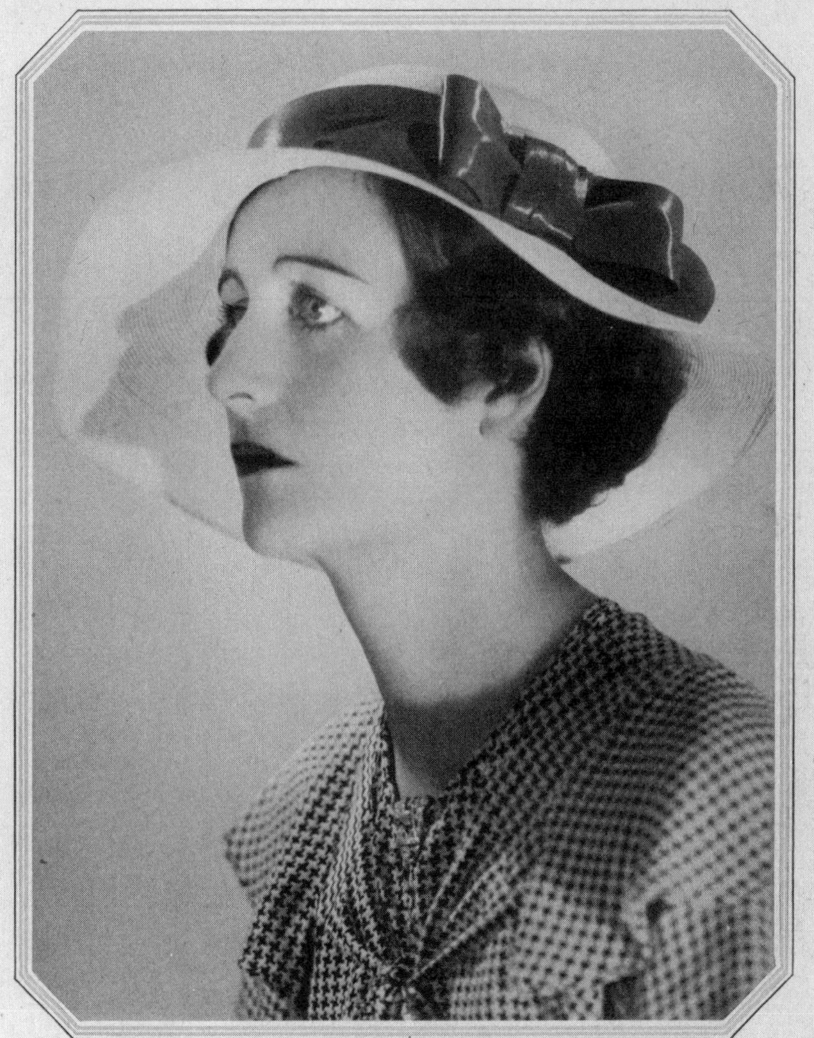

Yevonde, Victoria Street

ENGAGED: THE HON. NANCY MITFORD

The latest bride-to-be is Lord and Lady Redesdale's eldest daughter, whose engagement to the Hon. Peter Rennell Rodd was officially announced last week. The Hon. Nancy Mitford is not only charming to look at but also extremely intelligent and an entertaining conversationalist. She has written two novels, "Highland Fling" and "Christmas Pudding," both of which have had a distinct success. Her fiancé is the second son of Lord and Lady Rennell. Lord Rennell, formerly Sir Rennell Rodd, is an ex-Ambassador, and was Member for Marylebone from 1928 to 1932. His Barony appeared in the last New Year Honours List

a

Nancy on the cover of *The Tatler* in 1933, on the occasion of the announcement of her engagement to Peter Rodd.

Sir Oswald Mosley in his pomp, 1936.

Unity in the 1930s, dressed in the female uniform of Mosley's British Union movement, talks to an SS Colonel outside the Brown House (Nazi Party headquarters) in Munich.

Neanderthal men with him and they fell tooth and (literally) nail on anyone who shifted his chair or coughed'. This would not have gone down well. Later Diana described Mosley's guard as 'a disciplined body of men [who] were allowed to use only their bare hands when ejecting troublemakers or resisting attack'.[20]

Worse still came when Nancy – black shirt consigned to the dustbin – wrote a satire on the Fascist movement entitled *Wigs on the Green*, published in 1935 and portraying Mosley as 'Captain Jack', leader of the Union Jackshirt Movement. As it were incidentally, the book also contained an ambivalent commentary upon the married state. Her wedding to Peter Rodd, or 'Prod', as he became in Mitford parlance, had taken place on 4 December 1933 at St John's, Smith Square. Nancy wore a very lovely white chiffon dress, paid for by Bryan Guinness. Among the guests was Adelaide Lubbock, a cousin of Nancy's through the Stanley connection, who within five years would become one of Peter Rodd's girlfriends. Unlike Hamish, Peter was extremely heterosexual, but this too posed its problems.

Nancy's decision to fall for Peter – who had, according to legend, proposed to several women on the night she accepted him – revealed itself, quite quickly, to be a bad bet ('Fantastic what a girl will do on the rebound,' as a character in her novel puts it). She remained loyal to him for far too long, putting a very good face on the situation, as was her way. The couple set up home in Strand-on-the-Green, near Kew Bridge, and Nancy took a wifely delight in playing house; she had her mother's gift for making a home attractive, she had her two French bulldogs – Milly and Lottie – and she was, at last, freed from the stigma of 'the shelf'. Her new husband was extremely bright, a Balliol man, and from a good family: his father Lord Rennell of Rodd had been British ambassador in Rome. (Later Nancy would conjure him as the stately, vacuous Lord Montdore in *Love in a Cold Climate*, and delightedly plundered her mother-in-law's worst traits for the 'she-wolf' Lady Montdore.) Peter, however, was childish and self-destructive. Not a bad person; although Harold Acton, who thought he treated Nancy abysmally, called him 'a superior con-man'.[21] But he was simply, and hopelessly, unable to live the life that he ought to have had. Rather like David Redesdale, he grew up in the shadow of a paragon older brother, and this seems to have made him fatally rebellious. He could stick at nothing, was terrible with money – 'One feels a little scared about the young couple,' wrote Lord Rennell ominously, 'and I am wondering whether their house is healthy or whether they get enough to eat and keep warm'; this at a time when Peter had just chucked a job worth £600 a year. The couple lived in the main off Nancy's writing and an allowance from the Rennells. Diana's £2,500 a year from Bryan (a sum that was her right to name, as the 'innocent' party in a divorce suit), had been a deliberately frugal demand; to the Rodds, who lived on about one-fifth of that amount, it would have been wealth beyond their dreams.

By 1935 Peter was already seeing another woman: Mary Sewell, the daughter of Edwin Lutyens. Later the affair with Adelaide Lubbock would begin (in 1950 Nancy wrote that for the past twelve years Peter had 'considered himself as married to her'). The assumption is that there were others along the way. He had been sent down from Oxford for having a girl in his room; in fact the wilful flagrancy of his womanizing had something in common with Mosley's. It is unlikely that Nancy was ever truly in love with him, despite his blond beauty (described by Evelyn Waugh as 'the sulky, arrogant looks of the young Rimbaud'). For one thing he was simply too boring. His mind was encyclopaedic, about everything from the Norman kingdoms in Sicily to the tollgate system in England and Wales ('the Old Tollgater' was a secondary nickname), but there was simply no edit button: out it all spilled, and it is hard to imagine that Nancy – with her intolerance of 'crashers' – would have held her peace. Clearly other women did. And the humiliation of this would have half killed her, not least because it followed so hard on the heels of the dreadfully public non-affair with Hamish St Clair-Erskine. She was no Diana, who could sit in smiling silence, waiting for her roving dog to return after a night à la chasse. Nancy's façade was immaculate but it cracked easily; at a bridge party with the Sewells she stood up and fainted, a desperate cry for the situation to stop. 'She's only trying to get attention,' Peter said, carrying his wife briskly out of the room before returning to his mistress.

So it is unsurprising that *Wigs on the Green* holds so much dry disillusionment, a sense of cynicism fashioned, with some effort, from disappointment. 'A girl must marry once,' says a character in the book. 'You can't go on being called Miss – Miss all your life, it sounds too idiotic. All the same, marriage is a great bore... It gets one down in time.' The 'time' had not been very long: Nancy started the book just a few months into her marriage. The central character, Jasper Aspect, bears a strong resemblance to Peter, to whom the book is dedicated. Perhaps Nancy did not mean him to come across as quite so unlikeable, but he does. He steals money from women's handbags, just as Peter did from hers, and when told that wives are not expected to keep their husbands he replies easily: 'I never could see why not. It seems so unfair.' Although the novel is a brilliant little piece – like almost everything that Nancy did – there is a peculiar coldness, a not-quite-natural toughness in the passages relating to Jasper, essentially at odds with the *benevolence* that characterizes her subsequent works. It is not, somehow, a novel written by a happy person. And the will to happiness was, in Nancy, at least as strong as Captain Jack's will to achievement; but that, for her, came later.

Wigs on the Green was not, therefore, designed entirely as a satire on the Fascist movement. The Union Jackshirts are all part of the comedic landscape – in itself a way of making them seem facile. Nevertheless the joke on them is a pretty good one. The airy teasing was too much for Diana to take; with all the cool, alarming strength of which she was capable, she demanded that Nancy remove parts of the book. The sacred Mosley had recognized an enemy in his midst, and this meant that Diana, too, must view her sister with suspicion. Although political ideology relishes combat, it really does not like being laughed at; this, too, the modern age reminds us. And from the time that *Wigs on the Green* was published, in June 1935, the relationship between Nancy and Diana changed: there was no absolute rupture, and later came a resumption of closeness, but a certain wariness remained. As much as anything Diana would have been pulled up by little asides such as: 'Well, it's not usual for ladies to be divorced, you know,' which seemed to mock the months at Eaton Square, when each had succoured the other in their despair, and Diana had written 'Darling you are my one ally' to her sister. 'Oh dear,' Nancy remarked about *Wigs on the Green*, 'I wish I had called it mine un comf now because uncomf is what I feel whenever I think about it...'

She had seen a need, no question, to make light of the darkness in her sister's life. Oddly enough, however, *Wigs on the Green* was not entirely critical of the Fascist creed. One Jackshirt speech inveighs against a society 'rotten with vice, selfishness and indolence. The rich have betrayed their trust, preferring the fetid atmosphere of cocktail bars and night-clubs to the sanity of useful country life.' This echoed a typical robust Mosley pronouncement – 'Conservatives have chosen the financier, Fascism chose the British farmer' – but it also prefigured Nancy's attacks on capitalism in *The Pursuit of Love*. Perhaps, in that sense, she *had* responded to the BUF call. And perhaps her jibes sprang from a source that was not entirely disinterested: an envy of Diana's palpable fulfilment with this man. Nancy saw through Mosley, but she also saw the charge between him and Diana, which was different altogether from her wobbly loose connection with Peter. Nonetheless she was quite sincere in her ridicule when, for example, a character in *Wigs on the Green* describes a 'non-Aryan' as:

> 'The missing link between man and beast. That can be proved by the fact that no animals, except the Baltic goose, have blue eyes.'
>
> 'How about Siamese cats?' said Jasper.
>
> 'That's true. But Siamese cats can possess, to a notable degree, the Nordic virtue of faithfulness...'

The young woman parroting this stuff is Eugenia Malmains, a splendid daughter of Gloucestershire with 'eyes like enormous blue headlamps' and 'the gait of a triumphant goddess', who makes speeches on 'an overturned wash-tub in Chalford village green'. To a young man who responds to her greeting of 'Hail!' with 'Snow', she is severe: 'If you continue to be facetious at the expense of our Movement I shall be obliged to degrade you before the comrades. In fact I will cut off all your buttons with my own dagger.' Nobody takes Eugenia very seriously. When she sets up a Union Jack rally in a country-house garden and writes a speech for George III beginning: 'Hail! And thanks for all your good wishes, we are happy to be among our loyal Aryan subjects of Chalford and district,' this seems merely silly, rather endearing, the behaviour of a schoolgirl in the throes of a crush; one that will soon, when everybody comes to their senses, be over and done with.

Given that Eugenia was a portrait of Unity, this may be interpreted as wishful thinking on the part of her sister, whose need to see the joke in everything had come to the place where the laughter stopped.

VI

'Hallo, Fascist!'

That was the greeting offered to Unity Mitford by Oswald Mosley, when he arrived at Eaton Square for tea on the day before Diana's divorce hearing and offered her a party emblem to wear. She had been accepted as a member of the BUF.

It was June 1933. During the early part of that year Unity had attended art school while living in a house on Grosvenor Crescent, rented by her parents for the season (Rutland Gate had been let, as usual). Forbidden though she was to visit Diana's little house nearby, she nevertheless did so, and inevitably got to know Mosley. She also became closer to Diana, her senior by four years and her physical near-twin. She observed her glorious sister, the strength of her purpose, her devotion to this glamorous man who spoke so brilliantly and had all the Mitford confidence, burnished with bombast. She may, too, have fallen a little for Mosley: that is supposition, but also quite possible (years later her aunt 'Weenie' would say that Mosley had actually tried to seduce her, an improbable story that – according to Diana – came from Unity herself, and as such should have been instantly dismissed). Anyway it was exciting for Unity to be in on the illicit Eatonry set-up, supporting the pioneers against the reactionaries: it would have been surprising, in these circumstances, had Unity *not* become a convert to the Fascist cause. It was not Diana's fault, nor her responsibility. But her influence upon her bold yet uncertain sister was surely powerful, merely by the fact of her highly particular qualities, her very existence. 'Weenie' later accused Diana of unleashing the rebellions of both Unity and Jessica; on that occasion, her sometimes wayward spite found its mark.

Thus art school lost its interest for Unity, as another outlet – a daring alternative to the world of white dresses and callow dance partners – presented itself. It is somehow shocking to see Unity's name appear in the court pages in connection with normal dutiful debutante things: selling programmes at a royal charity screening of *The Good Companions*, attending society weddings, going to Royal Ascot the week before her induction into the BUF. Her friend and fellow deb from the 1932 season, Mary Ormsby-Gore, would later claim to have seen the development of her political obsession. According to Mary, who quickly got engaged, Unity criticized her fiancé by saying that one could see that he had 'Chinese blood'. The Mitfords, said Unity, were 'pure bred Aryans'.[22] By that time she had gone to Germany with Diana, and the die was cast.

During her teenage years at Swinbrook, Unity's close companion had been Jessica, and this too in its way prepared the ground for what was to come. Both were fidgety, intermittently discontented. Jessica was the more politically aware, and later described herself as thinking in the same terms as Diana about the wider, troubling world: 'By the time I was thirteen [1930] major storms were brewing outside the Swinbrook fortress. Whole population centres were designated "distressed areas" by the Government. I read in the papers of the great hunger marches, the great depression of the early 30s hit the country and police and strikers fought in the streets...'[23] One has a sense that the cut-off, law-unto-itself, English fairytale upbringing of the Mitford girls – which in Nancy was turned to imaginative use – bred in Diana and Jessica a kind of hunger for what lay beyond, almost a romantic relish for its brutal hardships, which they were not called upon to share. Of course this instinct took them in absolutely opposite directions; but were they so different, really, when all was said and done?

Unity's politics were not of this kind. There was nothing thought through about them; they filled some strange emotional chasm. It has been suggested[24] that their origins dated back to 1930, when – aged fifteen – she acquired a copy of *Jew Süss*, a novel that portrayed a Jewish financier in such a way that the Nazis made use of the character when promoting anti-Semitism. Certainly the book may have worked upon the underlying Mitford tendency towards the Teuton, the towering Siegfried; but probably this came later. In Jessica's recollection, she herself was fifteen and Unity eighteen by the time they had chosen their opposing political positions. Rather too old, one might think, for what they then did in the room that they shared at Swinbrook: the 'DFD', or Drawing from the Drawing room. According to *Hons and Rebels* this was divided into two, with one side a homage to Fascism, the other side to Communism. Jessica's reading of her childhood is prone to *a posteriori* reasoning, and there is a convenient glibness about this image of the schizophrenic DFD. Nevertheless it is very Mitford, and quite possibly true. When a guest of Pamela's was taken to Swinbrook, he was asked whether he was Fascist or Communist. 'I am a democrat,' he replied. 'How wet,' was the response, followed by peals of loud scornful laughter. The sense of play-acting, of showing off, is powerful. But the times could easily turn display into reality, if one allowed them to.

Naturally Unity attended BUF rallies. So too did Nancy. In 1934 Pam sat in the front row at the Albert Hall, where a spotlit Mosley made a strutting entrance to martial music; the spectacle is unlikely to have impressed her, although two years later she would marry a Fascist sympathizer, the scientist Derek Jackson. He seems a surprising husband for the passive Pam. 'Being married to Derek was never an easy proposition,' wrote Deborah, who as a girl had had a massive crush on him (chiefly because he was an extremely good horseman, who rode thoroughbreds to hounds with a jockey's short leathers). A divorcee when he became engaged to Pam – who married in black, trimmed with astrakhan – he had six wives in all, plus homosexual tendencies. Except for his love of animals he was not particularly nice. Deborah, who did not go in for sensationalism, nevertheless claimed that Derek took Pam on a particularly bumpy car journey through Norway when she fell pregnant; she also speculated as to whether the miscarriage led to her sister's dislike of children.

The mystery of Pam deepens further when one pictures her with this forceful little husband. Derek was a brilliant physicist and a professor at Oxford, a rider in the Grand National, the heir to the *News of the World*, and a man whose eccentricity was expressed through arrogance. On one occasion he tried to board a train with Pam and found the first-class doors locked. He marched furiously through third class then pulled the communication cord; when approached by a guard he forestalled any arguments, holding up a glove to show the mark left by the dirty chain, demanding that the glove be cleaned immediately. This sort of behaviour would be funny only in retrospect. According to Diana, he had been in love with most of the Mitfords, including Tom. This theory, with its *Brideshead* theme, is convincing: 'So true to life being in love with a whole family, it has happened in mine,' Nancy wrote to Evelyn Waugh after reading his novel (she may also have been thinking of

James Lees-Milne). In marrying Pam, therefore, Derek was marrying the Mitfords – with the exception of Nancy, whom he was said not to like.[25] He preferred his women to be adoring rather than amused; as did Mosley. Derek had a twin brother, Vivian, to whom he was intensely close and whose name Nancy filched for Eugenia Malmain's horse in *Wigs on the Green*. The news that Vivian had been killed in an accident greeted the Jacksons when they arrived in Vienna for their honeymoon, and may explain some of Derek's more *outré* behaviour; the kind of man that he was would express extreme grief in that fierce and oblique way.

Pam did not interfere in Derek's Fascist allegiances – which included friendship with Hitler's then closest confidante, Putzi Hanfstaengl – but there is no indication that she shared them. With regard to Deborah, meanwhile, one of her cousins claimed to have taken her (together with Sydney) to one of Mosley's big rallies in London,[26] although there is no corroborative evidence whatever for this. Deborah's attitude to the whole thing was probably best summed up by a letter sent to Diana in 1933. Thanking her sister for an expensive evening bag, she added lightly: 'I even forgive you being a fascist for that.'

So the score among the sisters was: Fascists 2, Communists 1, Neutrals 3. Then there was Tom: definitely present at Earl's Court, where he gave the Fascist salute to Mosley as he passed. The complexity of Tom's attitude is typical of his withdrawn and reticent character. And in the same way that the sisters had argued about their mother, with their conflicting memories becoming less about Sydney than their relationships with each other, so too they would bat back and forth opinions of their brother's politics: each side trying to claim him for their own. What Tom had actually believed became less important than what the sisters *wanted* him to have believed, and what that said about his loyalty to each of them.

In 1980, the five surviving Mitford girls took part in a BBC documentary about Nancy.[27] Jessica, sensing an opportunity for what Diana called 'tiresome political spite', agreed to appear only if she was allowed to read out a letter written by Nancy in 1968. Referring to the publication of *My Life*, a memoir by Mosley, Nancy wrote to Jessica: 'He says he was never anti-Semitic. Good gracious! . . . Also I'm very cross with him for saying Tud [Tom] was a fascist which is untrue though of course Tud was a fearful old twister and probably was a Fascist when with Diana.' In reply Jessica claimed that Tom was a Communist when he visited *her* and that her first husband, the violently left-wing Esmond Romilly, had adored him.

Jessica's insistence upon making this letter public hauled to the surface the giant, coiled, semi-submerged monster of the Mitfordian past. Diana wrote to Deborah that it 'shows the depth of seething hatred Decca feels for us'. Deborah, less personally involved, soothed and cajoled, while remonstrating with Jessica for 'revealing' that Tom had hated Mosley (who was then very old and frail). Diana and Jessica both wrote to Pam, pleading their different cases and seeking her support. Nancy, still agitating from beyond the grave, was mysteriously held to be the guiltiest of them all.

Diana's default position was that Nancy lied about everything. This was not the case, but with regard to Tom she was certainly making assertions unsupported by fact. It was typical Nancy to exonerate or reinvent the people she liked; when she portrayed her father as the fearless, funny, immutable, German-hating force that is Uncle Matthew, it was almost as if she were willing David to be that man again – the best side of himself. Similarly with Eugenia in *Wigs on the Green*: she was the enchanting, harmless Unity who *could* have been. And with Tom, whom Nancy worshipped, and often saw during the war – it was quite natural that she should want him to have been the Tom that he was with *her*, sceptical about Germany, highly critical of Diana's relationship with Mosley. If he had been a member of the BUF – 'which he just *was*', as Diana said[28] – then that was a joke, a meaningless act, like Nancy's own attendance at Olympia; and like his (undoubtedly) pretended belief in Communism in the presence of Jessica.

Tom was wise to bob and weave in this way. But it was simply not true to say that he had hated Mosley (although he had opposed the break-up of Diana's marriage); nor that he was entirely affecting an allegiance to Fascism. According to Diana he had completely agreed with Mosley about politics, which was not quite true either: he categorically rejected anti-Semitism (Mosley did this too, but one begs leave to have one's doubts). Tom did, however, attend several BUF rallies. In 1935 he went to Nuremberg, and in 1937 to a Nazi rally.

Of course he was, by nature, a lover of Germany; and as such had influenced his childhood companion Diana. He had chosen to live in Austria after Eton and his then host, Janos von Almasy, later close to Unity, was a Nazi sympathiser. Back in 1928, when Tom was staying in Berlin, he was visited by Diana and Bryan. He described the high tensions in the city between Communism and Fascism – which Hitler would later use to such advantage – and said that he himself found Communism unacceptable. Therefore, he admitted, if he were a German he would probably be a Nazi.

As an endorsement this was hardly unequivocal, not least because in 1928 a Nazi was not necessarily a crazed Jew-hater. Nevertheless the testimony of his friend James Lees-Milne takes Tom a little further down the road. In 1944 they dined in London, and Lees-Milne asked whether Tom still had sympathy with Nazism: 'He emphatically said "Yes".'[29] The best Germans, he said, were Nazis; this is near impossible to understand from somebody who shunned race politics, yet such was Tom's belief in the ideal of Germany. He was, indeed, a mystery. But also, as Diana put it, 'very deliberate in his actions always'. Having joined the Territorial Army in 1932 – while pursuing his career at the Bar – Tom became a second lieutenant in 1938, and was quick to react to the unsatisfactory truce at Munich. 'He was,' Lees-Milne later wrote, 'overwhelmed with misery and misgiving in fear that England was throwing away its traditional title in the European hegemony. And so ... with his usual thoroughness [he] threw himself heart and soul into what to him was a new-found romance – the science and art of warfare.' His family affections 'trumped his principles, even if they affronted him'.[30] Which meant what, exactly? Perhaps that none of his sisters, so confident in their beliefs – even when these were a belief in nothing that was on offer – quite understood the ambivalence of his own.

VII

Unity, for instance, had been wary of introducing Tom to Adolf Hitler. She had thought her brother insufficiently pro-Nazi, and in the sense that she meant this was true. But all was well: 'He *adored* the Fuhrer.' They lunched with Hitler twice. 'So really I think no harm is done...'

This was from a letter to Diana, written in June 1935. By then Unity had known Hitler for four months. By the time that war broke out, just over four years later, every member of the Mitford family – except Nancy and Jessica – would have met him.

Back in September 1933, the decision to go to Germany with Diana came about almost accidentally. Unity had wanted to visit France. Diana wanted to go somewhere – anywhere – while Mosley was on his motoring tour with his sister-in-law Baba Metcalfe. Earlier that year she had met Putzi Hanfstaengl, a long-standing friend of Hitler's who dealt with the British press on his behalf (and who claimed to have invented the chant 'Sieg Heil'). Now Hanfstaengl – smooth, supremely connected – suggested that Diana attend the forthcoming Parteitag at Nuremberg: the first major rally of Hitler's chancellorship. There she and her sister, those fabulous specimens of Aryan womanhood, could meet the new German leader himself. Presumably Hanfstaengl thought they might be of some use, somewhere down the line.

Even at this early stage, Unity was extremely excited; nevertheless she did not manage to meet Hitler in 1933, and her obsession with Fascism might therefore still have been a teenage phase, like her love of cinema, with the Führer in the guise of Errol Flynn. Jessica, of all people, wrote to Diana after the visit to Nuremberg, in a manner that makes a fond joke of the whole thing, and refers jauntily to Unity's 'semi romance' with Hanfstaengl. It was the Redesdales who saw danger. David, who was anyway in a prolonged rage with Diana, wrote to her: 'I suppose you know without being told how absolutely horrified Muv and I were to think of you and Bobo accepting any form of hospitality from people we regard as a murderous gang of pests... What we can do, and intend to do, is to try to keep Bobo out of it all.' Thus David revealed an awareness of the susceptibility in his daughter – and of his own essential powerlessness.

In 1937, Unity would be a part-agent in Putzi Hanfstaengl's fall from grace, when she informed Hitler, in her apparently inconsequential way, that Hanfstaengl had criticized him. Four years earlier, when he first met her in London, the power was his. He recalled that she was 'very much second string to her sister, tagging along'.[31] He was also frustrated by the attitude of the British press towards the Nazi regime. 'Hitler will build a great and prosperous Germany for the Germans,' explained the urbane and exasperated Hanfstaengl. 'If the Jews don't like it they can get out.' The first camp was established that year at Dachau, holding Socialists and writers as well as Jews, but not yet a death camp. As Clive James later wrote, in reference to Mosley's claim that the Jews were not under dire threat at this time: 'Before the war, apparently, Dachau had been like Butlin's.'[32] The great question of how much was known, or feared, about the regime is answered to an extent by *The Brown Book of the Hitler Terror*, a prophetic piece of writing, listing 250 murders committed by the Nazis after the burning of the Reichstag (which led to the declaration of a state of emergency, then to dictatorship). This was published in Britain by John Lane around the time of the Mitford girls' visit to Nuremberg, and in 1935 seized upon by Jessica. Later Diana would say that she 'did not pay much attention to it'. The book was quite easily dismissed as a Communist production. With politics, after all, people generally hear only what they want to hear; Jessica was equally willing not to know about Stalin's murderous propensities.

The Nuremberg rally was not exactly an epiphany for Diana. She had already had hers in the ballroom at Cheyne Walk. But to see a crowd of some 400,000 *sieg heiling* and marching was to see the Fascist dream realized: 'a demonstration of hope in a nation that had known collective despair'. Which it had, after the First World War. The exigent demands of the Treaty of Versailles were still gaping wounds; unemployment was at 7 million; civil war raged on the streets: it is not hard to see why a figure like Hitler could unite and dominate as he did. Nor, given the Communist threat, is it impossible to grasp why he was welcomed by some members of the British Establishment; or why, given the prolonged depression, 'what we need is an 'Itler'[33] became a refrain within certain parts of British society. What is almost incomprehensible – even without hindsight – is that a non-German could be a witness to that quasi-religious spectacle of mass hypnosis, could listen to Hitler's screaming voice with its razor rasp, its death rattle, and find it something magnificent: even beautiful. Diana claimed to Unity that this was her own experience, although her interest in Hitler actually developed when they talked privately and he behaved very differently. But Unity really did respond like a disciple. Although she too was at conversational ease with Hitler, Deborah wrote that in his presence 'she was shaking all over'. The image of her at the Parteitag, removing her lipstick – as Hanfstaengl instructed – then putting it stealthily back on again, has something of a schoolgirl's juddering excitement as she waits at the stage door. At the same time it was as if the semi-dormant madness in Hitler had found the same thing in her, and let it loose.

Back home, Unity became ever more possessed with her cause. Her social behaviour grew more extreme. There was a fashion at the time for recording one's voice on to a disc, and Unity's friend Mary Ormsby-Gore recalled them doing this together at Selfridges: Unity's recording allegedly consisted of a Blackshirt chant, 'The Yids, The Yids, We've got to get rid of the Yids.' This from a girl who in her first debutante season had attended a ball for her friend Nica Rothschild, and who had happily accompanied the producer John Sutro to watch a day's filming at Elstree (Sutro seems to have fallen into the category of 'I don't like Jews, but you're different'). Unity continued to appear at the aristocratic houses of London, for instance a ball at the Howard de Waldens on Belgrave Square, which ended in a dawn walk through Covent Garden with none other than Hamish St Clair-Erskine. But a fellow deb recalled – presumably accurately – that Unity would also spend her days in the East End (where the Blackshirts marched through Jewish areas) to play ping-pong with 'the boys', meaning Mosley's muscly young followers. One can imagine it, the comfortable sense of *de haut en bas* shot through with dark intimations of lust. Just as Diana had responded to Oswald Mosley's rather more manicured seduction techniques, so Unity was getting a serious kick from the straightforward hard-edged maleness of the Fascist movement. 'All those men,' as Nanny Blor had said; how right she had been! The nature of Unity's sexual curiosity was hinted at when she planned what she called 'an orgy' at Diana's Eaton Square house. Of course it was nothing of the kind. 'Everybody had been sick, and there had been a lot of necking,' recalled an art-school friend, who was told about it after the event. That too was probably an exaggeration. But the mere fact that Unity talked in this way – half sincere, half seeking to shock – hints at how fascinated she would have been by her sister's affair with Mosley, and what pleasure she might have got from being the centre of attention among all those uniformed young men.

Blackshirts, for the time being; not yet Stormtroopers. Later there would be lurid tales of her ritualized sexual antics with 'the darling storms', but this is just the kind of thing that *would* be said, as it were translating Unity's mysterious passions into the recognizable. Even the alleged affair with Tom's friend Janos von Almasy is unproven, as is the rumoured liaison with the SS officer Erich Widemann. In 1970 Nancy spoke to Unity's future biographer, David Pryce-Jones, and was rumoured to have told him that Hitler had wanted to marry Unity but was put off by her promiscuity with SS men. This 'information' was never printed. If Nancy said such things, she did so at a time when she was ill and made excessively spiteful by pain. In fact the only evidence of Unity's sexual activity, such as it is, is that she saw a gynaecologist for contraception advice.[34] She expressed a passionate desire for children – the life that she might have had – yet there was always something of the Joan of Arc about her, something virginal and untried, as perceived by her childhood governess.

In early 1934 Unity achieved her desire of living in Munich when she arrived at the home of the Baroness Laroche, who took girls *en pension*. It is unbelievable, really, that the Redesdales let her go. She was already a debutante; she did not need to be 'finished', as her older sisters had been, and Jessica would be, in Paris. Her parents had expressed horror at the recent visit to the Parteitag. So who knows what their idea was; other than that the baroness was a woman of the utmost respectability, and that Unity's nagging may have been such that it was simply easier to let her get this energetic obsession out of her system. Unity was on a girlish high. Might she still have come down from it, had the Redesdales refused to let her return to Germany? Diana thought not – 'Unity was a revolutionary' – and she knew her sister very well. Nevertheless Unity's cousin Clementine, who stayed with her in 1937 and who, to a lesser degree, succumbed to the Nazi spell, later said: 'In no way was she a person who wished to escape her background. I think she would always have come home.'[35]

Unity's intention in 1934 was to meet Hitler. And again, there was something in this of the schoolgirl, dreaming that she will catch the eye of the man on her bedroom wall. However hard it is to see Hitler in that light, there is no doubt that *Unity* did: up to a point. Then there was another factor, the desire to compete with the sublime Diana. All right, so Diana had Britain's Fascist-in-Chief in tow, smouldering at her across the dinner table and chatting in baby talk down the telephone. But Hitler: do admit. That was something more. The man with the real power, the one who had *putsched* his way to the top and had the whole of Germany swaying to his oratory, whom even hard-headed British people sought to encounter on their visits to Munich. If Unity were able to write to her sister and say oh, by the way Nard, you'll never guess who I've met... Well. In that sense, therefore, Hitler represented something comprehensible in the context of a young girl's imagination, a bizarre crush plus an ace of trumps in the lifelong Mitford game of sister whist. Yet there was also the unknown factor, the dark and terrible tide in whose shallows Hitler already swam, to which Unity responded in the same way as Diana did to the Mosley rallies. The times in which this pair lived were terrifying: most people crossed their fingers, shut their eyes and prayed for it all to be over. For reasons that can never quite be explained, these aristocratic young women embraced it instead.

So Unity, frantically learning German, began visiting the same restaurants as Hitler (as Deborah later put it, today she would have been arrested as a stalker). This is where that extraordinary blithe Mitford confidence played its part. She seems to have had no doubt that she could command the attention of this player on the world's political stage: if she sat there, in all her Anglo-Aryan splendour, the Führer would recognize her for what she was. Most people (assuming that they actually wanted to meet Hitler) would have worried about what to say, how to hold his interest and seem like something more than just a power groupie. Unity had no such fears. She would chat away, as Mitfords did, and she would amuse him. As indeed she did. In June 1934 a friend summoned her to the Carlton tearooms where the small Hitler party had just arrived. She wrote to inform Diana of the sighting. The following month she wrote to Nancy, warning her that she could not possibly publish *Wigs on the Green*. By this time her tone, although buoyant and brisk, held a faintly manic quality;

'No I didn't fumble with Röhm at the Brown House' was her PS to Nancy. The reference was to Ernst Röhm, who a couple of weeks previously had been dragged from his bed and shot on Hitler's orders (the Brown House was the Nazi HQ in Munich). Around a hundred brown-shirted officers were executed in what became known as the Night of the Long Knives, an efficient purge leaving the way clear for the ultra-loyal black-shirted SS led by Himmler. To read of this in the Mitford idiom is to come up, about as hard as is possible, against the sisters' adamantine mystery. 'I am so *terribly* sorry for the Fuhrer – you know Röhm was his oldest comrade & friend,' wrote Unity to Diana.

Around this time Sydney and, surprisingly, Jessica visited Munich. So again Unity was receiving encouragement, rather than disapprobation; it was beginning to seem that the 'murderous gang of pests' had been forgiven. Either that, or the Redesdales wanted to keep an eye on their daughter (David would go to see Unity in early 1935). Sydney, who had visited Tom in Austria back in 1927, now discovered that she rather liked Germany. Nevertheless her attitude to her daughter's hysterical saluting and so on is ambivalent; in her letter to Nancy, Unity wrote that Sydney 'isn't in a *very* good temper. I am though.'

The two Fascist girls again attended the Parteitag in 1934, after which Diana took a flat for them both in Munich. Possibly Diana was staying away from home deliberately, with the aim of bringing Mosley to heel; he was still pursuing his affair with Baba Metcalfe, cheered on from the sidelines by Irene Ravensdale. He was also charged with an allegation of 'riotous assembly' – in Worthing, of all places – along with the BUF member William Joyce, later known as 'Lord Haw-Haw'.[36] They were acquitted in December. That same month a dance was held for Jessica, then seventeen, at Rutland Gate. The court pages calmly reported that dinner parties were hosted before the ball by Mrs Winston Churchill and Mrs Somerset Maugham, Lady Cunard and Lady Rennell; the known world still spun on its axis. In March 1935, Jessica was presented at Buckingham

Palace wearing a white satin dress by Worth of Paris, which was later dyed purple and sold to help fund her life as a Communist fugitive. In tribute to her beloved Boud, who had stolen writing paper from the palace, Jessica snaffled some chocolates and hid them in her bouquet. Hons and rebels, eh. By that time beloved Boud had met her Führer: they spoke for the first time at the Osteria Bavaria restaurant in Munich on 9 February.

VIII

Hitler's sexuality has been much speculated over, but there is no doubt that he responded favourably to women of Unity's type. Although she still wore the red lipstick that had so distressed Putzi Hanfstaengl, in every other way her strong, fair, healthy youth was perfectly designed to please. He said, she later recalled, that she had beautiful legs. Diana almost certainly attracted Hitler in the conventional way; like most men whom she met, he found her beautiful and desirable. She in turn found him immensely good company. It should be emphasized that she was not alone in this. Hitler was courteous to women, he had old-fashioned manners of the kind to which the Mitfords were accustomed, albeit with Teutonic embellishments; and he was capable of commanding love, particularly that of unstable girls. Eva Braun, his mistress since 1932, attempted suicide twice; Hitler's adored half-niece Geli Raubal killed herself. Years later, in a television documentary, Winifred Wagner – daughter-in-law of the composer, and the director of the Bayreuth Festival during the war – would attempt to explain the nature of her friendship with Hitler ('Wolf'), his kindness to her children, his 'Austrian tact and warmth'. It was quite clear that, to those inclined to see him in that way, he had the ability to step away from the Nazi backdrop – 'I except Hitler quite generally from that whole crowd,' said Winifred Wagner, meaning creatures like Himmler – and produce a direct stream of high-octane charm. The truth, of course, was that the Nazi backdrop was always there, a dark shimmer behind the eyes, and this was the root of the attraction. The idea of talking to the Führer as a *man* was thrilling because he was the Führer; he had a dual identity that could never be divided: there is nothing more exciting, to the susceptible, than a man who is more than a man. The whole time that he and Unity were sharing jokes, they remained the devil and his disciple.

Why he wanted to share jokes with her is another story. 'Bobo said whatever came into her head, and spoke to him as she might have done to anyone, and he loved it,' was the recollection of Clementine Mitford, and this seems to have been at least part of the truth. If Hitler could turn on charm, the Mitfords embodied it. And Hitler, it would seem, fell for Unity's particular version. At their first meeting in February, he sent the restaurant owner to invite her to his table. Then they talked for half an hour – about Wagner, London, films (his favourite being *Cavalcade*)[37] and so on. And one can imagine the appeal of such a girl, talking in what Nancy called the family's 'loud sing-song voice', fearless in the face of somebody who operated on terror. She was like a great blonde lion cub in a pit full of black mambas: not incapable of violence herself, but without the smiling glint of malice aforethought. In the next four and a half years she and Hitler would meet some 140 times. She was treated like an honoured guest at rallies, at events such as the Berlin Olympics of 1936 and the Bayreuth Festival; she was twice invited to his retreat at Berchtesgaden. (Eva Braun was not happy about this. 'She is known as the Walküre and looks the part,' wrote Braun, 'especially her legs.') Effectively Unity was admitted to Hitler's inner circle. They were almost certainly not lovers, although naturally this has been claimed. Diana thought that Unity would have slept with Hitler had he asked, but he never did. She later dismissed a book claiming that the pair were seen, by a maid, on a sofa at the Wagner house in Bayreuth, 'in a compromising position' (as Winifred Wagner made clear, Unity never actually stayed at the house[38]).

Recently a story emerged that Unity had given birth to Hitler's child:[39] a fascinating notion, but there was no real evidence. Anyway one has the sense that Unity was in a preferable position to a mistress, more protected because not dependent upon that mutable physical tie. She could sit and babble away as a mistress would never have dared. Her intimacy with Hitler was odder than that. She was light relief, a combination of younger sister, court jester and talisman; he may also have enjoyed the fact that his henchmen did not really want her there, but could not say so. He was impressed by Britain, fascinated by its ability to command an empire, and like so many people he was compelled by the British aristocracy. In his way he was probably impressed by Unity herself. Quite simply he felt happier with her around, calling him blissful Führer and laughing at his impersonations of Mussolini. Whereas with Diana he engaged in the cautious dance of semi-courtship, and she herself was always careful to display decorous respect, the relationship with Unity was more relaxed. In photographs she has an air of compliance, but she also looks as though she belongs next to Hitler. On one occasion he showed his temper, in what must have been a terrifying scene, and 'thundered – you know how he can – like a machine gun', wrote Unity to Diana. 'It was wonderful.'

So Unity was obsessed with Hitler, and by what she saw as a miracle he took pleasure in her company. But this was the world of the Nazis, and blissful Führers looking to conquer great chunks of Eastern Europe are not content merely to chat with a fresh-faced young girl. It is impossible not to think that Unity was by Hitler's side because of *who* she was, as well as what she was. She was a hotline to England with her connections (not just Mosley and the Churchill family; early on, for instance, Hitler mentioned the pro-German Rennells of Rodd, only to find out that Unity's sister Nancy was married to their son). Unity gabbled out opinions – von

Ribbentrop was the wrong man to be German ambassador in London; Hitler should not have received the Londonderrys, as the political hostess Lady Londonderry was not a *true* admirer – and within the nonsense there would have been something to learn. Of course he had official channels, but her very indiscretion was a gift of sorts. He admitted as much in a recorded conversation: 'She and her sisters are very much in the know, thanks to their relationship with influential people.'[40]

Conversely she was also a potential liability, to either side. Although Hitler was not at this point Britain's enemy, the then ambassador in Berlin Sir Nevile Henderson – who met Unity at a party held by Himmler, where 'she squeaked "*Heil* Hitler!"' as she and Henderson were introduced – was very aware of her loose tongue. He reported her conversations back to London: 'Subject to certain reservations I have little reason to doubt the accuracy of what she occasionally tells me.' It is rather amazing that London did not worry more about this. On the Munich side, Hitler's inner circle were wary of both Mitford sisters, but the Führer himself seems never to have been suspicious of Unity, at least. His instincts must have been pin-sharp, and as it happened he was right to be sure of her loyalty, both to Germany and to her own country. In 1935 he reached a naval agreement with Britain, and noted that an 'Anglo-German combination would be stronger than all the other powers.' The following year he discussed the idea with Unity. As she reported to Diana, 'he said that with the German army & the English navy we could rule the world. Oh if we could have that…' It is perhaps unsurprising that Unity began to see herself as a figure of some importance within the regime, the one who could bring about the Grand Alliance between the two nations that she loved.

That same year, Hitler saw Unity's influence in action. In 1935 David Redesdale had stayed with his daughter in Munich; although he did not meet Hitler, one has the sense of a clever puppet-master pulling his strings when he wrote a fiercely pro-German letter to *The Times* in March 1936 – 'If our persistently un-English treatment of Germany is the result of treaties and pacts, would it not be wiser to disentangle ourselves' – and made a speech to the House of Lords that could have been written by Dr Goebbels himself. The anti-Nazi propaganda in Britain was absurd, he said, with 'the greatest exaggeration in such matters as the Nazi treatment of the Jews'. After reading British newspapers, 'the last thing one would expect to see was a Jew, but the place was full of Jews.' They were everywhere, said David, and nobody interfered with them, 'so long as they behaved themselves and adhered to the regulations laid down for Jews'. If the Germans thought that they were a danger, the Germans should be allowed to deal with that danger. Hitler had countered Communism, restored German self-respect, and now longed to live in peace with his neighbours. After such a speech, which represented a volte-face of staggering dimensions, it is hardly surprising that David (and Sydney) attended a dinner of the Anglo-German Fellowship at the Dorchester Hotel, along with the Londonderrys, and a reception for the von Ribbentrops at which Lord Londonderry proclaimed the Fellowship 'a great factor for good'.

Meanwhile Diana took Mosley to Munich in April 1935, and Hitler gave a rather dull lunch for him. The following year she suggested to Winston Churchill that he should meet Hitler – she was the only person in the world who could have introduced them socially – and although Churchill refused it was, in some way, an opportunity missed. (Churchill did quiz Diana about the German leader. She told him that Hitler found democracies problematical: 'One day you are speaking to one man, the next day to his successor.') Some thirty years later the memoirs were published of Baldur von Schirach, leader of the Hitler Youth and later a prisoner at Spandau. He wrote that Diana and Unity 'strengthened Hitler's belief that there were two elements in Britain': one dominated by Jews and Parliamentarians, the other recognizing the blood relationship with Germany. Idiotic though this sounds, it is not so far from the philosophy of Houston Stewart Chamberlain, as admired by both Hitler and the sisters' paternal grandfather.

The Minister for Propaganda, Josef Goebbels, who by rights should have been delighted by the prize of the two Mitford girls, was in fact extremely suspicious. His diary references to them – stark, charmless, narrow-eyed – give a glancing but vivid sense of what was going on, the sheer grim oddity of the whole thing, and how those on the outside (including MI5) must have wondered and gossiped about it. 'Again to the Führer,' wrote Goebbels in 1936. 'Mrs Genest [Guinness] there. Three short films of the Mosley party. Everything is still very much at the beginning but it will probably work out. We, also, began that way.' (If he thought that then Goebbels was less clever than his reputation.) Diana's motive in showing these films was to ask for money; the subs from Mussolini had come to an end. Even when the BUF was at its height in the mid-1930s, it was haemorrhaging cash, and by 1936 the organization was nearly bankrupt. Mosley himself had put in £100,000. Hitler must have authorized something because Goebbels wrote of funds being released by the Führer in December. But in February 1937 he said: 'Mrs Ginnest wants more money. They use up a fortune and accomplish nothing. I am having nothing more to do with this thing.'

The daring of Diana is breathtaking. Or perhaps not, to her; she was used to asking for, and getting, what she wanted. She must have known that Goebbels was resistant to her charm, as a small number of people were, but it seems not to have bothered her. The thought of being in a room with such a man, with his ventriloquist dummy eyes watching one's every move and calculating its motive, is somehow very frightening – more so than the thought of sitting together with an attentive, mannerly Hitler, although that does not conjure an image of ease either. Of course there is hindsight at work here, but by 1936 the Nazi regime had revealed plenty about itself: the occupation of the Saar, the Nuremberg Laws that enshrined Jewish repression in the constitution; although Diana agreed with the first, she would not have denied the dire implications of the second. Perhaps she simply did not find these men sinister. Goebbels, she later wrote, 'was clever, good company, always ready with a sarcastic witticism'. Hitler 'was exceptionally charming, clever and original'. At the same time there is this vague, powerful impression that she liked sailing close to the darkness. Some women do, and sometimes these are privileged women: posh girls who go out with gangsters, idealistic girls who form relationships with lifers in jail, and the like. Diana was bored by too much comfort, not bodily but spiritually, intellectually. Although supremely female, she required more than a straightforward female life. Mosley had opened this up to her. Now the proximity of the Nazi high command – whose cruelty she later condemned unequivocally – fulfilled something similar but in one sense greater; because they had power.

She was also using these men for Mosley, perhaps demonstrating to him the strength that she herself possessed, that remarkable persuasive allure. She asked Goering about the possibility of setting up a commercial wireless station on German wavelengths, broadcasting light entertainment programmes and generating funds for Mosley's political career. The BBC had a monopoly of the wavelengths in Britain. It therefore made sense to ask Germany. Advertising revenue was extremely healthy for commercial radio (some £1,700,000 in 1938) and could, in theory, have bankrolled the BUF movement. A company was set up, from which Mosley's name was carefully omitted; those involved in negotiations included the brother of the then Home Secretary (Deborah's old skating partner Sir Samuel Hoare, later a leading appeaser). MI5 would subsequently find it hard to believe that there had been no propaganda intention in this, and one sees their point. What the Germans thought, it is hard to say. Diana was turned down flatly by Goering in October 1937, but her persistence was formidable. She went with the proposal to the top man, who expressed himself willing to discuss it. The agreement for the station was finally granted in 1938. She had sat long into the night with Hitler, pleading Mosley's cause, talking, enjoying herself.

'Nothing', she wrote to Deborah at the end of her life, 'would ever make me pretend I was sorry to have had this unique experience.'

IX

For Unity, who had all her sister's bravura but none of her sophistication, the friendship with Hitler was without this kind of ulterior motive; it simply delivered complete happiness. When Mosley, some forty years later, said that Unity's was the 'simple, tragic story of a gel who was what we called stage struck in those days',[41] he was not entirely wrong. But there was a madness in Unity, an instability that had been hinted at when she left the security of home for boarding school, and which now found its fatal response in the shiny black world of Nazi Germany.

In June 1935, she wrote a letter in German to *Der Stürmer*, a publication edited by the raving anti-Semite Julius Streicher. 'If only we had such a newspaper in England! The English have no notion of the Jewish danger. English Jews are always described as "decent". Perhaps the Jews in England are more clever with their propaganda than in other countries. I cannot tell, but it is a certain fact that our struggle is very hard...' The letter ended with a PS: 'If you find room in your newspaper for this letter, please publish my name in full... I want everyone to know I am a Jew hater.' The question of how truly Unity believed what she wrote is impossible to answer. She was in the grip of hysteria by this time, and more than anything she sought to impress Hitler. But perhaps she herself would not have wanted this defence, such as it is; perhaps she meant every word.

The fact that Streicher not only printed Unity's letter, but headed it with the information that she was related to Winston Churchill, suggests in turn that he, at least, saw value in this girl. She was invited to make a speech at the midsummer festival at Hesselberg. 'Call me early Goering dear/ For I'm to be the Queen of the May,' Nancy wrote to Unity, as if the Mitford mockery might yet work its magic: not a chance. A photograph from the festival shows Unity to have the eyes of a fanatic, fixed yet vacant. The news of the Hesselberg speech made it into the British press, and the Redesdales summoned Unity home. Then they let her go back again. It was almost as if they were faintly in fear of their daughter, or at a loss as to what to do with her if she did *not* return to Munich. According to Jessica in *Hons and Rebels*, that summer Unity tried to pin up an autographed photograph of Julius Streicher in the Swinbrook DFD. It was also said that she visited some friends and was found shooting with a pistol in their garden. Practising to kill Jews, she explained. The gun was a relatively new acquisition, of uncertain provenance.

On her return to Germany, Unity attended the 1935 Parteitag at Nuremberg with Diana and Tom. By this time Sydney had also met Hitler ('He said he would like to see Muv'), at the Osteria Bavaria in April. Unity effected the introduction with the jittery excitement of a child introducing her playground boyfriend, but was disappointed in her mother's non-conversion: 'The most she will admit is that he has a very nice face' [sic], she wrote to Diana. Nevertheless the Redesdales were edging closer to the pro-Nazi position that David would publicly express the following year. It was as if they, too, had been hypnotized by the Hitler of Unity's imagination.

In 1936, however, when Sydney took Unity, Jessica and Deborah on a cruise, she was probably hoping that it would restore some kind of normality to Unity's behaviour. In fact it simply gave her a new stage on which to show off. She continued her political arguments on board ship, and was set upon in Spain for wearing a swastika badge. More realistically, Sydney may have been trying to amuse Jessica, whose discontentment was becoming transparent. Deborah rather poignantly remembered the holiday as a succession of jokes shared with her sister, although Jessica would later write, coolly: 'as I remember us in those days, we weren't all that adoring.'[42] There is little doubt that her first debutante season had done nothing for her, and that she longed for something different; as in her way Unity had found.

The cruise was also an escape from England at a time when David – whose relentless financial incompetence had reached crisis point – was disposing of Swinbrook House and 1,500 acres of precious Oxfordshire land. At first the estate was let, then finally sold in 1938, as was customary with David at the bottom of the market. He sold the Swan pub, the adjacent cottage beside the mill, the trout fishing, the coverts. He got rid of furniture. Diana, in the process of moving with Mosley to a beautiful house in Staffordshire – Wootton Lodge – rescued the better stuff: a Heppelwhite bedstead, a Sheraton sideboard, all bought with just a few pounds of Bryan Guinness's money. Nobody except David and Deborah had liked Swinbrook, but its loss was powerfully symbolic. Although the Mitfords still owned the cottage at High Wycombe, from now on the collective memories of chubb-fuddling, hunting, the Hons' Cupboard, would live only in the world of Nancy's novels. Many years later Deborah wrote to Nancy that leaving the house, riding for the last time through the woods, 'broke my heart.' Back in 1935 David received a letter from Unity. 'Poor old Forge, I AM sorry you have had to leave Swinbrook... I do think it's dreadful for you.' This was a glimmer of the real girl, now lost as surely as her home.

After the cruise Unity went back to Germany. She and Diana attended the infamous Olympic Games in Berlin – as did Nancy's in-laws the Rennells – then stayed at the lakeside villa belonging to the Goebbelses. Magda Goebbels had become very friendly with the sisters, although her husband remained wary: 'I had a row with Magda about the visit.' Nevertheless it was at Dr Goebbels' ministerial house in Berlin that Diana married Oswald Mosley in a ceremony on 6 October 1936, attended by Hitler. 'That's not all right with me,' Goebbels spat into his diary. 'But the Führer wants it to be so.' Diana told her parents, who were glad to have her union with Mosley regularized, and also told Tom. Unity, renowned for indiscretion, was not informed. The marriage remained a secret until the birth of the Mosleys' son, Alexander, in November 1938. As Mosley revealed all, the newspapers blared that Hitler had been his best man (untrue), and the two Curzon sisters – that mini Greek chorus who had stood on the sidelines of Diana's life chanting imprecations of doom, and now raged with a sense of betrayal – declared war on Mosley also.

Two days before the wedding, the violence generated by his movement – now called the British Union – had reached an apotheosis with the Battle of Cable Street. A giant march had taken place through the East End of London, with Mosley strolling along at the head looking like Errol Flynn in his suave double-breasted jacket. It was met by predictable resistance, and finally brought to a halt in a barricaded Cable Street. Two thousand police had been called in, almost one for every Blackshirt. The police were attacked with bricks, chair legs and milk bottles; their horses slid on the marbles thrown into the street. The vast majority of the eighty-five arrested were anti-Fascists, and Mosley's men were, in a sense, the innocent party, unless one believes that an act of such deliberate provocativeness rendered them guilty. Having brought the march to an abortive end, as the police now asked him to do, Mosley addressed his neatly assembled Blackshirts: 'The Government surrenders to Red violence and Jewish corruption. We never surrender... within us is the flame that shall light this country and shall later light this world.' The response from the London District Committee of the Communist Party was: 'This is the most humiliating defeat ever suffered by any figure in British politics.'

To those inclined to see Communism as the most fearsome force of the time, the relative impassivity of the Blackshirts in the face of such extreme aggression (they did not retaliate as they had at Olympia) would have seemed like proof of 'Red violence'. At the same time Mosley – described in Parliament as being 'surrounded by his bodyguard like a dictator or a gangster' – was recognized as a hugely incendiary figure, and even he later admitted that he had been wrong to dress his Blackshirts in military-type clothes (these uniforms were now banned under the new Public Order Act). A week after Cable Street a gang of Fascists ran through the East End attacking Jews. This behaviour was dismissed by the BU as contrary to orders. To the sane people of Britain it must all, every bit of it, have read like a horror show.

To Jessica Mitford, meanwhile, the Fascist and Nazi sympathies of her sisters were the springboard from which she could jump into the arms of the other side. It has been said[43] that much of Jessica's dissatisfaction with her privileged upbringing came after the moment of her leaving it: that she was on the whole a joyful girl, until she decided upon a cause that required her to have been unhappy. And there is surely truth in this. However aware she was of the scarred landscape beyond Swinbrook, however much she dreamed of some idealized school where she would exchange unknown thoughts with enlightened people, the image of herself – as portrayed in *Hons and Rebels* – as a frustrated activist among smug socialites is a literary construct, rather than the more ambivalent reality.

That said, there is no question that Jessica's left-wing politics were genuine. As a writer, she became a fighter for noble causes such the civil rights movement in the US; in 1961 her car was torched by white supremacists in Alabama, which may have made her proud. Anyway it was not something likely to happen to certain other Mitford sisters. In middle age Jessica's stance was, in fact, pretty much that of the straightforward liberal left, and in some respects shared by Nancy (for instance in 1967 they both signed petitions in *The Times* criticizing the Vietnam War). Not that Jessica herself necessarily saw it that way. She robustly dismissed Nancy as a 'Gaullist' (as if this were akin to 'Mosleyite') and Deborah as a 'Conservative policeman'. Both were simply anti-extreme – one more to the left, the other to the right – but this was the thing that Jessica could never bear to be. She sought to be a radical, like Diana and Unity, and in a way that would purge their allegiances. Whether this was *really* her nature is an imponderable. It must have been, in the sense that she embraced radicalism so fully; it is hard to believe that she would have done this, had the others not gone before her. Like Unity, she was intensely susceptible to influence.

Jessica's extremism is more acceptable to history than that of her sisters. Such is the luck of the left. Nevertheless she remained a Communist until 1958, by which time there was no excuse for being unaware that the Soviet regime under Stalin had not been not much different to the Nazi one. Two years earlier a speech by Khrushchev had been published, a sort of Communist confession to the mass murder committed by his predecessor, but still Jessica hung on: 'I had never been as thoroughly convinced as most comrades were of Soviet infallibility,' she wrote. 'Terrible as the revelations were it seemed to me that the very fact that Khrushchev had seen fit to lay them out before the world signified that the Soviet leadership was set on a course of fundamental change.'[44] This was reasonable, in the sense that Khrushchev sought 'de-Stalinization'. But Jessica admitted that she had been wrong to believe him so wholeheartedly. As for Stalin: it is often said that he killed more people than Hitler, although very recent research suggests otherwise, that Hitler killed some 11 million non-combatants to Stalin's 6 million.[45] These figures, so grotesquely casual on the page, are not merely disputed but in a sense an irrelevance. The two men were both liquidators of life. Stalin's Great Terror, in which the Soviet version of ethnic cleansing obliterated an approximate 700,000 people, took place in 1937: the year that Jessica became a full convert to the cause. To be fair, she was hardly alone in this. Communism was the intellectual creed of the time, although many on the left felt betrayed by the Nazi–Soviet pact of August 1939 ('*Susan* Stalin how could you let him' was Nancy's reaction: for reasons unknown, she and Jessica called each other 'Susan'). When the pact disintegrated and the Russians entered the war against Hitler, George Orwell – who fought on the Republican side in the Spanish Civil War – wrote in his wartime diary: 'One could not have a better example of the moral and emotional shallowness of our time, than the fact that we are now all more or less pro Stalin. This disgusting murderer is temporarily on our side, and so the purges, etc., are suddenly forgotten.'

Communism and Stalinism were not the same thing, of course. As Jessica said, she was not a Soviet apostle. Her own Communism was in one sense an expression of natural left-wing instincts, therefore perfectly honourable. But she was directed towards extremism by circumstances: of the times, and of the family.

Nancy – whose iconoclasm derived from a kind of extreme common sense – believed what she wrote in *Wigs on the Green*, that with women the personal counted above the political. The mere fact of saying this was probably designed to annoy. As usual, she was making light of the dark passions aroused by the 1930s, hoping thus to dispel their clouds. At the same time, she had a point. Jessica's act of rebellion – throwing in her lot with her Communist cousin Esmond Romilly – was ideologically motivated and also a consequence of being a Mitford girl, both at the same time. The simple catalyst for her particular act of rebellion was Unity's move to Munich. Political, therefore, but also deeply personal. How could her Boud jump ship so boldly, and leave her Boud on the deck in her white satin from Worth? Deborah later speculated that Jessica had been jealous of Unity, all the attention and excitement she was getting. Peter Rodd, who was no fool despite behaving like one, thought the same thing (he told the *Daily Mail* that Jessica had become a Communist to 'get even' with her Fascist sister). Yet Jessica also admitted to jealousy of Deborah, and this had nothing to do with politics: it was personal envy of her sister's looks – Jessica was remarkably attractive, but believed Deborah to be 'much prettier' – and her well-adjusted character. (Deborah had privileged status as the adorable youngest, although she herself thought that Jessica was Nanny Blor's favourite.) Jessica had a tricky position within the sororial hierarchy, squashed down the bottom, but even there hemmed in by Deborah. She was fascinated by Nancy, with her casual, gallant demeanour and her crisp satirical talent. She hero-worshipped Diana, so much so that her perfect older sister later became the focus of her anti-family rage (nobody ever had weak feelings about Diana). She was bracketed with Deborah as the two 'little ones', but their 'Honnish' closeness seems to have generated odd frustrations. With Unity, companion in 'Boudledidge', the relationship was intense and fond; she never found Unity unforgivable as she did Diana. Perhaps she saw Unity's behaviour as having been inspired by Diana, which was surely *au fond* correct, although Diana was also right to disclaim responsibility; she could not have predicted the mad force of her sister's commitment. Diana clearly distanced herself from acts such as Unity's letter to *Der Stürmer*, and from Jessica's later claim that she was complicit in this rabid anti-Semitism, that she had called the lunatical Julius Streicher 'a kitten'. This was rubbish, as Diana put it, and one completely believes her. She was not a Nazi. She admired what the regime had achieved in rebuilding Germany, she had views on race that were rigid, a product of heritage and of faith in Mosley (yet contradicted by her circle of Jewish friends). Although she refused for years to acknowledge the sheer scale of the Final Solution, she condemned it – and Hitler – absolutely; but it did not suit Jessica to nuance this kind of thing.

So Nancy was right: the personal did come first; but because of the times, the personal and the political became indecipherable, and in ways that Nancy herself could not encompass. That first decisive act of Diana's, the cool shattering of every convention that went with setting herself apart from society as Mosley's mistress, set it all in train. From then on the competitive, combative relationships between the sisters would carry on until the causes had been used up; because of the times, those three with the radical strain in their natures were taken to limits that they would not otherwise have reached. And, because they were all young women, there would always be a man in it. As Nancy wrote in *The Pursuit of Love*, when her heroine Linda takes on the Communist creed of her second husband, Christian. 'Linda has always felt the need for a cause,' says her cousin Fanny, to which the novel's touchstone of worldly wisdom, Lord Merlin (a portrait of Gerald Berners), replies: 'My dear Fanny, I think you are mixing up cause with effect. No, Christian is an attractive fellow...' Nancy had hit the nail on the head, but perhaps it was the wrong nail.

X

Jessica's man was Esmond Romilly: Mosley with a red flag. Diana, naturally, did not see him in that way. Some years later, Romilly's comrade Philip Toynbee wrote a memoir of himself and his friend, which Diana took apart in a typically dry review:

> The highly disciplined Communist party, to which they naturally turned in their revolt from bourgeois society, also failed to make them conform and found them intractable material, useless for its purposes. Perhaps they did not become Communists because of any positive ideological agreement with Communist political theory, but for the same reason that they stole dozens of top hats from Eton boys while they were in chapel. *He only does it to annoy, because he knows it teases…*

But to the debutante Jessica, prancing through balls looking as pretty as a porcelain doll, willing herself to dislike every second of it, her cousin Romilly was a convenient god. 'She was ripe for change and it happened to be him,' Deborah later wrote, adding 'he was such a strong personality and so against EVERYTHING.' But Mitford girls had a weakness for strong men. And Esmond, among all the other things that he was against, was specifically anti-Fascism. He and Toynbee protested at Mosley's meetings (Diana would have retained a piercing memory of this). He ran away from Wellington, where he had tried to incite rebellion. Together with his brother Giles he distributed pacifist literature, refused to join the Officer Training Corps and edited a left-wing magazine called *Out of Bounds*. 'Red Menace in Public Schools! Moscow Attempts to Corrupt Boys', was a *Daily Mail* headline in 1934, an example of the hysterical fear of Communism that then raged. He was sent briefly to a remand home, then wrote a book – again entitled *Out of Bounds*, a portrait of his life to date – which was well received. Nevertheless his mother, Nellie Romilly, effectively gave up on him, which may have increased his sense of alienation and, to Jessica, his romantic aspect (vulnerable beneath the bravura). Aged just eighteen, he joined the International Brigade and went to fight in the Spanish Civil War, where he took part in the battle at Boadilla del Monte before being invalided home with dysentery. He wrote another book, *Boadilla*, published in 1937 (and reissued in 1970, as Jessica proudly proclaimed to Deborah). So although he was, in Nancy's view, 'the most horrible human being I have ever met',[46] he was also by any standards formidable and courageous.

Temporal proximity to the Second World War has made the war in Spain seem a relatively minor conflict. Yet as a fight between Republicans – democratic, but supported by the USSR – and General Franco's Nationalists it was, in some sort, the great struggle of Communism and Fascism made flesh, and a lot of flesh died. The casualties were estimated at around half a million, with atrocities and executions carried out by both sides (by far the greater part by the Nationalists). Esmond's company lost two-thirds of its number in twelve days. Britain and the US took a position of neutrality, which was opposed by the perhaps naïve, but well-intentioned left-wing intelligentsia; Orwell, Hemingway and Laurie Lee were among those who travelled to support the International Brigade. In 1939 Nancy and her husband Peter Rodd went to Perpignan to help war refugees – in fact Nancy, who absented herself philosophically from the times, did more actual war work than the rest of her sisters put together – and she was confirmed for good and all in her hatred of ideology. 'How odd the Spanish upper-classes must be,' says her proxy Linda in *The Pursuit of Love*, 'they don't raise a finger to help their own people, but leave it all to strangers like us.' Her brother, who is fighting there in the person of Esmond Romilly, replies: 'You don't know Fascists.'

It was during a dinner at the home of Esmond's kindly, de facto adoptive mother that Jessica met the battle-hardened boy, in early

1937. She knew about his exploits – said she was already half in love with him, which was probably true, such is the girlish imagination – and he behaved much as Christian does with Linda: 'planted his elbow, bare through the rent, onto the table', thus dismissing one of the dinner guests completely, and focused his attention upon the lovely girl to his other side. Esmond was not as handsome as Christian – he was short, thin, with a fierce and unyielding Churchillian face – but his intensity was compelling and probably rather sexy. According to her own account, Jessica asked Esmond whether he would take her to Spain. He said yes. And that was that.

Here, then, was an encounter to compare with those *coups de foudre* experienced by her sisters; but Esmond – as Jessica saw it – was on the side of the angels. Which he was, at the moment of their meeting. She told him that she had £50 saved: her 'Running-away Account', as she called it in *Hons and Rebels.* He told her to travel as his secretary. Together they wrote a letter that purported to invite her on a trip to Dieppe with some friends. Back in London, the letter was opened by Jessica in the presence of her mother. Sydney not only agreed to the holiday, but gave her £30: this was to be spent on clothes for a world cruise that had been planned for Jessica and Deborah. Cruises seemed to be Sydney's solution to everything – she knew that Jessica was not entirely content in her role as debutante, and surely did not want another rebellion on her hands; frosty and inadequate though she may sometimes have been, one can only feel pity at the thought of her pleasure at this excitingly extended holiday for Jessica, and her fingers-crossed hope that it would bring her daughter happiness. On 7 February 1937 she and David took Jessica to Victoria Station. David gave her £10 spending money and the Redesdales waved goodbye as Esmond lurked in the shadows. From that time David never saw his daughter again; a few years later, when Unity asked in her direct way whom her father would most like to see walk into the room, he answered instantly: 'Decca.'

And it is hard to think of what these parents went through, when it transpired that Jessica was not in Dieppe, nor anywhere that could be imagined. 'I nearly went mad when it seemed you had quite disappeared,' Sydney later wrote to her daughter. 'I knew you were unhappy, but the cause of it all was beyond me, except that like many girls you had nothing to do. I ought to have been able to help you more… Farve is better now but it was frightful to see him so down, I have never seen him like that.' It was indeed from this point that the fine and handsome David, who was not yet sixty, became an old man.

'You were the first one of the family to be on posters,' Nancy told her sister. 'Boud was so jealous.' But before the time for jokes there came a period of cold despair, lasting some two weeks, in which the Redesdales sat beside the telephone and simply waited. 'I don't think she ever realized the effect it had on all at Rutland Gate,' Deborah wrote to Diana some sixty years later. 'It was just as if someone young had died.' She recalled the absence of the sound of the gramophone, which had previously played all the time. She was still perplexed by how Jessica could have done what she did, in the way that she did it; and still, palpably, distressed by the memory. Forty years after the event, however, Jessica contested the implied accusation – that she had brought such pain to her family – in a letter to Deborah. 'I honestly think you've revised all that, somehow, in yr. mind.'[47] But that was not Deborah's style. And the description of those attenuated days of agony was surely not exaggerated.

In Deborah's view, Jessica had been in Esmond's thrall. Yet she had been a willing prisoner. And – very much like Diana, which neither would have admitted – she was determined to have been right: in *Hons and Rebels*, written more than twenty years later, she described Esmond as a beautiful comrade-in-arms, an 'orchid upon a dungheap' (this particular phrase was a little too much for Deborah). One reviewer reacted to the book in a way that the sisters saw as closer to the truth: Jessica and Esmond were described as 'an alarming couple', with 'a mutual amorality which at moments approached the sublime'.[48] Evelyn Waugh wrote to Nancy that the book made Esmond 'quite detestable' (well, he would say that, Jessica would have replied): 'She not only gives a nasty impression of the people against whom she has conceived grievances, but about those she presumably loves.' Certainly there was a great charge of feeling between Jessica and Esmond, in which attraction and a cause each served to strength the passion of the other. There was the glory of defiance: would Romeo and Juliet have fallen quite so hard had there not been that barrier between them? And there also seems to have been an obscure desire for revenge, upon something about her past life that could not quite be identified. Diana had perhaps felt that too, even towards her first husband, although her temperament was such that she expressed it differently, not through a dramatic rupture but with a calm, withdrawing finality. Unity did not: she was the simplest and the happiest in her rebellion.

After two weeks, Esmond's mother received a letter from him, explaining that he and Jessica were probably married by that time and that any attempts to force her back to London would be met with a leak, to the newspapers, of the 'truth' about Unity and Hitler. This was fairly typical stuff. Esmond had already revealed his true colours to Jessica in Bayonne, where the couple were waiting for her visa. They had been in a café where some locals were tormenting a dog; like all Mitfords, she loved animals dearly, and begged Esmond to intervene. He responded with righteous anger. 'What right have you got to impose your beastly upper-class preoccupation with animals on these people?' In England, he said, dogs were fed on steak and people left to starve; true, but one sort of cruelty does not justify another; if anything could have sent Jessica home at that point, it was this, yet she stayed. It was as if she was determined that the political should override the personal. On receipt of her visa she sailed with Esmond to Bilbao. There they were accepted into the press corps, living at some distance from the war zone, and Esmond sent bulletins to the *News Chronicle*. Soon he would find a job with Reuters. He *was* impressive – for a boy of nineteen he was extraordinary – but his toughness had a repellent quality. He embodied the antithesis of the Mitford charm, and seemed to relish the fact. When Nancy later said that he changed Jessica, who, despite continued affections, in some fundamental way set her face forever against her family, one sees what she meant.

As the family pinko it was Nancy who was sent to try to persuade her sister home. Unity, who had travelled back from Munich in early March, had been considered for the job and swiftly discounted. Unity's letters to Jessica from this time are fascinating: they show the acuity that she possessed beneath her mania, and the absolute disregard for her sister's conversion to the enemy. 'Your letter is really *extraorder*,' she said; 'on reading it again I can hardly believe you wrote it yourself, it's so unlike you.' Which was Nancy's perception, translated into the Unity. She went on to write that 'the vile aunt Weenie' had said that Jessica would be better off dead, and that Weenie probably thought the same about her and Diana. Her last, almost amusing shot was to inform Jessica that she had persuaded Hitler to keep the story out of German newspapers. For by this time the publicity around the 'elopement' was intense, 'Another Mitford Anarchist' and so on. Thanks to the Churchill connection, the then Foreign Secretary, Anthony Eden, had cabled the consul in Bilbao. The British ambassador had also become involved. Communists though they were, Jessica and Esmond were commanding the attention of the highest authorities, like the members of the upper class that they also were.

Eventually they were forced to board a destroyer, the HMS *Echo*, together with some 180 refugees; the ambassador had the wit to tell them that if they did not do so the refugees would not be evacuated, and they would be blamed. On 10 March *The Times* reported that Jessica and Esmond were 'returning to London this evening', but this was optimistic intelligence from somebody who did not grasp whom they were dealing with. When the destroyer had reached St-Jean-de-Luz – which was as far as Esmond was prepared to travel – the couple were met by Nancy and Peter, the moment of reunion played out in front of a chorus line of reporters. 'We saw them at the end of the gangplank,' wrote Jessica in *Hons and Rebels*, 'Nancy, tall and beautiful, waving at us with her gloves...' According to this account Nancy spoke to her sister in a highly frivolous tone – 'Nanny keeps saying you didn't have any suitable clothes to fight in' – although in a letter written at the time, in July 1937, Jessica took Nancy to task for telling her that living with Esmond was not respectable. Meanwhile Peter, who thought that he could handle any situation, simply hardened her resolve. 'He was dying to be the heroic brother-in-law who rushed out... (expenses paid by Farve) to bring you back,' wrote Unity. Peter told Esmond that if they returned to England, Jessica would be given an allowance by David. He was right to think that Esmond wanted money (within a couple of months the young couple would be begging from Sydney), but it was still very much the wrong thing to say to a man who posed as being above such concerns.

It was Sydney, in fact, who resolved matters, if not in the way that she would have wished. She visited Jessica, now in Bayonne, who confessed to her mother that she might be pregnant (which indeed she was). A return to England was no longer the issue; now a wedding became the priority. This had been the couple's intention, but they were prevented from marrying at once because both were under age. Sydney also confronted Esmond, accusing him of cowardice for not having approached David properly to ask for Jessica's hand: 'what you would expect from a Communist'. He appeared to accept this, but vengefulness was in his nature, and back in England Sydney received a series of very nasty letters: first Esmond suggested that he and Jessica might not bother to marry after all, then he threatened to bar Sydney from a marriage ceremony that she herself was arranging. His dislike of the Mitfords had quickly become non-negotiable. He would have told himself that this was because they were all Nazis (his loudly expressed view), but it was – as so often – the personal that was guiding him: a hatred of their charm, their correctness, their sense of entitlement; a guilty grudge against their wholly legitimate distress. It was illogical, yet it became Jessica's view also. For the Redesdales, the Romilly marriage – which took place in Bayonne on 18 May 1937, in fact attended by both mothers – was comfort of a sort, but not much. They knew perfectly well that Jessica was lost to them.

Yet Sydney wrote bravely to Deborah about the wedding, telling her of the silk dress from Harrods that she had taken for Jessica to be married in, and of the gramophone that she had bought as a joint present from Deborah and Unity (it may be imagined what Esmond made of this tainted marriage gift, and of the necklace sent by Diana.) In the end it was probably David who suffered the most. He did not know that he would never see his daughter again – although at the time he did not *want* to see her – but he had borne the full force of the publicity that her behaviour had generated. Reporters had doorstepped him at Rutland Gate and demanded a statement. The *Daily Express* had blasted the story across its front page, naming 'The Hon. Deborah Freeman-Mitford' as the daughter who had disappeared. With Tom as a member of her legal team, Deborah was awarded £1,000 for the damage to her reputation; but at the High Court in June it was said that David had supplied 'certain information' to the press (in other words, had blabbed hopelessly) in the belief that it would help 'in the trouble which had arisen. He was very greatly distressed at the time...' Thereafter he was trapped in the sticky maw of the newspapers, where his name appeared repeatedly. Sydney handled these things far better. When the *Daily Express* reporter asked whether he might know when consent had been given for the Romilly marriage, she replied that he could ask but she would not answer. David, in contrast, was absolutely without the worldly wisdom that would have helped him to deal with this kind of person; he was like a great ageing bear, cleverly baited, lashing out with force but no accuracy. Subsequently he tried to allege press intrusion, but was fobbed off with the usual 'public interest' defence.

This was a very long way from the behaviour of Uncle Matthew, who in *The Pursuit of Love* is similarly besieged when his daughter Jassy absconds to Hollywood, and chats merrily to reporters about her intention to track down and marry a film star named Gary Coon.

Nancy, as was her way, had sought to dispel the nightmare by rendering it ridiculous (and, using the other part of Jessica's story, by giving a charismatic yet deadly Communist husband to Linda). As was also her way, she had urged her fictional father back to his old, magnificent, seemingly indestructible self when she wrote of journalists braving his stock whips and sneaking into his house: 'Isn't that the damned sewer I found under my bed?' Uncle Matthew would say, devouring one of their ludicrous reports. 'He greatly enjoyed the whole affair,' wrote Nancy. She added: 'He also seemed greatly to enjoy reading about himself in the newspapers and we all began to suspect that Uncle Matthew had a hidden passion for publicity.'

As Nancy was all too aware when she wrote this last sentence, it would become even more remote from the truth after the outbreak of war.

XI

From Esmond Romilly's point of view, it may well have seemed that the Mitford family were all Nazis. Consider the evidence, as a person with his affiliations might have seen it.

When he and Philip Toynbee tried to disrupt the Blackshirt meeting at Olympia in 1934, Nancy and Unity were in the audience. When they similarly protested at the meeting at Earl's Court in 1939, Diana, Unity and Tom were present – also, just possibly, Deborah and Sydney (see page 157) – and Tom gave a Fascist salute. Nancy's *Wigs on the Green*, which set her right-wing sisters so firmly against her, should have been evidence of scepticism, but the tone of the book was infinitely too frivolous to exempt her from a metaphorical execution.

In 1935, when Unity was in Munich, Tom lunched twice with his sister and Hitler. That same year Unity was visited by Pamela (who the following year would marry a Fascist sympathizer), and again there was a meal with Hitler, who had been struck by Pam's marvellously blue eyes. Her stolid nature was proof against the nonsense of extremism, but Esmond would not have seen it that way.

Then there were the Redesdales; where the evidence does indeed pile up. Sydney had met Hitler first in 1935. The following year her husband began evincing pro-German sentiments in the House of Lords. The couple attended dinners of the Anglo-German Fellowship, whose supporters included the Duke of Wellington, David's old friend Lord Nuffield and Edward VIII, who was soon to abdicate but held fast to his pro-Nazi views. (In the *Anglo-German Review* of December 1936, a German observer was reported as saying: 'You have a splendid King. Why don't you let him out of his cage?') In 1937 the Redesdales attended a reception at the German Embassy, along with the Duke and Duchess of Kent, the Churchills and the Chamberlains – as Nancy put it, von Ribbentrop's embassy was the most elegant in London (although there, at least, *she* was in the clear. Peter Rodd had replied to an invitation in Yiddish). In reciprocal spirit the Londonderrys held a reception for the ambassador, attended by the prime minister, at which the Redesdales were again present. This, more than anything, proves Nancy's later assertion that when it came to the German embassy, 'everybody went. They deny it now, of course.'[49] As the historian Andrew Roberts wrote: 'There was no shortage of people in 1930s Britain who would have viewed a British accommodation with Hitler positively, if not with enthusiasm. This feeling extended far beyond the lunatic fringe of anti-Semites…' Imperialists, conservatives, press barons, businessmen – they all contained advocates of appeasement within their ranks. 'Perhaps most interestingly, a significant proportion of the British aristocracy had strong pro-German and sometimes even pro-Nazi leanings.'[50] Ribbentrop won over plenty of people. Lord Derby invited Goering to his house for the Grand National.

So the Redesdales were not so exceptional, although it was somewhat out of the ordinary that, in the summer of 1937, Sydney should have taken Deborah to tea at Hitler's flat. Writing to Jessica about this, Sydney said: 'He is very "easy" to be with and no feeling of shyness would be possible, and such very good manners.' He had, she reported, asked after 'little D[ecca]'. One would suspect a desire to enrage, but that is not the tone of the letter; rather Sydney seemed eager to placate, to deny this foolish insistence upon political divisions. If so it was beyond naïve. Deborah probably did better by making a joke of the episode. She wrote to tell Jessica that their mother – 'wasn't it killing?' – had asked Hitler if there was a law specifying the quality of flour in German bread. At just seventeen, and with part of her attention on Royal Ascot the following week, Deborah was inclined to see the whole thing as a romp; or perhaps she deliberately chose to do so. Like Pamela, however, she was essentially immune. She described Unity 'shaking so much she could hardly walk' as if this were a natural but alien phenomenon. Of Hitler she wrote, in her diary, that he looked less hard in the flesh than he did in his photographs. Years later she expressed her lasting amazement that he had delayed his departure to the Obersalzberg, his mountain retreat at Berchtesgaden, for two hours simply to talk to them all.

In the autumn of 1937 the Redesdales, along with David's sister-in-law Helen (whose daughter Clementine was then a follower of Hitler), attended the annual Parteitag. They would do so again in 1938: 'Lord and Lady Redesdale have arrived in London from Nuremberg,' as the court pages of *The Times* politely reported. But before that, in March, David had given another remarkable speech to the Lords. He launched a long defence of the *Anschluss*, Hitler's annexation of Austria. It was, he said, childish to think that any part of the hysterical welcome had been staged. He, Redesdale, was 'firmly convinced that the change which had taken place in Austria was one which was the sincere desire of the majority of the Austrian people', and he hoped that friendly talks would be opened with the German government.

It was, replied another member of the Lords, the argument of German propagandists. David had learned his stuff well. Little wonder that Diana wrote to Deborah in June, informing her that the Führer had 'talked a lot about Farve and his speech' and was extremely grateful. Furthermore: he '*specially*' wanted Deborah to attend the Parteitag that year! 'Isn't he kind and sweet.' This, Deborah did not do.

The views that David expressed in the Lords were Unity's, who had written to Winston Churchill explaining that the *Anschluss* was a wonderful thing. He replied civilly that a 'fair plebiscite' would have shown a large majority of Austrians to be against Nazi rule. Yet Unity herself had watched the scenes in Vienna, which to a believer seemed undeniably pro-Hitler, and in high manic mode wrote to Diana, describing how Austrians would ask her – in tones of quasi-religious awe – if they could kiss the hand that the Führer had touched. Sometimes, inevitably, Unity displayed competitiveness with her beautiful sister over their relationship with Hitler, and sought to prove her particular closeness. 'Fancy you being in Berlin again,' she wrote rather sharply in 1937. 'I imagine the Führer is there isn't he?' – for all the world as if he were a potentially unfaithful boyfriend. Diana, in turn, gives an occasional sense of stoking up Unity's passion. Again in 1937 she related, in great detail, an evening with Magda Goebbels, at which the guests played 'Analogies' and decided that if Hitler were a flower, he would be a Madonna lily. She also described a photograph of Hitler at the 1929 Parteitag: 'it makes me cry with rage to think we were alive and yet missing *everything*.' Can that really be true? Well, perhaps.

What is certainly true is that by 1938 Sydney had fallen under the spell of Hitler, rather than of mere theoretical 'Fellowship' (he is, wrote Nancy, 'her favourite son-in-law'). So too, to a degree, had her husband. David had dealings with Hitler when Unity fell ill in August, oddly enough after a performance of *Die Walküre* at Bayreuth, where she was an honoured guest. With the force of the disciple she rallied to attend a huge march-past in Breslau with

Hitler – 'of course I would rather have died than miss that' – and took a different aeroplane back to Bayreuth as she was terrified of giving him her flu. In fact she had pneumonia. Hitler asked Winifred Wagner to look after her, and at 3 a.m. called out his private doctor. 'The Fuhrer is the kindest man in the world isn't he?' replied Diana. Again, can she really have meant it? But these actions had an effect upon David that the rantings at Nuremberg may not have done. Hitler had paid for Unity's stay in hospital, a bill that David – replacing his wife at their daughter's bedside – insisted upon reimbursing. In the course of this transaction he met Hitler several times, man to man, and found him likeable.

At the end of the 1938 Nuremberg rally, Hitler made promises to the Germans in the Sudetenland that were effectively a provocation, and a threat to the Versailles agreement of 1919. The Sudeten Germans in Czechoslovakia wanted to join the Fatherland: who could deny them this right? Three days later, the prime minister Neville Chamberlain flew to Munich in an attempt to avert war – an outcome that far more people wanted than they would later admit – and the Czechs were required to hand over the Sudetenland. The blissful Führer was clawing back his Rhineland, chunk by chunk. After the talks, Chamberlain told his aide Alec Douglas-Home that he thought Hitler was mad. Unity, too, was showing signs that a blind person could scarcely have missed. Earlier that year, after two Sudeten Germans were wounded in a tavern brawl in Czechoslovakia, it was reported in *The Times* that 'Miss Unity Mitford, who has been wearing a swastika on her coat in Prague, was held up today on her way to Carlsbad by motor car when entering a zone in which special military regulations are in force. She was detained and then released after a few hours.' She had been parading herself in the most flagrant way, flaunting her Nazi insignia. Afterwards she complained of her treatment at the hands of the hated Czechs, who had accused her of carrying Hitler's photograph. Her behaviour, still that of a hysterical young show-off, was also ragingly dangerous; she was an oversized out-of-control child playing chopsticks around the nuclear button.

As early as 1934, Peter Rodd had written to David telling him to get Unity away from Munich. Beyond question he had more brains than most of the Mitfords, but according to Nancy his letter was dismissed as 'impertinence'. Four years on, however, it is truly remarkable and dreadful that the Redesdales did not force Unity to leave Germany with them. Of course they would have believed that, as long as Chamberlain succeeded in achieving an agreement, Hitler would view it as binding. But the apparent acquiescence in Unity's view of the Führer was beyond naive. And there is a strong sense that David, certainly, was in a bewildered state that led him towards Germany because he no longer knew what to think. He did not want a war – who would? Perhaps there was a chance that Unity and 'the man Mosley' (as he called him) were right, that Britain and Germany could indeed be friends? Sydney was obdurately against war, and remained so even throughout its entire six years. Like her politicized daughters, she was incapable of abandoning an opinion once it had been fully formed. But this is not really the point: the Redesdales' desire for appeasement did not mean that it was going to happen. Rather it was as though, having lost two daughters, they were determined to hold on to this one by giving her everything that she wanted.

Back in London, Sydney had a final Mitford girl to present to society, and dealing with the entirely satisfactory Deborah, buying dress material at John Lewis and Ascot hats from Madame Rita's in Berkeley Square, created the necessary illusion that the world had not changed. Nor had it, if the court pages were one's guide. In the same old faithful way they transcribed Deborah's progress through her debutante season: a coming-out dance at Rutland Gate in March, for which Pamela gave a dinner party; a ball attended in Eaton Square; a presentation at the Palace in May, at which not a sheet of writing paper, nor a single chocolate, was stolen.

This normality may have been Deborah's own particular form of rebellion. What better way to thumb her nose at her fanatical family than by spending late August 1939 at a house party for York races? Or perhaps, like Fanny in *The Pursuit of Love*, she was simply born sane. And, like the divinely pretty 'Northey' in *Don't Tell Alfred*, she was made to charm: a 'violent little fascinator', in Nancy's phrase. Northey is a fairly exact, if exaggerated, portrait of the young Deborah. She has eyes of brilliant blue and a habit of wriggling like a puppy as she speaks. She is obsessed with animals (her pet badger builds a sett on the back lawn of the French Embassy). Almost every remark made to her ('Is that a badger's sett?') is met with the refrain of 'oh you *are* clever'. She is also, beneath the twinkling and sparkling, very much on the ball. Deborah had to be: she had to trace the steps of the pavane with care. Her sisters had cast a shadow across the family name. Worse, they had made it something of a joke. To the press, the girls were the Hon. Kardashians, styled in black shirts and red flags. Deborah herself had been named in the *Daily Express* as having eloped with Esmond Romilly, and newspaper apologies are never quite as noticeable as they might be. In April 1938, bang in between Deborah's coming-out ball and presentation, Unity was attacked by a crowd in Hyde Park. A newspaper headline read: 'At it Again, the Mad, Mad Mitfords'.

In June Unity was back in the papers again, this time for her provocative antics in Prague. At the same time, in a different world, Deborah was at a dance held for the daughters of Joe Kennedy, now US ambassador in London. She became friendly with the family. At a ball given by Lord Mountbatten she danced with Jack Kennedy, whose presidential inauguration she would later attend; in her diary she wrote that he was 'rather boring but nice'. She met her future husband Andrew Cavendish, second son to the Duke of Devonshire, just two weeks into her debut season. 'That was it for me,' she later wrote: she had found her man. If Deborah had ever seen herself as a package of perfect goods damaged by the brutal knocks from those around her – what eligible type would marry into a family of nutters? I mean, what would the mater/the vicar/nanny think? – then there was no sign of relief at this early entrance of Lord Right. Not that she would have admitted to such a thing.

Andrew, who was then at Cambridge, was not the type that

Mitfords usually fell for, and this perhaps added to his appeal: unlike those forceful egomaniacs he was languid, humorous and self-deprecating. He had an immense capacity for pleasure, and his charm was the kind that did not have to try. As a young girl Deborah had had an immense crush on Derek Jackson, who in style could not have been more different, although both men were dedicated to racing. (Andrew was also an elegantly fervid gambler: 'chased by a Ladbroke's man the length of a train at Victoria station'.[51]) But Deborah had sense, she had seen her sisters coping with strident alpha males who knew it all yet sulked like little boys when thwarted. Later Andrew would say that Deborah was the bossy one: 'but I like that in a woman'. In August 1938 the couple, plus a friend, descended suddenly upon Wootton – this was still technically forbidden to Deborah, as the Mosley marriage had not yet been announced – where they found the great Sir Ogre fishing peaceably, surrounded by children. They stayed 'literally ten mins', as Diana wrote to Unity. The men, she said, 'seemed incredibly babyish' (Diana, one senses, was born a woman). Certainly the eighteen-year-old Andrew would have cut a callow, bashful figure compared with the jackbooted chaps with whom Diana was then consorting. He was, according to Nancy, a 'dear little fellow' (although to Evelyn Waugh she later wrote that he reminded her somewhat of Lord Sebastian Flyte in *Brideshead Revisited*, by which she meant, presumably, a casual intensity of aristocratic charm.) Again, this was surely part of what Deborah liked.

They did not marry until the spring of 1941. Although not good-looking, Andrew was popular with women; it was reasonable that he should wait until the great age of twenty-one before plunging. Sydney, meanwhile, had been unsure. She was worried by examples of what she saw as Andrew's nonchalance, as when Deborah drove to Oxford to meet three trains, all of which he had failed to board. Nevertheless by the first summer of her season Deborah regarded herself as unofficially engaged, and was invited to meet the Devonshires. Her mother – still anxious, still clinging to the rules – wrote her a stiff letter, saying that she hoped the invitation had come from the Duchess herself, not merely from Andrew. This was the Sydney of old, in the days before her power had been overridden. It reads absurdly, in the face of other events. Yet there is something pathetically staunch, indeed admirable, in her attempt to make sure that this daughter, at least, achieved a happy ending.

Deborah also visited Jessica, who had returned to London and now had a baby named Julia. The Romillys were living in the working-class area of Rotherhithe, slum-ridden at the time, close to the docks that would soon be bombed by the Luftwaffe. Jessica wrote brightly to her sister in December 1937, when Julia was just two days old, saying that the baby was very strong '& you could have seen me and at any time if you hadn't been such a young germ carrier': Deborah had had measles. But in fact it was not easy to see Jessica, as Esmond was so opposed to visits from any Mitford. (Tom was an exception, evidence of his ability to be all things to all men.) When Deborah finally went to Rotherhithe, and found Julia suspended in a cradle from an open window, Esmond was not at home; there were, however, a couple of ghastly occasions when she did see him. He was, Deborah later recalled, extremely nasty about her mother. He was probably left ignorant of the fact that Sydney had been driven to see Julia by Unity, in a car full of things for the baby including a dress from Diana, for which her sister Jessica wrote a graceless letter of thanks asking her sister not to send any more presents, 'as Esmond doesn't like it'. The fact that Bryan Guinness, now remarried, was made so welcome at the house probably says as much about the couple's attitude to his former wife as about Bryan himself. Nancy was persona non grata after her 'betrayal' at St-Jean-de-Luz, as was Pamela for having married a Fascist. And so it went on, life according to the gospel of Comrade Esmond.

What Jessica thought of the reality of working-class life in the 1930s – a world of zinc baths, chamber pots, houses 'where the cracked walls were held together by layers of bulging wallpaper'[52] – is impossible to know. She and Esmond worked at J. Walter Thompson's advertising agency. He was a copy-writer (unlike Gordon Comstock in *Keep the Aspidistra Flying*, he did not view this job as the gateway to the evil Money God), she was in market research, and for the first time she mixed with the people whose cause she espoused. Jessica was honest enough to admit that her feelings were ambivalent, as they were when she met the Labour Party men whose company Esmond purported to favour; she was accustomed to certain refinements of behaviour, and was uncomfortable without them. She was always protected to an extent, simply by who she was – like the downwardly mobile posh girl in Pulp's *Common People*, if she called, her daddy could stop it – and she remained Mitford enough to employ a maid. Nevertheless the distance between Rutland Gate and Rotherhithe Street would have been unfathomable. Did she achieve anything, by her great leap from SW7 to SE16? Life experience, of course, but surely that was too solipsistic to be the point. She was *proving* a point, but what? As a reviewer of *Hons and Rebels* put it: 'There is something rather touching about the notion of these young people [Jessica and Esmond] that they were missionaries of Progress as well as buccaneers... A Leftist young woman of the present day [1960] might well find this book deplorable in its resolute concentration on family jokes, private languages, and activities from which the comrades of the party are automatically excluded.'[53] Po-faced criticism, but it hit its mark: without the Mitford background to rebel against, there was no meaning to the rebellion, and not much more to the book.

Similarly with Esmond. Two years later he would say: 'I wasn't a Communist, I am not now, and I never will be.' He was something less defined, perhaps even to himself. He despised the modish aspect of Communism as an abstract creed, and one sees why: most members of the intelligentsia would never have met a working-class person in their lives; a man like Anthony Blunt would have fainted clean away if required to live in Rotherhithe without a Poussin to pore over. At the same time it is hard to know just what Esmond himself was trying to prove, other than that he had the guts to practise – for a time anyway – what he preached. He, too, was protected by who he was. As Diana suggested in her cool destruction of his politics; as Deborah and Nancy implied in their analysis of his character; as even Jessica admitted, when she called him 'a gifted hater' – he was *against* rather than for, a natural anarchist rather than an idealistic left-winger like his wife. This can carry its own glamour (think Russell Brand) but it is surely a dead end, as the barricaded Cable Street was to Mosley's Blackshirts. Esmond attacked Jessica for any sign that she was behaving like a Mitford, like the upper-class person that she harmlessly was. He attacked her family. And this new life was what she had said she wanted; was it not? The only possible response was yes; the only possible attitude was acceptance. If Jessica ever had doubts of the kind that may have assailed Diana when she sat alone in Eaton Square, then she, again like the sister who was now excised from her life, would have died before admitting it.

Nevertheless when Julia died, at the age of five months, she must surely have wondered. The baby caught measles – this, ironically, after the care taken to protect her from Deborah – when an epidemic surged across Rotherhithe. A local clinic, assuming that Jessica had had the disease, informed her that breastfeeding would give the baby immunity and there was no need for inoculation. Measles developed into pneumonia. Her parents watched as Julia's life ebbed painfully away in an oxygen tent.

And one may imagine the wildfire of chit-chat, rampaging through the society that the Romillys had disowned, blaming them for trying to raise a helpless child in a slum district, for making Julia the sacrificial victim to their 'ideals'. Esmond had alienated so many, not just by his rhetoric but with his brash Robin Hood antics: he and Jessica would go to parties held by the kind of people they vociferously loathed and steal from their homes. Doubtless Esmond would have regarded aristocratic Fascists as fair game, and Jessica would have gone along with his view, but now their behaviour was being repaid with all the cruelty of which gossip is capable.

The problem, for Jessica, was that she may in her heart have believed that the gossipers were right. Her mother had always thought that Julia looked sickly. Even Unity saw that she had legs 'like Marlene Dietrich's'. The image of the baby suspended from a window is disquieting. Sydney had offered to send Blor, who had so much kindly understanding of children, but Esmond had refused to allow a nanny in the house (yet he had a maid). He wanted Jessica to be like the working-class mothers of Rotherhithe, surviving and coping as a real woman should. But Jessica was not such a woman; she had not been trained in the tough business of life; she was a formidable spirit play-acting at something that she truly believed, but did not truly grasp. And she had been very much isolated. None of her family attended the baby's funeral, which surely was not Jessica's real wish. The questions raised by Julia's death were harsh: why, after all, should this baby have been spared, when others in Rotherhithe would die of disease, just because her parents had the means to have possibly saved her? Was that what Communism meant, sharing evils that might have been averted by the deployment of tainted capitalism?

The solution, to these unanswerable things, was escape. The couple went to Corsica, leaving behind them some gigantic bills: Jessica had assumed that electricity simply came like magic. On their return to London they took a bedsit in the Edgware Road. In the autumn of 1938, for reasons unknown but surely connected to the loss of Julia, Jessica underwent a termination (some twenty years later she would write with brave candour about this experience, and campaign for the legalization of abortion). Then, in early 1939, the Romillys each did something very typical. Jessica travelled to Swinbrook to find her childhood pet, the now ageing sheep Miranda, which was standing amid a flock but hobbled across the field toward Jessica's call. Esmond went with Philip Toynbee to Eton and returned to London with a collection of stolen top hats: 'gallant symbols,' wrote Toynbee, 'of our hatred of Eton, of our anarchy, of defiance'.[54] More typically yet, Esmond sold the lot. He and Jessica took the money – along with £100 that she had inherited on her twenty-first birthday – and travelled to New York.

XII

Back in the summer of 1937, when Hitler's predations into the Rhineland were still being batted aside as not *quite* anybody else's business, Unity wrote a letter to her Boud. Its friendliness and affection was undiminished; they might have been back in the DFD, squabbling idiotically, rather than living out the truth of their divided allegiances. Unity told Jessica about the heat in Munich. She also described how she had gone to the Englischer Garten and, in a semi-pagan ritual, had taken off her clothes in the park and sunbathed naked. Then she had wondered whether Sydney, somehow, knew what she was doing: '& I laughed till I ached, if anyone had come along they would have thought me mad as well as indecent'.

Was she mad? Surely yes: although she need not have been. She was a seeker of attention, a boldly confident girl who nevertheless recognized herself as a misfit, not stupid but without sense or control, who fell into the wrong times and the wrong hands. She harboured great and undirected passions. 'Bobo would have been a religious girl,' a friend later said. 'She found it in Nazism instead.'[55]

She was not evil, although her terrible ravings against the Jews read that way. She was surrounded by evil people whose good opinion she sought. Perhaps they found the evil in her, as well as the madness: like a *folie à deux*, in which the stronger party can induce the other to commit and take pleasure in murder. Yet she had had the power of commanding deep affection. 'It was not that those who loved her forgave her her beliefs,' wrote Deborah many years later, 'they went on loving her in spite of them.'

By 1939 the days in Germany, which had brought her the happiness she so clumsily craved, were coming to their conclusion. There were other endings also. Nancy's journey to Perpignan with her husband was a brief revival in her marriage, in that it made Peter Rodd somebody she could think well of – which *she* craved. However, her miscarriage at the end of 1938, after five years of trying to fall pregnant, was a kind of death knell: it was not the end of the relationship, but it did end any hope that it might succeed in the long term. 'The really important thing,' she would write in *The Pursuit of Love*, 'if a marriage is to go well, without much love, is very very great niceness – *gentillesse* – and wonderful good manners.' How true that is. But it was hard-won knowledge, as those were the very qualities that her own marriage lacked. One of the best things about Nancy's novels, and key to their infinitely consolatory air, is the easy grace with which she hands out wisdom that she herself had struggled to acquire.

She spent the lead-up to war in a house in Maida Vale's Blomfield Road, with Peter (mostly) and with her beloved French bulldogs, Milly and Lottie, which produced the babies that she could not. Milly, she told Robert Byron, 'is very anti-appeasement'. She was also editing the letters of the Stanleys of Alderley, whose sane Whig politics and settled belief systems constituted a wondrous respite from the present day; and from Peter. The first volume of letters, *The Ladies of Alderley* (1938), contained an acknowledgment of the encouragement given by 'my husband'. The second, *The Stanleys of Alderley* (1939), did not. The books, cleverly done and well reviewed, were a fillip to Nancy's treasured pride. Nevertheless her life, at this time, held no particular promise. War would at least provide a solution as to what happened next. Her judgment upon the world situation – and by extension upon her family – was bored, despairing and somehow detached. 'There isn't a pin to put between Nazis and Bolshies,' she wrote to the family friend Violet Hammersley. 'If one is a Jew one prefers one & if one is an aristocrat the other, that's all as far as I can see. *Fiends!*'

Swinbrook had gone, and now David advertised the house at Rutland Gate as to be sold, or let, furnished. His daughters were all 'out'; there was no need of it any longer, although in fact the war would forestall the sale. By 1938 the Redesdales' main home was an island, Inch Kenneth, off the west coast of Mull, with a single large dwelling, a chapel and a private boatman. David bought it after meeting the man who had built the house at his club, a characteristic childlike impulse: he was very like Unity in that sense, heedless and eager, without much thought as to consequences. Dr Johnson and Samuel Boswell had been entertained in the original house, 'an elegant retreat' in Boswell's phrase. Its replacement was less beautiful ('something of a Home Counties mansion').[56] It was also exceedingly remote. Reaching it required an overnight sleeper, a long ferry ride to Mull, a fifteen-mile drive, then a boat trip; what Nancy called 'the worst journey in the world'. Deborah later wrote that she 'veered between wanting to live there for the rest of my life, and hating it'. The weather made more difference to Inch Kenneth than to anywhere else that she knew: it was sublime in sun and grim in gloom. Sydney, who had spent so much of her childhood surrounded by sea, found an affinity with the place. David had Scottish blood – the Airlie mother – and like most men of his class he loved Scotland. But the impression is that he was hunkering down, like a tired old animal. One wonders what he thought about his marvellous girls, who had danced through their childhood, teasing and provoking, making him their fantasy lord and master, weaving a spell of enchantment in his immutable Oxfordshire acres.

One also wonders whether David sensed what had to come, as the Munich accord was revealed as a sham, Hitler strode on towards Prague, and he himself reverted – with some relief, as if the hypnotized conversion at Nuremberg had never been – to his old hatred of Germany. Sydney, meanwhile, became more pro-Hitler than ever, and raged against the idea of war. Still 1939 had to play itself out. Unity moved to a new flat: 'it belongs,' she wrote, 'to a young Jewish couple who are going abroad.' Unforgivable? Yes, beyond a doubt. In March she wrote to Diana as if nothing much had changed. The Führer 'was in his very sweetest mood', sympathetic because England and Germany were becoming enemies. In the summer she visited London – again, how was she ever allowed to go back to Munich? And with a car full of furniture given by Sydney for her new flat? She attended the Mosley rally at Earl's Court. Outside the house at Rutland Gate, she said a fond goodbye to the parlourmaid, Mabel. 'Don't say Hitler's name to me,' Mabel warned. 'Mabe, you don't know Hitler, you'd like him.'

But by July, as she wrote to Diana, the sweet Führer 'was in his least forthcoming mood, you know, all preoccupied'. The two sisters went to Bayreuth, where Unity was greeted with flowers, and they watched *Götterdämmerung*. They lunched with Hitler. Conversation was sober, adult; at least between Diana and the Führer. She told him that Mosley would continue to campaign for peace for as long as this was legal, although he might not be the right man to avert war. Hitler replied drily that by doing this he would risk assassination. He also said to Diana, with regard to a British declaration of war: 'I am afraid they are determined on it.'

After lunch Unity told Diana that she did not wish to live if England and Germany went to war. Nevertheless she asked her sister to return for the Parteitag that year, as if such a thing still might happen. Diana went home to Wootton, where she prepared for the baby she was expecting, and for war. Unity lunched with Hitler on two more occasions. Presumably they discussed the situation; they always had in the past, and she may have been urging peace even then. Albert Speer wrote in his memoirs that 'Lady Mitford', as he called her, 'even in the later years of international tension persistently spoke up for her country and often actually pleaded with Hitler to make a deal with Britain. In spite of Hitler's discouraging reserve, she did not abandon her efforts through all those years.' A friend of Unity's, Rudi von Simolin, later said: 'She had been on a pedestal, and therefore was mistaken into thinking she had influence.'[57]

The British consul ordered her to leave Germany, but she replied that she did not need to as she had Hitler's protection. Her father sent a series of desperate telegrams, but it was too late now for persuasion. Through the last days of August Unity was alone in her flat, whose previous owners had gone who knows where. She listened constantly to the wireless. On 1 September she lunched for the last time in the

Osteria Bavaria. The next day she sent another letter to Diana, still in the familiar Mitford voice, saying that Chamberlain should be hanged. She expressed concern about her dog, a gift from her sister. 'I fear,' she wrote, 'I shan't see the Fuhrer again.'

The following day she put her gun to her head in the Englischer Garten.

PART III

'And, you know now I am well again, I can't bear life.
I mean, this war!'

Letter from Unity Mitford to Diana Mosley,
20 November 1941

I

In fact Unity did see Hitler again, at a hospital in Munich. Her life was over, but she had failed to end it. The bullet from her little Walthur pistol lodged itself at the back of her head, in a position too precarious to allow its removal. It stayed there, playing upon her central nervous system, causing her to become wholly childlike in her moods, her lack of co-ordination and her incontinence. Yet somehow she remained very much herself. An exaggerated self, but that she always had been.

Whether it was guilt, affection, or both that caused Hitler to assume responsibility for Unity and pay for her treatment, it was something resembling human emotion. She was found almost immediately after dropping to the ground beside a park bench. So many people seem to have known that she intended harming herself, although none of them managed to prevent it. Rudi von Simolin, who on the morning of 4 September would receive a letter from Unity, explaining that she was now dead, had been shown the pistol. Deborah later wrote that the family also knew of its existence. To Tom and Diana, Unity had said that she would commit suicide if war was declared. On the morning of the 3rd she had visited the office of the gauleiter, Adolf Wagner, and asked whether she would be interned, to which he replied she would not; it is unclear why she wanted to know this, given her already fixed intentions. Wagner was concerned by her demeanour and put two men on her tail. Later she returned to his office and gave him an envelope containing a suicide note. Her shadows had temporarily lost her by that time, but a woman in the Englischer Garten heard the shot, and watched as Unity was driven away in an official vehicle. News of what had happened was suppressed, a state secret.

Hitler visited Unity on 10 September, when she did not recognize him, and again on 8 November. By this time she had tried again to commit suicide, by swallowing her swastika badge. But she now knew Hitler, and was able to understand when he asked whether she preferred to stay in Germany or return to England. 'England,' she said. He therefore began to make arrangements for her to be taken to neutral Switzerland, from where she might travel on to her home.

When war was declared, Unity's parents were on their island with Nancy and Deborah. It was a similar situation to the one that they had endured two and a half years earlier, with Jessica's disappearance. Different in the sense that they knew where this daughter was; but everything else was unknown, and terrifying. Through the British consul they received a letter from Unity: 'This is to say goodbye… I send my best love to you all and particularly to my Boud.' No real intelligence got through. There were stories of Unity's arrest, of internment in a camp: 'a sort of poetic justice', as Nancy put it to Violet Hammersley. Nancy had travelled back to London on 3 September. On the way to the station she picked a quarrel with her mother about Hitler. Now that war had begun, her exasperation with the pro-German side of the family was ever more legitimate, yet there was also a sense in which she was relishing those discredited sympathies; she was surely justified in any antipathy towards a mother who liked Nazis. 'Muv has finally gone off her head', she wrote, not without a certain glee. She meant that Sydney was still supporting Hitler, which was true, although she could hardly fail to see that her mother was also delirious with anxiety. In fact Nancy would make efforts of her own to find out what had happened to Unity, about whom she too was deeply concerned, beneath her pose of detachment. Nevertheless she could not do the simple thing and offer sympathy to Sydney, and the unyielding quality in her mother did not make it any easier. Writing a letter of thanks for the stay at Inch Kenneth, Nancy went on to describe her immediate plunge into war work – she was driving an Air Raid Protection car every night, and soon would be working at a first-aid post near Paddington Station (where she began her 1940 novel *Pigeon Pie)*. The message to Sydney was pretty blatant: *some of us* are doing the honourable thing.

In mid-September, the Redesdales received a letter from Janos von Almasy's brother, László.[1] Unity, he wrote, was ill and in hospital. Another month on and they were told what they had surely already known, that she had tried to kill herself. By then the story was out. *The Times* reported in October: 'News has reached Lord and Lady Redesdale that their daughter… is seriously ill in a hospital in Munich,' but such restraint would not be typical. A journalist rang to ask if Unity was dead. Sydney hung up. Nevertheless a headline blaring her death made the newsstands. Jessica, now in Washington DC (where Esmond had a job as a door-to-door salesman), heard wild rumours: for example that Unity had been executed on Himmler's orders. It was not until December 1939 that the Redesdales, back in London, were telephoned by Janos von Almasy. He passed the receiver to Unity, who was now in a clinic in Berne. She asked her parents to bring her home. At this point they still had little idea of her condition, although Almasy's guarded manner must have been some sort of warning.

On 3 January 1940, it was reported that Unity was expected at Folkestone. Accordingly the press assembled, and something like a nightmare ensued.

Sydney and Deborah had travelled together to Berne. The clenching terror of seeing a person for the first time in hospital is always, fatally, underpinned by hope, but here it was instantly clear that there was none: Unity was alive, and that was all. She had been unable to bear anybody touching her head, and her scalp was dense with blood. Her face had collapsed into itself. Her teeth, never good, were orange. The early paralysis had worn off, however, and despite extreme vertigo she was able to walk. So the grim journey to Calais began, in an ambulance carriage attached to a train, which stopped and started continually. Every jolt sent a shot of agony into Unity's head. The family spent two nights in a hotel, surrounded by journalists. The *Daily Express* offered £5,000 for an interview. The *Evening News* reported that the special carriage had been 'supplied by Hitler'. Meanwhile David waited for three days at Folkestone, with no clue as to what he would find when he saw his daughter again.

'Elaborate precautions were taken at the harbour,' *The Times* reported, in reference to an armed guard that stood on the dock. This would later be seized upon. For now, there were other issues. As Unity was taken from the boat on a stretcher, photographers crowded in: a picture shows her holding a blanket to a face that has become suddenly old, her eyes blank yet very sad, her hair prettily combed by her mother. The ambulance that drove the family away broke down immediately, so they were forced to return to Folkestone for another night; David's suspicion of sabotage was surely correct. The car containing her luggage, fourteen pieces that had been searched at length at Calais, was also stopped by a puncture. The Redesdales, according to Nancy, had not handled it cleverly;[2] but how would they have known any other way? In all it took four days to take Unity from Berne to the cottage at High Wycombe, from where she moved to the Radcliffe Infirmary in Oxford. There the family was told that she had been well looked after and there was nothing more to be done. Time would do its best or its worst.

In fact it did both: Unity would improve, but she would never recover. Newspaper reports, however – 'Miss Mitford will probably return home in the near future in order to complete her convalescence' – gave an impression of a minor disruption to a life of wholly undeserved privilege. So it is understandable that the public reaction was not kind. This, after all, was 'the girl who loved Hitler'. Unity was already a familiar figure in the press; like a politician caught fiddling the till, she was a semi-joke – which the British love – but a joke in bad taste. When she appeared at events or marches in London, it was hot and delicious news. In 1938 she was attacked at Hyde Park Corner, where Stafford Cripps was making a speech, and gangs of Fascists and Communists began one of their usual dust-ups. Unity, who was by nature drawn to these explosions of violence, suddenly found herself its focus when her swastika was torn off. She retaliated; anti-Hitler chants began; she was attacked with punches and stones, and there was a threat to throw her in the Serpentine. Eventually a policeman and two other men shielded her on to a bus, which some of the crowd attempted to board. Such was her notoriety by this time: which she herself professed to enjoy.

Therefore when newsreel of Unity staggering from a stretcher, helped by her father, was shown in cinemas in January 1940, it was greeted with catcalls and abuse. It was said that the suicide attempt was a concocted story whereby she could evade arrest,[3] that vast sums had been spent on bringing her back to Britain. A 'fake' film was broadcast by Paramount News, a harsh satire in the modern vein, in which footage of Unity's return was accompanied by a ribald commentary in verse and by mocking shots of aeroplanes flying overhead in formation. A letter to *The Times*, apparently from a disinterested correspondent, protested against this 'degrading' production. 'They have spared no-one – even the tragic face of Lady Redesdale and close-ups of the girl herself are given, while the commentator makes unpleasant jokes.' The question of this film – and the trickier problem of Unity herself – were raised in the House of Lords. The 'elaborate precautions' at Folkestone were criticized: why had an armed guard been posted? The reply was that the guard had been there anyway, which it may well have been, and that Lord Redesdale's sole request had been for the local commandant to prevent reporters from questioning his daughter. This had been deemed reasonable, but it would later be alleged that men with 'bayonets' had come between the press and its prey. With regard to the Paramount News film, Lord Denman remarked: 'To magnify the return of Miss Unity Mitford to this country into a matter of national importance, as this film seemed to do, was really absurd.' As for the voiceover: 'Considering the unhappy plight in which she returned home, to pour ridicule on her as was done in this commentary was ... an unfair and ungenerous proceeding. The gibes at Lord Redesdale's expense, with no pity for the anxiety he obviously felt, were uncalled for.' These comments were backed by the Marquess of Dufferin and Ava: 'as an example of sadistic brutality the Unity Mitford film would be hard to beat.' And yes, one can imagine some of the reaction to this: those wretched toffs, that bunch of old Fascists, clubbing together the way that they always do. Unity, as so often, had presented a paradox. Was she more deserving of pity or opprobrium? In truth, it is still unanswerable.

In the Commons, Labour's Herbert Morrison did not let up. He asked Neville Chamberlain to detail what steps the government had taken to facilitate 'the return of this young lady to this country after she had been assisting the Nazi government'. The prime minister tried to bat him off, saying only that the US Embassy had been given a list of British subjects in Germany, including Unity, and asked to help them in any way it could. This was hardly damaging, but was so little to the point that it sounded evasive. In fact David had also had a guarantee from the Secretary of State for War that Unity would not be arrested on arrival in Britain. This was not mentioned.

Then Morrison went in for the kill. 'If this had been a working-class person, would the same thing have been done?' To which the answer is: probably not. Meanwhile Paramount News was also stoking the fires. In a letter to *The Times*, the company's general manager wrote of widespread approbation for the film. Naturally. As Oswald Mosley had quite rightly perceived, a scapegoat is a very useful thing. Referring to the infamous armed guard, the letter also asked: 'Why was Miss Mitford seemingly accorded military protection?' That 'seemingly' was a get-out – the reason for the guard's presence was unclear, however bad it looked – but the letter continued, relentless in its semi-hypocritical rectitude: 'Neutral observers might have deduced that the British persons most dear to the official mind are those who reserve their deepest admiration for Hitler.'

Parliamentary questions about Unity continued into March, when the Redesdales attempted to take her to their home at Inch Kenneth. These remote islands were part of a prohibited area, and in the House it was asked why she had been allowed to enter it. 'Is the Home Secretary aware,' came a further question in July, this time from a Scottish MP, 'that as late as June 2nd Miss Mitford was met by her father at Oban and taken to that island, and that in Scotland we are concerned as to how well-known Fascists [note the plural] can live in these islands while perfectly loyal people cannot visit their relatives?' Again, this was an understandable grievance, and it was reasonable that Unity should be forbidden this particular freedom. In fact the other Fascist banned from Inch Kenneth was Sydney, although from the wording of the question it would appear to be David. But he, having 'recanted like Latimer' (Nancy's phrase), was not deemed a security risk, which did not convince those who saw him as 'an old Nazi baron' (Esmond Romilly's phrase).

Unity, no longer trapped in vacancy but returned to perpetual childhood, was blessedly oblivious to it all. 'Oh, Boud, I have a Goat!' she wrote to Jessica in February. 'Oh Boud, I AM so sorry to be short, but will write again soon!' Yet she knew that something was wrong. She believed that doctors had made a hole in her head. 'Am I mad?' she asked repeatedly. Nancy's poignant tease of a reply – that she always had been – again raises a question that cannot quite be answered; other than to say that the *potential* for madness had always been there, and that every single circumstance had allowed it to develop.

Years later, Nancy would say that Unity's behaviour 'wasn't an embarrassment. It was a terrible sadness.'[4] When Unity asked her sister: 'You're not one of those who would be cruel to people, are you?' Nancy answered gently that she was very much against that. The family looked on helplessly as the enormous girl rampaged around the cottage in High Wycombe (described in an American magazine as 'a fabulous mansion'), as lacking in physical control as a Great Dane puppy, shouting at random, spilling her food. She wore Tom's shoes, as her feet had grown along with the rest of her. The parlourmaid Mabel, who had moved to the cottage to help Sydney look after her, recalled finding Unity in the bath, up to her neck in water, completely still. 'Now, no games with me, I said and pulled her out. She was not herself, oh no.'[5] Deborah, who lived at the house at the time, wrote a letter in which even her fearless spirit seemed subdued. The situation, she told Jessica, was 'extraordinary and awfully horrifying'.

For David, exposed not just to the ruination of his Valkyrie daughter but to the worst excesses of the press, it was almost beyond enduring. He was a private, uncertain person beneath his aristocrat's confidence, stumbling around an unfamiliar world with eyes thickened by cataracts. Uncle Matthew's jousts with journalists, his suspected taste for publicity, belonged to another man altogether; as Nancy knew only too well, when she pictured him through the light-filled prism of her imagination.

Her fictional father would move closer to reality in her last novel, *Don't Tell Alfred*, although Nancy could never quite bear to allow Uncle Matthew to give up, as David had done. He has a fine carapace of dogged bravery, but beneath it he is weary: 'he was not well-preserved. He had gone through life with one lung... I can often remember, as a child, seeing him fight to get his breath – it must have been a strain on his heart. He had known sorrow, too, which always ages people. He had suffered the deaths of three of his children and those his three favourites...' Back in 1940 the actuality of a dead child was still to come for David. But Jessica was gone, Diana had not been seen for eight years, Unity was lost – they had surely done for him, his bright daughters.

And then there was this public loathing, these accusations of Nazi sympathies. A letter to the Home Office in 1940 put the question: 'Why should British food be used to feed traitors like

Mosley, Mitford and Redesdale?' It was the sort of thing that David himself might have asked, had he not been among those tainted by the handshake of Hitler. His wife's continued sympathy for the German regime – whose very existence had reduced Unity to a dribbling, halting wreck – was untenable. He blamed Sydney for the perception that their daughter was a fraudulent invalid: she had been quoted as saying that Unity was 'recovering well'. According to Nancy, the doctors in Oxford had given her mother a degree of hope that they had denied to David.[6] This was probably true, but at the same time Sydney was protecting herself, stating publicly that Unity would get better because it was what she had to believe. Her refusal to turn against Hitler may have been part of this delusion: if only Britain could have made peace with him, instead of agitating for war, Unity would still be herself. To David, the argument presented itself the other way around. The couple had the same wrangle about it during every wireless bulletin. It is possible that Sydney was obscurely glad to defy her husband, now that their thirty-six-year marriage had reached this arid place. There was so little left of the man she had married; his splendid animal ease in his own environment had hidden a complete inability to cope outside it. David would have freely admitted that Sydney was the stronger character. If he had given his daughters their ineffable charm, their toughness came from their mother. He had dominated the family throughout the playground years of the 1920s – had behaved foolishly in business, but it hadn't seemed to matter too much; somehow he had bounced back to his magnificent self. Yet from the moment of Diana's defection he had begun to crumble. Everything he had ever done seemed wrong. Now it was Sydney who accepted each day without regrets, who took over. She cared for Unity with a saintlike patience: teaching her to crochet, giving an hour of lessons, taking her for unsteady walks, while David watched his daughter through eyes like cloudy marbles, and could not deal with what he saw. 'Muv has been *too* wonderful & absolutely given up her whole life,' as Nancy wrote to Jessica. 'Farve simply beastly, hardly goes near her.' To Sydney, he had become useless, shamefully so. Yet in a different way she was useless to him – there was no comfort to be had from that impressive, insensitive woman – and the symbol of this rupture was none other than Adolf Hitler.

In February 1940, David told Nancy that he felt he could no longer live with his wife. Sydney moved back to Swinbrook, to the stone cottage next door to the pub, beside the busily rustling mill; a very beautiful setting, a metaphorical retreat to the childhood that Unity now inhabited, just a few steps from the churchyard where she would be buried. David removed himself to Inch Kenneth, taking with him a parlourmaid named Margaret Wright, with whom he formed a close (presumably sexual) relationship. She treated him as no other woman now did, as if he were still a man of importance, and this was essential to him. He maintained a closeness to Nancy, perhaps because he intuited that she shared some of his feelings towards Sydney. For 'personal and private reasons' he resigned as director of the National Employers' Mutual General Insurance Association, the last in the succession of his many dutiful public posts, although later – as if in an act of atonement – he would pull himself together sufficiently to join the Home Guard in London. And in March he wrote to *The Times*, a long letter that was his own bewildered *De Profundis*.

> I have had, during the last few months, to put up with such a volume of publicity in certain sections of the Press, invariably followed by a flood of anonymous letters of abuse, that I am prompted to ask if you will be so generous as to allow me a short space in which to make a statement.
>
> All this has now been resuscitated by the decision of His Majesty's Government to refuse to allow me to take my daughter to my home in Scotland... It would be highly improper of me to question it. What I do resent, however, is the undoubted undercurrent of suspicion and resentment created by the publicity to which I refer...
>
> My only crime, if it be a crime, so far as I know, is that I was one

> of many thousands in this country who thought that our best interests would be served by a friendly understanding with Germany. In this, though now proved to be wrong, I was in good company… there is many a man in this country who has changed his mind on this matter since the days when the Prime Minister flew to Munich. I could not pretend that I have ever rendered this country any signal service. But I am satisfied in my own conscience that my military record is one of which I have no reason to be ashamed, and certainly today my only desire is to see the earliest possible victory for the Allies. One other matter which I find very wounding is that I am constantly described as a 'Fascist'. Now, I am not, never have been and am not likely to become a Fascist…

Reading this sincere and hopeless document, it is not hard to understand why Nancy – who knew her father's weakness, and reproached him for it, but held to the memory of his strength – offered him the gift of Uncle Matthew, with his eternal hatred of the Hun.

II

Had Unity returned to Britain hale and hearty, she might have been imprisoned under the Emergency Defence Regulations. Whether anything worse would have happened to her, it is impossible to know. The usual charges against her – that she was a friend of Hitler, an admirer of the Third Reich – did not equate to traitorous activity. But Herbert Morrison had flung out the accusation that she had assisted the enemy. Doubtless there were many who did believe that she had been some kind of agent for the Nazis. What would one have thought, as a member of the public back in 1940? Probably just that.

How much truth there would have been to such a perception is difficult to say; and this nuance, this need to draw a line between pro-Nazi sympathies and unpatriotic sentiment, between those who wanted peace with Germany and those who supported German aims, would become a peculiarly vexed, quasi-philosophical point. Of course it was not really a good time for arguing subtleties of this kind. War was not High Table. And it was quite natural, to see present guilt within past allegiances. Whether it was *justice*, to condemn outright those whose behaviour had formerly been legal, if distasteful, and now looked suddenly dangerous, is another question. But such was war. The enemy was also anybody who had ever supported the enemy.

Well: Unity had certainly done that, and in her *sui generis* position she had also been a potential conduit for information, from Germany to England and the other way about. In 1937, for instance, she had nonchalantly told the British ambassador that Hitler did not like Mussolini. And Hitler had remarked, in a recorded conversation, that the Mitford sisters 'are very much in the know, thanks to their relationship with influential people'. He had then said something else: that on one occasion, in 1939, Unity had 'exclaimed that in the whole of London there were only three anti-aircraft guns!' Diana, who was present at the time, was described by Hitler as staring at Unity 'stonily'. She was used to her sister's loose-cannon behaviour, but this was something rather more. Later, Diana was at pains to make clear that Unity was probably repeating newspaper gossip; that she was in no position to hold such lethal information in 1939. Nevertheless what Unity said teetered dangerously close to treason. Britain *was* ill prepared for war. The fact that Germany would have known that anyway was hardly the point. Perhaps it was simply the old desire to tell Hitler things that would please, with no thought to what they might really mean. Unity, in Diana's words, 'was incapable of disloyalty to England'.[7]

In April 1941, however, the Commons was again contesting this assertion. Unity had been seen in public that month at Deborah's wedding to Lord Andrew Cavendish, at St Bartholomew's church in Smithfield. Some families might have thought it politic not to have her there, but the Mitfords (and the Devonshires) were not the kind to be influenced by what 'people' might say. Unity was Deborah's sister and that was that. Ever alert, the press glimpsed a woman among the guests who put a small handbag in front of her face; like a clue in a bad detective novel, the bag was embossed with the letters 'U.M.'. So the furore started up again.

There is no question that in a photograph of the wedding, showing Unity outside the church with her old friend Mary Ormsby-Gore, she looked almost as good as new – certainly far better than her father. This was illusory, but it was understandable that a Labour MP in the House should have seized upon Unity's resumption of her social life. Now that she was 'recovered', should she perhaps be detained? Perhaps her illness would be best described as 'Quisling-itis',[8] for which the most appropriate treatment would be found on the Isle of Man, in an internment camp?

Herbert Morrison, by this time Home Secretary in Churchill's coalition government, clearly knew more about Unity's true condition and had subtly shifted stance. If her health and circumstances changed, he said firmly, then her situation would be reconsidered, but at that time it was unnecessary. 'What my honourable friend is putting to me is that I should put people I do not like under detention, and I cannot do that.' When a Conservative MP asked, disingenuously, why Morrison did not like Unity, there was a Labour heckle of: 'Hitler does.'

Another MP referred to the 'widespread feeling' among the public that Unity had been given special privileges. To this Morrison said: 'It is not a special privilege for a British citizen to be at liberty.'

A dignified reply, in the face of the urgent desire for retribution against Unity; but if she had not been damaged, if she had not replaced her love of Hitler with that for her goat, would the principle thus stated by Morrison have been upheld? At the start of the war,

Nancy had written to Deborah, saying that everybody she met asked whether their parents had been interned yet. This was Nancy in teasing-cum-righteous mode, although it was true that Lord Londonderry, that erstwhile supporter of Anglo-German fellowship, had been obliged to deny publicly his own detainment. There is something almost comical about the thought of these former appeasers, running around excitably and proving their patriotism. Sydney, however, did not do so. Quite the opposite. In October 1939 she had written to her MP to complain about attacks upon Hitler. 'Last war she would have found herself in jail,' wrote Nancy to Jessica, in a spirit of shared leftism, before going on to say that another family Fascist, Oswald Mosley, was going about his activities unchecked.

Again, with that peculiarly Mitfordian conflation of the personal and the political, Nancy – who had never liked Mosley – was now even more antagonistic. This was not just because of the war, but the war conveniently justified any dislike. Similarly, she was also both irritated and obscurely pleased by the new closeness between Sydney and Diana, who from this time on would be conjoined in a mutual loyalty and affection. Nancy stood outside that particular enclave: her relationship with her mother was what it was, and there had been no rapprochement with Diana since the publication of *Wigs on the Green*. Ordinarily she would have minded, but the outbreak of war had, in a sense, freed her from the cling of those tiresome old emotions. The resentment of her mother, the jealousy towards Diana, could be channelled into the fact that they were a pair of old Hitlerites: most satisfactory. Nancy's mood, febrile from all the dark nights at her first-aid post scribbling away at *Pigeon Pie*, was full of enjoyable fury towards anybody who was insufficiently anti-German. This did not include her husband, who had straightaway applied for a commission in the Welsh Guards. Diana's husband was a very different matter; as the authorities were all too aware.

It was pretty much true that Sir Oswald Quisling, as Nancy now called him, was still engaged upon his usual business, although he would not be for much longer. The BU fought three by-elections between the outbreak of war and May 1940, and received pitifully few votes (as *The Times* put it, Mosley's party held 'the blue riband of the deposit-forfeiting world'). Their hour was over – their old headquarters in Chelsea was attacked, as was Mosley himself – but the leader was unwilling to accept it. 'The question has been put to me why I do not cease all political activity in an hour of danger to our country,' he wrote in May, as the Germans marched towards Paris and the British retreated to Dunkirk. 'The answer is that I intend to do my best to provide the people with an alternative to the present government if, and when, they desire to make peace with the British Empire intact and our people safe.' Even as this proclamation was appearing in the BU magazine, so the government was rushing through an extremely wide-ranging Emergency Powers Act. Within it, as detailed in Regulation 18b, was the ability to detain in prison 'any particular person if satisfied that it is necessary to do so'.

Special Branch had, naturally enough, been investigating the BU since the declaration of war. It had learned a key fact: that Mosley, whose name had been carefully kept off all official documents, was involved in an agreement to broadcast from a German wireless station. There is no evidence that this was anything other than a commercial venture. Yet it could hardly have looked more suspicious; particularly when William Joyce – who had been a prominent BU member – began his propaganda speeches on German radio in the guise of 'Lord Haw-Haw'. Nancy's 'Phoney War' novel, *Pigeon Pie*, made a very good joke on this. She created a character named Sir Ivor King, a popular old English songster who is kidnapped by the Nazis and forced to make broadcasts for them. ('"Good night dears," said the old König, "keep your hairs on. By the way, where *is* the Ark Royal?"') To the authorities, however, Mosley's activities looked supremely unfunny. Eventually Special Branch reported that the BU was 'not merely a party advocating an anti-war and anti-Government policy, but a movement whose aim it is to assist the enemy in every way it can'.

Was this true? Or was it an assemblage of circumstantial bits and bobs, which when collected together looked like guilt without actually being it? Mosley had spoken in favour of a negotiated peace with Germany. From the modern perspective, which has seen the footage of Auschwitz, this seems rather dreadful. At the time it was nothing like so simple: the possibility of peace had not ended with the declaration of war. Hitler offered it several times between October 1939 and July 1940. He may not have meant it. Yet he did mysteriously order his troops to halt in France, thus allowing the evacuation at Dunkirk. In May 1940 even Churchill – by then prime minister – was discussing a negotiated peace with the War Cabinet (although that particular door was quickly closed). Meanwhile others in support included impressive men like R. A. Butler – later a friend of Sydney's – as well as the usual suspects such as Lloyd George, who admired Hitler at least as much as Mosley did and had likened giving independence to Poland to giving a monkey a pocket watch. As late as 1942 there were those who still dreamed of withdrawal from the fray, leaving the Nazis and the Soviets to get on with it.[9]

So Mosley's desire to reconcile with Germany was not outlandish. And in May 1940, even as he was still promulgating peace, he made this statement: 'However rotten the existing government, and however much we detested its policies, we would throw ourselves into the effort of a united nation until the foreigner was driven from our soil.' Many members of the BU *had* gone to fight; one of them would later be arrested in front of his men on the parade ground. (Meanwhile Esmond Romilly had been handed a white feather by his mother for having moved to America: 'if it is your sincere conviction not to come home there is nothing more to say – but if Decca is holding you back from your country in her hour of anguish remember Uncle Winston's words…') Mosley himself tried to join his old regiment. He had never preached against *fighting* the war, only against the war itself, and in this he was not alone. It is hard, therefore, to see how he could be directly accused of being a non-patriot. It would have been just as easy to say it about Sydney Redesdale, and to have her interned. The problem, of course, was not what Mosley said, but what he was. This had always been the case. He had promoted the BU as a band of disciplined men, who obeyed police commands and never initiated violence; up to a point this was true, if one accepted that any aggression was enacted against official orders. Yet the mere existence of the organization was a provocation, a challenge to democracy, and Mosley's rhetoric was a supreme exhortation to conflict. And now, not quite accurately but quite understandably, his movement was being equated with Nazism.

But could a man be detained under Regulations 18b, simply for the nebulous crime of being Sir Oswald Mosley? The threat of invasion was certainly making it desirable. Might he become Hitler's puppet dictator in Britain, a Whitehall Quisling? Was he actually working for the Germans towards that end? Irene Ravensdale was summoned to the Home Office and asked whether she had any evidence that Mosley was a Fifth Columnist. Two years earlier, before she had learned about the secret marriage to Diana, she would have done her best for him. Now personal considerations were too powerful to be overcome. Since the death of Mosley's first wife in 1933, Irene had given her life to him. She had cared for the three children of that marriage, and had even paid his share of the upkeep at Savehay – the family home in Buckinghamshire – while he chucked money at the BU. He had made a fool of her; she had been more than willing to let him, but that probably made it worse. So when the Home Office put its questions, she replied with lethal care for her words. No, she had no *evidence* against Mosley. Nevertheless: if he believed that a version of National Socialism, in conjunction with Hitler's regime, would be good for Britain, then 'he might do anything if he got angry and thought we were mucking [up] the whole thing'. An interesting sophistry, in which patriotism and treason became one and the same. 'He [her questioner] said I had given him all he wanted,' wrote Irene in her diary.

Still the Home Secretary (Morrison's predecessor, Sir John

Anderson) reported to the Cabinet that he had no power to detain Mosley under Regulation 18b. Yes, the man had met Hitler twice; there were strong rumours that Mussolini had put money into the then BUF; there was the uncomfortable fact of the radio deal, in which Germany owned more than 50 per cent of the company. And there was the great weight of all that past speechifying. Mosley was 'too clever to put himself in the wrong by giving treasonable orders', said Anderson, although that was not the end of the matter. 'Notwithstanding the absence of such evidence, we should not run any risk in this matter however small.' Rules were rules, in other words, but they could always be changed. Regulation 18b was amended to catch Mosley in its net. The government could now order the detention of members of any organization deemed 'subject to foreign influence or control', whose leaders had associated with 'any power with which His Majesty is at war'. The BU denied these accusations; nevertheless it had become inevitable that Mosley, along with some 600 members of his movement, would be detained. On 23 May he was arrested at a flat in Dolphin Square to which he and Diana had recently moved, and taken to Brixton jail. 'After Winchester,' he later said, with a throwaway gallantry that commands a certain admiration, 'prison was nothing.' His son Nicholas, who did not share his politics, later wrote: 'It was not in his nature to complain.' In a further act of defiance, Mosley passed the time – which was by definition of an unspecified duration, since there had been no trial and no sentence – in teaching himself German. He also studied psychology, by which he was unconvinced. 'The world', as he put it, 'is character.'[10]

'We were told at that time by Sir John Anderson that people were not put in prison for their opinions', Diana later said, 'and we took his word.'[11]

As Sydney Redesdale later bravely wrote to *The Observer* – which did not publish her letter – this was contrary to Magna Carta, which stated that 'no Englishman may be kept in prison without trial.' It was ironic, she suggested, that Britain had been fighting for freedoms that it did not itself uphold. This indeed was the paradox of war, and it has not gone away. 'Sir Oswald and his followers were imprisoned because they opposed the war with Germany, on which our politicians were resolved, and for no other reason at all.'[12] Of course there *were* other reasons; with the threat of invasion, a frightened and angry public could not stand to see such a man still on the march. And the BU had been an authoritarian movement, had itself sought far-reaching powers of this kind. Nevertheless Sydney was right, in that 18b was all about what had happened and what might happen, what a person represented and what they were perceived to believe, rather than the proofs that peacetime would have required. Mosley's remark about the need for scapegoats had been proved quite true. Now the scapegoat was him.

The idea that a successful German invasion would give Mosley the power he craved was almost certainly absurd. His relationship with Hitler was not strong – his admiration had mainly been for Mussolini – although in May Hitler did express the belief that 'Mosley's role hasn't run its course yet'. However, as the historian Andrew Roberts wrote: 'It is doubtful that, even if he had been prepared to serve (which is unlikely considering his orders of 9th May 1940 to fight "until the foreigner is driven from our soil"), Mosley would have been chosen to govern Britain. The BUF's dismal political record in peacetime would have left any Blackshirt ministry far too transparently a puppet government.'[13] Thirty years after the war Diana expressed the same sentiment, albeit through her particular viewpoint: 'As to the insulting suggestion that Mosley would in some way have benefited from a German occupation of England, it is enough to say that from 1932 he never ceased to press for rearmament, and that given his character and record it is impossible to imagine him as the lackey of a foreign power.'[14]

Her loyalty was astounding; one might even say magnificent. Especially so, given what her connection to Mosley would now bring upon her.

III

Like her husband, Diana was imprisoned for who she was. Like him, she was also betrayed.

Her former father-in-law, Lord Moyne, had been extremely fond of her during the marriage to Bryan Guinness. Remarkably, he had also helped her when the marriage was over. In 1935 she had driven to visit Mosley at Savehay (the day after his other mistress, Baba Metcalfe, left the house); a couple of minutes into the journey, her little Voisin car was hit by a Rolls-Royce, and she smashed through the windscreen. She was taken, half conscious and asking desperately after her dog (which was unhurt) to St George's Hospital in Hyde Park. There her wounds were stitched with coarse thread. Any woman would have been distraught about her face – a fabulously beautiful woman would have been out of her mind – but not Diana. After she was reassured about her dog, her thoughts were for Mosley; afraid that he would read about the accident in the newspapers, she insisted upon telephoning to tell him that she was all right. What saved her face was the intervention of Lord Moyne, who immediately summoned a leading plastic surgeon. When he had done his work, not a scar was left to be seen. Perhaps her father-in-law had been unable to contemplate the wreck of that Canova perfection; perhaps Bryan had urged his help; but the fact is that while Mosley went off on holiday to Italy – admittedly with his children – it was Diana's abandoned associates who had rescued her.

When war broke out, Bryan wrote to Diana: 'I am afraid this must be a time of more than ordinary difficulty and anxiety for you than for most people… your sympathy with the German regime conflicting with the great love I know you bear for your own country.' Bryan was now happily remarried to an extremely nice woman, Elizabeth Nelson, but he retained his closeness to his former wife. Obviously they had two sons together, Jonathan and Desmond, whose care they shared. But Bryan's generosity to Diana – for example he wrote to congratulate her on the birth of Alexander, her first son with Mosley – verged upon the superhuman. Anger and sadness had been apparently dissolved by his new life. Nevertheless when he met Diana by chance, fifty years after the end of their marriage, he said it was the first time he had seen her 'and not wept'.[15] Lord Moyne surely knew this, and therefore surely still burned with resentment at the anguish she had caused to his sweet-natured son. So it is hard not to think that personal vengeance was in his mind when he replayed his old trick of setting somebody to spy upon her. As he had done with private detectives back in 1932, so now he asked Desmond's governess, Jean Gillies, to report to him any signs of Nazi sympathies in the lady of the house.

In June 1940, Diana was visiting Mosley once a week at Brixton, planning to move her family to the home of Pam and Derek Jackson – Rignell House in Oxfordshire – and clearing up the muddled situation at the BU (paying wages and so on). She tried to publish the movement's magazine, *Action*, but desisted when – as she later put it – 'every time anybody started printing it, they were put in prison.' In fact the BU was now banned by the government, which was much the most sensible thing.

Although BU members were being detained en masse, Diana seems to have had no sense that she herself was under threat. Lord Moyne, however, had written a letter to the Chairman of the Defence Security Executive, a secret body headed by his friend Lord Swinton; as with the plastic surgeon summoned to Diana's hospital, Moyne was pulling vital strings. 'It has been on my conscience for some time,' he wrote, 'to make sure that the authorities concerned are aware of the extremely dangerous character of my former daughter-in-law, now Lady Mosley.' He went on to detail the evidence collected by the governess. 'It is widely believed by those who are aware of Lady Mosley's movements that her frequent visits to Germany were concerned with bringing over funds from the Nazi government' (ah, that fateful radio station). 'I also enclose a list of the dates on which

Lady Mosley went to Germany, which the governess has extracted from her diary.' Furthermore Jean Gillies – a truly valuable secret agent – reported private conversations. Mosley, she dutifully informed her employer, had said that Hitler would be justified in invading Czechoslovakia. When Belgium was overrun Diana had made 'no secret of her delight in what was happening'.

Lord Moyne was naturally genuine in his vehement anti-Nazi stance (it is a grim irony that within four years he would be assassinated by the Stern Gang, a Zionist terrorist group). So too in his fears for national security. The lawns of Sussex were rumbling with tremors from the guns in Dunkirk and Dieppe. Spies were seen everywhere, Nazis in the guise of nuns and so on. A woman named Olive Baker was charged with 'intent to assist the enemy' after sending postcards scrawled with propaganda, one which read: 'What a lot of English people are pro-German!' and was signed 'Unity Mitford'. That particular family association did not help Diana's cause.

So Moyne was doing his duty, as he saw it. But his bitterness towards Diana is palpable. The tactics employed against her read shabbily, and his report contained an alarming amount of hearsay. After reading the letter the Home Office took the view that Diana should be observed, not arrested. Lord Swinton, however, was ahead of them. Without hesitation he set in motion the order for her detention, whose co-signatory wrote to the Home Office: 'I understand that the presence of Lady Mosley at large is the subject of wide and universal comment... In view of present circumstances I do feel very strongly that this extremely dangerous and sinister young woman should be detained at the earliest possible moment.'

Put like that, it sounds unanswerable. Described in those terms, it is easy to see Diana as a terrible figure. Those pale fanatic's eyes, that appalling charisma. Far more than Mosley, she had the power to compel adoration. The fact that so many people loved her, for those characteristics of cleverness, humour, kindness, tolerance, warmth and charm that gleamed above her political beliefs – is this enough to exonerate her?

Diana had her own intricate belief system, constructed with her own fierce logic, underpinned by a refusal to repent. It made complete sense, and no sense, at one and the same time. To her, Germany was a 'success story'. Of course she said none of this at the time, having no public profile; but later she wrote: 'The economic revival of Germany under the National Socialists was speedy and impressive. Hitler's thesis, that a country's riches consist of the quality of its people *(Volk)* made him reject the idea that it was ruined... It was their work that could enrich it. Industry, agriculture and the building of a modern infrastructure absorbed the unemployed, and Germany became prosperous in a remarkably short time.'[16] This was what she admired in Hitler and his Reich, and what she believed – or wanted to believe – that Mosley could replicate in the tired, confused, bankrupt Britain of the 1930s. She wrote that 'attentive audiences listened to Sir Oswald Mosley's economic and social policy for what was then a very sick country with over two million unemployed'.[17] She despised the compromises of democracy. After the war she became an advocate of a united Europe. What she would have thought when the Eurozone began its descent into hell, the tumult that raged in noble countries like Greece, who knows: probably that Mosley should have been in charge. She believed in large solutions, grand plans, big men. The fact that such thinking carries with it the inevitable implication of destruction, including that of the civilizations that she valued so dearly, did not seem to worry her. In a part of herself, she liked it. And it was – to be frank – part of what fascinated those who fell under her spell: they bathed in the light and wondered about the darkness.

How much of this thinking was Diana's, and how much Mosley's? The quality of Diana's loyalty was such that she would continue to support his aims, long after it had become apparent that he had no political future. What she herself would have believed, had the love of Mosley not entered her soul, is impossible to say: perhaps she would still have thought all these things. More likely not. The other elements in her nature would have allowed for scepticism. She expressed a faint hint of this when, in 1966, she wrote to Deborah – always the person to whom she could speak most freely – that she had faith in Mosley as 'an outstandingly clever person who is about eighty per cent right in his ideas'. Back in 1940, there was no room for even twenty per cent's worth of doubt. Having come this far with Mosley, Diana had above all to convince herself that she had not set herself apart from society on account of a bunch of deluded buffoons in jackboots. As with Unity and the Nazis, there was a powerful sense in which she had been caught up in a *folie à deux*.

But it had been her decision to associate with the Nazis in Germany, and there is no denying that she had enjoyed it. She had glimpsed their evil and deliberately shut her eyes, even though she herself was not evil. For this she *would* later repent, although she did not do so in the full-blown confessional way that would have convinced, and few really believed her. Meeting Hitler ruined her life, she would say, and that of her husband. It is difficult to understand how so intelligent a woman could not have foreseen this at the time. What she had thought would happen – whether she had believed that there would be no war with Britain, or that Germany would help to advance her husband's career – is another imponderable. In her way, again like Unity but without the madness, she had seen herself as playing a part in politics, the old-fashioned woman's part that cajoles and suggests, that achieves by flattery. *She* had been flattered, by the regal, sidelong position in which she had been placed by men of power. It was such a bizarre and interesting deployment of her beauty, which made its own rules. That, she had probably been unable to resist.

Perhaps some natural law decrees that if a woman is given every single gift, the Wicked Fairy at the christening must also have her say. One cannot help but wish that it had been otherwise, and that Diana had channelled all that she had in some other direction. The editor of her collected writings later wrote, astutely: 'If Britain liked intellectuals in the way France does, she might have wanted to be one'[18] – that indeed was what she most naturally was, albeit of the radical tendency.

If she herself ever thought this way, that she had taken a fundamental wrong turning, she would never have admitted it. Her own choices had brought their consequences, and she dealt with them like the person that she was: one in a million, for good and for ill.

In October 1940, she was questioned like all other detainees by the Advisory Committee, which met at a hotel in Ascot. Its chairman was Norman Birkett, for whom Tom Mitford had once worked as a junior barrister. One of the members sent Diana a bottle of claret for her lunch. There was a sense, still, behind the formalities, of Diana being treated in a particular way because of who she was – 'lovely *One*'; except that it was precisely because of who she was that she was there at all. Diana was not the only woman interned under Regulation 18b. But she was the most notable, and she suffered correspondingly. Whether one likes it or not, a woman will always be blamed more than a man for the same transgression, unless she seeks forgiveness in appropriate self-abasing style. That is the way of the world. And Diana, who looked so feminine, was indeed beautiful to a degree that would have aroused great envy, scorned to conduct herself in a manner appropriate to these looks. She was forbidding, restrained, 'masculine' in her self-containment. To the public she was a hate figure, as only a woman can be. She was exposed to the equivalent of today's Twitter mob (#bangupmosleybitch). The Advisory Committee would have been all too aware that Diana risked physical attack if she were freed. House arrest at Rignell was an option, but it would have been so deeply unpopular. As Diana spoke, she knew this.

Her interrogation was a long one, and her brave, cool answers are extraordinary, oddly reminiscent of Anne Boleyn some four hundred years earlier, who had also been found guilty of crimes framed to achieve that particular end. Diana 'made no pretence of being anything other than contemptuous,' wrote Nicholas Mosley. In one exchange she was asked whether Hitler was still a friend of hers. She replied: 'I have not seen him for some time.'

'Absence makes the heart grow fonder. Do you still entertain the same feeling for him?'

'As regards personal and private friendship, of course I do.'

'Did you hear the bombs last night? That is Mr Hitler, as we suggest. Does that kind of thing make any difference to you – the killing of helpless people?'

'It is frightful. That is why we have always been for peace.'

She was asked about the proposed radio station, and her answers were convincing with regard to its purely commercial intent. The damage, as far as the Committee was concerned, was rather the way in which the concession had been won: because she was so close to Hitler.

'Did you convey to him,' she was asked, 'the idea that you were rather sympathetic towards his point of view?'

'Well, yes, I was.'

'That is quite honest. And therefore you conveyed that idea to him?'

'Yes, I suppose so.'

'That was rather siding with him against this country?'

'No, of course not.'

'It was rather saying, "My country is in the wrong"?'

'Not my country. I absolutely differentiate between my Government and my country.'

How remarkable she was! Whatever one thinks of what she said, one can hardly deny her that. Similarly, when asked whether Hitler was somebody who could be trusted, she replied: 'We should not put ourselves in a position where we should have to trust.' And the Committee, compelled by her despite itself, as so many people were, was forced to say: 'You are exceedingly intelligent on these matters… you do betray, in the real sense of the word, an intelligent view about these things.' Doubtless they had expected something like Diana's fearless display, the image of glacial superiority that she presented; nevertheless it must have impressed them, and perhaps confirmed the belief that she could indeed be dangerous. But she was unable to behave otherwise. She would not deny what seemed to her the truth. In fact she seems almost to have taken pleasure in making it sound worse than it was; certainly that is the impression, as if Diana were conducting a perverse and deadly Mitford tease. Yes, she had liked Himmler. With regard to the reports she had read about the Gestapo: 'I did not believe them very much.' Yes, she knew Streicher. 'He is a very simple little fellow… I do not know that he is as bad as he is made out to be.' No, she was 'not fond of Jews'. This was in contradiction of the fact that she had a number of good Jewish friends. Of course she did not then know all that would happen to the Jews. Years later she would write to Deborah that Hitler was 'a part of history, a terrible part, but important'.[19] Yet to have said what she did in 1940 is a self-indictment: the irreducible part of Diana that cannot be explained or excused.

To the Committee, she refused to move beyond her stated position that Britain should negotiate peace with Germany, that the retaking of German 'colonies' had been Hitler's right. Asked why he had then marched on to Belgium, she replied in her unmistakeable, unshakeable Mitford voice: 'Hitler does not want Belgium. If you have ever been to Belgium, you will know it is a horrible place. It is just because they have to have the ports to fight on.' When the war was over, she said, Western Europe would again be free. Her belief that the East would fall into the hands of the Soviets, which would be a bad thing, was indeed correct.

Expressing herself as she did, there was no sense in which Diana could 'win' her arguments, yet she did score one intriguing victory. Do you, she was asked, 'have a great contempt for democracy?'

'Yes.'

'And so has Hitler?'

'Yes.'

'How can you say then that he admires this country, which is a democratic country?'

'Because he admires England tremendously for its general characteristics.'

'But I should have thought the characteristics of this country for years were democratic?'

'I do not think it was democratic when we got the Empire and so on. We did not go to the Negroes and say, "Look here, you vote to have your rulers." We went and took bits of the world.'

'I see what you mean...'

Diana's argument against her detainment was extremely straightforward. What she and her husband believed was not the issue. Now that the BU was banned, and therefore neither she nor Mosley had any propaganda vehicle, there was no reason to detain them. They had no desire for a German victory over Britain, and would never do anything to advance this: 'my husband is the most tremendous patriot and adores his country. I feel it very strongly.' And she was right, which made not the slightest difference. What she represented to Britain was something unacceptable. This was the other side of the issue, the public view. Two days after the hearing, the Committee wrote that she was 'an attractive and forceful personality' – quite true – who 'could be extremely dangerous if she were at large': most unlikely. It was also suggested that 'the views of Hitler on the British statesmen have been to some extent coloured by the views put forward by Lady Mosley.' Diana admitted to discussing Churchill with Hitler (and vice versa), although what she had said – that Churchill was 'hurrying on with our armaments as much as he can' – was hardly in the realms of treachery.

The most succinct exchange came when the Committee asked Diana why she thought she had been detained. She replied: 'It was because I had married Sir Oswald Mosley.'

But there was more, as she later came to believe. It was also because she was the sister of Unity Mitford. The 'crimes' of which Diana was accused were more truly Unity's; the questions she had been asked would have been more aptly put to Unity – but Unity, who had always been vulnerable in a way that Diana was not, had escaped a public trial and sentence. Therefore Diana had to endure it for her. This was not something that could be proved; nevertheless there is a logic to it. When the desired scapegoat is elusive, another must be found in its place. And so because of who Diana was, who her husband was, who her sister was, she was transported away from

Ascot, back to Holloway jail. 'My darling Boud,' she wrote to Unity in December, 'We have just been told that we may write one extra letter (for Christmas) so of course I shall use mine to you.' Unity replied: 'Oh Nard, I do so HOPE you had a lovely and beautiful Christmas, I prayed about it a terrific lot.'

IV

When Diana was first taken to Holloway, on 29 June, she had just finished packing up at Savehay, where she and Mosley had moved after the disposal of Wootton at the end of 1939. Now Savehay was to be requisitioned in two days' time, and she was preparing to go to Pam's house. She was sitting in the garden, reading, beside the pram that held Max, her eleven-week-old baby. When the police arrived, she was told that she could take Max to Holloway with her. She thought it better not. She was also told that she would probably be detained only for forty-eight hours: this was said to most of those arrested under Regulation 18b. On the way to London she asked the car to stop so that she could buy a breast pump, in order to resume feeding the baby when she returned.

Holloway was a terrible place for any woman. One can hardly say that it was worse for Diana because she was used to a life of comfort, extreme cleanliness, good food and beautiful things around her, but the shock of transplantation would have been extreme: like being kidnapped. The first four hours after admission were spent in a metal cage measuring four feet by four with a wire-mesh roof. Then she was locked in a dark cell with one tiny window blocked by rotting sandbags. There was no bed, just a mattress and some dirty blankets.

This was E wing, which also contained the execution shed. It was so damp that the mattresses were soaked through. Diana sat all night with her back against the brick wall. Almost immediately she realized that she would not be leaving in two days.

The physical effect of having been torn, almost literally, from her baby was an expression of the emotional torment: her breasts were excruciating and she was terrified to touch them, for fear of the dirt. She was told to wash down the prison landing, but could not move her arms. Another prisoner helped her. From the first, her status singled her out, and made her something of a heroine with the other BU women in the jail (Mosley held the same position at Brixton). Some of the warders sought to belittle her, remarking that it was all a bit different to what she was used to, eh? She would smile at their jibes in the Mitford way, which denied the concept of shame.

But the sudden enclosing horror of it all, and the knowledge that there was no sense of when it would end, was almost beyond imagining. As she would put it: 'Those who have not been in prison can scarcely imagine how revolting are the lavatories, how uneatably disgusting the food, how freezing the cells in winter, what complete nonsense the idea that prisoners are being trained for a trade, or fitted for life outside, or that anything at all is being done except to degrade their bodies and unutterably to bore and depress their minds.' The state, as she perceived, preferred to lie to itself about the redemptive powers of prison: 'the ponderous machinery of English hypocrisy is always set in motion when anything "unpleasant" is under discussion, whether it be sex, or crime, or capital punishment, or just the diet of some poor wretch condemned to sit for a stretch in one of HM Prisons.'[20] This was a typical Diana sentence, in which the natural Mitford clarity of thought is tuned up by her particular quality of rigour; it is the kind of writing that makes one wish, rather passionately, she had not deployed her citrus-sharp brain on justifying the darkly indefensible.

The sanitation at Holloway was indeed a disgrace: 'one never stopped dreading the lavatory,' she later wrote to Deborah. One outside privy was marked with a red cross, for use only by those with venereal disease; more than once sewage flooded the stone floor. Meals, which were served with the pudding on the plate alongside the main course, included a fish pie that even the prison cats could not eat, although Diana found the corned beef 'delicious'. The cocoa was covered with a layer of grease, which the women used for face cream. They also borrowed books in red bindings from the library, rubbed the cloth with their fingers and transferred the colour to their lips. These small vanities were essential. 'One of the saddest sights in prison,' wrote Diana, 'was the piebald heads, with a few inches of golden, crimped hair hanging down below the black, brown or sometimes grey.'[21]

Soon she was transferred to F wing, along with the other internees, and this was better. The women were allowed to wear their own clothes. There was a small kitchen, in which they would fry up tiny potatoes found in the garden; they were also permitted to order in small amounts of food and in one letter Diana, whose standards remained refined, asked Pamela to send her some dill. The cells were very dark, especially during air raids, so there was no possibility of reading after lights out. Nevertheless books were a great solace. In prison, as Diana said, 'The need is for either beauty, wit and elegance, or for what the Germans call "*das Erhabene*" (which can be more or less translated as "the sublime").'[22] Where others might have sought mindless escapism, Diana read Racine. Mosley sent her a whole Stilton, and for weeks she lived on this, together with a small glass of port. She received one half-hour visit per fortnight, usually from her mother, who would later bring Deborah, and Diana's children. At first she was allowed just two letters a week, and these were from Mosley. If he felt any guilt about the pass to which he had helped bring his wife, he did not show it, but neither would she have wanted that – far better was his cheerful encouragement: 'You are such a brave and wonderful Percher.' (This nickname came from the magnificent white Percher horses, which Mosley thought she resembled; tellingly implying strength as much as beauty.)

A very early letter had come from Gerald Berners, perfect in his lightness and loyalty, never remotely embarrassed about Diana's situation. He had written to ask whether he should perhaps send a peach containing a small file? The Home Office kept the letter for months.

When the restriction on post was lifted in August, Deborah – equally immune to the notion of shame – wrote: 'Oh, I do long to see your cell.' Deborah's world at this time was a lesser hall of hell, despite her engagement to Andrew Cavendish. She was living at the Swinbrook cottage with Unity, who had taken possession of the small sitting room and had conceived an irrational dislike of Deborah ('she *so* hates me'). To be normal within such a family was a strange situation indeed. The bright good humour of Deborah's letters is therefore all the more impressive, although she later condemned herself for selfishness, saying that her thoughts at that time were almost wholly with Andrew, and very little with her sister and mother. At the age of sixty Sydney moved doggedly back and forth between Swinbrook and Holloway, where the buses stopped to the conductor's cry of 'Lady Mosley's suite!' (good old English humour, nothing like it). Diana's admiration for her mother now hardened, as the true quality of Sydney's character revealed itself. On one occasion she did break: she confessed that she was at her wits' end with Unity. 'And you, Diana darling, who could do something with her, locked in here…' But it was a brief moment of weakness. Generally, all was strength. She sent warm clothes; she put money on account to be spent in Harrods: *malgré tout* these women remained who they were. She wrote repeatedly to MPs about her daughter's imprisonment without trial. The question of 18b was raised in the House by some of its braver members. Churchill was also increasingly uneasy; he asked for the detainees' conditions to be improved (and for Diana to have a daily rather than a weekly bath, a concession that amused her for its naïvety. Such a thing was impossible in Holloway).

But to be jailed with no notion of when one will be freed is a peculiarly refined kind of torture. Hope remains – perhaps this will be the day? – then as the day passes, and nothing changes, hope becomes merely a mockery. When the bombs fell on London in 1941, and thirty-eight incendiaries exploded in the grounds of Holloway jail, what Diana minded was the noise; the possibility of death was an irrelevance. What she had said to the Advisory Committee, that she did not think a woman in her situation would be imprisoned in Germany, was a bad joke (as she surely knew). Yet her words were powerful: 'I am sure they would never take a woman from a tiny baby.' This separation without end, not just from Max but from her three other sons, was endured in the knowledge that other BU women with young children had been released by Christmas 1940. She spent a night in her cell, waiting for news, while Jonathan was taken to hospital for an emergency appendectomy: permission to see him was denied by the Home Office. Alexander, aged two, was brought to see her; he 'often had to be forcibly dragged away from Diana, his tears soaking her clothes'.[23] After a visit, his nanny wrote that Alexander 'enjoyed his day I am sure but the time was far too short. He keeps saying "Mummy today".' Whatever Diana had done – and she had done nothing, really, except be who she was – this was surely itself a kind of evil? The children spent time with Bryan at Biddesden but in the main were cared for by Pam, who took them in with their nanny. In one letter Diana wrote asking her sister to give 'Miss Gillies' her love.

After eighteen months the nanny moved with the boys to Diana's former home, Swinbrook House, in which they stayed as paying guests (they also visited Deborah, where Alexander and Max told her 'not to talk at table'). For Diana this was a relief; many years later she wrote to Deborah of how she had dreaded Pam's letters. Pam seemed unable to perceive what Diana was suffering, separated from her children. On one occasion she boasted merrily of taking Alexander for a walk through a field full of thistles. 'It's not her fault, she doesn't like babies.' She also wrote, quite as if giving normal news, of having Diana's beloved dog and mare put down. 'It would have been better *not* to tell me about the animals.' This was not cruelty on Pam's part; she had offered to have the children, which in itself was a kindness. She was not spiteful, nor capable of the kind of glancing darts shot by Nancy or Jessica (although Diana later said that her children would have been better off in Nancy's care). Pam was deficient in imagination, which was strikingly unlike the rest of the sisters. Her muted obtuseness had begun in childhood, partly due to her attack of infantile paralysis, and no doubt also to Nancy's brittle teasing. It would have helped her to cope with Derek, now in the RAF and flying night raids over Germany with his usual brusque efficiency ('he behaved much as he had on the racecourse,' wrote Deborah). It made her unaware of what she was doing to Diana. It was not until more than thirty years later that she suddenly said to her sister: 'I'm afraid I wasn't always kind to Nanny & the boys.'

It is perhaps inappropriate to say that Diana showed bravery in prison, given that there was nothing she could do but live through what was happening to her. Yet her spirit was unbowed: a very Mitford quality. They *were* brave women. They passed through calamitous events and remained themselves. Even Unity did, in so far as she was able. This was Sydney's nature, although not David's. Much of the fascination of the Mitford girls lies in this indestructible sense of *One* that they carried so lightly. Even the image of Diana in jail does not convey abasement or ugliness; rather a tall, straight, undiminished figure, glowing with the fervency of outrage.

She had spoken a little scathingly of Churchill to the Advisory Committee – 'He is more interested in war than anything in the world' – yet it was he, more than anybody, who was working on her behalf. Baba Metcalfe, a less bitter woman than her sister Irene, had approached Churchill to ask if something might be done for Mosley, who was declining physically. Tom Mitford, now a serving officer in the King's Royal Rifle Corps, also sent a message to Churchill through his son Randolph. Tom had visited Diana several times in Holloway and knew what she wanted more than anything except freedom: to be imprisoned with her husband.

Whether impelled by family loyalties, or a sense that justice required him to do so, in November 1941 Churchill sent a letter to Herbert Morrison. 'Feeling against 18b is very strong,' he wrote. 'Sir Oswald Mosley's wife had now been 18 months in prison without the slightest vestige of any charge against her, separated from her husband.' Morrison felt unable to order the Mosleys' release, given how strongly the public wanted them to remain in jail. Nevertheless he did what he could: the order was given that the fifteen couples held under 18b be transferred to married accommodation. A separate block at Holloway, formerly the parcels office, was prepared to receive three of these couples, including the Mosleys.

Diana's husband moved in with her on 20 December. She later wrote that 'one of the happiest days of my life was spent in prison'. The two years that they would then spend together in the Parcels House, growing vegetables, occasionally having their children to stay, fused their marriage into indissolubility. Out in the world, Mosley had been a rover and a bounder. Now, in this little island of domesticity within the cold clutch of Holloway, he was Diana's only. She had seen off all the competition: the Curzon sisters, the army of Blackshirts. And Mosley was a good companion, full of jokes and kindness towards the woman whose life he had destroyed.

Although it was he who had given cause for jealousy, it is not surprising that he was the one who displayed it: Diana would never have been unfaithful, but Mosley knew exactly what most men thought of her, and there was surely a sense for him, too, of holding her captive at last. This possessiveness would grow stronger after their release. It had already been made apparent, as Diana suggested many years later, when she wrote to Deborah that her husband had perhaps felt safer when she was living at Wootton, away from all her adoring friends. Indeed her removal in 1936 to that house in Staffordshire, beautiful though it was, had marked an end to her London life (Germany was another matter). Yet to Deborah she wrote that, such was her love for Mosley, 'I look back on Wootton as a dream of happiness.'

In its way, it *was* a great love story. And in jail these two remarkable people were bonded as few couples are: by separation from the outside, by an intensity of shared suffering, by a knowledge of their pariah status. Diana's love for the man who had taken her down with him was now absolute. Any choice about that, had she wanted one, was gone. Another woman might still have reneged on him, but that was not her nature. Instead she went the other way and dedicated herself to him even more completely. It was Mosley's greatest triumph, this subordination of his wife. For Diana, it had to have been worth it. Otherwise, what had it all been for?

V

What Diana did not know, and would not know for another forty years, was that another person had been involved in her betrayal to the authorities.

Probably these private interventions – as made by Lord Moyne – made no difference. Once Mosley was detained, it was perhaps an inevitability that Diana would be too. But Nancy had not been sure of this, back in May 1940, when she wrote to her friend Mark Ogilvie-Grant: 'I am thankful Sir Oswald Quisling has been jugged aren't you but I think it quite useless if Lady Q is still at large.'

And so Nancy, still high on her particular cause, did her bit to ensure that Diana would be detained by ringing influential acquaintances, including Gladwyn Jebb at the Foreign Office. When Diana was arrested, Nancy may have believed that this was her own doing. The following day she was summoned to an interview with Jebb. The jolt of reality might have led her to pull back, to speak in Diana's defence, but instead she did her very best to ensure that there was no early release or house arrest for her sister. Diana, she told Jebb, was 'an extremely dangerous person': that phrase again. She 'advised him to examine [Diana's] passport', to see how often her sister had been to Germany. Nancy had known that Diana went to Berlin, but not that these visits were usually to discuss the radio station; she would anyway have put a sinister interpretation upon that deal. One can picture the scene, the distinguished questioner in his stately, secretive office, the elegant woman in her patched-up clothes, sipping from the Crown Derby and speaking in her quick, light drawl the words that would condemn. 'Not very sisterly behaviour,' she wrote to Violet Hammersley, 'but in such times I think it one's duty?' The question mark suggests a faint desire for reassurance. Yet the mere fact of confession implies a belief that she was right. Everybody was suffering because of men to whom Diana had played the silken confidante; why therefore should she not have her own term of trial?

Nancy had done precisely what she threatened to her mother, when she wrote that she would 'join hands with the devil himself to stop any further extension of the disease [of Fascism]'. So had she acted out of principle? Was this her answer to the sisters who had fallen into the arms of ideology – that she should embrace non-ideology with the same fervour, and act to destroy what she saw as her own enemy? It is possible. Nancy also suggested that Pam and Derek Jackson should be kept under observation, given their Fascist tendencies. They were, she told Jebb, 'anti-Semitic, anti-democratic and defeatist'. Given Derek's RAF exploits and Pam's apolitical nature, this was nonsense; but perhaps Nancy believed it.

There is no doubt that she was fierce in the matter of the war. 'The huns must be fought,' as the heroine of *Pigeon Pie* put it. Like any Londoner Nancy was in the thick of it, trying to laugh to scorn the bombs that were shredding her nerves, doing her stint for the war effort. After working at the first-aid post she took a job finding holiday billets for ARP workers, and later served as a fire-watcher. In October 1940 she moved back to Rutland Gate with her father – her

Maida Vale home was dangerously close to the target of Paddington Station – and had the care of a number of Polish Jews ('my sweet refugees'). She loved this, of course. It enraged her mother so much. Sydney, she claimed in a letter to Violet Hammersley, had refused to live at the house after the Jewish evacuees had been there. Then she added: 'Exaggerated?' Surely yes, by Nancy herself. Her mother did complain about the dirt at Rutland Gate, which was absurd and unfair in the circumstances. But then Sydney was living under near-intolerable pressure. They all were. Given Nancy's run-ragged days and sleepless nights ('oh dear there are the sirens again what a horrid life'); her fears for Peter in France and for Tom Mitford, her comrade in war service; her sadness when she contemplated her father, who agonized still over his brief alliance with the enemy; her memories of the pitiful refugees in Spain and the militaristic chaotic horror of the Blackshirt meeting at Olympia – given all this, it may be that she was genuine in her motives when she informed on her sisters. She may have seen herself in the position of somebody who, today, fears that a family member has jihadi sympathies. What does such a person do? Society expects them to inform. If they put personal considerations first, they are politically complicit.

In a way, the fact that Nancy also informed on the Jacksons is her 'alibi' for the crime of denouncing Diana. Otherwise one might have suspected her of pure and glinting spite. Actually, one *does* suspect her. The alibi was probably of her own making, a means to deceive her conscience. The Jacksons were not going to be sent to jail; for Diana, however, the consequences of betrayal were great, and Nancy knew this. Had she been writing about herself in a novel, she would have made it all too clear that those who purport to act out of principle are rarely as noble as they think they are – take Lord Moyne, for instance, with his little Jane Eyre spy and his friends in high places. In a novel, Nancy would have mocked him, and herself, with a delicate ironic sorrow. But life does not always welcome that kind of clear-sightedness. Otherwise Nancy would have recognized that few people could have done what she did. Jessica, perhaps; after the gift of baby clothes sent by Diana, she turned against her sister for good. The fact that she did not do this with Unity confirms the idea that Diana received all the hatred in Unity's stead, simply because of who she was: invulnerable, glorious, enviable. With Diana, always, it was personal. The emotions that she aroused in people were so dreadfully strong. For Nancy, the twin power within the Mitford sisters, they were a powerful aperitif of affinity, respect, resentment; above all of jealousy. 'I think', said Deborah, 'that Nancy was jealous of Diana all her life.'[24] There had been mutual anger over the publication of *Wigs on the Green*, which had not dispelled in the intervening five years. Diana had expected her sister to abandon the book, and the much needed money that it might bring, in case what she wrote offended the damn Leader. Nancy had expected Diana to come to herself and laugh about it, even the digs against divorced women. The way in which they reacted to the rupture was typical: Diana, instantly withdrawn and unmoving, Nancy similarly stubborn yet uneasy beneath her cascade of defensive jokes. ('I saw Diana at a lunch,' she wrote to Mark Ogilvie-Grant in 1935, 'she was cold but contained & I escaped with my full complement of teeth, eyes etc.')

But this wrangle held so much more for Nancy, after all those years of growing up with that beautiful, unchanging, calmly smiling face in one's midst. How hard it would have been, dealing with such a sister! Without lifting a finger Diana had compelled admiration from those whom Nancy wanted for herself: Evelyn Waugh, Robert Byron. And there were other things, more difficult still. Nancy had miscarried a few weeks before the birth of Alexander in 1938. This wretched piece of timing happened again in 1940, when Max was born. She was obliged to swoon over Diana's sons (whom she did in fact adore) even as she suffered those sad, bloody little endings. 'Fancy favourite aunt how blissful' she wrote to Diana in Holloway, having connived at the separation of these children from their mother. Even Diana's relationship with Mosley – ridiculous though he appeared to Nancy – revealed the aridity of her marriage to

Peter Rodd. How, then, to resist delight, when Mosley was toppled like the statue of a fallen dictator, and dragged Diana through the jeering crowds behind him? She could have done, of course; but she chose not to.

This was the central relationship of the Mitford girls, this push-and-pull between Nancy and Diana. For Nancy, denunciation was a means to even the score with one quick, almighty stroke. Yet it seems that the first attempt had not quite achieved her aim: in November 1943, when the Mosleys were released under house arrest, Nancy strode briskly into MI5 to tell them that the Home Secretary's decision was wrong. Diana, she reminded them, sought 'the downfall of England and democracy generally'. It is impossible that she should have believed this, although many others did. There was a public uproar after the release, as nasty in its way as Nancy's scheming. A crowd marched in Trafalgar Square, carrying Mosley's crude effigy hanging from a gibbet. By now they could not plead a legitimate fear of invasion: this was merely and grossly vengeful, like the ludicrous press stories about the Mosleys' personal maid, about their private supply of coal, about a fashion show staged for Diana's benefit. On one occasion Mosley sued for libel and won the case (the proceeds were spent on a fur coat to protect Diana from the desperate Holloway cold). More usually the Home Office was obliged to deny the stories. They need not have bothered, as everybody had made up their minds. The Mosleys were in the position of today's 'sexual predators': no argument about proofs or degrees of guilt was possible.

Nor would the public believe the main reason for the Mosleys' release, which was their state of health. Mosley had recurring phlebitis and, despite his staunch efforts to maintain fitness, had lost almost fifty pounds in weight. Diana was skeletal and white, with a low body temperature and feeble pulse. She became too ill even to play with her children when they visited. During an apparently incurable attack of gastric flu, she fell into a deep coma for four or five days when a fellow internee, the former BU member Major de Laessoe, cluelessly medicated her with an opium pill ('one would have felt so awful for the poor Major if one had died'). Take castor oil, said the prison doctor, if it happens again. But Churchill was deeply uneasy about the prolonged imprisonment without trial. Sydney had visited his wife Clementine (who, in another life, had been bridesmaid at her wedding to David Mitford) to make a last desperate appeal. Soon afterwards, a medical report was sent to the Home Office, suggesting that to keep Mosley in jail for another winter might lead to his death and subsequent martyrdom. Herbert Morrison, nervous of his party, remained against the release. Nevertheless Churchill persuaded the Cabinet; it was back to the conundrum of what was Britain fighting for if not justice, even for the vilified; although these arguments meant little to a public worn down by bombs and bereavements. It is quite astonishing, at this remove, to consider what the government braved by releasing this couple, who would surely have been hated less had they been devoid of physical glamour. As it was they loomed like two great waxworks in the collective imagination: the pale-eyed Nazi bride and the rapacious Dracula, who could be pictured without rage only when contained within their cells. Once sprung from jail they provoked abusive mail, protests from the TUC, an angry debate in the House, and an open letter from Jessica to Churchill that read: 'The release of Sir Oswald and Lady Mosley is a slap in the face of anti-fascists in every country and a direct betrayal of those who have died for the cause of anti-fascism.' Nancy, no stranger to deceit, remonstrated with Jessica for writing what she did.

In the face of this, it is easy enough to see why Diana clung to Mosley as her companion in dishonour, and why she found such precious treasure in her mother's loyalty: the quality that she came to value above all others. There was no logic to this public opprobrium. It simply served a purpose of expiation. Britain had suffered, and to attack those it had branded as traitors made it feel better. Let them suffer too. It was human nature, like Nancy's *et tu Brute* betrayal. Nancy, said Diana many years later, 'was the most disloyal person I ever knew'.[25] In that sense, assuredly, the women could not have been more different. Yet in other ways they were very much alike, and recognized each other as such. Nancy, like Diana, could behave with great warmth and kindness. Both were abundant in humour, intelligence and imagination. Within them lay a well of emotions that went deeper than in the other sisters (except Unity?), a passionate capacity to feel, an inability to put up barriers without some cost to themselves. Nancy did not present the same mystery as Diana; she was deeply complex, 'a very curious character' as her mother put it; but she could be explained. Yet both sisters did things that cannot be excused.

Back in 1941 they were exchanging kindly letters: Holloway had, at least, healed the breach caused by *Wigs on the Green*. Nancy's jealousy or rage against Diana had been assuaged by her act of treason, which would need to be repeated after the release from Holloway. Diana gave her sister money with which to buy herself presents – stockings, a Guerlain lipstick – 'it brings tears to the eyes,' wrote Nancy, probably sincerely. In November 1941 Diana arranged for grapes to be sent to the University College Hospital in London, where Nancy had been admitted after being seized with agonizing stomach pains during a stay with friends in Oxford. It was an ectopic pregnancy; her condition was serious and required immediate surgery. She begged the surgeon to preserve her fertility, but awoke from the anaesthetic to be told that her fallopian tubes had been removed. 'Therefore,' she wrote to Diana, 'I can never now have a child.'

To her mother, Nancy had confessed that she could not bear the thought of the scar. 'But darling who's ever going to see it?' It was also at this time that a doctor asked Nancy whether she had ever been infected with syphilis, and Sydney admitted to having employed a nursery maid who had had the disease. As ever with Nancy, the truth of what she wrote is hard to establish. Yet there is a powerful sense of a failure of sympathy in her mother: this, surely, she did not entirely invent. It was absurd, but not entirely incomprehensible, that Nancy thereafter blamed her mother for her inability to carry a child to term.

The baby had not been Peter Rodd's. He had been posted to Addis Ababa, so how she would have explained any new arrival is an imponderable. Despite Nancy's best efforts to admire her husband for his instant plunge into war service, he had thrown her attempts right back at her. On his leaves in London he would dance smartly past his wife to an ARP post run by Nancy's cousin, Adelaide Lubbock. This affair was almost certainly going on when Nancy fell pregnant back in 1940, but juggling females had never posed a problem to Peter.

Nancy believed in marriage as an institution, and tried to have faith in her own for longer than she probably should have done. To Violet Hammersley she wrote that she would struggle on with her 'wretch' of a husband, despite the friends who urged her to leave. She was made very unhappy by Peter's behaviour; it is not necessary to love somebody to suffer from their infidelity. She had tried to be a good wife, but she lacked the calm insouciance that might have brought Peter closer to heel and her sharp, crackling asides did not naturally endear her to men – not, at least, as a mate. Nevertheless Peter betrayed her, as surely as she did Diana. He drained her, not merely emotionally but financially. As ever she was very poor, and Peter very profligate with what little money they had. Nancy's allowance from David had been cut (he was rather broke also); the death of her father-in-law had stopped that particular source of income; and the money from her husband came erratically. Always thin, Nancy became spare, living only on a kind of hysterical adrenalin. 'My hair is going quite grey,' she wrote to Mrs Hammersley in late 1940, in a letter whose subtext seethes with the pain of her marital failure. 'I feel older than the hills [she was thirty-six] – not a bit young any more isn't it horrid and my own life has honestly ceased to interest me which must be a bad sign.'

Nancy reached a kind of nadir at this point. *Pigeon Pie* had been a failure. It was a joke on the Phoney War, which by the time of the book's publication was over. By 1940 people really did not want to read that 'countries were behaving like children in a round game, picking up sides'. Yet it is an entrancing novel, and can be seen as a transition between the chilly, faintly forced satire of Nancy's first three books and the benevolent natural flow of what came after; starting with *The Pursuit of Love* in 1945. The tone of *Pigeon Pie* is authentic Mitford, relaxed and chatty and cool. The heroine, Lady Sophia Garfield, is a delightful creation. She yearns to be a spy but finds herself temperamentally unsuited to the work: it is not her nature to leave her house on a top-secret mission 'after she had had her bath and changed her clothes'. This is the sort of remark that only Nancy could make with such bright and frivolous honesty. It was part of her gift to write the things that women think but do not bother, or dare, to express. And, as she would often do, Nancy used Sophia as a conduit for the easy worldly wisdom that she herself found so hard to achieve. Faced with a difficult man, a slightly more satisfactory Peter, Sophia behaves with all the innately feminine calm that Nancy could not conjure in reality. When her lover shows interest in another woman, 'Sophia saw that she must look out. She knew very well that when a man is thoroughly disloyal about a woman, and at the same time begins to indulge in her company, he nearly always intends to have an affair with that woman.' Too true. So Sophia, vexed but unfazed, tells her lover that she is dining with another man: 'he must be taught a lesson.' It was something that Nancy also needed to learn, as she knew all too well.

By the time the book had died, it seemed that the avatar of Sophia had become an irrelevance. Peter was not there to be handled and beguiled. Anyway he no longer even wanted to be. Yet Nancy *had* been taught something by *Pigeon Pie*, although it probably did not seem that way to her. She had primed her authorial voice for the next subject, which would be the re-creation of the ruined Mitford family: an imagining of the past that would give her a future. And, more subtly, she had identified in Sophia a philosophy that would sustain her. 'Sophia had a happy character and was amused by life': simple words, but they would become Nancy's creed, her version of Voltaire's 'I have decided to be happy, because it is better for my health', and she would hold to it as firmly as Diana and Jessica did to their ideological causes. It was not yet possible, as the bombs fell – 'Ten hours is *too* long, you know of concentrated noise & terror in a house alone' – and the image of Peter with Mrs Lubbock pranced grimly round her head, together with who knows what thoughts of the wreckage of her family. But it would become so, even though in many ways life became much worse, from March 1941.

It was then that Nancy wrote to Violet Hammersley, casually offering the news that a friend at the War Office had asked her to infiltrate what she called 'the Free Frog Officers' Club' and try to pick up snippets of information. The Free French, headed by de Gaulle, had set up in London to work against the Vichy regime established in France after the country's occupation by the Nazis, and headed by the puppet Marshal Pétain. Nancy reported that the Officers' Club was rumoured to be full of spies; one particular operation planned in Africa had been leaked to Vichy. 'Isn't it tricky', she remarked to Mrs Hammersley. 'Seriously I don't see what I could do…' It sounds a rather exciting proposition, yet Nancy was essentially reluctant. Unlike Sophia, it seems that she did not hold even the illusory desire to be a secret agent.

For whatever reason, however – probably her sense of duty – she did use her social contacts to gain an entrée to the club; and all changed. 'I live in a slight world of frogs now,' she wrote to Jessica in July. 'You can't imagine how wonderful they have been, the free ones I mean.' It was the first time that Nancy had been surrounded by men who truly *liked* women, who enjoyed them, who did not exactly make her feel young but, better yet, gave her to understand that youth was merely a phase: that a woman in the full bloom of sophistication was equally desirable. And she did now bloom. When happy, she looked years younger than her age, although that was no longer the point. Had she not known the French, Nancy could never have created Madame des Rocher-Innouis in her 1951 novel *The Blessing*: a sublime woman of about eighty, rich with humour, dressed in cutting-edge couture and emanating 'great billows of sex'. As a girl Nancy had loved Paris, had stood on the Avenue Henri-

Martin and felt a joy almost beyond bearing. Now she invested all her adult capacity for happiness in the image of France, which she saw reflected in these brave, courteous, laughing officers. She was ripe for new experience, but this one gradually revealed itself to be what everybody craves: a world in which they are appreciated for who they are. Furthermore it was a world free from the cling of her family. This, she was starting to need. They did not bring out the best in her. They could have Germany. She had France.

It was around this time that she began an affair with an attractive, cultured officer named Roy André Desplats-Pilter, codename André Roy, the father of the baby that had rendered her barren. The hysterectomy was a ghastly thing for Nancy. But it, too, represented a kind of liberation.

VI

Thirty years after writing her open letter about the Mosleys, Jessica was gracious enough to admit that it had been 'painfully self-righteous and stuffy'.[26] It had led to an invitation to join the Communist Party in America; on the application form, beneath the question 'Occupation of Father', she fortuitously remembered his days prospecting for gold in Canada and wrote: 'Miner.'[27]

Although she disliked the tone in which she had written about Diana, she never changed in her attitude towards her sister, and saw her only once more after her marriage to Esmond Romilly. Was this, then, the division of the 'DFD' made flesh, a pure commitment to the belief that Fascists and Communists must be separated at all costs? Or was Jessica's fixation upon Diana born of something more obscure and ignoble?

In 1947 she wrote to Nancy that Diana 'would melt us all down for soap if she could catch us, most likely.' This was absurd, and especially so given Jessica's lifelong affection for the real Nazi sympathizer, Unity: 'she was easily my favourite sister'.[28] Perhaps that would have changed, had Unity remained her robust old self throughout the war, but somehow one feels not. What is odd is that there is also a sense in which Unity's fanaticism was part of what Jessica loved in her, what bound them together. As for Diana – Jessica had worshipped her as a girl, and seems to have felt that her older sister had let her down: that here was another family betrayal. Perhaps the identification of Diana with the war – the desire to blame her – was also a sublimation, a way of holding her responsible for what had happened to Unity. Perhaps she felt, as did others, that Unity was an innocent, which Diana had never been.

Certainly it was irrational to hate Diana all the more when Esmond was killed in 1941. Yet that was Jessica's stance, from which she did not outwardly deviate. Mitfords didn't, on the whole.

The Romillys had left home for America before the outbreak of war, where they worked their way around the country. Jessica took jobs as a salesgirl, Esmond as a door-to-door salesman. Among the contacts that they been given – the sort of thing that could never have happened to a member of the working class – was Katherine Graham, whose father, owner of the *Washington Post*, loaned Esmond money with which he started a bar in Miami. He was a figure of some interest in the US press. In 1939 he was interviewed by *Life* magazine, and said: 'If England is drawn into a war now I shall go back and fight... but I have no illusions about England fighting for democracy.' The war, as he put it, was 'imperial England against imperial Germany'. What this meant, if anything, was surely that he would enter the war only on *his* terms. The letter that Nellie Romilly wrote to her son, accusing him of having fled the war scene, was not entirely just; whatever else he was, Esmond was not a coward. He joined the Canadian Air Force in 1940 and volunteered to serve in Europe. 'I'll probably find myself being commanded by one of your ghastly relations,' he said to Jessica. (His relations too, as it happened. In fact the man whom he sometimes claimed for his father was by now in charge of the whole shebang.) Having entered in the ranks, Esmond applied for a commission as a pilot officer; he justified this apparent endorsement of the hierarchical class system with the argument that commissions were based on performance rather than social background. Having an answer for everything was another of his characteristics.

Jessica was now living in Washington DC, a semi-permanent house guest with a family called the Durrs (the husband was high up in broadcasting, but crucially – fortunately for one's principles – they were all Democrats). Her social life was cosmopolitan. Being introduced as the wife of Churchill's nephew did her no harm with people like Lyndon Johnson. Again, there was nothing notably communistic about this lifestyle, but she found the direct American manner more congenial than the roundabout, oh-you-are-kind Englishness that she nevertheless could use to her advantage.

If she missed the Mitfords, there was no particular sign of it. Yet she stayed in close touch through letters. She had been devastated about Unity, and refused large sums to talk about her to the American press. Her mother told her of the pitiful conditions in which Diana was living; her reply to that is not recorded (perhaps just as well). Deborah wrote in her familiar 'dear old Hen' style and from Swinbrook gave news of Unity: 'I think Bobo is a bit better but I don't know.' Pamela wrote to say that 'Air Force blue' suited Derek's eyes – something oddly touching about this – '& I expect it suits Esmond also'. In very different tone, and as if in league against their pro-Germanic tribe, Nancy wrote often. Her droll, dry, elliptical letters suggest a kind of relaxation with Jessica, who would get all her jokes and for whom she felt no uncomfortably strong emotions. She was rarely able to resist a little dig about their mother's politics ('she is, I fear, very unsound at heart') and emphasized her own status, of which she was proudly aware, as the only sister to be contributing to the war effort ('you see I WORK Susan'). Although Nancy always made great play of her hatred of America – the butt of many jokes in *The Blessing* – and teased Jessica about living there, she may also have empathized with her sister's desire to escape the Mitfords by moving to another country. In fact Jessica intended to return to England, and it is interesting to imagine what her life would have been had she done so; but this did not work out as she had planned.

In February 1941 Jessica gave birth to a daughter, Constancia, who this time was strong and healthy (also very beautiful). Three months later Unity sent congratulations to her sister, apologizing for the delay and explaining that she still wrote very slowly: 'You know I got shot in the head.' In June, Esmond visited on leave then sailed to England, from where he was to fly in nightly operations over Europe. Jessica, who had again fallen pregnant, miscarried in August but wrote to her husband: 'I don't mind a bit about it any more, and I hope you don't. The Donk [Constancia[29]] is so frightfully nice and companionable, she is really all I need.' Except Esmond, of course. She was still deeply attached to him. Like the Mosleys, whom the Romillys would have scorned to resemble, this marriage that had cut them off so forcefully from their previous life was obliged to succeed: the love was sincere, but it was also a necessity.

Meanwhile Esmond was unhappy and nervous, with good reason. His brother Giles – to whom he was extremely close, his fellow public-school rebel – had been taken prisoner at Dunkirk, then held in Colditz (Giles survived the war, but killed himself in 1967). The night flights were wearing, terrifying. Only a man like Derek Jackson – who with typical perversity barked orders in German as he buzzed through the air – would have relished them. Jessica wanted to hitch a ride on a 'lend-lease bomber' and meet Esmond in England, but for a time he sought to discourage her; he was lost in despair after losing four of his closest friends to the war. Yet by November 1941 his attitude had shifted, and he sent Jessica a reflective, kindly, stoical letter, a hint towards the man that he might have become. He recognized that Jessica wanted to return to her home country, and felt that he was selfish to dissuade her on account of his depression. 'I want', he wrote, 'to be with you again more than anything in the world.' Then he continued:

> This whole business has made me realize one thing very deeply – ie that this sort of thing is infinitely worse for the wives etc. of the people concerned than themselves. The thought that when people are missing, it is of course a very long time before any definite news can be reached of them, ie as to whether they have landed somewhere and been captured. In a very large number of cases this turns out to be the case... one always imagines the worst somehow, which is utterly irrational.
>
> Incidentally if, which I certainly think is an inconceivable improbability, I should ever find myself in this sort of situation, I have absolutely determined to escape in some way or another...
>
> Very much love, darling angel,
> Esmond

No doubt the brave reasoning contained within this letter was what convinced Jessica that she should not believe 'the worst' when, three days before she was due to sail for England, she received a telegram that read: 'REGRET TO INFORM... YOUR HUSBAND PILOT OFFICER ESMOND MARK DAVID ROMILLY MISSING ON ACTIVE SERVICE NOVEMBER 30.'

Churchill, impressively loyal once more to his family ties, left Jessica a message to contact him during a visit to President Roosevelt. She rang the White House, spoke to Roosevelt's wife and was given an appointment to see Churchill the next day. Again, Jessica was who she was; however much she sometimes did not want to be. When she saw Churchill he was in bed, working. She had Constancia with her and, as he wrote to Nellie Romilly, 'looked very lovely': painfully young to be the widow that he knew she had to be. As gently as he could, Churchill explained that Esmond had surely drowned in the bleak North Sea. There had been a search, but fog had halted it; the water was icy, and nobody could possibly survive its temperature. In an attempt at consolation he then talked of Diana, thinking that Jessica would be glad to hear that conditions at Holloway had improved and that her sister was now imprisoned with her husband. Jessica exploded like a firecracker: the Mosleys, she said, should be put up against a wall and shot. It may have been that single moment, in which Churchill's wildly misguided remark penetrated the great tumult of her grief, that hardened Jessica against her sister thereafter. Shocked by his mistake – he had not known that Jessica felt so violently towards Diana – he then compounded it. He offered to find her a secretarial job with Lord Halifax, his former rival for the post of wartime prime minister, now British ambassador in the US. This too she flung back in his face. Finally he gave her $500. She bought a pony for the daughter of her hosts, the Durrs, and donated the rest to the Communist Party.

Deborah wrote to Jessica with the utmost sincere kindness, saying that she was thinking of her sister the whole time. To Diana she took a slightly different tone: 'Thank goodness she has got her pig' (she meant Constancia). 'It is so much worse for her anyway because of her being so queer.' Even Deborah, who had managed to maintain closeness with all her sisters, was pulled this way and that within that complex weave of loyalties. Yet despite her own political conservatism, her wish for the whole bunch of extremists to start behaving like normal people, one has the sense that she was most herself when writing to Diana. She had not liked Esmond, as was understandable given his obdurate loathing for the Mitfords, but many years later she expressed the view that the Romilly marriage would undoubtedly have lasted, because the couple were so right for each other. This did not mean that Jessica shared the same character as Esmond, although her willed hatred for Diana was very much his style. She had more warmth, more humour, a kind of humanity that he had not displayed in his horribly short life – he was twenty-three when he died – but to a degree he had changed her, and as she mellowed she would probably have changed him. His death cannot really have been a shock, as she knew the risks of what he was doing. Yet the arrival of the telegram, even as she was preparing for her journey across the ocean – rather as Vera Brittain received news of her fiancé's death in the First World War, in a telephone call to the hotel where she was tremulously waiting to meet him – was the kind of blow from which one does not really recover. Nor did she accept it, for quite some time after Churchill's insistence that she should. Like the Mitford that she was, she sublimated her emotions into a display of bright, tough smiles, but she remained dedicated to Esmond by her separation from her past. (Again, this was very much like Diana, that martyr-like dedication to the Mosley shrine.) Mrs Durr, an extremely nice woman, wrote secretly to Sydney, saying that she felt Jessica might do better at home: 'She is so essentially English, and so bound to England by her affection that she could never be anything else. She has been hurt so much both by circumstances and her own fierce pride that I cannot bear for her to have the further hurt of feeling unwanted.'

Sydney, who wanted nothing more than for Jessica to return, wrote begging her to do so. The temptation must have been there. At times it may have been overwhelming. For one thing Jessica had very little money, only a six-month pension from the Canadian government worth less than $400; but the rejection of Churchill's money was symbolic of her dogged determination to live in her way, not that of her family. It was admirable, if not entirely supported by logic, and it cannot have been easy. She found a part-time job with the RAF delegation in the British Embassy (thus not entirely remote from Churchill's offer), which meant that Nancy's self-righteous contention – that she was the only Mitford girl who actually did any war work – was no longer true. And in mid-1942 Jessica went it completely alone. She moved from the comfort of the Durrs' large farmhouse into the centre of Washington, placed Constancia in the care of a neighbour and began a typing job at the Office of Price Administration, which formulated policy on rationing, price controls, petrol usage and so on. The spirit of the place was left-wing and idealistic, as described by Jessica's future husband Robert Treuhaft, a Harvard-educated lawyer who drew up OPA regulations during the war: 'We were gung ho for enforcement of the price and rationing laws that were in effect at that time. J. K. Galbraith, the economist, was one of the people on the staff of the OPA at that time. There was still a lot of New Deal spirit in Washington, and also a very powerful anti-Fascist, anti-Hitler spirit. And there were lots of young people in the Office of Price Administration, and we were all dedicated to our work.'[30]

This, to Jessica, was a kind of nirvana, to be surrounded by those whose beliefs were formed in a new, clean, egalitarian system. Quite soon, after fiddling the facts by claiming a degree from the Sorbonne (actually she had been 'finished' in Paris), she was promoted to take on investigative work. She was now self-sufficient, earning the equivalent of £500 a year, living in a way of which Esmond would surely have approved. And she may well have heard his distant applause when she wrote to her mother: 'I know you realize I could never come & live with the family. After all I was told once never to come home again, which I know wasn't your fault' [her father had said it, in the throes of the anguish caused by her disappearance with Esmond], 'but it still means I never shall… Of course I do hope one day I'll see those members of the family I'm still on speakers with; probably after the war.'

It was a hard letter for Sydney to receive, as she coped with the wobbling liability that was Unity and the horror of 'All change, Lady Mosley's suite!' as she took her bus journeys to Holloway. But the DFD had been divided for ever: only by denying Diana could Sydney receive the gift of Jessica.

Later, however, Jessica semi-apologized for the tone of her letter. 'I really didn't mean to tease when I wrote about being turned out by the family,' she wrote to her mother in 1943. Clearly she still had feelings for all those Mitfords, and perhaps it was the very strength of that cocktail of guilt, love, rage and sadness that made it so hard to swallow. Jessica would never live in England again: 'all our ideas are so tremendously different and opposed that it would be impossible to go back to an ordinary family life.'[31] By this time she had married her second husband. She told her mother only when the deed was safely done. Robert Treuhaft – aged thirty-one, small, dark and very clever – later conjured a wry portrait of the compelling and dignified girl that he had first met the previous year:

> She was dressed in black, and she seemed to be a private sort of person, but she was quite beautiful, and I was tremendously enamoured of her right away as soon as I met her. And I took her to lunch the next day at the cafeteria... she would eat a salad and put the empty plate down below the counter; and at the end she'd take a cup of coffee and I'd pay for it, and that would be five cents. That was her way of life. She was making $1,200 a year, and had a baby daughter, and had to have somebody at home to take care of her. So I thought, such frugality, I can't pass that up. It was a very cheap date.[32]

This is a very American idiom, like a piece delivered to camera by Woody Allen and attractive as such, although Nancy later wrote of Treuhaft: 'I quite like him but *oh* Americans.' In fact he was a formidable person, urbane and far more mellow than Esmond Romilly, but similarly dynamic. Like Jessica he was keen to join the Communist Party in America, which reached into the underworld of public bodies – the top brass remained conservative – and claimed many of their brightest minds. Nevertheless he said: 'A lot of it didn't make terribly great sense, because none of us were proletarians. We tended to be middle class in our point of view and in our way of living. A proletarian is someone who has nothing but his job and the clothes on his back.' This, indeed, was the same paradox that had exercised Romilly, who had raged against the public-school intellectuals who read Marx whilst lounging in the comfort of their parents' Wiltshire drawing rooms. Treuhaft, however, saw the support that the Communists gave to the unions, and crucially to the civil rights movement, then in its formative days: as early as the

1930s the Communists had organized pickets of baseball stadiums where blacks were not allowed to play, and later Treuhaft took on many cases of racial discrimination (including within unions, which were then segregated). His influence upon Jessica was profound, utterly remote from anything Mitford, and essentially benevolent. His causes became hers. Eventually he would give her the insights into the commercialized con of the funeral industry which led her, in 1963, to write the hugely influential – and controversial – *The American Way of Death,* and which ironically (given the book's anti-business ethos) made her very rich.

So it is unsurprising that she wrote to Sydney as she did, as if from a world where the systems and beliefs of the Mitfords looked absurd, indeed meaningless. To his own mother, giving news of his relationship with Jessica, Treuhaft began by saying, rather quickly, that she was the sister of Unity and Diana – thus far had their notoriety travelled – but she had, not to worry, been disowned by her family as a radical. 'Besides being beautiful she is exceptionally talented and shines with a kind of fierce honesty and courage.' True enough. Deborah, in the very different idiom of their shared childhood, reached out to Jessica: 'Do write and tell if Mr Treuhaft is a Hon, I'm sure he must be a tremendous one.' Better than that: he was a Jew.

VII

Nancy's insistence that she was the only worker among the sisters had always been slightly ridiculous, as Unity and Diana were hardly in a position to contribute to the war effort. Pamela had had charge of Diana's children and was back in her familiar role of running a farm, at Rignell House. The cost of cattle feed meant that she could not maintain her herd of Aberdeen Angus, and she lamented the death of the bull: 'poor Black Hussar!' She did not have the luxury of being sentimental about Diana's mare, Edna May, but perhaps she would not have been anyway. Jessica was delicately parodied in *Pigeon Pie* as the character Mary Pencill, who spouts anti-Nazi politics but does no real work; her latest behaviour contradicted this portrayal, although Nancy could always wave her hands-on dealings with Spanish and Jewish refugees in her sister's face. Deborah also came under Nancy's unrelenting fire, criticized for 'having a wild time with young cannon fodder at the Ritz etc'. In 1942 Nancy refused to attend a ball thrown by her sister, on the grounds that Tom was in Libya and Peter Rodd in Ethiopia. In fact Deborah worked at a servicemen's canteen at St Pancras Station in 1940, and four years later at a YMCA canteen in Eastbourne, where everybody imitated her accent. (Nancy had the same experience in her office finding holiday billets; she was also told that she could not lecture on the subject of fire-watching, as her voice annoyed her audience so much that 'they want to put you on the fire.'[33]) Deborah did admit to Diana that she hated the canteen: 'I do disgusting work now, do be sorry for me'. Actually Nancy felt the same way. 'Oh Susan isn't work dreadful', she wrote to Jessica. Later Deborah would exert herself devotedly in the cause of Chatsworth House, and Nancy in the cause of her books; but those were rather different jobs.

Deborah had been granted a gap in her war service by the fact of her pregnancy, following marriage to Andrew Cavendish. 'You have either got to marry that girl or stop asking her here,' the then Duchess of Devonshire had told her son at the end of 1940. In March 1941, a month before the wedding, Deborah wrote to Diana in a light and merry manner, clearly striving to involve her sister without inflicting torment. She gave airy details about the dress, with its skirt 'such as has never been before for size', and said that Nancy had been 'teasy' about the ring. Twelve years earlier Nancy had likened Pamela's engagement ring from Oliver Watney – eventually given to Hitler –

to a 'chicken's mess'.[34] That was Nancy: she could not resist, when it came to her sisters.

The wedding reception was held at Rutland Gate, from which the refugees had now departed. Just a couple of days previously a bomb had sliced two nearby houses in half, shaking Deborah as she lay in bed in the mews behind. 'The poor old house (no. 26), quite empty with all the ballroom windows blown in... looks slightly dreary,' wrote Sydney to Jessica, describing how it had nonetheless been magically enlivened by the blooms of giant red camellias sent by the Devonshires, 'from the tree planted by Paxton[35] 100 years ago'. Jessica – determinedly not giving an inch – sent a faintly sour telegram, saying that Deborah had 'nearly' got her duke (Andrew was a second son). Unity, unaware of the press who had watched her every move, wrote happily to Diana: 'Well, Nard, about the Wedding!!!! Well, it was quite heaven... The only person who looked ghastly was dear old Farve; he looked so sad.' David, now a private in the Home Guard, wore his uniform, 'which was also rather depressing as it wasn't even long enough. Horrors!!' Unity was quite right about his appearance. He had the air of a man close to death, a study in accustomed grief. But Deborah – 'she looked MARVELLOUS' – was as flower-like as the great camellias in her tall wreathed headdress, and an abundance of white tulle like foam on the waves: the dress, by Victor Stiebel, had been made six weeks before the start of clothes rationing and would have taken all her coupons for years to come.

After the honeymoon in one of the Devonshires' many homes – Compton Place at Eastbourne – Andrew was posted to the 5th Battalion Coldstream Guards, and Deborah moved to the Rookery, a rather dark and damp house on the Chatsworth Estate. As she later wrote: 'Rationing and coupons ruled our lives.' She described asking the butcher for a tongue – offal was not rationed – and being told that she was thirty-sixth on the list. A soldier home from Italy brought with him a lemon, which by this time had become an unimaginable luxury. He placed it on the counter of the local post office and charged tuppence for the Red Cross to let people smell it.

Deborah wrote bravely to Diana when her first baby was born in November, a premature son who died almost immediately. It was, she said, nothing like as bad as when Jessica lost Julia, because she had never known the child. What she did not tell Diana was that after the birth the gynaecologist had barked at her: 'You don't expect the baby to live, do you?' Sydney had been there and was, she wrote, 'quite wonderful'. Nancy said the same thing to Diana about their mother, when Sydney visited the hospital after her daughter's hysterectomy: 'Muv was wonderful.' But she meant it very differently, that her mother was reacting with a vagueness that was too funny to be believed: asking who would ever see the scar on Nancy's stomach, casually recalling the syphilitic nursery maid. Deborah was cared for by Sydney at Swinbrook after the loss of her baby. Nancy left hospital to go back to her life in London. It is impossible to know whether the fault lay with the mother who did not offer comfort, or with the daughter who appeared not to want it. Something of both: a kind of emotional stalemate.

Deborah would have three healthy children – Emma, Peregrine and Sophia – and Jessica two sons, Nicholas and Benjamin, with Bob Treuhaft. But only Diana was truly fecund. Deborah's pregnancies became a business of creeping through the days, not daring to buy new baby clothes, in a state of desperate hope that was dashed four times. She had another miscarriage in 1945, as it happened a twin. The other twin was born only slightly premature; after eight hours he suffered a brain haemorrhage. 'The village nurse... called me Your Ladyship through all the most undignified parts,' Deborah wrote to Nancy, striving for the Mitford lightness. She lost another baby in 1953. The dead children were named, and baptized – without her knowledge at the time – by her mother-in-law. Meanwhile Pamela had undergone surgery in 1937 to help her fertility, but miscarried that year after Derek drove her over the bumpy roads of Norway. Later both Deborah and Diana would speculate as to whether Pam's dislike of children proceeded from this vexed personal history. As ever with Pamela, the question is difficult to answer, but there is probably something to her sisters' belief. Despite her husband's fairly obvious reluctance she did fall pregnant again, and lost a baby at six months towards the end of the war.

Unity, meanwhile, had wanted a family of her own; and even now still longed for one. A friend of Nancy's, Mollie Friese-Greene, later recalled her saying 'when I get married, I should like to have ten children.'[36] Naturally enough, Unity had also found God. 'Nard, I am in the Choir!!' she wrote to Diana at the end of 1940. After her confirmation she visited a Christian Science practitioner; this was somehow discovered by the *Daily Express*, which reminded its readers of the movement's strong links to Nazism. Later, however, Unity would try other churches, and spoke to Mollie about her desire to become a Catholic.

Her condition had improved somewhat, and would do so increasingly, at least in a physical sense. By 1941 she was able to go for little expeditions on her own and take the bus into Oxford. There she would lunch at the British Restaurant – a wartime café where meals cost a shilling – but her appetite was uncontrolled, as were her table manners. She would go up for a second meal, which was not really done, especially for Unity Mitford; Nancy, not unkindly, said that one could get an extra bowl of soup by wringing out Unity's sleeves after she had eaten. She worked briefly in a canteen in Burford, until the woman who had employed her was told that she had to go: 'You can't have her in the house.' More intriguingly, a Home Office file – classified under the 100-year rule, but opened prematurely – suggested that Unity had had a boyfriend: a married RAF test pilot, with whom she was said to have been 'consorting' in November 1941. The problem with information of this kind is that it is extremely hard to assess – who reported it? How reliable was their judgment? Does the detail of the pilot's married status imply malice on the part of the informant? And who was this RAF man, who got his kicks out of dallying with Hitler's brain-damaged lady friend? It is not impossible that Unity did have a bizarre little romance, but the hard evidence of her sisters' letters – as written at the time – do not portray an image of a likely adulterous seductress. Unity's own letters, meanwhile, make the scenario seem even less feasible.

So too does the recollection of Mollie Friese-Greene, who worked with Nancy at the bookshop Heywood Hill in Curzon Street, where Unity would occasionally visit when she and Sydney were staying in London. Nancy had taken the job of managing the shop – at the suggestion of James Lees-Milne – in March 1942. She was still thin and fragile after her hysterectomy, but the work was a civilized delight to her; not merely because it paid £3 10s a week. Heywood Hill himself became a friend, and she made the shop into something like her own club. The enchanting interior was filled with her old friends, de facto members like Evelyn Waugh, Cecil Beaton, Harold Acton, Gerald Berners, the Sitwells. (It was in Heywood Hill that Osbert Sitwell, after the result was declared in the 1945 General Election, ran in and seized the till, crying 'Labour has begun!') Heywood Hill was indeed another heavenly boost to Nancy, along with the entrée to France and the affair with *le capitaine* Roy. The admiring Acton later described her crisp, chic vigour – she walked from Maida Vale to the Mayfair shop every day – and her 'Sir Joshua Reynolds' prettiness. She sent quantities of books to Diana in Holloway, and wrote to tell her of the shop's merry social ambience; a delayed revenge, perhaps, for the days when her friends had decamped *en bloc* to worship at the feet of the young Mrs Guinness in Buckingham Street.

Mollie Friese-Greene, who was Nancy's assistant at Heywood Hill, later recalled how one day a 'stranger came up and said, Do you think it is wicked to commit suicide? I don't think I've ever thought about it, I said, let's have a chat.' This was her first meeting with Unity, who would come to the shop in between afternoons at the Curzon cinema across the road – she had always loved films. The sweet-natured Mollie would sit with Unity looking through a newspaper called the *Matrimonial Times*, a sort of dating agency publication (imagine turning up with your carnation to find Unity

Mitford waiting for you). Again, this does not suggest that Unity was having a genuine love affair. Nor does the way in which Nancy would say, in a tone of brusque fondness: 'Now Miss, you're being a perfect nuisance, go away.' It was, as Mollie put it, 'like having a child'. The Mitfords were typically unembarrassed by her, and in 1946 – for instance – she would spend Christmas at Edensor House on the Chatsworth Estate, although care was taken to keep her away from the vicar as (according to Deborah) she was liable to ask if clergymen enjoyed sleeping with their wives. In public, however, she could still provoke an uneasy reaction; even when the war was over a crowd of women were angered by the sight of her waddling down a London street: 'Oh! it's disgusting.'

Another imponderable is how aware Unity was, how restored her memory of the recent past and what she now thought about it. Although her mental age was said to be that of a ten-year-old, and her letters prove that she had difficulty in writing, she still had her skewed Mitford sharpness, as with her remark about her father's too-short Home Guard uniform (very much the sort of thing that Nancy would have said). James Lees-Milne observed that she expressed herself like a 'sophisticated child'. And she does seem to have remembered a certain amount. As early as May 1940 she was rather surprisingly taken to a tea party, together with Deborah and Sydney, at Ditchley Park in Oxfordshire, where Churchill held secret meetings during the war. Among the guests was Duff Cooper, who had been chief among anti-appeasers and had resigned after the Munich agreement. ('Such little influence as he was able to exert in the 1930s was a dangerous influence,' Diana later wrote: she despised Cooper.) In a letter to Jessica, Deborah remarked that she feared for a moment that Unity would not shake his hand at the party: 'however she just did'. Unless Deborah was merely showing concern for her sister's manners, this of course implies that Unity knew precisely who Duff Cooper was, and what he represented.

In November 1942 Unity attended another party, this time thrown by Nancy, who by now was back in her Maida Vale home.

Nancy was good to Unity; she found disinterested kindness easy. She 'crammed' her sister into one of her own dresses, perforce left undone down the back but covered with a coat. Unity refused to make up her face, but André Roy – the most good-natured man Nancy ever had relations with – did it for her. 'So in the end,' Nancy wrote to Diana, 'she looked awfully pretty.' However another guest at the party, Osbert Lancaster, took a different view. Nancy had placed him next to Unity, with Roy to her other side, and Lancaster later recalled 'this Mitford giantess, unmistakable, aggressive'. When Roy suggested politely that she spoke better French than he did English, she reportedly fired back: 'Thank the Lord, not a word of the beastly language.'[37] There were suggestions that she held to her fanatical pro-German stance, although her way of showing this was surreal. Another friend of Nancy's, Billa Harrod – upon whom she based the sane, calm, satisfying Fanny, narrator of *The Pursuit of Love* – was asked to 'be nice to Bobo, she runs up to everybody like a huge big dog wagging her tail, and nobody is nice to her'. Billa recalled Unity again saying that she wanted children: 'the eldest to be called Adolf'.

Diana, Deborah and Pamela protested strongly against the biography of Unity in which such information appeared.[38] Nevertheless James Lees-Milne, who saw her at Swinbrook in 1944, reflected similar views in his diary, writing that Unity 'talked about the Führer, as though she still admired him'. Despite the damage to her brain, her memories of Germany and Hitler appeared intact. As to her opinion of them: her old friend Mary Ormsby-Gore did recall one strange, sudden moment when Unity asked: 'Why didn't you stop me?' 'We tried to,' said Mary. Yet when she saw footage of the liberated concentration camps Unity apparently dismissed it as propaganda; perhaps she had to do so, to protect herself from too much reality. Diana did the same thing, to an extent, but with Unity the evidence is especially confused as her mind had always been a mystery; 'the inner Boud is almost impossible to describe', as Jessica put it.[39]. How much more so now that she was still herself, but a ruined self. James

Lees-Milne wrote that he found the sight of this heavy, plain young woman extremely sad; although he did not seem to think that Unity was unhappy.

Which makes her first question to Mollie Friese-Greene an interesting one: was Unity referring to her previous attempts at suicide, asking whether her act had been a wicked one? Or was she thinking of trying again? How deep, in other words, was her sense of her essentially hopeless situation? At times she appeared contented, lumbering about with her peculiar gait, writing excitedly to her sisters about their new babies and enjoying occasions such as Deborah's wedding. Her obsession with going to church was a consolation, a conduit for her vast emotions. Yet she had expressed appalling frustrations when Deborah was living with her at Swinbrook, raging randomly, taking a fierce dislike to her sister. To Osbert Lancaster, who spoke to her of his fear of the air-raid sirens, she said: 'It's so odd for me, because I want to die.'

She was deeply distressed when told that she could not see Diana in jail; although in late 1941 this restriction was lifted, at which she expressed similarly excessive joy ('Oh, Nard! Oh, Nard!'). In the spring of 1943, by which time the Mosleys were together in the Parcels House, a report was written on one of Unity's visits: 'Lady Mosley was most anxious to hear what [her children] did but Miss Mitford didn't wish to talk about it. Somebody had told her that she was very beautiful but she did not make the best of herself [was this the kindly André Roy?] and she was anxious to have Lady Mosley's opinion.' Diana would have been patient, wonderfully reassuring as she could be, but the strain must have been great; and worse still the realization of what her mother had to bear every day with the incessant gabbling questions, the inability to concentrate or engage, the delusional desire for children (and, every night, the incontinence). It was around this time that Sydney at last confessed to Diana her despair: 'I don't know what to do with her.'

From July 1944, after D-Day, Sydney was allowed to take her daughter to Inch Kenneth, where they would thereafter spend half the year. Sydney farmed sheep, kept Shetland ponies, goats and – her old standby – hens. She made butter and cheese, while Unity wound a sheet around her waist to serve as a cassock and took possession of the island chapel. This, then, was a kind of peace.

Nevertheless a woman whose family ran the post office on the mainland, who held Unity in some affection, later said that she had not seemed happy: 'You would see it in her eyes. I often think she'd known what she'd done.' Wisdom after the event, perhaps. Yet it was confirmed, in a sense, by the letter that Unity had written to Diana in November 1941, in which she explained her situation as well as could be done, with a simple grasp of its complexities. 'You see, when I first came back, I thought all this was a play, and I was looking on. Now, I know I have a part to play, & I can't bear acting it!'

VIII

After their release from Holloway early on the morning of 20 November 1943, the Mosleys went to stay with the Jacksons at Rignell House. This was where Diana had been planning to go when she was arrested more than three years earlier. Savehay was still requisitioned, and they were forbidden to live in their flat in London. (Clementine Churchill had anyway told Sydney that there was a danger they would be lynched on the streets if released; Sydney replied coolly that they would take that risk.) By this time Derek was working as Chief Scientific Officer at Fighter Command Headquarters. He was not often at home, but Diana was nervous of imposing upon a man who did not even particularly like Mosley, despite his sympathy with the Fascist ideal. Nevertheless Derek showed his mettle. 'Of course they must come.' Pam, too, was impressive. She had not liked Mosley either but was shocked out of such judgments by his sickly appearance. Neither Jackson was frightened by the thought of the encroaching press, the crowd that had gathered at the gates of Holloway waving banners. So much anger, still, from so many people; while Desmond Guinness sent a letter to Diana from his school that began: 'Darling Mummy, What News!' Herbert Morrison, heckled loudly as he made a public speech, proclaimed: 'This issue is a conflict between a dangerous emotionalism and mob rule and a reason respect for law and the constitution.' George Bernard Shaw bravely, and truly, wrote of a situation in which the public could buy *Mein Kampf* in a bookshop but would not allow Mosley to defend himself. The Home Office, overwhelmed with letters of protest, stated: 'Lady Mosley's release is an almost greater source of aggravation than her husband's.' Such was the woman's fate.

'Nothing so beautiful was ever seen by human eye,' Diana later wrote of the autumnal Oxfordshire landscape through which she and Mosley were driven, on their way to spend their first evening at Rignell. Sydney, who had used her month's allowance of petrol, was waiting there with Deborah; Pam had used her stock of anthracite to feed the boiler; there was wine and clean linen. The idyll was brief, however. The house was instantly under siege: the phone rang incessantly, reporters hid behind every tree, Pam was shadowed and bellowed at as she walked her dogs. What Diana later described as the 'sub-stockbroker' Rignell was described in the press as the Mosleys' stately home retreat. 'Woman is being simply too killing,' Diana wrote to Nancy, recounting how Pam would rush outside and say to the pressmen: 'I dislike you intensely.' Of the demonstration in Trafalgar Square, where Mosley's effigy dangled from a gibbet, Diana – at her most mysteriously Mitford – said: 'I wish I could go.' Nancy replied that a friend had been caught up in the protests while trying to catch the Underground, and that only by chanting 'Put Him Back' was she allowed to join the queue for the tube.

Diana's sang-froid was extraordinary, like everything else about her. Perhaps the joy of release was so great that nothing else mattered.

At the same time it *did* seem as though the world outside meant nothing to her. It had, after all, done its worst. Hence the mantra of 'being hated means nothing to me'. If any other woman on earth had said those words, one would doubt their truth. Not so with Diana. She had achieved a state in which the blithe Mitford confidence reached a heightened and insurmountable level. She genuinely did not care what anybody thought of her: a near-unique condition. The exception to this was Mosley, of course. *His* opinion, she would bend herself to accept. For the others, she trusted to the imperishable magic of 'lovely *One*': as long as people allowed her to do so, she knew that she could still cast her spell.

Derek, magnificent despite his oddity, and a renegade of the Mosley stamp, fought to keep his house guests after the Home Office informed him that they must go. Derek was privy to highly secret scientific information; Mosley – somewhat amazingly, given that events were turning so inexorably against Germany – was still considered a security threat. Perhaps suspecting that the real reason was official bloody-mindedness, Derek rang the Home Office and demanded to speak to Herbert Morrison (whom he knew to have been a First World War conscientious objector). Again amazingly, he was put directly through. He said to Morrison: 'When you've got the DFC, the AFC and the OBE for valour, you can tell me what to do.' This must have been rather satisfying, but it was also pointless; the Mosleys were effectively on the run, and finding an empty house at the time was almost impossible. Sydney suggested that they move to a half-derelict hotel near Swinbrook called the Shaven Crown (doubtless what some of the protesters would have liked to do to Diana). There they spent a strange Christmas with Diana's four children; before she went searching, accompanied by police and still in a very weakened state, for a more permanent home. Eventually she found Crux Easton near Newbury. It was a large manor house with ten bedrooms: almost as if nothing had changed.

Whatever else happened to him, Mosley always had money to live somewhere nice – he gave £3,000 for Crux Easton – and to pay for staff. Within a short time, Diana had made a home for her king, with servants including a wonderful cook who had formerly worked for Gerald Berners. Mosley bought a cow. They had their own vegetables, and eggs from Sydney. People began to visit: Nancy, who had asked immediately if she could stay; Pamela; Tom, home from Italy; Deborah, back at Swinbrook while Andrew was on active service; the children, including Mosley's three from his first marriage. There were also friends such as Osbert Sitwell – who wrote that 'to have been unjustly deprived, as you have been, of a period of time, is beyond bearing' – and Berners, who remarked of Diana's police escort that nobody but she could now afford two footmen. John Betjeman later found a prep school willing to take two young boys with the devil's surname. Life was an island, as it had to be. It was house arrest, as well as almost total social ostracism; the Mosleys could not own a car, nor travel beyond a seven-mile radius. But it was a return, *en petit*, to the cosmopolitan broad-minded civilization that Diana loved, in the face of the political beliefs that she refused to deny.

And this paradox was a nonsense, yet she would not change. She could not, had she wanted to, because Mosley was all. Because of him, the couple's good friend Randolph Churchill was not invited to Crux Easton. ('Why will they see Berners and not me?' he asked Nancy). The simple reason was that Randolph's father had urged war with Germany, and Mosley blamed Churchill indirectly for his and Diana's imprisonment; despite her appeal to the old friendship with Clementine, Sydney also held Churchill responsible. This was really rather outrageous. Randolph had carried the message that brought the Mosleys together in Holloway, and his father had got them out of the place. Yet Mosley never forgave Churchill, whom he seemed to view as the demon agent of his own political downfall. Therefore Diana, of whom Churchill had always been very fond, did not forgive either. She had delicately mocked him to the Advisory Committee in 1940: 'I think in his own character he is a person who enjoys war, and always saw himself as a great leader.' Plenty of others had shared this view. Probably it was not too far off the mark. But ten years after the war, when the devastation of much of Europe – as predicted by Mosley – had revealed itself and Communism had triumphed in the East, Diana knifed Churchill with all the delicate ferocity of which she was capable when she reviewed his own account of the war. 'He wishes,' she wrote, 'to show the world how great was the effort he made during the last year of the war to avoid the results of his colossal errors of judgment.' Her argument was that Churchill's sole focus – upon defeating Hitler – blinded him to 'Russian intentions in Europe': that going to war to free Poland from the Nazis had delivered it to the Soviets.[40] She had a point. But in making it she closed her eyes, in that way she had, to certain unanswerable questions.

So too did Sydney, who was still unable to accept that the war had been necessary. Perhaps, like Diana, she felt that she would lose too much by that admission. Her response to all the ruptures was to plough on regardless and hope that family affections would win out in the end. She sent Jessica news of the Christmas of 1943, omitting all mention of the Mosleys. Perhaps seeking to please with a display of egalitarian ideals, she wrote brightly that she imagined few people would seek to return to 'a house full of servants' after the war. (Actually a lot of them wanted nothing better, Diana for one; post-war novels such as those by Agatha Christie are positively obsessed with the dream of good staff.) 'Things like carrying coals and keeping fires going and ordinary housework are *so easy* and quickly done,' Sydney nonetheless wrote, and she for one was probably sincere. She was now sixty-three, condemned to what would have surely seemed like a life sentence with Unity. Yet the sheer busyness of the war suited her. Such a capable woman; rather wasted by that marriage to odd, handsome David. Today she would probably be a CEO, dealing calmly with whatever was thrown at her (which would almost certainly not include seven complicated children).

Given Sydney's truly unusual strength, her supplicating letters to Jessica are peculiarly touching. She was so determined not to let her daughter go completely that she endured Jessica's jibes against her beloved Diana, simply behaving as if they had never been made.

Perhaps it was the same attitude that she had adopted when Unity had longed so much to be in Munich; let her daughter go with a good grace, let her do what she wanted, else she might never forgive. Sydney was like this with her girls. It could be seen as a kind of evasiveness, a refusal – even a reluctance – to confront them; or perhaps it was a brave willingness to make difficult compromises. Either way it was an attitude that never seems to have been extended to Nancy: the difficult eldest, who had come shrieking into Sydney's life when she was young and not naturally maternal, and who made affection so hard to give. When Nancy wrote that her mother disliked her, this was surely an exaggeration. Nevertheless, it is very hard to imagine Sydney writing to Nancy in the way that she wrote to Jessica, although Nancy – a susceptible character beneath her metallic veneer – would probably have been more fundamentally receptive.

Jessica did not even reply to the letter about the family Christmas, so Sydney wrote again. Then came the explanation, with its grudging coda: 'The main reason I haven't written… is because you haven't told me about the Mosleys. I see in the papers that they are now living in Shipton [at the Shaven Crown], so I suppose you do see them. I was so disgusted when they were released… that it actually made me feel like a traitor to write to anyone who had anything to do with them. However I see that it is difficult for you, and not your fault…'[41] This, too, was starting to read like nonsense. The Mosleys were not responsible for the war. They had obviously endorsed anti-Semitism, which was in itself unforgivable, but their private lives did not uphold those grim idiocies. The Communist Party of which Jessica was now a signed-up member had done its own share of killing – Jessica could not distance herself entirely from that knowledge – and had its own authoritarian tendencies. As with Diana, great questions remained unanswered in Jessica's blind faith. Indeed the similarities between the two sisters were remarkable, each adhering to beliefs no more substantial than Unity's imaginary services in the chapel on Inch Kenneth. Yet Diana had more forgiveness in her nature. Years later she wrote to Deborah that she was unable to forget the public statements made by Jessica after the Mosleys' release from jail – 'in my wildest nightmares I cannot imagine myself doing that about either of her husbands' – but there was no desire in her for revenge or retaliation.

Jessica had taken a direct hit with the death of Esmond. But the thought process whereby she attached blame to Diana was absurd; according to that argument Nancy could have blamed her sister when, for instance, her adored Robert Byron was drowned at sea after his ship was torpedoed in 1941. Not such a terrible loss, of course, although Byron's mother wrote to Nancy: 'He loved you the best.' Yet the principle remained the same. If Diana could be held symbolically responsible for one death, then logically this was true of *all* the deaths; also of the fact that Mark Ogilvie-Grant languished in a German prison, and that Hamish St Clair-Erskine had been captured at Tobruk. The laughing aesthetes had become men of war, as had Deborah's merry young dancing companions. In 1944 she lost her four best male friends. That same year her brother-in-law Billy Hartington was killed at the age of twenty-six. Part of the Allied advance after D-Day, he was marching ahead of his battalion at the Belgian border when he was shot through the heart.

Four months earlier, Billy had married Kathleen Kennedy ('Kick'), sister to Jack and a friend of Deborah's from her debutante days. There had been a strong *Romeo and Juliet* style opposition to the match: the Devonshires were 'Black Protestants', the Kennedys were Irish Catholics. Eventually it was agreed that any boys would be brought up Protestant, and any girls Catholic, although Kick's mother Rose, tough bird that she was, remained antagonistic to a marriage that would have made her daughter the Duchess of Devonshire. Not long before the wedding Billy had contested the Derbyshire West by-election, a seat that had been held by the Cavendish family since the sixteenth century. But as Nancy would observe throughout *The Pursuit of Love*, the landowning classes, with their belief in *noblesse oblige*, no longer held their appeal (except in novels). In a prefiguring of the General Election the following year, Labour won the seat – which Deborah deplored, as she would the result in 1945; she disliked 'any Socialist government and their pretences', and had no fear whatever of saying so. Albeit indirectly, the loss of the by-election led to Billy's death. 'I am going out now to fight for you at the front,' he proclaimed to cheers after the result was announced; a woman next to Deborah muttered: 'It's a shame to let him go, a great tall man like he is, he's such a target.' In fact what had made him so visible was his absurd officer's outfit, pale trousers and a swagger stick.

Andrew, now the Devonshire heir, wrote to Deborah how glad he was that she had moved back to the Rookery on the Chatsworth Estate, with her daughter Emma (born 1943) and her new son Peregrine (nicknamed, and always known as, 'Stoker'). She would, he said, be a great comfort to his parents, for whom Deborah did indeed have deep affection (although she always respectfully called them 'Duchess' and 'Duke'). The grief-stricken Duke of Devonshire, Eddy, never went to Chatsworth again, except for the occasion of his daughter's wedding. In his letter Andrew mentioned, as it were in passing, that he had been awarded the Military Cross – 'most undeserved'. This, Deborah commented, was typical of her husband, to make light of courage. He had received his MC for 'the cheerfulness and leadership he displayed' in Italy, when his company had dug in under heavy shelling and was trapped for thirty-six hours with neither food nor drink.

Thereafter Deborah's fear for Andrew was ever more intense. 'Oh dear, I am nearly off my head,' she wrote to her mother, when she received the news that he would come home for good in December 1944. For Peter Rodd, Nancy had feared in a more oblique way (bearing in mind that on his leaves he would, as Harold Acton later wrote, 'ask me not to tell Nancy that he was in London'). He had returned from Italy in Easter that year; it had been, he told Nancy, 'hell on earth'. To Jessica she wrote casually, in reference to the old family nickname for her husband: 'He is toll-gating round the place.'

Meanwhile Tom Mitford, who had fought in Libya and Italy with the King's Royal Rifle Corps, came back to England in 1944 as a major. He underwent administrative training at the Army Staff College in Camberley, from where he visited Diana at Crux Easton. In July he was in London on leave. By chance, he and Nancy met James Lees-Milne outside the Ritz. 'He almost embraced me in the street', wrote Lees-Milne in his diary, 'saying "My dear old friend, my very oldest and dearest friend", which was rather affecting. He looks younger than his age, is rather thin, and still extremely handsome.'

It was while dining with Lees-Milne on this leave that Tom admitted that he still had sympathies with the Nazi viewpoint, that the best Germans he knew were Nazis and that he did not wish to kill them. Yet he was not anti-Semitic; that has never been suggested, rather the opposite (similarly, his friend Janos von Almasy was a Nazi who had no dislike of Jews). By now the first camps, at Sobibor and Treblinka, had been liberated by the Russians. So the paradox of Tom's 'confession', so late in the war, can be resolved only by reference to his deep love of Germany, of some romanticized idea of the German identity as conjured by Wagner, rather than Hitler. But it is almost impossible to understand. His commanding officer, who thought very highly of him, said that Tom 'was not the easiest man to get on with. He held strong views which he defended with skill and wit and he did not suffer fools gladly.' Perhaps this unyielding quality, very much like that of his sister Diana, was what drew him similarly to a stern creed. Lees-Milne, who loved the Mitford family but Nancy the least of them, once wrote: 'There is a vein of callousness in her that almost amounts to cruelty.' He added: 'All the Mitfords seem to have it, even Tom.' How true this was; while at the same time they were capable of warmth, passion, generosity, all the things that Lees-Milne found in his boyhood lover: yet this tough snaking wire was what held them firm as they drove through life. It lay within their jokes, and enabled them to withstand blows that would have destroyed other people. It was certainly very apparent in Nancy, although Lees-Milne was wrong to imply that it was especially strong in her; alone among the Mitfords their father did not have it.

Over dinner, Tom – whose complexity extended to his love life – said that he thought he should get married after the war. He was, after all, the future Lord Redesdale; and from the look of his father that future was not too far away. He listed all his girls, those he had slept with, those he might love, those he merely liked, and asked his friend's advice. 'If I were one of these girls and knew how you were discussing me, I wouldn't dream of marrying you,' said Lees-Milne, adding: 'he roared and roared with laughter.' Then he wrote: 'Tom makes me sad because he looks so sad.'

Tom, who preferred to fight the Japanese rather than the Germans, went out to Burma at the end of 1944. He requested a transfer from Staff to a fighting battalion, and his letters home were resolute and cheerful. In March 1945 he led a force against a small group of Japanese armed with machine-guns, against which his battalion sheltered behind some sheets of corrugated iron. The cover was insufficient. Tom was hit several times in the neck and shoulders, yet he remained conscious and was taken quickly to a field hospital. Like Unity, he was found to have a bullet lodged inside him: in his spine. Although paralysed, he was expected to survive, and was accordingly transferred to another hospital. There he contracted pneumonia. He died on 30 March at the age of thirty-six.

For the Mitfords, the war had finally done its worst.

IX

In her letter to Jessica describing the Christmas of 1943, Sydney had written: 'Very horrid not being with Farve and I greatly hope that next Christmas we may be together.'

By 1944, things should have been a little better. Diana was released. David had an operation for his cataracts, which was successful, although he was obliged to wear very thick glasses (he looked, wrote James Lees-Milne, 'like a piano tuner'). Jessica, happily remarried and now a US citizen, had given birth to her son, Nicholas. For the first time in seven years her father reached out to her: 'Just to send you my love and every good wish for him and his future. Some day, when things are in a more settled state, I greatly hope to see you all, and judging from all news and the look of things it seems to me that there is some prospect that I may last that long – I should much like to. Much love, Farve.'

Sydney got her wish of being with her husband for a time, in so far as she and Unity – now permitted to visit Inch Kenneth – joined him on the island in the summer. Yet Deborah, who stayed with them in August, described the situation as 'misery'. If there was regret for the end of her marriage on Sydney's side, there appeared to be none on David's. In Deborah's view, he seemed to hate his wife. His housekeeper-cum-lady friend, Margaret, was in occupation as surely as the Germans had been in France. She was a boring woman, unfriendly to the Mitford sisters, the sort who took possession of the teapot in order to show Sydney who was boss. But her sheer ordinariness – and lack of political opinions – made her some sort of solace to David. After dinner, at which he sat in grim silence behind his distorting lenses and Margaret talked banalities, the pair scuttled off to the kitchen to do the washing-up together. Unity dragged her mother and sister to the island chapel, where she staged a service with herself in the guise of clergyman. Like a fractious child she became angry and mortified when she forgot the words to the Te Deum and Jubilate, and stomped back to the house alone.

After this, Sydney did not visit the island when her husband was in residence, although she was staying there with Unity when David's telegram came, from London, to say that Tom was dangerously wounded. For Unity, it was consolation that her brother had been fighting the Japanese, not the Germans. One wonders whether she and her mother had ever talked about what was happening in Germany, the remorseless march of the Red Army towards Berlin and the heavenly Führer in his bunker. The city of Breslau was now under siege; this was where, almost seven years earlier, Unity had watched a march-past, 150,000 people by her account, all clamouring for their leader: 'I never expected to see such scenes again,' she had written ecstatically to Diana. What did Sydney now think about her cosy tea party in Hitler's flat, when she saw the footage of rubbery, flaccid bodies piled into pits? She never spoke of it, so far as is known; as with Unity's denials of the mass murder supervised by her old friend Himmler, there had to be an element of self-protection. One wonders, too, whether by March 1945 Sydney had allowed herself to hope that Tom would be saved. She believed it for a while after the arrival of the telegram. 'As the days passed,' she wrote to Jessica, 'we grew hopeful, and the shock when it came was so bad I nearly went mad.' She continued: 'I had to learn from you darling, for your great courage was an example for anyone, but you always were such a brave little D.'

Scorning the rule that confined her to a seven-mile radius of Crux Easton, when Diana received the news about Tom she instantly hired a Daimler and drove with Mosley to Rutland Gate, her police guard beside her. At the mews she found Nancy with Peter, Deborah with Andrew, Pam, the family nanny Blor, and her parents, together perforce. Diana had not seen her father for thirteen years, but she strode into the room in all her dynamic serenity, without embarrassment or hesitancy, and he greeted her affectionately. In James Lees-Milne's account, which he had from Nancy, she 'at once, like the old Diana, held the stage and became the centre of them all'. If Nancy had been capable of jealousy at such a time, she might have then felt it; but she was not. She had adored Tom. To Jessica, she wrote: 'It is almost unbearable oh *Tud* if you knew how sweet & nice & gay he has been of late & on his last leave.'

He had been necessary to the family, a shadowy but steady magnetic pole. Whatever their other feelings, they were united in the fact that they all loved Tom: a man who had known Mosley and Romilly and had found the respect and liking of both. His death had come less than five months before the end; had he not sought to fight the Japanese instead of the Germans, he might have been spared: in that sense he was, like Unity, a casualty of that mysterious affinity. 'I do envy Tom,' she said, in one of her lightning moments of strange acuity, 'having such fascinating arguments with Dr Johnson now.'

Seeking to comfort, Nancy wrote to Jessica that 'Muv & Farve are being simply wonderful & much much better than we had feared at first.' It was not true. Again to Jessica, Sydney described her husband as 'sadly down'; this, too, was understatement. She could not look for consolation from David for the death of their son. Now he would retreat still further into his lair, and move to Redesdale Cottage in Northumberland with the wretched Margaret, leaving Sydney to the wilderness of life with Unity. It was a strange end for the couple who had shared such beguiling beauty, had inhabited the English fairytale world of Asthall with that lively, leaping litter of children. The steep stumbling descent that had begun in 1932, when Diana left her marriage for Mosley, had at last come to an end. Yet even now, when he might have sought it, David could make no full rapprochement with Diana. As she left the mews he insisted on escorting her to the car – his manner still survived – until she explained gently: 'Farve, the man Mosley is waiting for me in the motor,' at which David let her go. The divisions in the Mitfords, which Tom might have bridged had he lived, were now as fixed as the wall that would soon be erected across Berlin; indeed some would outlast it.

Nor did the hand that David had stretched towards Jessica receive an answering grasp. Before Tom's death, his father had made Inch Kenneth over to him; but Tom died intestate, perhaps as a bright wave to fate that he intended to get through the war, and according to Scottish law the island now passed to his sisters. They all chose to hand it to their mother for her lifetime. All, that is, except Jessica, who wrote that she wished to deed her share to the Communist Party in England: 'to undo some of the harm that our family has done, particularly the Mosleys, and Farve when he was in the House of Lords'. A vein of callousness indeed. Given the circumstances in which Jessica had received the bequest of Inch Kenneth, her action was cruel: it was not something that many people could have done. It was also terribly silly. David struggled to a meeting with Jessica's appointed attorney, to whom he suggested that on such a very small island neither the family nor the Communists 'would be happy under the circumstances'. The Communists wanted nothing to do with it either, and clearly thought the arrangement quite mad. Jessica, as was her nature, could not back down. Her share of the island was worth just £500, but she ranted on to her mother that she wanted that much – more if possible – because 'money is an important political weapon... I don't know whether developments in the last ten years have yet proved to you what a criminal thing it was to have supported Hitler and an appeasement policy...' From her new position with the Joint Anti-Fascist Refugee Committee, she stood pure and fiery on the side of the righteous. The behaviour of the Red Army in Berlin was proof, at that time, that the capacity for evil lay not merely within Nazis, but in human nature itself; the point was not made, however, as nobody was willing to speak to Jessica at the time. Only her mother continued to write the letters that ignored it all and reached out to 'Little D'. In the end it was agreed that Sydney alone should keep the island as her home, but that Jessica would hold on to her own share, on a point of political principle.

On one sixth of Inch Kenneth, as across tracts of Europe, the red flag flew.

PART IV

'There they are, held like flies, in the amber of that moment – click goes the camera and on goes life.'

From *The Pursuit of Love* by Nancy Mitford (1945)

I

It was now Nancy's job to reimagine the family that no longer existed, and make of it an enduring English myth.

She herself had moved into a different world, so much so that even the death of Tom could not entirely pierce her happiness. She had met her own life-changing man, the one who would allow her to move away from the Mitfords and inhabit the landscape of her imagination; not just in books, but in France. Although Nancy's love for Gaston Palewski would create its own kind of thraldom, he was also, paradoxically, the means to a glorious freedom.

It was in September 1942, in the garden of the Allies Club in Park Lane, that Nancy was introduced to Palewski, then aged forty-one, a colonel (as she would always call him) in the Free French forces and *chef de cabinet* to his revered Charles de Gaulle. She encountered him in very much the same circumstances as Grace, the heroine of the 1951 novel *The Blessing*, meets her Frenchman: he had been in Ethiopia at the same time as Peter and offered news of him. In *The Blessing*, Charles-Edouard de Valhubert – who brings news of Grace's fiancé – is a tall, dark, superbly elegant viscount with the usual collection of houses, who very soon announces: 'Perhaps I will marry you.' In almost every respect, Nancy's real-life situation was different. Palewski was a small man with a small moustache, he had pitted skin and receding hair, his family was of Polish descent. He had a flat in the Rue Bonaparte and that was all. And he could not propose marriage, even if he had wanted to, given that Nancy was *hors de combat*. Yet her feelings for him were exactly those of Grace: she was 'in love as never before'.

Palewski was an *homme aux femmes*, practised in the art of seduction to the point of social notoriety, although not to his own satiation (one story had him inviting a married society lady to lunch at his flat, and opening the door to her stark naked). He could resist no pretty woman – and Nancy had been rendered very bright and lovely by André Roy – and his way of speaking to her, of courting her, was that of all those Free Frogs combined to the power of ten. The laughing, formal flattery of the men at the Officers Club had made her buoyant, but Palewski had the remarkable power of concentration, of making a woman feel singular, singled out, even as he cast half an eye upon the new arrival in the doorway. 'Fabrice talked to her, at her, and for only her…' Thus she described the first Frenchman of her novels, *the* Frenchman, Fabrice du Sauveterre in *The Pursuit of Love*, the man who launches himself into Linda Radlett's life with the same bowling force as Palewski did into Nancy's.

'Linda was feeling, what she had never so far felt for any man, an overwhelming physical attraction. It made her quite giddy, it terrified her.' Fabrice, like Palewski, is short and stocky and physically unremarkable. He is also – the Pemberley touch – a rich duke. But long before Linda knows this she has fallen, hard and irrevocably, just like her creator. After Peter Rodd, with his sulky little-boy handsomeness and scuttling, showing-off affairs, this was a man at last; his extraordinary confidence with women was something entirely new to Nancy. And she had never before known that love could be *fun*. Palewski was amusing and amused; within the formal French *vous-vous*-ing, the civilized familiarity with Proust and every species of porcelain, there lay an anarchic lightness of spirit that called to the same thing in Nancy, and made her almost alarmingly alive.

For him, she too was different, not a bit like the smart little 'Veronicas and Sheilas and Brendas' (Fabrice's phrase) who were cautiously obsessed with his reputation and whispered about him avidly over their gin and limes. Nancy was clever, nervy, as enchantingly English as a Wedgwood teacup yet somehow detached from the society that she knew too well: already she was hearing the siren call of 'La Marseillaise'. And she had an eagerness, beneath her polish. She was oddly untouched despite the liaison with André Roy, which now dissolved swiftly into the smoky wartime air. That had been a sophisticated affair, taken for what it was. Neither party had allowed the image of Nancy's wrecked fallopian tubes to touch their kindly feelings for the other, and that was the behaviour of grown-ups rather than deluded romantics. Yet with Palewski, who had knocked her sideways, Nancy reverted to a kind of girlhood state: despite her innate discretion she could not help showing off about him, revealing to dinner party guests that she had been with him 'all night' and getting a kick out of their fascinated shock, laying out her heart like an open hand of cards for him to assess and play accordingly. He was a very adult proposition, and she was able to cope with him as such. Yet the tsunami of emotion that had swept over her and carried her off to his bed, where she enjoyed herself as never before, was too great for concealment.

She was still no Sophia in *Pigeon Pie*, calmly retaining control as she picked her way towards fulfilment with her tricky, desirable lover. She was Linda, 'telling' all. Not to her sisters; they were only partly aware of what was going on; although Peter Rodd clearly knew something was afoot, and on his return to England in 1944 marched into Heywood Hill in a towering rage. Like many serial adulterers, he was peculiarly affronted when his erstwhile victim played him at his own game. 'He puts Nancy on edge,' wrote James Lees-Milne, who dined with the couple at Claridge's, 'and makes her pathetically anxious not to displease him. Now why should a husband put a wife under such an obligation?' Nancy was not a natural at infidelity; for all her Mitford airiness she had a powerful sense of guilt, and indeed of correctness. At the same time she was fearful that Peter's perversely possessive behaviour would make her affair impossible. In fact she was unsure how it would continue at all. Palewski was back in France; he visited London briefly in June 1944, then returned for the liberation by the side of his triumphant general. 'Yes I do feel gloomy without the Col,' wrote Nancy to Violet Hammersley (who, having asked plaintively, 'But what of Roy?', now counselled caution), 'but I don't believe it will be another year before I see him again…' She wrote him so many letters that, in allusion to her grey Harrods envelopes, he referred to a '*charmante avalanche grise*'. This hurt her, and he made efforts to retract. But she knew that she was the one in literal pursuit of love, *l'une qui aime*, while he was the *l'un qui se laisse aimer*. He, above all, was the person whom she had 'told'.

This was a wrong move at the very start of the game. When Nancy wrote, in her biography of Madame de Pompadour, that in every successful love affair the man has the upper hand, she was possibly telling herself that she had done the right thing in giving Palewski so much power. Theirs was not a mutual love, she felt more for him than he for her, and of course he knew that. Yet with a very worldly mixture of *gentillesse*, elusiveness and experience, he found an equilibrium that kept the uneven seesaw in play. 'I love you, Colonel,' she would say; to which he would reply '*I know*.' It was a game indeed, although the price that Nancy paid to her opponent was higher than he deserved.

It was not quite as simple as that, however. Nancy never looked at another man after meeting Palewski, and in a sense he became her life. In September 1944, by which time he had returned to France, she wrote to her mother: 'Oh to live in Paris, I'd give anything.' Almost exactly a year later, she did just that: like Jessica, she prised herself from the cling of the past and gave herself to an unknown future in which, by sheer force of will, she found happiness. Her stated reason was to set up a Parisian connection for Heywood Hill (as Evelyn Waugh put it, 'selling Cobbett's *Rural Rides* to the French'). This was her own idea, and she was doing it for Palewski.

'I *can't* live without that military gentleman,' she wrote to Diana. But it was something else too: 'Life *is* more agreeable here.'

She might have gone anyway. What was left for her in England? The grieving parents, the irreparably damaged sister, the errant husband; the grey bombsite of London; the daily work at the bookshop, in which she had been invited to become a partner but with whose nine-to-five she was now heartily bored. It is hardly surprising that, as much as with the man, she had fallen in love with the mirage of Paris. When she wrote of Charles-Edouard de Valhubert that he was 'the forty kings of France rolled into one', that is also what she felt about Palewski. Had he been English, the impulse to love would have been so much weaker. He symbolized a Fragonard world of elegance, prettiness and courtesy; a world of the past, certainly, but that was what Nancy now sought to inhabit, knowing full well that it was where her kind belonged. This was the France that she would describe in *The Blessing* – one of sumptuous parties full of gorgeous people untouched by war and obsessed with *placement*, with houses full of possessions miraculously saved from the Germans – and in which she utterly believed. Indeed she would find it for herself, at the golden embassy presided over by her friend Lady Diana Cooper (whose husband Duff was appointed ambassador after the war), at the *maisons de couture* run by Dior and Lanvin, in the words of Voltaire and St-Simon. If it was not quite the reality of Paris, that did not matter. Like Diana, she had the ability to close her eyes to what she did not wish to see: the aftermath of Occupation, the summary reprisals against collaborators, the women with viciously shaven heads. The most powerful aspect of Nancy was her imagination; to her, therefore, the gleaming France that she inhabited was *not* illusory, it had an absolute truth. 'They were all exactly like ONE, that's the truth!' she wrote of the court of Louis XV. The eighteenth century was what now called to her – rational, amused and civilized – although it left out the part of her nature that had been formed in childhood, which was romantic and emotional and entirely English.

Yet this faith in France, which was just as strong as her sisters' belief in ideology, was what compelled her. It was a writer's faith, above all. With the death of her hopes of children she moved inexorably towards a life of creativity, where perhaps she had always been destined to be. And Palewski was subsumed within it; however real her feelings for him, it was the literary variation upon them that she treasured, the rose-scented affair beneath the Parisian skies that defines Linda Radlett's existence. Love is always, in some measure, a matter of illusion. Look at Diana with Mosley. Nancy had never chosen men with whom she might have had a contented, 'normal' life. When she could have had a rich, steady, sensible husband like Sir Hugh Smiley, she had instead conceived a passion for the openly homosexual Hamish St Clair-Erskine, and accepted a nonchalant proposal from the blatantly unsatisfactory Peter Rodd. Now there was Palewski, unfaithful as they come, stating quite plainly that even if Nancy were to obtain a divorce he could never marry her because General de Gaulle would not like it.

So was she, as has been suggested, simply a bad picker? Or is there in fact no such thing: one picks the people that one wants, often these are the wrong people and, in some obscure way, that was the intention. Again, look at Diana. Without Mosley, her life would have been immeasurably different. Judged by an outsider, it would have been infinitely better. But if anybody ever had the power of choice, it was she, and Mosley was what she had wanted. Nancy, an extremely attractive woman, could also have chosen 'better': a man like André Roy for example, who was able to handle her somewhat 'unfeminine' brains and treated her impeccably. Another Free French officer, the Prince de Beauvau-Craon, was immensely keen on her ('do you think of me a little bit?') but he aroused no interest. It was as though the as yet untapped talents within Nancy led her, in some way that she herself may not have acknowledged, to men who would leave her free. 'If anybody wrote to me like that I'd be sick,' she would later remark, tellingly, about the publication of Lord Curzon's wildly effusive love letters.[1] 'Oh goodness how greatly I prefer the Colonel's respectueusement.' Although she had tried very hard with her marriage, her ambivalent remarks about her pregnancy in 1938 – '2 Peter Rodds in 1 house is unthinkable' – suggest that in her most mysterious self she did not want the normal woman's fate.

'*Faute de mieux*'[2] was Deborah's crisp judgment on the life that Nancy did achieve, that of an enormously successful writer. Deborah, being what she herself called a 'total female', sought a husband who would give her a proper, secure, family environment, within which unhappiness would be incidental, rather than in the nature of things. The men that Nancy chose were absolutely *bound* to cause her suffering. And, however unnecessary that had been, it was real. She had tried to kill herself over Hamish, was made bitter and distraught by Peter. For Palewski she would eventually pass through fires. Yet her romantic imagination, the part of her that drove her art, was entirely fulfilled.

> 'Oh Fabrice, I feel – well, I suppose religious people sometimes feel like this.'
>
> She put her head on his shoulder, and they sat for a long time in silence.

As early as 1942 Nancy had been scribbling away beneath the bombs at what she called 'my autobiography'. *The Pursuit of Love* was dedicated to Palewski, who inspired its exquisite later passages, but she did not write it for him, nor because of him. In October 1944 she was offered the partnership in Heywood Hill, which would have been easily manipulated into setting up the Paris connection; yet she was dismissive and suggested that they wait until after the war. What she most wanted, at that moment, was to write her book. 'My fingers itch for a pen.' She was given three months' leave, and it all poured out. It was there, perhaps, that Palewski had his influence. Through him she understood *how* to write *The Pursuit of Love*: the sublime directness of its style. '*Racontez – racontez*,' says Fabrice to Linda, urging her on to tell stories of her family in her 'sing-song

Radlett voice'. '*La famille Mitford fait ma joie*,' Palewski had said to Nancy, as she enchanted him like Scheherazade throughout their early courtship, the evenings spent à deux in her Maida Vale house, where he would turn up outside the window whistling snatches of Kurt Weill. With her peculiar childlike clarity, her magpie instinct for the glinting detail, she conjured for her kindly, ironic, war-weary lover the magical English fable of her vanished upbringing. And this 'telling', this straightforward act of narration in the first person, was the key that finally opened the gate to her gift. For the first time there were no devices, except the writer's trick of shaping fact to make truth. She told her own story, in her own way, and by the grace of art the Mitford family was made indestructible.

II

'This family again,' Sydney wrote curtly to Jessica, after reading a couple of chapters of *The Pursuit of Love*, and expressing scepticism about Nancy's claim that it would make her £1,000. (In fact it made £7,000 within six months: 'I sat under a shower of gold.')

Her father, meanwhile, had 'cried at the end', as Nancy wrote to John Betjeman: 'He had read a sad book once before called *Tess of the d'Urbervilles* & had hoped never to read another.' His sublime reimagining as Uncle Matthew, the man he had in part been, must also have struck at his heart. So too the transformative mystery whereby the Mitfords were given back their leaping vitality, and seemed to spring like hares across the land he had once owned.

What Sydney did not see – would not have tried to see – was that the book would do more than any public recantations could ever have done to remove the taint upon the family name. As the popularity of *The Pursuit of Love* spread out to a million readers, and its authorial 'voice' grew as delightfully familiar as that of Noël Coward, so the word 'Mitford' would come to symbolize the World According to Nancy. Charm, 'creamy English charm' (in Waugh's immortal phrase), would triumph over causes. Slowly, by degrees, Unity and her swastika would become a doolally posh-girl fashion statement, Diana a blonde icon of enigmatic cool, Jessica a sweet-faced Rosa Luxembourg preaching to the comrades in the accents of the lacrosse captain at Benenden. But *The Pursuit of Love* was far more profound than it was sometimes seen to be. In telling her story, Nancy was also laying out her philosophy of life. Amid the furore that followed publication in December 1945 – in modern parlance, the book went viral – it took a John Betjeman ('oh you clever old girl') to perceive as much. Like all the best art it contained paradox at its heart, a slow-burn of elegiac melancholy set beside an abundant faith in joy. This was Nancy's faith, the courageous belief that happiness was something that one could choose: it was lightly expressed, and most seriously meant.

And it was her great gift to her family, to distil them into this creed. Of course it left out other things, as did the novel; *The Pursuit of Love* contains no portrait of Unity, no Diana; war comes to the book, but the wrecking ball of the 1930s does not swing among the Radletts with that same annihilating force. The revolt of the children against parental control is portrayed as a collective act of youthful folly. 'This,' wrote Nancy, 'was the year when the parents of our contemporaries would console themselves… by saying: "Never mind, just think of the poor Alconleighs!"'

One year of hell? If only. The aftermath of the Mitford rebellions endured along with rationing. As late as 1947 graffiti scarred the door of Diana's London flat in Dolphin Square. Mosley had a private line to the police in case of attack. The couple remained social pariahs: Evelyn Waugh, who had bowed down in worship before the pregnant belly of the young Diana Guinness, wrote a polite reply to her delicate reopening of civilities ('how very nice to have a letter from you. I think of you often...') but reserved his intimate friendship for Nancy. 'You are not to say you are infamous & unfashionable it hurts my feelings,' Nancy wrote to her sister. 'Anyway *nobody* so beautiful & beloved.'

The goddess façade remained in place, but at a cost. After Tom's death Diana had fallen ill again, the trauma of the years in prison revived in her, and she had nightmares in which she was torn from her sons and taken back to Holloway. To blame Mosley – as almost any other woman would have done – was unthinkable. Soon Diana would begin suffering from the debilitating migraines that recurred throughout her life, every one of them surely a symbol of the suppressions that raged beneath. Mosley, who had sold Savehay, bought sight unseen a house in Wiltshire – Crowood – plus acres of land to farm. In order to do so he asked Diana to return the family jewels that he had given her so that he could put them up for auction; she did so without a murmur.

But what Mosley really sought was a return to politics. In a way, one can only admire; whatever else he was, he was a life force. Perhaps his greatest talent was to believe in his own rightness about everything. His son Max would later state that Mosley renounced Fascism after the war,[3] and there is no reason to doubt the sincerity of this statement. Max Mosley is a truth-teller, just as his mother was. He is also a democrat, yet as a young man he saw no difficulty in supporting his father's politics. The problem, as ever with Mosley *père*, was that the nuances of his undoubtedly able brain – which were apparent in what he wrote, and even in some of what he said – were overwhelmed by the theatrical, rabble-rousing, supremely unsubtle things that he *did*. In November 1947 he announced his intention to form a new party: the Union Movement. Some ten years before the signing of the Treaty of Rome, it sought to bring about a union of the European nations, but that was not the end of it. Mosley went on to state that Jews who had not had their roots established in Britain 'for about three generations' would be resettled: presumably in the convenient new State of Israel.

In May 1948 Diana wrote to Nancy that she had attended a meeting in Mosley's old stamping ground, the East End of London (how the government must have wished that he was still restricted to that seven-mile radius). The police presence was strong, but 'we always seemed to be almost *in* a terrifying procession of young & very strong looking Jews who were chanting "Down with Mosley"...' If this was different from what had gone before, it was frankly hard for the casual observer to see any changes. Mosley's old BU loyalists rallied round the flickering flame, although the person most enjoying the sound of his voice was surely himself. Meanwhile Diana knew only too well that her husband's hour, such as it had been, was past. But she clung on with him, her mighty Ozymandias, in the splendid ruin of his near-isolation.

Diana was Nancy's chief correspondent at this time. Their letters were frequent, mutually flattering, abundant with good will. This was probably because Nancy, for once, felt that the power was hers. After a couple of peripatetic years, moving to and fro between London and various Paris billets, she was now – money having smoothed the way – living in a supremely smart apartment in the *septième* (Rue Monsieur, £25 a week), prancing around in her exquisite New Look outfits, socializing with the *gratin* and with the kind of company (the Coopers, Cocteau, Coward) who stimulated her to the limits of her fantastical wit: 'She really *is* the belle of Paris' was a remark that Diana generously reported back to her sister. It was to Diana that Nancy retreated for a few months in 1947, when the dedication of *The Pursuit of Love* – for which Palewski had expressly asked – apparently threatened to cause him embarrassment in his political career. Nancy suffered a great deal over this, even more so since she knew that she had done nothing wrong but dared not quite say so.

In a sense, Diana was also the supplicant in her own relationship: what Mosley wanted was what happened. She did not see it that way, and she was right to the extent that she had chosen her role. Her willingness to close her eyes – to smile her way through her husband's vigorous rants and demands and infidelities – was a deliberate decision. It had its price, but she always believed herself beloved and necessary: as indeed she was. She therefore viewed Nancy's relationship with Palewski as a far more tragic business than her own marriage. 'I think,' she later said, 'he was always slightly hoping that she would go back':[4] meaning to London. With regard to the scandal over the dedication, which had sent Nancy scurrying obediently from Paris into exile, it was Diana's belief that Palewski had semi-fabricated the problem. The left-wing newspaper that had intended to run a damaging article – beneath the headline 'Hitler's mistress's sister dedicates book to Palewski' – had in fact gone on strike (as Palewski would have known) and never printed the story at all. 'I haven't seen it,' Nancy wrote to Diana, '& the Col won't let me because it is apparently too revolting...' In this instance, her trust in him was total. Another woman, more experienced in the handling of love, might have been suspicious when Palewski hustled her out of the country, saying that de Gaulle (always a metaphorical sword between them) must not be upset. Nancy, it seems, was entirely deceived.

Yet she too had chosen her role; and one might say that, for all the '*horror* of love', it caused her less grief than did Diana's thraldom to Mosley. Nancy's life had become so charmed. 'She greets you in a Dior dress, her waist so small that one fears it might snap at any moment.' Thus wrote Evelyn Waugh, describing his epistolary soulmate in her Rue Monsieur *mise-en-scène*. 'This is the only waspish thing about her; all else is sweetness, happiness and inexpressible levity.'[5] Her status as an author, reinforced in 1949 by the publication of her second masterpiece, *Love in a Cold Climate*, reached the exalted position for which writers pray, in which every single thing that they publish is received with rapture and no failure can really touch them. Her social life was a glitterball whirl. Even her brisk daily promenades through the grey-and-dusk boulevards, scattering beams and *bonjours* to all she beheld, brought waves of pleasure. 'I feel almost too much on top of the world,' she wrote to

Diana in 1949. Did the fractured affair with Palewski really have the power to undermine such a very lovely life?

A complicating factor, however, was the sullen appearance of none other than Peter Rodd, who in 1948 decided to plant himself in Nancy's flat, probably with the idea that she would pay him to go away. One evening she was dining with him and his dismal nephews in a restaurant where Palewski was at a table with another woman. In an untypical state of hysteria, convinced that he had proposed marriage to his dinner companion, she telephoned him as soon as she reached her home; and, compounding her error, rang again the next morning to apologize. 'The rights of passion have been proclaimed by the French Revolution,' he replied. It was kind, it was adult, it defused the situation; but it was also a calm, distancing admission of the fact that she loved him in a way that he would never love her. As was her way, she used the sentence in *The Blessing*, when her heroine Grace similarly confronts her unfaithful husband; the difference, of course, being that he *was* her husband. 'The fact is I *couldn't* live through it if he married,' wrote Nancy to Diana. 'He says I take a novelist's view of marriage [true enough], that if he marries it will only be to have children & will make no difference at all.'

But here lay the other issue: Nancy was barren. It is possible, theoretically, that had she been younger and fertile – like a royal bride – Palewski might have considered her as a wife. (He always claimed that de Gaulle had an antipathy to divorce; although that, too, may have been an excuse of sorts.) It is also highly unlikely, although Nancy may have tormented herself over the thought.

Diana, however, viewed her sister's childlessness as tragic in its own right. An oddly conventional view, from such a storming radical; yet it is what she professed to believe. According to Diana, Nancy's will to happiness was brave but it was merely a shopfront: not a philosophy of life at all. 'Unsuccoured'[6] was Diana's word for her sister's relentless snip-snapping humour, her insistence that one would find a joke in the journey to the guillotine. It was a brittle and highly polished carapace, behind which lurked Nancy's own particular darkness, her despair and her spite. This, for Diana, was the real woman. She thought as much, despite familial affection, even before she knew that her sister had informed against her during the war; her wariness seems to have begun with the writing of *Wigs on the Green*, which – encouraged by Mosley – she viewed as a profound betrayal. When she learned of Nancy's more serious act of treachery, she would naturally feel herself to be vindicated. 'Diana hated Nancy,'[7] as a friend put it, towards the end of Diana's life; which was a kind of truth, although not the whole truth.

Nancy could indeed hiss out a sudden jet of poison, as if something serpentine lay twisted inside her. 'My mother used to say she planted a dart in people,'[8] said Diana (a very Sydney remark; if lack of love had bred the spite in Nancy, then her mother surely bore some of the blame for that). James Lees-Milne wrote that her remarks contained a 'sharp little barb, barely concealed'. She could, undeniably, pull one up short. When Deborah miscarried in 1946 after an aeroplane trip, Nancy wrote to Diana: 'Flying nearly always does it, you'd think people would know by now, but perhaps she's really pleased.' Even to Diana herself, very much favourite sister at that time, she was unable to resist wielding her wicked needle. In 1947 she asked if Diana's house was on the procession route for the then Princess Elizabeth's wedding: 'or is there an 18b stand?' Quite funny. Not kind.

Yet Nancy *could* be kind, forgiving, generous – 'the warmest of them', as Betjeman said, and was not he a judge to be reckoned with? She was very good to Diana's and Deborah's children. Diana's son, the perceptive and intelligent Alexander, remembered her as 'a wonderful aunt… a wonderful person to have known'.[9] And to Palewski – 'I know one's not allowed to say this but I love you' – she revealed a capacity to feel that perhaps no man could ever meet. To Deborah, it was 'absolute courage'[10] that led her sister to sublimate her emotions, allowing her romanticism to bloom through her imagination, while rationally seeking the most direct means to happiness. The sudden effusions of spite were a by-product, not the whole. To Diana they were the bedrock of Nancy's nature, albeit covered with all those layers of *millefeuilles* deliciousness. 'Of course' – she wrote to Deborah – 'we know that it was all part of her unhappy life & I don't blame *at all*...[11] Deborah was not as obsessive on this point as Diana, although she essentially agreed about her sister's inner emptiness. After Nancy's death she wrote in a kind of raging sadness: 'I really think she had a FOUL life... I know she had success as a writer but what is that compared to things like proper husbands & lovers & children.'[12]

Nobody can know how much Nancy truly suffered from being denied her female destiny. She was a concealer; even the 'telling' of her passion for the Colonel was a kind of deflection. And as her sisters were not fully in her confidence at the time – they knew of Palewski, but not the true, complex nature of the relationship – they could not really know how Nancy felt about it. From the outside, of course, it looked bad: other people's love affairs quite often do. A woman in her forties, mooning helplessly over a man who fitted her in between General de Gaulle and any juicy peach who allowed him a squeeze? How sad, how pathetic, how silly. But that was not the whole of it. She did, indeed, go through the pangs of disprized love, but that was, as she knew, the deal. Palewski brought her priceless pleasure. And he loved her in his way. He treasured her company, which could be among the best on earth. As for the lack of children: Nancy's thoughts on this were not consistent, they could hint at ineffable pain or intense relief, although either way the subject was raw. The flicked quip about Deborah's miscarriage may have been an involuntary expression of this. To Evelyn Waugh she wrote: 'Don't... tease me about not having children, it was God's idea, not mine.'[13] Yet that does not mean that what she had was purely compensatory: mothers sometimes assume this, but they are not always right.

What her sisters did not, perhaps, understand was that Nancy's life was fundamentally different from theirs: she was a creator, a writer, and as such experienced the world most intensely in her mind. 'N's life was all in fantasy world,' Deborah would later write to Diana, as if this were a rather sad thing. But what Nancy created in her imagination *was* real to her, in a way that they would never quite grasp. The love affair between Fabrice de Sauveterre and Linda Radlett was poignant; not just in itself, but in its fundamental difference from its real-life counterpart; this may have been painful to Nancy but, in her artist's heart, Fabrice and Linda were satisfying as reality could never be. When she said that she was happy, even when it appeared that this was impossible, she was probably telling the truth: such was the strength of the illusions that she could conjure. Such was the will to joy, in which Diana was surely wrong to disbelieve. Nancy's post-war correspondence with Evelyn Waugh is enough on its own to constitute a rebuttal. It is impossible to say which of the two is the funnier, but where Waugh is surreally dry, depressive and droll, Nancy darts with an aerial high-spiritedness that is too vital and effortless for fakery.

Similarly with those two exquisite novels. Although they see their world with absolute clarity they are not satires, as were the four books that came before (*Pigeon Pie* less so). Nancy was never a natural social critic – she is more E. F. Benson than Evelyn Waugh – and in her two masterpieces there is no judgment *whatsoever*, not of Boy Dougdale with his origami-like sexual proclivities, nor of Cedric Hampton with his taste for rough trade and eye to the main chance. What permeates them instead is a glad affirmation, a simple sparkling delight in the human condition. And so these are joyful novels, even when the story that they tell becomes tragic. There are some things that a novelist cannot hide – *Wigs on the Green* is full of wary discontentment about the married state – and Nancy's mature default position was not that of an unhappy person. 'Sophia was amused by life': yes, indeed. And yes, Nancy did want a life of bliss with Gaston Palewski, but not in the way that her sisters would have pictured it. Rather it was what Fanny perceives, through her creator, in *The Pursuit of Love*, when she describes her own deeply contented family life as 'composed of a series of pin-pricks': nannies, children, noise, boredom, housekeeping, her husband's unaccountable moods.

'These are the components of marriage, the wholemeal bread of life, rough, ordinary but sustaining; Linda had been feeding upon honey-dew, and that is an incomparable diet.'

Anyway there is – is there not? – something a bit rich about Diana's assertion that Nancy was pitiably deprived. As with Diana and Jessica: were these two sisters really so different? 'I've given up everything – my family, my friends, my country,' Nancy had once stormed at Palewski, upon which he roared with laughter, '& then of course so did I.' The same was true of Diana, and it was not a laughing matter. The marriage to Mosley had brought opprobrium, jail, the strain of enduring his recreational affairs, which resumed in the 1950s – and *that*, if you like, was spiteful. (It also proved that even then there were women who could not resist him.) Diana's sons were a priceless gift, but she fought with her husband over the Mosley boys, particularly Alexander; the only subject on which she did confront him. So was the knowledge of Mosley's love – deep, but deeply selfish – sufficient repayment for what Diana had offered? Were her splintering migraines not the equivalent of Nancy's sudden shafts of malice: the inevitable fissures in a life sustained by illusion? Not that illusion is necessarily a bad thing, so long as it can be maintained. Both Nancy and Diana preferred it that way; both were able to keep their intelligence separate from their hearts. And these profound similarities made the differences between them – Diana was never disloyal, rarely spiteful and always controlled – all the more apparent.

What is especially interesting is that Diana showed a willingness to forgive Jessica for the kind of behaviour that she reviled in Nancy. This was despite the fact that Jessica would not shift from that obdurate stance against her Fascist sister: 'the public Decca is somebody unforgivably callous & hard', wrote Diana to Deborah. But, as she also wrote: 'The private Decca is Decca.' Given Jessica's behaviour towards Diana, this was a remarkable statement. It was an absolute reversal of the judgment upon Nancy, whom Diana viewed as a delightful social being with the cold blood of a lizard. It was also fiercely reminiscent of the way in which Jessica forgave in Unity what she could not in Diana. In other words, the twin queens among the Mitford sisters were both judged according to their dominance: with a harshness that the rest did not excite.

At the same time – and this was entirely typical of the complexity within that six-ply weave – Nancy and Diana had enjoyed a kind of laughing alliance against Jessica. Together they mocked what they viewed as her righteous pomposity. In 1947, for example, Jessica had written to Nancy lecturing her quite seriously on the dangers of forgiving Diana. By this time she had given birth to her second son, Benjamin, and was living near San Francisco, where she had become deeply involved in the Civil Rights Congress – formed around this time – and in raising money for the American Communist Party. There was a touch of Mrs Jellyby about her, bustling about angrily for her causes, leaving her household to fend for itself. Her mother-in-law, Aranka – Hungarian by birth, a custom milliner in New York – was critical of this attitude, and could not believe the sordid back-yard in which the children played, but Jessica became very fond of her. She thought her a warm woman: unlike Sydney. Nevertheless when Nancy met Aranka in Paris (for the fashion shows), she reported gleefully to Diana that Aranka had moaned incessantly about her daughter-in-law: '"My Bob never thought of being a communist till he met her".' Diana replied by quoting Mosley, who had suggested that when all was said and done only one Mitford had ever harmed a Jew: 'Decca.' Which was, incidentally, an off-colour joke in the Nancy style.

In 1948 Sydney, now aged sixty-eight, flew to California to visit Jessica (whose children – Lord knows what they can have been told – believed that they would have to bow to their grandmother). It was an impressive show of intent, of the desire to heal a breach that was ostensibly about Sydney's pro-Fascist sympathies but that had, as ever, run far deeper into the territory of the emotions; as was proved when during the visit Jessica launched a sudden missile attack, screaming and storming at her mother as they stood together in her kitchen. The obsession with school recurred – why, she wailed, had Sydney refused to allow her to go? This, in itself, was a symbolic grievance: of what, it is hard to say, other than a generalized feeling that Sydney had been an inadequate mother, that the home life she had created had not been the one that Jessica had wanted. From a grown woman who had caused her own share of grief to the family, this display of hysterics was not overly attractive. It may even have struck Sydney as rather American. *Nancy*, at least, would not have behaved like that; but one also wonders whether Sydney would have reacted as gamely if she had. She made great efforts with Jessica, even to the point of meeting her Communist friends (did they know that she had shaken the hand of Hitler?) She liked her son-in-law; who was, as it happened, quite clever enough to make up his own mind about becoming a Communist. To that extent, the visit was a success, although it did not prevent Jessica from returning to the theme of her awful upbringing in *Hons and Rebels*, nor allying with Nancy against their mother in later life.

Diana, of course, was enraged by that. She loved Sydney, who had shown such stalwart loyalty during the war, with an intensity of protectiveness. And she was disgusted by Jessica's desire to demonize their mother, just as she was by the same urge in Nancy. Yet Jessica did not *bother* her in the same way. When Nancy showed reluctance to make the dire journey to Inch Kenneth, Diana asked Deborah the tentative question: 'She hasn't got much heart?' but made no such comment about Jessica, who did not visit their mother at all. Nancy had skipped off to France, yet she did not sever ties in the definitive way that Jessica had done, leaving Sydney to cross the Atlantic with an olive branch in her ageing hands.

Devotion to Mosley meant that his allegiances were Diana's also, and he disliked Nancy. Diana wanted to see her, but she was always made aware of her husband's teeth-grinding antipathy, and felt obliged to share it. There may, however, have been something more: something to do with the simple, infinitely difficult sister relationship, which in the Mitfords was writ so large. It is clear enough that Nancy was jealous of Diana. But was the opposite also true? Did Diana envy that creative gift, that perfect little novel, which used their shared past and won acclaim for Nancy alone – did she even envy the freedom to lead that effervescent Parisian life, while she was glued to the side of her tempestuous man? Possibly. And what of the friendship with Evelyn Waugh, whom she had once held so easily in her thrall? Later Diana reviewed the published correspondence between Nancy and Waugh, and without much evidence posited the idea (to Deborah) that Nancy had been hurt by Waugh's teasing 'Open Letter' in response to the 'U and Non-U' furore: it seemed to be something that Diana *wanted* to believe. She was at pains to make clear that his last letters had in fact been written to *her*. They were both passionate women, these two Mitford girls, although one sought to hide this beneath a slightly cracked veneer, the other more successfully within the guise of a smiling Madonna. Whatever emotions Nancy felt for Diana, these would surely have been reciprocated in strength.

After Nancy found soaring success as a writer, all her sisters sought to emulate her – even Pamela considered a book ('it would be nearly all Food!!!') – and colluded in their different ways with the fame that *The Pursuit of Love* had brought them. Like the public, albeit with reservations and self-awareness, they bought into Nancy's mythmaking. As Nancy wrote of *Hons and Rebels*, 'In some respects she has seen the family... through the eyes of my books':[14] it was true, in a way, of all the sisters. Just as Diana had led the troops into the darkness of battle by her defection to the Fascist cause in 1932, so Nancy did the same with her shift into the sunlight of public adoration. Because of Diana, they had become the 'mad, mad Mitfords'. Because of Nancy, they all – with however great a show of reluctance – became the Mitford girls.

Above: Deborah in her favoured sportswoman mode, at a point-to-point in 1938 with the Hon. Pamela Herman (*left*) and Lady Margaret Ogilvy.

Right: Unity in 1938.

Le mystère de la disparition de Miss Unity Mitford, celle que Hitler appelait « l'idéal de la femme nordique parfaite », n'est pas prêt d'être élucidé. Peut-être ne le sera-t-il jamais.

L'opinion du prince Nicolas Orloff, — il vient d'arriver ces jours-ci à Belgrade, — qui fut jusqu'à la guerre speaker anglais à la radio berlinoise, est catégorique.

— Unity Mitford s'est suicidée avec son propre revolver, le 3 septembre dernier, dans son appartement de Munich. Elle fut transportée dans un hôpital de la ville où Hitler lui envoya des fleurs. Lorsque le bouquet arriva, Unity était encore en vie, mais les médecins n'avaient que peu d'espoir de la sauver.

Quant à connaître le pourquoi de ce suicide au revolver, inutile. Aucune hypothèse n'est seulement avancée. Et la presse allemande est muette sur toute la ligne.

Seconde version : désespérée par la guerre qui a éclaté entre son pays natal et son pays d'élection, la jeune et belle Anglaise aurait absorbé du véronal, après une entrevue orageuse avec le seigneur de Berchtesgaden. Elle l'aurait elle-même expliqué après son transfert à l'hôpital où elle aurait repris connaissance.

Enfin, troisième version : l'Égérie d'Adolf Hitler serait tombée sous les coups de fanatiques des Sections Secrètes, le jour même de l'ouverture des hostilités. Et ceux qui se disent renseignés mettent en avant l'arrestation de l'aide de camp du Führer chargé de veiller à la sécurité de Miss Unity Mitford, ainsi que les coupes sombres opérées parmi les S. S. munichoises entre les 2 et 10 septembre dernier.

Tout cela est en effet troublant. Mais, à vrai dire, en dehors d'un télégramme de Munich annonçant la tentative de suicide, on ne sait rien d'autre. La mort même n'a point été confirmée. Ce qui fait que toutes les suppositions — y compris celles d'une arrestation et d'une « exécution » — demeurent permises.

UNE FAMILLE QUI FAIT PARLER D'ELLE

Miss Unity Valkyrie Freeman Mitford n'était autre que l'aînée des six filles de Lord Redesdale, le puissant magnat des Compagnies anglaises d'assurances.

Vétéran de la guerre des Boers, britannique cent pour cent, ennemi de tous les

en savait-elle trop

Suicide? Assassinat! Disparition!

Portrait tout récent de Miss Unity Mitford. (F. P.) (N° 16442.)

QUAND GŒRING OFFRE... DES PISTOLETS AUX FEMMES

En 1930 à une époque où le nazisme commençait son ascension au pouvoir, Hitler avait fait choix, pour conseillère intime, de sa propre nièce, Greta Ranbal qu'on disait ardente sous tous les rapports.

Pour son anniversaire le maréchal Gœring lui offrit des fleurs et... un superbe automatique parabellum à crosse nacrée.

— C'est toujours utile, fit-il avec rondeur.

Peu après, Greta Ranbal... se suicidait d'une balle en plein cœur.

On l'inhuma à Vienne et Hitler assista secrètement à ses obsèques.

Unity Walkyrie eut aussi son « petit anniversaire », cet été. Des orchidées et... un automatique Walther, don du souriant Gœring.

— On ne sait jamais... fit cette fois encore le maréchal.

L'existence de ce pistolet est d'autant plus connue que Unity l'a montré à des amis. Elle était d'ailleurs très satisfaite d'avoir obtenu du chef de la Gestapo de Munich, Albert Wagner, l'autorisation spéciale de le porter sur elle. Peut-être pensait-elle avoir à s'en servir contre ses ennemis personnels.

Quels ennemis ? Policiers, S. S., ou bien des gens de l'entourage immédiat de « my Führer ».

Toujours est-il que le prince Nicolas Orloff a cru pouvoir affirmer à un correspondant de la presse anglaise :

— Unity s'est suicidée avec ce pistolet, le 3 septembre.

Étrange, cette histoire des pistolets de Gœring que les Égéries de Hitler se repassent comme des flambeaux.

Plus étrange encore qu'on ne puisse dire ce qu'il est advenu du corps de la belle Anglaise... si toutefois le suicide est prouvé. Ce suicide duquel on ne donne aucune raison satisfaisante...

Mages et astrologues, compagnons de lutte et généraux, amies et conseillères, on disparaît singulièrement vite et sans bruit dans l'entourage de « my Führer ».

Il est vrai que Gœring ne s'en porte pas plus mal...

M. Vidal.

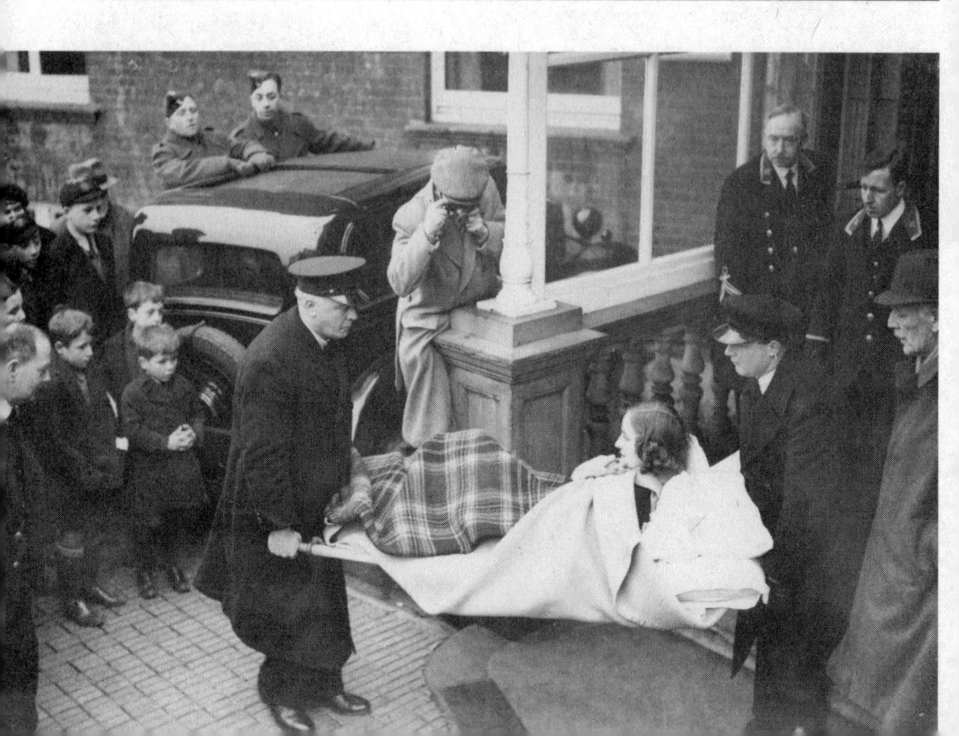

Above: Jessica in 1940 with her first husband, Esmond Romilly. The couple briefly ran a bar in Miami.

Top left: A 1939 article in *Partout* magazine speculating on the fate of 'Unity Mitford: the Führer's Muse'. Unity's name appeared constantly in the British and overseas press.

Opposite: Unity in 1940, after her suicide attempt, being transported on a stretcher from the port of Folkestone to her home in High Wycombe. Her father (*extreme right*) looks on.

Above: Diana and her second husband, Sir Oswald Mosley, under house arrest after their release from Holloway in late 1943.

Right: The Mill Cottage at Swinbrook, formerly owned by David, later rented by Sydney as a place of refuge for Unity.

Opposite: Deborah's wedding day in 1941. She was dressed by Victor Stiebel; her father wore his Home Guard uniform.

Nancy in the 1950s, at her beloved apartment in the Rue Monsieur, holding one of her writing notebooks.

The young Duchess of Devonshire:
Deborah in 1954.

Jessica in 1966 with her second
husband, Robert Treuhaft.

The graves of Nancy, Unity and Diana in the churchyard of St Mary's, Swinbrook.
Diana's grandson Alexander, who died in 2009, is buried to her left.

The Mitford children in 1935, with members of the Heythrop hunt behind.
Left to right: Unity, Tom, Deborah, Diana, Jessica, Nancy (plus French bulldog), Pamela.

III

At the start of May 1948, Sydney returned home from San Francisco. She was visited in London by Diana, who wrote to Nancy that their mother having a bad time – yet again – with Unity, 'who had spent a guinea on some dead roses for her & then was taking it out of her like mad by saying she had a temp of 103 . . .'

The ambivalence of Nancy's feelings towards Sydney – the fact that she did not actually want to dislike her – had previously expressed itself, in her sidelong way, by a real concern about the impossible strain of the life that her mother was leading. She had suggested to Diana that they – and Deborah, who was of the same mind – pay towards a separate establishment for Unity, 'with an attendant & an ample supply of bed linen', but she was uncertain as to how she could broach the subject. '*Oh* for Tom.'

Sydney was, indeed, terrified by the thought that she would die before Unity. What, after all, would become of her? 'I believe', wrote Nancy, 'she half thinks Boud will be on the streets like a poor stray dog.' Somebody could indeed have been paid to look after her, somewhere close to one of her sisters (they too must have dreaded the prospect); but the patience displayed by Sydney was unlikely to be replicated elsewhere. Unity remained physically strong, as well as immensely irritable, and in 1947 had taken a part-time job in a hospital in High Wycombe, washing up and serving tea. But the bullet in her brain was like one of those bombs buried in wartime: at the slightest touch it could decide to become active. The high temperature that she complained of on her mother's return from America may not have been invented out of pique. Diana's letter was written on 2 May, at which point Unity had twenty-six days to live.

She and Sydney took the long journey to Inch Kenneth, the place of refuge that catastrophe would soon visit once more and – as with the death of Tom – acquire a peculiarly nightmarish quality. At first

Unity seemed well enough, but a couple of weeks after arriving on the island she went to bed with a fever. Sydney's communications with the mainland were not made by phone, or in any remotely convenient way, but by hanging a black disc on a garage door that could be seen through binoculars: via these means, a doctor was called. The high winds and rough sea meant that he was delayed for several days. By the time he reached Unity her temple was bulging, her temperature very high. 'I am coming,' she said suddenly. Then her mother knew that she was dying.

Nevertheless attempts at treatment continued for what had now been diagnosed as meningitis, caused by an infection from the bullet. The mother and daughter went by boat to the mainland, and penicillin was administered at the hospital in Oban. As arrangements were being made for ambulance transport to a specialist neurosurgery unit – a journey much like the one made from Folkestone eight years earlier – Unity had an epileptic fit and lapsed into unconsciousness. She died the same day, aged just short of thirty-four.

Death, which had sat fidgeting in the waiting room since the first day of war, had at last risen to claim great galumphing Boud, who had rampaged through life like an innocent puppy but had held so much unfathomable darkness. In a strange way she had been the happiest of the sisters. Yet she had had not a clue as to how to live. She had been entirely at the mercy of her giant capacity for passion, for which she had sought a vessel of equal magnitude: the times being what they were, she had the evil luck to find one, and paid an equally all-consuming price for it. For Sydney, who had endured pain beyond imagining with her daughter, there was surely a degree of relief; not least that Unity would not now outlive her. But the real grief would have been for the girl who had existed before the suicide attempt – 'How cruel it was, really, to bring her back to life,' wrote Diana[15] – or perhaps before the first visit to Munich.

After Unity's death, Diana wrote to Nancy (who, rather to her own surprise, was devastated by the loss of her sister). The letter said that Sydney was greatly distressed by a remark that Nancy had made, suggesting that Unity should never have been taken so far away from her doctor at the Radcliffe Infirmary. There was no reproach in Diana's tone – the relationship between the sisters was still close at that time, and Diana was at pains to say that their mother must have misunderstood – but she wanted Nancy to give some reassurance. Nancy, meanwhile, was appalled: she had said nothing of the kind, she wrote to Diana, all she had done was *mention* the doctor. On this occasion, one believes her. It was, certainly, the sort of accusation that Sydney would have made only against this particular daughter, who had after all made the grim visit to Inch Kenneth after Unity's death. Of course Sydney was in a state of great grief; increased, perhaps, by a sense that she should *not* indeed have taken her daughter to the island. If Nancy had even hinted at such a thing, she may have touched a nerve of guilt. But Sydney's ability to stir the same emotion in Nancy was always very strong. 'I can't bear her to think I feel that anything different should have been done.' She wrote to her mother, saying as much, but the fundamental impasse between the two women remained.

As did the protectiveness that her sisters felt towards Unity; for them she remained vulnerable after death. When her biography was written in 1976 the surviving Mitfords returned to war in their particular, inter-familial way. Mosley – who, in a television debate coinciding with its publication, described Unity as 'a sweet gel, an honest gel'[16] – attempted to have the book suppressed, as did the Devonshires. Jessica, who had co-operated with the author David Pryce-Jones, was blamed for having done so. Deborah's view had been that nobody who had not known Unity could possibly portray her, so contradictory was her character: 'it would just be Nazis all the way'. (She added: 'I do wish people would stop writing books.')

When the biography was sent to Diana in proof, she wrote to Deborah: 'It is very nasty.' She deplored the interviews with Mary Ormsby-Gore and, especially, with the family's former parlourmaid Mabel, by then aged ninety and in Diana's view not a reliable witness. Mabel had, for instance, claimed that David Redesdale had said to her: 'I can never lift my head up again' – admittedly most unlikely from such a proud, withdrawn man. Diana was also appalled by the amount of material concerning the crazy anti-Semite Julius Streicher, and by what she perceived as the attempt to imply an affair between him and Unity. 'He was about two feet high and wildly unattractive' (the least of his problems, one might think). Diana longed, she said, to defend Unity, while recognizing that this was almost impossible. Oddly enough, it was Pamela who was the most enraged of all – beneath the passivity lay the Mitford steel – and accused Jessica of stealing a scrapbook of photographs for use in the book. Jessica furiously denied this to Pam and wrote a letter, both defensive and emollient, to Deborah. 'I can't make a break with her,' was Deborah's resigned conclusion to Diana. Thus, deep into middle age, the divisions and alliances remained as alive as ever. Of course the objections to the biography were slightly disingenuous, although several interviewees did claim to have been misquoted (fearful perhaps of the Mitford Furies?). Nevertheless the book was remarkably researched; it sought to understand rather than condemn, and the fact remained that Unity *had* associated closely with the Nazi regime. Did the Mitfords really believe that such behaviour remained, as it were, within the family; that the loyalty of friends was to be commanded, in the face of what Unity had said and done; that there were no public implications? This was an extraordinary expression of their peculiar confidence, if so, and it seemed as though it *was* so.

Unity was buried at Swinbrook, a place she had loved. Towards the end of her life she had amused herself by planning her funeral, although it was Sydney's choice to engrave the line from Clough on her tomb: 'Say not the struggle naught availeth.' The Mosleys attended the ceremony, and although David did not speak to Diana's husband she later received a letter from him apologizing for this: he had not meant any snub. To his wife, however, he gave no sign of lasting reconciliation. He had travelled to Oban to meet her, and they returned together to Swinbrook with their daughter's coffin. Yet in July, just six weeks after Unity's death, Nancy ran into his housekeeper Margaret, quite by chance, at the palace of Versailles. To Diana she described the encounter. Their father rang or wrote to Margaret every day, she said, and in her casual way she remarked how glad she was that David had found love: 'One can't say there was ever much of that from Muv who didn't even like him particularly – not that I blame her.' This, from the woman who had created the eternal partnership of Uncle Matthew and Aunt Sadie, in all its configurative contentment, and who even then was reconjuring it in *Love in a Cold Climate*? Did she really believe what she said? In a sense, perhaps, although the desire for detachment (and perhaps the ever-present urge to shock) made her too sharp. She had loved her father, and she admired her mother. He was the warmer, unquestionably, although so much the weaker. This is hinted at in Nancy's novels, which portray Sadie sitting vaguely 'on her cloud' while her husband – who is never quite happy away from her (unless it is with somebody like his gamekeeper) – does most of what she wants. Despite his theatrical displays of temper, his children never really fear him or his disapproval. It is Sadie whose good opinion they seek. When Linda disappears with the glamorous Communist Christian in *The Pursuit of Love*, it is her mother's imagined reaction – sorrowful, guilt-inducing – that worries her. Yet for all this, the veil of benevolence that Nancy throws over her parents' fictional marriage embraces it completely. There is never a moment's doubt that it is happy, nor that it will not last until death. However ironic this seemed by the time the novels were published, it surely contained something of the truth of the Redesdales' past: it was their children who destroyed them and their life together.

Despite the death of Unity, the unspeakable irruption of Peter Rodd into her life, the terrible evening stuck with him at a restaurant table while the Colonel flirted merrily at another, Nancy wrote to Evelyn Waugh with this typically teasing exclamation: 'Heavenly 1948.' He replied – similarly in character – 'What an odd idea of heaven. Of course in my country we cannot enjoy the elegant clothes & meals & masquerades which fill your days.'

In France, it was true, Nancy was leading a life that England forbade. One of her aunts, her father's sister Iris, wrote rather nastily, accusing her of not wishing to share in the austerity. Who, wondered Nancy, could actually wish such a thing? Waugh's not wholly joking riposte was that she had voted for the government that was imposing these exigencies, then fled their consequences.

After the war, when the top rate of tax rose to 19s 6d in the pound, Derek Jackson had simply upped sticks with Pamela and moved to Ireland. They lived at Tullamaine Castle, in the hunting country of Tipperary. For all his love of horses – he rode in the 1946 Grand National – he rather quickly tired of the lack of intellectual stimulation and began working in the scientific laboratories at Dublin University. There he met a young woman named Janetta Kee, who would become the third of his six wives. For Pamela, impenetrable though her emotions were, this may have been something of a relief – as Deborah later guardedly remarked, Derek was 'not like others'. It may even have been a joy, when she discovered the size of her divorce settlement. 'So glad Woman is to roll,' Nancy wrote to Diana in 1950. Plenty of people would have seethed over Pamela's effectively unearned wealth, but in some ways Nancy could rise above the pettiness of jealousy; she did not seem to mind, for instance, when Jessica rivalled her success as a writer (despite the imitative aspect of *Hons and Rebels*) and she even told Evelyn Waugh that Diana's memoirs, begun in 1962, were 'dazzling and screamingly funny'. In another mood, of course, she might have said differently. Beyond all else, Nancy was unaccountable. What did she think, for instance, when Deborah became Duchess of Devonshire, chatelaine of a house that made Batsford look as bogus as an example of a Barratt Homes Georgian?

In 1946 Deborah and Andrew had moved to Edensor, close to Chatsworth House, which that year was vacated by its wartime residents, 300 girls from Penrhos College. The rooms of the great stately home were cold and echoing: the contents had been stashed away, Old Masters stuffed casually into drawers, and the clocks, which were wound once a week, struck loudly in the emptiness. The Duke of Devonshire had taken little interest in Chatsworth since the death of his heir, although he was persuaded by his librarian that it should be run as a proper business. Two Hungarian sisters, together with a small team of Eastern European women, took on the job of dusting and polishing the rooms, which at that time numbered 178. The duke, who had removed himself to another family home, Compton Place at Eastbourne, spent his time drinking and chopping wood. He also handed over most of his fortune to the Chatsworth Settlement Trust, which required him to live a further five years if his descendants were to avoid death duties. He died of a massive heart attack in 1950, aged fifty-five, fourteen weeks before the time was up. His death certificate was signed by Dr John Bodkin Adams, who had treated Deborah's two oldest children for whooping cough and the following year was accused of murdering a patient: he was later suspected of killing some 160 others.

The post-war tax regime now had the 11th Duke and Duchess of Devonshire in its grip. Death duties were levied at a rate of 80 per cent on what was, undeniably, a massive estate: a house in London's Mayfair (the old town house on Piccadilly, where Sydney attended her first debutante dance, was long sold); Lismore Castle in Ireland; great chunks of Derbyshire; land in Scotland; and Chatsworth House itself – dreamlike despite its substance, its flattened dull-gold frontage seeming to float in the air – with its Sculpture Gallery full of Canovas, its great gardens designed by Paxton, its roof spanning 1.3 acres. Nevertheless the debt was harsh – four-fifths of the estate had to go – and this would have confirmed Deborah, if such a thing had been necessary, in her dislike of socialist governments. In 1945 Andrew had stood as a Conservative candidate for the Chesterfield constituency, which he lost by more than 12,000 votes. While canvassing he was heckled and spat at, and on one occasion a car in which he and Deborah sat was rolled repeatedly until it almost turned over. Unlike some of her sisters, she got no kick out of this kind of political agitating. Like Uncle Matthew she believed in public duty and the sanctity of land ownership; believed therefore that Andrew was the custodian of his inheritance, and understood that responsibility better than the state. She was, in that sense, a true conservative. She would probably have been baffled by the fact that Nancy could express a nostalgic longing for those same ideals in *The Pursuit of Love* while voting for Mr Attlee. (It was indeed a paradox, although – one might say – by the by in that family.)

But Deborah also understood – as did Nancy – that the world had shifted away from her kind. She was above all a pragmatist. As her father had done in order to survive, Andrew sold: in this case thousands of acres, magnificent furniture and several paintings, including a Rembrandt that was later found to be a 'studio production'. In 1954, when the debt to the Exchequer was in the process of being discharged, Nancy wrote an acid little aside to Evelyn Waugh, saying that she would sympathize more with the Devonshires if they actually cared about these objects (she also suggested to Deborah that the drawers-full of Old Masters had made her sister's fingers 'itch for an india-rubber'). Perfectly true that Deborah was not an aesthete by nature; also true that Nancy was joking; but the serpentine glint is surely discernible in Nancy's remarks. At the same time she would have fairly relished the fact that her sister was a Grade One Duchess, who had placed the Mitfords in the impenetrable aristocratic sphere that fascinated Nancy as much as it did her readers. And for all her socialistic sympathies, which are sometimes so hard to detect, she would have believed that the Devonshire legacy was best handled by the Devonshires. In fact the debt to the government was not cleared until 1974. The money that might have restored Chatsworth for the nation had been returned to the nation. But the job of the house had begun: Deborah, who hated work, would find in it fulfilment.

In 1950, meanwhile, the year that Deborah became a duchess, Diana and her husband took the decision to leave Britain. It had perhaps been inevitable; although the Mosleys were now less isolated, they were in a sense exiles within their own country, and their new faith in the European ideal led them to France (and to winters in

Ireland, where their son Max loved to hunt). With their extraordinary talent for finding beautiful houses, which never deserted them even in the worst days of excoriation, they bought a dilapidated white house with a Palladian facade, the Temple de la Gloire, at Orsay. It was a palace, albeit in miniature: 'It's charming, but where do you live?' asked Diana's friend (and companion semi-outcast) the Duchess of Windsor. Just as Deborah was doing in Derbyshire, Diana absorbed herself in restoring the house, which could have been conceived by a designer as the perfect stage setting for her statuesque beauty: at forty she was quite undiminished in looks and would have been ideally placed on top of one of the Temple's Corinthian columns. A frequent visitor was Nancy, from nearby Paris: 'she very very often came,' as Diana later said, although Mosley 'would have much preferred she hadn't, but I always wanted her. They got on outwardly all right, because of me I suppose, but they must have both been making an effort. I suppose manners – !'[17] The sisters spoke every morning on the phone; one can imagine Mosley's pacings and tuttings as the middle-aged Mitford girls gossiped and shrieked. Diana was habitually torn, made to feel uncomfortable, required to show nothing of her feelings, as her husband's possessiveness extended to the relationship with her sister. It was rather monstrous. It was as though, whatever Diana gave her husband, he would merely ask for more. There is no question that he loved her, but love is filtered through character, and therefore Mosley's love was an egotistical one. One might even say that it was sadistic, that he took pleasure in seeing the goddess at his feet. What a sense of power that would give – especially with a woman like Diana! The fact that she would always retain her dignity, that it was in fact impossible to bring her low, meant that she had his absolute respect; meant, too, that the game of maintaining her thraldom would always be fun to play.

He was right, however, to be suspicious of Nancy. Whatever Diana privately thought of her, their closeness ran very deep – again through mutual respect, a sense of equality – but proximity meant that the latent jealousy in Nancy reared up again. If Diana had hoped that her sister would effect a smoothing of the entrée into Paris society, she should surely have known better. Nancy did not particularly want her glittering friends to meet the Mosleys. For some time she tried to keep Palewski away from them. Some instinct of privacy perhaps directed her; although she would not have especially wanted to hear the Colonel's rapturous hymns to her sister's deathless allure.

The Mosleys were unwelcome at the embassy, now presided over by Sir Oliver Harvey, with whom Nancy was very friendly (she described his replacement of the celebrated Diana and Duff Cooper in her last novel, *Don't Tell Alfred*). Diplomats were forbidden to visit the Temple. Unsurprisingly, the Rothschilds had no desire to do so. So Nancy may have calculated that it would do her no good to bring the devil Mosleys into her circle; better to flutter around them in Orsay and institute a de facto seven-mile radius. Yet it is more likely that she was impelled by the memory of 1929, when her beloved aesthete friends, the Swinbrook Sewers, had defected to Diana. Having conquered Paris, how could Nancy bear to step aside again?

IV

For Jessica, the adherence to the Communist creed was making her life difficult, although she would have relished that: she had always liked a fight. In 1950 she and her husband had tried to visit England, but were refused passports. Instead Deborah visited America in 1952, and described to Diana how 'a figure appeared who somehow was Decca and yet *completely* different... Oh Honks.' True to form, Jessica claimed that she had stopped writing to Nancy on the grounds that she was 'living with [sic] a Gaullist'.

Yet by now there was far more to Jessica than the youthful posturing to which she reverted with her sisters. Her husband later described how the Civil Rights Congress appealed not merely to the black population, but to

> left-wing whites... My wife became interested in it. She became Secretary-Treasurer of the East Bay local [where she lived outside San Francisco] and devoted herself to it for ten years. Pretty much on assignment to begin with, from the Communist party. You had to find a place where you were going to be active – a 'mass organization' – and this was her mass organization. As lawyers, my partner and I were the only ones in the East Bay who would take these cases.[18]

In 1951, through her husband – and the Civil Rights Congress that handled the defence – Jessica became involved in the case of a black Mississippi man named Willie McGee, who was sentenced to death for the rape of a white woman. With three female friends she marched bravely on Jackson, where lynching was commonplace and Ku Klux Klan membership quite normal, and organized a mass protest. She was not alone in her belief that the case against McGee was unproven and racially motivated. William Faulkner, Albert Einstein and Paul Robeson were among those who joined the international pressure on President Truman to reconsider the sentence. He did not: McGee was executed. In his last letter to his wife he wrote: 'Tell the people the real reason they are going to take my life is to keep the Negro down.' Jessica was left like Linda in *The Pursuit of Love*, helplessly lamenting the Scottsboro' Boys (nine black youths accused of raping two white women): 'I'll bet they'll be electrocuted in the end...'

Yet it had been noble behaviour. Jessica had displayed the bright aristocratic fervour of Eugenia Malmains in *Wigs on the Green* – she was frightened of nobody – but for once a Mitford cause had absolute right on its side. Not that it was portrayed that way in the press. In an America seized with the fear of Communism – rather as Britain had been in the 1930s – the McGee protesters were regarded as a bunch of rabble-rousers. The fear of Communism (Reds under the bed) had already shown itself during the war, with a government 'loyalty program' in place in Washington, and the Dies Committee established as a precursor to the House of Un-American Activities Committee. But by the 1950s, the nuclear era, a kind of hysteria took hold. The Treuhafts' phone was tapped. Both were under surveillance. In a report dated 3 October 1950, the FBI 'recommended that a Security Index card be prepared on the above captioned individual': Jessica. Her husband was sent a 'written interrogatory', which, as he later said, made it clear that there were no charges but nevertheless contained a real threat:

> 'We have information to the effect that you've attended social events where Communists and other subversives were present. Is it true that you subscribe to the *Daily People's World*?... Is it true that you contributed money and raised money for the Joint Anti-Fascist Refugee Appeal?' Well, these were the ones that came to me and I threw them right back... I went beyond denying. I really attacked their right to ask these questions.

In 1951 Jessica was subpoenaed by the California State Committee on Un-American Activities. Her interrogation is, again, oddly familiar: reminiscent of the questioning put to Diana by the Advisory Committee in 1940. Jessica was asked whether she had ever been a member of the Communist Party, or had maintained a bank account for the Civil Rights Congress. In mockery of her accent, she was asked whether she belonged to the Berkeley tennis club: rather like asking Esmond Romilly if he attended Royal Ascot. To all questions – except the ridiculous last – she pleaded the Fifth Amendment. When the procedure ended she fled to a safe house until the hearings were over. Yet the very real fear of being subpoenaed again lasted for several years, during which time she and her husband were effectively on high alert, their movements watched, their activities under continual suspicion. As late as 1971 she was named by the House of Representatives on a list of 'radical and/or revolutionary speakers'. In its perverse way, it was a little like being Sir Oswald Mosley, of whom Diana wrote to Deborah in 1966: 'He is really an *outlaw*'.

Jessica was rewarded ungenerously for her attempts to save Willie McGee, and not merely by Truman and the McCarthy brigade. In 1955, not long after the family moved to a new house in Oakland, California, Jessica's ten-year-old son Nicholas had embarked upon the usual boyish means to supplement his pocket money: a paper round. Cycling home one day, he was hit by a bus. His sister Constancia, who had been out looking for him, heard the sound of the crash. As she crouched beside her brother, who lay dying as she watched and waited for the ambulance, a neighbour remarked that this might not have happened if his mother had spent more of her time with her children.

It was Julia again, the baleful whispers that those feckless Romillys should never have had a baby that they could not look after. It was unspeakable: and Jessica never spoke of it. She was unable to mention Nicholas in her autobiographical writings, nor could she look at his photograph. Very much like Nancy, who, when the news of her brother's death came during a visit to Gerald Berners, sat down to dinner among the guests as if nothing had happened, so Jessica smiled and pretended as the grief twisted inside her. Having finally been granted a passport, she decided to take her husband and two surviving children on a trip to Europe, and find a kind of strange solace among Mitfords. The Treuhafts visited Sydney at Inch Kenneth, then Deborah at Edensor House. Deborah also gave Jessica the tour of Chatsworth, but confessed to Nancy she had not enjoyed doing so; she had sensed sanctimonious disapproval, what she later described as Jessica's 'bigoted sort of liberalism'; as if her sister might at any moment seize a priceless artefact and sell it for the Communists.[19] And indeed, what connection could there be between the glowing young Duchess of Devonshire, a Romney to the life, and the woman who, in her stern uniform of trousers and Eton crop, had marched on Mississippi? Only that sisterhood: frail, tenuous, yet somehow unbreakable. Then the Treuhafts made their way to Paris, to the Gaullist fraternizer. They arrived at the Rue Monsieur, as arranged, and found that Nancy was not there. Alarmed by Deborah's reports, picturing a gang of belligerent Americans drinking Coca-Cola from the Waterford, she had made her own visit: to Chatsworth. Oh these Mitfords.

Again, it was not kind. But Jessica was not the sort of person to whom one could show sympathy; for Nancy, her fellow concealer, it would have been particularly difficult. Their relationship was brisk, fond, sometimes arm's-length – 'I don't die for her as much as I pretend to,' Nancy later told Evelyn Waugh – although on other occasions she would write that Jessica was 'such a darling'. They had their own bond, especially against their mother. As Diana had it, they were both liars about Sydney – liars by nature – and both for the same reason, the unhappiness of their lives. It was true that Jessica and Nancy did collude in a kind of bitterness that the other sisters did not possess. It was also true that Jessica had sustained a series of appalling blows, which surfaced with a steely smiling courage at least equal to Nancy's. Yet both these women had a sense of profound fulfilment: their work was of primary importance, in a way that it was not for the rest. By now Diana had begun writing – in 1953 Mosley had started a new publication, the *European*, edited by his wife – and her reviews and diary were a cool, spare variation on the Mitford voice that resonated with quality. But this was not her life, it was done first and foremost for Mosley. For Jessica, and especially for Nancy, it was different. Not *faute de mieux*, simply the way it was.

In the end – because her sense of guilt was strong, except with Diana – Nancy returned to Paris and found the Treuhafts sitting peaceably in her flat, behaving like normal people, not even looking for a baseball report in *Le Monde*. She gave her sister £50, pretending that it was payment for some of Jessica's old books that she had kept for herself. They were worth a few shillings, if that. It was a typical gesture, oblique in its charity, neatly side-stepping gratitude. In fact all the sisters, including Diana, contributed with Sydney to a small amount for the Treuhafts, whose principles left them rather poor but did not extend to refusing the allowance (nor, when Jessica's writing made her rich, would she resist the decadent lure of Dior).

Fifty pounds was quite a lot of money in 1955, but by then Nancy's success was towering. 'How dull things would be without Miss Mitford,' as *The Observer* very truly had it. Her translation of the über-sophisticated André Roussin play, *The Little Hut*, had opened at the Lyric Theatre in 1950 and ran for 1,200 performances before transferring to New York. (To avoid travelling to the opening – Nancy's theatrical antipathy to America being what it was – she claimed to have been a Communist before the war: Peter Rodd's idea.) Her third novel, *The Blessing*, was published in 1951, a sublime take on the relationship between a naive Englishwoman and her attractive, amusing, compulsively unfaithful French husband. As she had often done in the past, she used the book to write a behavioural manual to herself: her advice was to be less romantic, more Parisian; despite her best efforts, she struggled in real life to follow these instructions. The novel was less well received than its two predecessors – the expectation had been more of the same – although Evelyn Waugh, to whom it was dedicated, was quite right to dismiss the criticisms. The novel was poised, wise, realistic to the point of extreme cynicism, illumined by the romantic view of France: as ever, only Nancy could have done it. 'They can't bear to see a writer grow up,' wrote Waugh, with the generosity of one entirely secure in his talent. 'Everyone I know delights in *The Blessing* and I am constantly buoyed up with pride in the dedication.'

Nancy also wrote a regular column in *The Sunday Times*, commissioned by 'handsome Mr Fleming' – Ian – and, in 1955, the essay on 'The English Aristocracy', with its strictures on 'U' and 'Non-U'. Boringly, and reductively, this short piece of writing would overwhelm the rest of her career for years to come (including in her *Times* obituary). True, it was the construct of a sweetly teasing agitator, which was definitively Nancy. But it was also perceived as the work of a snob, a woman who treasured a class structure that placed her on top, and she was more complicated than that: complicated, indeed, in every way.

Far more revelatory was the book that she published in 1954, her brilliant *Madame de Pompadour.* It was lit with the clarity of perception that characterized every word of her mature writings. Her grasp upon the difficult business of history was sure, strong, always directed by her unfailing instinct for human motivation. Some historians (notably a rather rude A. J. P. Taylor)[20] viewed this through the prism of their own snobbery – the intellectual kind – but in doing so they failed to see that politics *is* about the personal: as nobody knew better than a Mitford. More to the point, however, the book was a homage to the things that Nancy truly believed in, and that made life, in her view, a happy business: civilization, prettiness, formality, jokes, love conducted with an intensity of courtesy, the gardens at Versailles, France. And it ended, as events decreed that it must, at the moment when a shadow would begin to move inexorably towards them all.

In 1957 Gaston Palewski was appointed French ambassador to Rome. Nancy cabled to him from Venice, where she now spent her summers: 'O DESESPOIR. O RAGE. O FELICITATIONS. NANCY.'[21] The divorce that she had finally obtained from Peter Rodd – whose stubborn presence in her Parisian life had been unbearable, but had perhaps constituted some sort of shield against the knowledge that Palewski would never marry her – was now no more than a bagatelle in her life. A relief, no more; bringing with it a faint sense of melancholy, of failure and guilt. From that point, the will to happiness would be more necessary than ever, and Nancy did not fail to conjure it. But it was as she wrote in the last line of *Pompadour*, which falls like the thud of a blade upon the page: 'After this a very great dullness fell upon the Chateau of Versailles.'

It had fallen almost twenty years earlier upon the life of David Redesdale, and he now crept, without resistance, towards the death that had befallen two of his children. At the end of 1957 Nancy had visited him at the cottage in Northumberland that he shared with Margaret Wright, an icebox with its safe filled with firelighters. 'I loathe going there, it fills me with nervous terror,' she wrote to Theodore Besterman, the scholar with whom she was corresponding as she worked on her new historical biography, *Voltaire in Love*. Again she was impelled by a kind of guilt: 'I must see my relations who are getting too old to come and see me here.'

Before this, haunted perhaps by a sense of so much that had been lost, David had written further letters to Jessica, but still received no answering forgiveness for his nameless crimes. Yet he made a full rapprochement with his adored Diana, whom he visited at the Temple de la Gloire. He sent her a large cheque with which to curtain her giant windows: a Nancy-like gift in its indirect kindness. He also became friendly at last with 'the man Mosley' – who could be immensely charming, remarkably good company: how else could he have seduced as he did? Mosley, who behind his urbanity was also fundamentally frustrated by his native country's refusal to want him, had in 1956 seized upon a cause once more. The Union Movement was to be regenerated, like Dr Who. This time its focus would be upon the West Indian immigrants who had begun to arrive in Britain after the war, and who he believed would be ultimately destructive to the country's economy. 'Let the Jamaicans have their country back and let us have ours,' Mosley would argue, from his newly curtained Temple at Orsay.

He began hustling back and forth, using the pretext of politics to take in affairs on the side – just as he had done to Cimmie Curzon – and courting women in Paris and London. 'There is no jealousy like sexual jealousy,' Diana wrote to a friend, in the authentic voice of Nancy. She was still beautiful, and she could still have left. Instead she lent her support once more to Mosley as, in early 1958, he officially re-launched the Union Movement and began hurling his apparently reasoned rhetoric at a crowd of aggressive young men who had no desire to listen to ideas, only to have a punch-up.

The hoarse old warrior was now sixty-one. His followers had

been replaced, so too had his scapegoat, but in all other respects everything was the same; even the ensuing violence, whose vicarious outlet Mosley seemed to crave while, at the same time, condemning it. If it was true that the Notting Hill race riots of 1958 were not directly caused by the Union Movement, it was no less true that Mosley sought to exploit them. Through the battleground of the fighting, he saw his chance for one more shot at political glory. Without a thought for the time and dedication that Diana had expended on the venture, he abruptly closed the *European* and began spending money on support for his campaign to stand as candidate for Notting Hill in the 1959 General Election. He was right to believe that racial divisions were intense at this time, as they would remain (and as the Treuhafts could have told him). Nor would his economic arguments lose their sting; indeed, as UKIP voters might say, they still have not. And so his self-belief was high as he canvassed, scattering his 'Keep Britain White' leaflets in streets that fifty unimaginable years later would be home to bankers and film stars, but then were rife with post-war poverty, writhing miserably beneath the control of the slum landlord Peter Rachman. Yet the appeal of Mosley remained limited to a core of the discontented. He won less than 3,000 votes, around 10 per cent of the poll.

Himself to the end, he thought of bringing a legal suit to investigate irregularities in the poll, and he did not abandon hope. He remained in contact with extreme right-wing groups across the Continent; albeit with the aim of discussing a united Europe, which was then in its very earliest phase of development. Of course the past clung to him. In 1962 Nancy wrote to Diana – possibly with the idea of helping, or possibly stirring – with the news that French radio had claimed that Mosley wanted 'to send all Jews & Niggers out of England – not a word about making Europe. Is it worth his while to contradict this?'

In London that year, Mosley was subjected to a vicious physical assault (his son Max was arrested for defending him). He remained almost uniquely provocative, such a convenient hate figure – rather like Margaret Thatcher twenty years on, albeit without the power –

that in 1966 he actually sought to get the BBC committed for contempt of court, claiming that the corporation's output attacked him repeatedly, yet allowed him no right of reply. But at the same time, in an odd and very English way, he had become a more accepted figure: an eccentric part of the landscape, like Stonehenge. On one occasion he was lunching with Lord Longford, who as an undergraduate at Oxford had been set upon while protesting at a Blackshirt meeting in 1936.[22] They were approached by Michael Foot, whose politics leaned so far to the left as to topple him over, yet who said courteously: 'What a pleasure to see you again, Sir Oswald.' An interview with *The Times*, in which Mosley gave advance warning that he had written a first draft autobiography[23] totalling 225,000 words, confirmed this ambivalent status. Mosley set forth his belief in Europe as the only cure for Britain's balance of payments deficit (not so UKIP there); he was portrayed as a figure from the past, whose big ideas had had their day, but only scant trace of the sinister remained: 'From darling to ogre', the article concluded, in reference to his political journey from future PM to Fascist menace, 'and now, perhaps, a tiny step or two back?' He even stood one last time as a General Election candidate, in Shoreditch – his old East End connection – in 1966 (an event that Diana dreaded, as she admitted to Deborah). There, memories were longer. Mosley received 1,600 votes. It was over; it had been over thirty years earlier. 'I am afraid dear Kit can't win whatever he tries', wrote Diana, 'I wish to goodness he wd see it'. The Leader's occupation was gone.

But Mosley would never say, as David Redesdale did towards the end: 'All the savagery has gone out of me.' It was to his wife that he spoke these words. A kind of reconciliation was achieved with Sydney – indeed they had corresponded throughout the later period of their separation – when she visited him at Redesdale Cottage in March 1958 for his eightieth birthday. Margaret became part of the insubstantial present as the past returned to the fore: Sydney, together with Deborah and Diana, who later wrote: 'I shall never forget the expression on Farve's face when Muv appeared at his bedside, and his smile of pure delight. All their differences forgotten, they seemed to have gone back twenty years to happy days before the tragedies.' Three days later, when his wife and daughters had departed, David died. His funeral was held at Swinbrook, where a memorial had been erected to Tom, and where Unity lay in her grave. As Nancy described to Jessica, their once huge and vital father entered the church as a small box of ashes: 'the sort of parcel *he* used to bring back from London, rich thick brown paper & incredibly neat knots... Alas one's life.'

David left no money to Jessica, which amazingly made headlines ('Red Sheep Cut out of Will'). She had hurt him badly with her ridiculous attempt to give her share of Inch Kenneth to the Communists, the party that she and her husband in fact left in 1958. Nancy, ever generous in her spiky way, now gave her own share of the island to Jessica. Later, when she inherited some money from the Romillys, Jessica bought the whole thing and gifted it to her mother for her lifetime; thus that particular little saga, which like so much in the Mitford story had caused ripples of unnecessary hurt, came full circle.

The truth about why Jessica never saw her father after 1937 was not, however, entirely straightforward. She had agreed with her mother that she would visit him when she came to Europe in 1955, but wrote – quite jokily, if very much typically – that David would have to agree not to 'roar' at her family. 'Does he still?' Sydney, who could be so craven with Jessica, suddenly withdrew into chilling obduracy. 'Since you have imposed conditions it would be better not to see Farve.' It was an extraordinary thing to write to a woman who had just lost her son. Sydney herself had good cause to know that. Perhaps it was a sudden spurt of revenge for all the lack of sympathy that Jessica had shown in the past; perhaps she thought to protect the husband for whom she still had feelings of a kind: as ever, the complexities proliferate. But that act of coldness may help to explain *Hons and Rebels*.

Jessica notwithstanding, it seemed that David had been happier before his death than throughout the twenty years that preceded it. He had even, in his old way, entertained the women of his family: 'Remember me to the hall porter,' he called to Sydney, as she left for the Oban Hotel. It had something of the flavour of his exit from Nancy's last novel, *Don't Tell Alfred* – published in 1960 – when Uncle Matthew takes his leave of Fanny at the embassy in Paris:

> 'I shan't come and disturb you in the morning, Fanny – I know you've never been much use before seven and I want to be off at half-past five. Many thanks...'
>
> 'Come again', I said.
>
> But Uncle Matthew was gone.

V

Five years later, the same Mitford girls who had buried at Swinbrook the remains of their father were assembled, watchfully, on the island of Inch Kenneth.

Sydney, not easy to love, impossible not to admire, had lived out her late years with the regal stoicism that characterized her. The ghost of Unity flickered through the chapel, among the goats that Sydney still tended. The grief for her son did not alleviate. 'It was so kind of you to think of sending a word for Tom's birthday,' she wrote to Diana, in January 1957. 'I fear the sorrow for him gets no less.' She mourned her husband, perhaps more than he deserved. She did not show emotion, but she felt it; in this she was more like Nancy than she may have cared to admit, which perhaps was their problem.

When Jessica signed the contract to write *Hons and Rebels*, published in 1960, Sydney wrote to her: 'What exciting news... I thought a lot of yours so good, that you sent me.' This was a very different reaction from the dour 'This family again' that met the publication of *The Pursuit of Love.* Later Sydney would ask Jessica to remove some minor passages in the book, and later still attacked her for some of what she wrote. But she relented in a way that she did not towards Nancy, whose far less critical essay on her childhood – 'Blor', published in 1962 – caused her mother to withdraw into her icebox. Sydney never dared to go this far with Jessica. She intuited that beneath their joking veneers Jessica was a tougher character than Nancy, and might cut herself off completely; something that Nancy, whose nature comprised layers of spikiness and vulnerability, could never quite bear to do.

Interestingly, it was Sydney's sister 'Weenie' – who had no time for any of the tyrannical Mitford girls, and would have seen the entire Mitford myth as a nonsense built around some silly, self-aggrandizing show-offs – who flew at Jessica with a rant that came dangerously near the knuckle: 'I for one will never forget the savage cruelty with which you treated your mother and father. And now, you filthy little cad, you come back and write a lot of horrible things about your mother and come and sponge on her...' Which was a kind of truth, if you like, as surely as *Hons and Rebels* purported to be.

Meanwhile Nancy wrote to her old friend Heywood Hill that 'Diana is outraged for my mother.' Sydney had – as Nancy emphasized in her letter – stuck by Jessica 'thick and thin', but one would never have known it from the book. In fact all the sisters disliked *Hons and Rebels,* and to varying degrees viewed it as a travesty of the past, which in a way it was. 'She has,' as Nancy put it to Hill, 'quite unconsciously copied from my book instead of real life, & various modifications of truth demanded by the novel form are now taken as true.' *Hons and Rebels* was a construct, as was *The Pursuit of Love.* It used Nancy's novel as a springboard from which to leap towards the side of righteousness; and used it because Nancy's reimagining of the Mitfords was such magnificent value. Thus Jessica had it both ways. She could deplore what she plundered. But her book was also brilliant, and extremely successful. 'Oh dear,' wrote Deborah to Nancy, 'luckily it will soon all be over': which of course it never really was.

Jessica's capacity for guilt was small, or perhaps more accurately subsumed into her convictions. Nancy's was much greater. She spent the years leading up to her mother's death planning her autobiography, which would have laid bare the relationship with Sydney. Yet she was filled with the familiar furious wretchedness – reduced to the child who had had tantrums in the street – when her mother responded to her 'Blor' essay in 1962, writing: 'It seemed when I read it that everything I had ever done for any of you had turned out wrong and badly, a terrible thought, and can't be remedied now.'

Whether Sydney meant what she wrote, she *had* done things that turned out wrong: as who does not. Such is the nature of the family, which with the Mitfords was writ so peculiarly and dramatically large. In 1946 Diana had written to Nancy that she had seen a performance of Lorca's *The House of Bernarda Alba*, the story of a stern matriarch with five daughters, whose lives she controls and whom she confines to her house: 'It is all about Muv and us.' This was a joke, but it was another kind of truth. Sydney *was* the dominating force in the family. Her daughters had eluded her, but their mother remained inescapable. What Nancy and Jessica thought of her is yet another truth; so too what Diana thought; so too what each sister thought about the other. The interpretations of the play multiply, and in the end none is definitive, although, given the nature of the Mitford girls – the capacity for conviction that lay within them all – they probably believed that they alone had it right. They continued to debate it until only one of them, Deborah, remained. In her lack of complication, her basic honesty, her ability to accept the complexity of her sisters without distorting her own healthy character, Deborah was perhaps the final word on it all. But that very straightforwardness meant that hers, too, was only a version of the truth.

In 1959, when Jessica was in London seeing her publishers and completing her purchase of Inch Kenneth (which she would finally sell eight years later), Sydney – who still spent her winters in the old mews at Rutland Gate – was diagnosed with Parkinson's disease. Yet she battled on, back to the wilderness of her island, where she now lived with the help of a couple called the McGillvrays, turning her face to the sea spray as she had done when sailing as a young girl with her father: at the age of nearly eighty, she was as indomitable as the Scottish landscape that she loved. Four years later, however, her condition became critical. In May 1963 the sisters were alerted that they should visit. As it had done for Unity in her last illness, the fearsome, magnificent island exerted its power: although Sydney had two nurses, the doctor was delayed in attending her by the rough seas. Perhaps she did not really mind. 'So difficult to die,' wrote Deborah to Jessica, 'like so difficult being born.'

Sydney's dying was indeed a slow business. Again to Jessica, Nancy wrote that 'she has twice seemed to be going', then rallied: she was a strong woman. In the tone that had characterized so much of her dealings with her mother, Nancy fretted petulantly that Sydney was scolding her daughters for ' "dragging her back from the grave – what for?" But all we have done is given her a little water when she asks which isn't exactly dragging!' Then, also in character, the sudden softening. 'How she loves clothes & nice things. Even in the night she likes my dressing-gown.'

Eleven days before Sydney died, on 25 May 1963, she said goodbye to the daughters who sat beside her, then added: 'Perhaps Tom & Bobo, who knows?' In the dim island light of Inch Kenneth, it may have seemed as though the faces around her bed became beautifully indistinguishable from each other: her Mitford girls.

AFTERWARDS

NANCY

Remained in France for the rest of her life. After her last novel, *Don't Tell Alfred*, was poorly and rather unjustly received in 1960, she returned to historical biography with *The Sun King* in 1966, a life of Louis XIV. 'No more readable book has ever been written in my view!!!!' she wrote to Deborah. Produced as a coffee-table book, it sold vastly and made her still richer. In *The Times* she was described as one of those writers who 'change the talk and the behaviour of a whole generation'. Her fans were many and sometimes surprising: Bertrand Russell (a distant cousin) had made repeated visits to her hit London play, *The Little Hut*, and she was much admired by Field Marshal Viscount Montgomery of Alamein. 'I suppose you hate Monty – well I LOVE him,' Nancy wrote to Evelyn Waugh. The death of Waugh in 1966 took her best audience, the person who, for all his oddity, truly understood what she most valued in herself.

In 1967, Nancy moved from the Rue Monsieur to a little house at Versailles. She loved the proximity to the chateau, and cherished the romantic idea of a *champ-fleuri* garden, although the house itself was not attractive and it is hard to understand why she chose it. It has the air of a withdrawn resting-place, the last home of a quiet provincial widow. Despite her never more glittering career Nancy was tiring at last of *la haute société;* she was still spry and indestructibly elegant, but the merry fervour of her twenty years in

Paris had subdued. Many friends had died: Waugh, Mark Ogilvie-Grant, Victor Cunard, the *beau monde* of her merry middle age. Gaston Palewski had returned from Rome, but his departure – as Nancy had recognized at the time – had changed their relationship for ever.

In 1968 Peter Rodd died, with one of Nancy's letters in his hand. This, in its strange way, was also a grief. It was what Aunt Sadie called 'the dropping off of perches'; what Nancy called 'one more step towards THE END'; which was hastening rather swiftly by this point, although she still had her least popular but, in a way, finest book to complete: *Frederick the Great*, published in 1970. Deeply researched – Nancy had visited the battlefields of Potsdam, Dresden and Prague in the company of Pam – it showed the very remarkable path that she had taken from innately gifted debutante scribbler to serious yet wholly readable scholar. It was a homage to the power of self-education; whatever Jessica might say.

It was at the end of 1968 that Nancy first felt a pain in her left leg. The following year she began to feel unwell. 'What *can* it be?' she wrote to Diana in February 1969. Throughout her Paris years she had enjoyed perfect health and it was not her nature to believe in illness (only for housemaids, as Diana Cooper put it). Nevertheless she saw a doctor, who told her to rest in bed while awaiting tests. It was then that Palewski appeared at her house. 'Hallo Colonel, I've got cancer,' she said, which put him off his stroke. He had come to tell her that he was engaged to be married, to a divorcée named Violette de Talleyrand-Périgord.

From that point Nancy fought – the will to happiness was never stronger than when she was dying – but the last four years of her life are scarcely bearable to contemplate: she saw doctor after doctor, had tests, operations; and through it all she remembered the Colonel, his final, gently delivered betrayal. Jessica was adamant that Nancy should be told she had cancer – although this was not yet definitively stated – but Diana, surely rightly, was of the opinion that her sister lived by illusion and never needed it more than then. It was in 1972 that she was diagnosed with Hodgkin's disease, a cancer that fills the body with such agony that Nancy would, as Deborah said, simply 'sit in bed and cry with the pain'. In the night, she told James Lees-Milne, she longed for Blor.

But Palewski continued to visit, their friendship – which was a kind of love – did not diminish, and in 1972 his recommendation secured Nancy the Légion d'Honneur of which she had dreamed. It was Diana who half lifted her down the stairs to greet the Colonel, where he pinned the decoration to her dress as tears poured down her face. 'He was,' Diana later wrote, 'a kind old object.' Subsequently Nancy also received the CBE, and told Diana that what she chiefly liked about it was thinking how many people it would annoy.

As they had for their mother, so her sisters now gathered around Nancy's bedside; it was Pamela's calm presence that she craved. Diana braved the jealous tantrums of Mosley to drive to Versailles every day. Deborah asked: 'Is there *anything* I can do?' 'Nothing,' replied Nancy. 'But I would give anything for one more day's hunting.' Jessica came from California and saw Diana for the first time in forty years: 'She looks like a beautiful bit of ageing sculpture... God, it's odd.' The two sisters were polite, nothing more. Yet Jessica later admitted to treasuring the short, kindly letter that Diana sent to her after Nancy's death: 'That was so nice to get'.

It was Jessica, the victim of Nancy's most despairing snaps of irritation – a dim echo of all that mysteriously productive childhood teasing – who heard her sister whisper to the doctor: '*Je veux me dépêcher.*' But she waited to die: the Colonel was on his way. He arrived at the little house with his dog, and took Nancy's hand. Although she was barely conscious, he had the impression that she smiled.

'Oh! Fabrice – *on vous attend si longtemps.*'

'*Comme c'est gentil.*'

She died that day, 30 June 1973, and was buried at Swinbrook beside Unity.

PAMELA

Lived at Tullamaine Castle after the divorce from Derek Jackson, which had left her so delightfully rich, until 1960. Her companion there was another connoisseur of the horse, Giuditta Tommasi, a woman of Swiss-German-Italian birth: it was, according to Diana, 'a kind of marriage', although Jessica more bluntly stated that her sister had become a 'you-know-what-bian'. Pamela was also friendly with Rudi von Simolin, who had known Unity in Munich and been aware of her intent to kill herself. In 1958, Diana wrote to Deborah that although Giuditta Tommasi wanted to move to Rome, Pamela 'really has her eye on Bavaria & Rudi'.

In fact she remained in Ireland with Giuditta until 1962, when the two women moved to Zurich with Pamela's beloved dachshunds. Deborah later expressed surprise that her sister had never remarried. 'I suppose really Giuditta put a stop to it,' she said, which did not fully resolve the mystery of their relationship. When Giuditta died in 1992, Deborah described Pamela as 'wonderfully unmoved'.

Pamela was possibly the toughest of the sisters, and the best at hiding it. When Nancy died, she said to Diana: 'Nard, let's face it, she's ruined four years of our lives,' meaning the length of that atrocious illness. It was at least as shocking as anything Nancy ever said. Perhaps it was justified in Pamela's mind by memories of her sister's childhood jibes. Yet when Jessica's daughter Constancia met her aunts at Chatsworth she had the impression that they *all* made Pamela a butt of their jokes. Constancia thought it 'cruel – it was as though Pam came from a different family from the rest of you'. Which was, indeed, the impression given by Pamela herself. Yet her placid, muted manner and her wayward pronouncements were savoured, not unkindly, by Diana and Deborah ('Woman works in a mysterious way'). So too was her obsession with food. The chicken that she ate over lunch with Hitler was what she most remembered from that encounter.

She remained in Europe until her dachshunds died, telling a German magazine that they – the dogs – preferred living on the Continent. In 1972 she moved to Woodfield House, in the Gloucestershire village of Caudle Green, and returned to her countrywoman roots. She had eight acres, pigsties and stables, a superb kitchen garden and a black Labrador. She stood for the local parish council, carrying what Deborah called her 'Unscratchable' (a leather attaché case that she refused to allow anybody to touch). She was reconciled completely with Jessica after the row over Unity's biography, although the rupture had lasted more than a year. She also remained friendly with Derek Jackson. 'Hallo, horse,' she said to him when he walked into Chatsworth for the wedding of Deborah's daughter Sophia.

Gradually Pamela retreated further into the world of the other, numerous, unknown Mitfords, the ones who lived in the country and never ruffled its feathers: like her uncle Bertram, High Sheriff of Oxfordshire, who inherited the title of Lord Redesdale from David and kept a prize-winning flock of Hampshire Down sheep. Pamela acquired an additional home, a cottage at Swinbrook, close to the one where Sydney and Unity had lived during the war. She bred poultry, as her mother had done, and became an expert in her field. In 1986 Diana visited the Swinbrook cottage and was so cold that she lay in bed reading Strindberg while her sister fretted over the malfunctioning Rayburn.

As Pamela aged, so the effects of her infantile paralysis worsened. She walked with two sticks and, on a visit to London in 1994, fell and broke her leg. After an operation, she came round and asked Deborah what had won the Grand National. Three days later, on 12 April, Deborah was recalled to the hospital, where her sister had died ten minutes earlier from a blood clot. 'Hen. Please picture,' she wrote to Jessica.

The loss of Pamela affected the surviving Mitfords very deeply. It was as if something that they had thought immutable, like rain, had suddenly gone. Pam was buried at Swinbrook, together with three of her sisters; her grave stands separate from the rest.

DIANA

Suffered her own term of trial during the years of Nancy's illness, driving between Orsay and Versailles almost every day as the migraines flowered in her head. Diana visited Nancy with the staunchness that her mother had shown when she herself was in Holloway. But the duty to be with Nancy fought the pressure to be with Mosley: 'I longed to stay but it was impossible,' she wrote in her diary. 'If I had stayed he would have had his birthday completely alone.'

In 1977 Diana published her autobiography, *A Life of Contrasts*, which was received in predictable fashion: the style was greatly admired and the content criticized. Diana publicized the book and was interviewed on the BBC's *Russell Harty Show*. Her appearance was controversial, but she was serenely undisturbed except by the sound of her own voice: 'I think you *might* have died of laughing,' she wrote to Deborah, who had missed the programme. In 1980 she published a biography of her friend, the Duchess of Windsor. Mosley, possessive even of her time, asked her not to write another book, even though she had done her work at night.

By this time Mosley had been diagnosed with Parkinson's disease. Yet he remained strong until late 1980, around the time of his eighty-fourth birthday. Diana began helping him to undress, to go to bed. Throughout the night of 2–3 December she woke several times to check on him, and at 4 a.m. on the morning of the 3rd she found him lying dead on the floor. She held him in her arms, saying,

'Darling, darling, come back to your Percher.' The depth of her love, and her grief, were extraordinary: Diana's emotions had the magnitude of Greek tragedy. In 1981 she became partially paralysed, as if from a stroke. She was suffering from a large, benign brain tumour, which she believed had grown on account of her bereavement. Who can say that she was mistaken? – although she was almost certainly wrong to think that Nancy's virulent cancer had been caused by lack of love and excess of spite; this, surely, was 'wisdom' after the discovery of Nancy's wartime betrayal.

Diana recovered quickly from complicated surgery (during a visit from Lord Longford she was heard to murmur: 'He thinks I'm Myra Hindley'), but her despair did not lift. In December 1981, she wrote to Mosley's son Nicholas: 'Darling Nicky, One year today but for me it really seemed like the night before last, because that was the terrible night.' A year later, she would attack Nicholas fiercely for the first volume of his excellent, measured biography of Mosley, *The Rules of the Game*. It verged upon madness, this love of Diana's. But there was something very poignant about the way in which she wrote to Deborah, who had offered help during her illness. 'I only want Kit and he can't come.'

Eventually Diana resumed writing. *Loved Ones*, published in 1985, was a collection of pen portraits of friends and family (and, incidentally, a superb evocation of an era). She contributed reviews to the *Evening Standard* and *Books & Bookmen*. She produced not a word that was superfluous or inexact; her clarity of argument, even when arguing the case according to Mosley, was pure as geometry. James Lees-Milne thought her a better writer than Nancy. She was certainly more austere and refined, which he may have preferred (although he may simply have preferred Diana). But she lacked, perhaps, the vital creative flame; in her case that went into her life.

In 1989 Diana was a guest on *Desert Island Discs*. She spoke about her friendship with Hitler – 'I can't regret it' – and her husband's alleged anti-Semitism: 'He really wasn't, you know. He didn't know a Jew from a Gentile. But he was attacked so much by

Jews... that he picked up the challenge.' Asked about the Holocaust, she said: 'I don't really, I'm afraid, believe that six million people were killed. I think this is just not conceivable. It's too many. But whether it's six or whether it's one makes no difference morally. It's completely wrong. I think it was a dreadfully wicked thing.'

This, then, was her stance. She condemned outright the Final Solution, but she would not do so in a way that satisfied. She would not say what people wanted her to say. Those were her terms; except when it came to Mosley, she had always done everything on her own terms. And somehow, by means that no other woman could have achieved, this too became part of her fascination.

Diana left the Temple de la Gloire in 1999 and moved to a beautiful airy flat in the Rue de l'Université. Although now extremely deaf – she had not truly enjoyed a visit to the opera since 1965 – she had books, a love of literature as deep as anybody ever possessed, and she had family. The following year she celebrated her ninetieth birthday at the Hôtel de Crillon, with more than forty of her descendants.

Then there was the Mitford connection, between Diana and Deborah: the last pair standing, who alone among the sisters never deceived each other, whose mutual adoration was real and warm. In Deborah's case it encompassed the political beliefs that she neither understood nor shared, but which in the case of Diana she simply accepted, because this was Diana. Deborah held the view that Diana became almost 'saint-like' in later life; the unstated implication was that this remarkable generosity of spirit was a kind of expiation for what had gone before.

The two sisters exchanged letters to the end. Variations on the Mitford past was their major theme: 'My goodness how it all comes back.' They wrote to each other in the voices of girls; in that respect they never grew old. Nor did Diana ever lose her beauty, also a part of her.

With the reissue of *A Life of Contrasts* in 2000, she became a rather fashionable public figure. She had always commanded the most acute interest but, as with Mosley, the urge to vilify her gradually shifted into something more honest: the desire to penetrate her mystery. It could not be done, but she was worth the trouble.

In July 2003 Diana suffered a small stroke, after which she refused to go into hospital. She died on 11 August and was cremated at Père Lachaise cemetery. Diana had no religious belief; her faith had been in Mosley. She was buried next to Unity in Swinbrook churchyard.

Those who met her found her impossible to forget.

JESSICA

Published *The American Way of Death*, about the outrageously commercialized funeral industry, in 1963. It became a number one best-seller, earned her around $115,000 within a year and launched her into a career that was, for a time, as stellar as Nancy's. Jessica had found what she was truly good at: journalism. She was without fear, she loved controversy and publicity – adored reading her own reviews and cuttings – and she had a genuine social conscience. She subsequently wrote *The American Way of Birth*, followed by *Kind and Usual Punishment*, about the American prison service. Her collected journalism was published under the title *The Making of a Muckraker*: no other Mitford sister would ever have described herself in that way.

Apparently with much delight, Jessica became a media figure. 'From the extent of the brouhaha,' wrote *The Times*, in a 1965 article about *The American Way of Death*, 'it is clear that Miss Mitford's impact on the transatlantic scene is only slightly less than the Beatles', and may be a good deal more lasting.' Throughout the 1960s and 1970s she travelled to Europe more often. She allowed Nancy to drag her into couture houses and spent a large chunk of her royalties; in London she met the writer Maya Angelou, who would become a close friend (a de facto, and wonderfully non-Mitford, 'sister'). She went on book tours, appeared on television and was a brilliant speaker on the lecture circuit. She worked extremely hard, perhaps even harder than Nancy. Yet the *faute de mieux* argument – that success could not compensate for the sadness of Nancy's life – was never really applied to Jessica in the same way; although she suffered far worse tragedies. Jessica could irritate and enrage her sisters, but with Nancy the emotions went deeper.

Handsome like all Mitfords, Jessica was the only one who did not keep her looks. The others aged but did not change. Jessica became fat, bold and comfortable, like a grand Cotswolds landowner disguised as an American tourist; which in a sense is what she was.

She continued as an activist deep into middle age and was followed in this by Constancia, who had worked for the civil rights movement and had two sons by a leader of the extremist Black Power movement. It interested her sisters greatly that Jessica appeared to disapprove of her daughter's liaison: did she revert to type a little?

In 1978 she published a second volume of autobiography, *A Fine Old Conflict*. Pamela wrote to say that she had greatly enjoyed it, but that it was wrong of Jessica to say that she had remained in America because all the Mitford family were pro-Nazi. 'That was a sad figment of your imagination.' Jessica had a remarkable ability to shrug off such remarks. She also wrote a memoir of her friend Philip Toynbee – *Faces of Philip* – and a book about Grace Darling ('Grey Starling'), *Grace had an English Heart*, the writing of which bored her tremendously. Like Diana she appeared on *Desert Island Discs*.

In 1985 Jessica learned that her husband was having an affair with an old friend of the family. 'It sounds very bad, poor Decca,' wrote Diana to Deborah, although in fact the marriage survived. Diana never lost her fondness for the sister who had once adored her; all her life she wore a brooch that Jessica had given her before eloping with Romilly. For her own part, Jessica almost certainly came to regret a rupture that had become, in their relative old age, a near-absurdity, yet she also felt that it had now gone on too long for her to back down. When Mosley died, she wrote to Deborah asking her to convey sympathy to Diana, adding the rather hopeless postscript: 'you know how it is, Hen'.

Alone among the sisters, Jessica smoked and drank spirits: the Hemingway touch. In the mid-1990s her daughter, now a nurse, confronted her mother about her alcohol problem. To Maya Angelou, Constancia wrote that Jessica had given up instantly, by sheer will-power, which was not something she ever lacked. Her marriage improved thereafter. Smoking, however, was a tougher nut even than Jessica. In June 1996 she was diagnosed with lung cancer, and the end was very quick. This was mercifully unlike Nancy's illness, although Jessica's bravery was comparable. To Deborah she wrote: 'Here's the point Hen: SO much better than just being hit by a car or in plane wreck.' She went home for the last few days of her life; as the cancer spread like a blaze through her body, Maya Angelou came and sang to her. The night before she died, on 22 July, she spoke to her Hen on the phone. 'She knew it was me.' wrote Deborah to Diana.

After a simple service in a San Francisco hall, Jessica's ashes were scattered at sea. No American Way of Death for her. No English one either.

DEBORAH

Enjoyed what was unquestionably the most pleasurable life of any Mitford girl. She worked extremely hard for Chatsworth: but what a job.

As Fabrice de Sauveterre put it to Linda in *The Pursuit of Love*: 'In short, *madame*, I am happy to tell you that I am a very rich duke, a most agreeable thing to be, even in these days.' By the time that Deborah's rich duke inherited, 'these days' had become rather less agreeable, although everything is relative. As Jessica wrote to a friend, after visiting her sister in 1955: 'Because of the Death Duties the poor dears cannot afford to live in "the lodge" (which they own) in the village (which they own) and they make do with opening the house to trippers...'

'I don't want to be the one to let it go,' Deborah's husband had said. Yet it was an act of defiance against the times, trying to keep such an estate together in the post-war era. The Devonshires finally moved into the great house in 1957 and Deborah took up the challenge, set by Mr Attlee, of making Chatsworth thrive as a commercial enterprise. Andrew, who like most true aristocrats was without snobbery, was insistent that the public should enter through the main front door, that as much of the house as possible be open to them, and that they should wander and picnic as they wished in the gardens (only the Old Park is private: home to the deer). Then he left Deborah in charge of every domestic detail. Like her mother, she had the gift of an aesthetic sense – and of divine efficiency.

She later wrote that she had not employed a decorator, because she was too mean to pay somebody else for what she could do herself: 'besides, I loved every minute of it.'[1] Her friend Nancy Lancaster, whose interior designs Deborah much admired, said: 'If I had done this house for you, you would have had to sell it to pay me.' Later, and often, people would ask Deborah how she had done it. With a great deal of help, was her usual reply. She always robustly rejected the popular idea that she had 'saved' the great house: 'It was Andrew who was determined to keep Chatsworth independent.' Yet nobody could have been better suited to the role of modern-age chatelaine than Deborah, in whom the quality of good sense became something imperishably charming.

In 1960 Andrew became Parliamentary Under-Secretary of State for Commonwealth Relations, and the Devonshires took official trips to Africa and the Caribbean. The following year, they were invited to the presidential inauguration of Deborah's old dancing partner, Jack Kennedy. After the death of Billy Hartington's widow, Kick, in a plane crash in 1948, Deborah had kept in touch with the family, and later they would visit Kick's grave at Edensor in turn: Rose, Bobby, Teddy, Jack. Deborah became very fond of the president in the brief time before his assassination. He was, she said, rare among politicians in being able and willing to laugh at himself. She facilitated an easy relationship between Kennedy and the man she called 'Uncle Harold' – Prime Minister Macmillan – whose wife was a Devonshire relation; and Deborah was invited to accompany Macmillan to Washington in 1962, in order to help 'cement Anglo-American relations'. Later that year, in the middle of the Cuban Missile Crisis, Kennedy attended an exhibition of drawings from Chatsworth at the Washington National Gallery, and after a dinner at the White House invited Deborah to ring Jessica from the Oval Office. He certainly rather adored her; like the Führer, he could not resist that aristocratic confidence. 'Muv thinks you & Kennedy so like Birdie & Hitler,' wrote Diana.

But Deborah was also immensely feminine and attractive. The

spell she cast was less intense than Diana's, yet there were few who could resist it. Nancy dreamed up a series of teases over some of Deborah's friendships: with the playboy Aly Khan ('Jungle Jim'), who gave her one of his steeplechasers, and particularly with Kennedy. 'Our fast young sister went over that ocean & had long loving tete à tetes with your ruler,' she wrote to Jessica in 1961. This was, and always had been, typical Nancy. Nevertheless to Diana, who in 1963 had remarked upon the nonsense of marriage vows that nobody dreams of keeping – 'we're all adulterers & adulteresses' – Nancy had replied: 'It's not *quite* true, after all Debo's absolutely pure.' (Diana admitted that she had been thinking of herself and Nancy; and, intriguingly, of Pamela.)

The marriage was not always easy: Andrew had alcohol problems, about which both he and Deborah were utterly frank. Nevertheless they were essentially happy in the shared business of being Devonshires. Their life was magnificent, if exigent: receiving royalty; entertaining politicians; sitting for Lucian Freud – the first guest at Chatsworth, who painted several members of the family; attending occasions like the 1981 wedding of Prince Charles to Lady Diana Spencer ('she was mad of course,' Deborah wrote to Diana, after the Princess of Wales's death). Family life; the Chatsworth Estate; the shared passion for field sports and racing – Andrew owned one of the best race mares of the modern era, Park Top: it all created a life of wonderful solidity from which Deborah's incandescent Mitford spirit could soar freely. 'Oh Graceland,' she wrote to Diana, having visited the home of her beloved Elvis Presley in 1997.

Deborah wrote a history of Chatsworth – *The House*, first published in 1982 – and several autobiographical works, all in her plain and delicious idiom, giving the lie to Nancy's childhood joke that her sister could neither read nor write. In later life she became something of a magnet to the media. Journalists could not resist her. To the *Independent* in 2001, for instance, she expounded on her Elvis worship and on the fact that he was still sighted everywhere. 'I wish he would turn up in our farm shop.' The article was a homage to her brisk and deathless charm, her exquisite 'oh now *aren't* you clever' courtesy: 'These', wrote her entranced interviewer, 'are the sort of old-style manners that refuse to be defeated, no matter how hard you might try. At one point I suggest we do a house swap next summer... She doesn't miss a beat. "What a marvellous idea."'[2] Deborah was equal to whatever was thrown at her, and despite her round dismissal of most modern orthodoxies – she loathed Labour governments, the hunting ban, health and safety regulations – she was quite astoundingly popular. She strode dauntlessly through the contemporary landscape, while at the same time symbolizing a vanished past. It was very Mitford. And, as such, the public seemed to treasure it.

After Andrew's death in 2004, Deborah gave over Chatsworth to her son, the 12th Duke of Devonshire. She moved back to Edensor, where she had begun her married life during the war, and had paid tuppence to smell the lemon on the post office counter.

On 24 September 2014, at the age of ninety-four, the last Mitford girl died.

NOTES

INTRODUCTION

1 In fact 'Woman' was Pamela; 'Honks' was Diana; 'Stubby' or 'Stublow' was Deborah; and 'Bobo' was Unity.
2 'Farve' and 'Muv' were the names given to the Mitford parents. The Hons' Cupboard featured in *The Pursuit of Love*; based upon a large linen cupboard in one of the Mitford family homes, it was the secret place in which the children were assured of privacy.
3 Evelyn Waugh to Nancy Mitford, 5 March 1957.
4 By Julian Slade. It opened at the Theatre Royal, Bristol, in May 1967 and failed to transfer to London. Two years earlier, Nancy, who wrote the dialogue but not the lyrics, had contacted Diana to say that one of the songs – created for the character of their father – began with the line, 'I do want my girl to be a lady (changed by Nancy to 'I do want my girl to be a moron').
5 This was amazing. In 1971, Nancy agreed, in principle, to an idea from the then head of BBC Comedy for a series of half-hour programmes based upon the Mitford family. The proposed writer was the late Barry Took, who at the time wrote sitcoms, although an internal memo at the BBC suggested – with all seriousness – that the Mitford series might have 'the same sort of interest as *The Forsyte Saga*'. Fortunately the rights to *The Pursuit of Love* remained entangled in a deal struck with a film company back in 1946. After Nancy's death in 1973, the terrible idea was laid to rest.
6 Deborah Ross in *The Independent*, 12 November 2001.
7 Originally commissioned by Stephen Spender and published in

Encounter; reprinted in 1956 in *Noblesse Oblige*, together with a reply by Evelyn Waugh entitled 'To the Honble Mrs Peter Rodd On a Very Serious Subject'. Nancy claimed that it was Spender who had insisted upon the inclusion of the 'U' and 'Non-U' material.

8 By Mary S. Lovell in *The Mitford Girls* (Little Brown, 2001).

9 From a 1997 article for *The Sunday Times*.

10 The nickname was a vague rhyme for 'adultery', which the sisters found a hilarious concept when applied to their brother.

11 This began as Deborah's joke, later taken up by Diana and then used repeatedly in their letters. In the 1950s Deborah had attended a wedding at which, when the cake was about to be cut, the Queen Mother cried, 'The cake!' in an ecstasy of amazement.

12 Or 'Smartyboots', as the erudite writer and critic Connolly was called in the letters between Nancy and Evelyn Waugh. Apparently the nickname was originally conceived by Virginia Woolf, but they ran with it; Nancy once claimed that a madrigal, containing lines such as 'Sweet Bonny Boots', was all about Connolly.

13 Unusually this nickname came from Tom Mitford, who for reasons unknown had named Herr von Ribbentrop after an obscure medieval song: 'Go to Joan Glover, and tell her I love her . . . '

14 Nancy, who loudly proclaimed a not wholly sincere dislike of Americans, mocked President Kennedy – a friend of Deborah's – at every possible opportunity, and came up with this particular name after the president was photographed in a rather low-cut bathing suit.

15 According to Evelyn Waugh, Nancy used this voice rather indiscriminately. After reading *Love in a Cold Climate* he wrote, in a typically dry scolding tease, that although he could accept the book's heroine, Polly, talking exactly like the Radlett girls, the über-sophisticated Cedric was another matter. 'Cedric is a Parisian pansy. Oliver Messel doesn't talk like Debo.' Nancy did make a few adjustments to Cedric's speech, although in fact there is always a warning note of worldliness beneath his Mitfordian effusions.

16 Broadcast in 2010, this superb series had Rhys Thomas (as the journalist 'Gary Bellamy') meeting a selection of characters including 'the Combe sisters', spoof versions of Jessica and Diana, played by the heavily latexed Rosie Cavaliero and Lucy Montgomery.

17 Deborah said this in a 1980 BBC documentary made by Julian Jebb, *Nancy Mitford – A Portrait by Her Sisters*. The programme was enchanting, although it caused the usual familial ructions (see p. 157).

18 *The Independent*, 12 November 2001.

19 Diana appeared on *The Russell Harty Show* in April 1977, to coincide with the publication of her autobiography *A Life of Contrasts.* A mild furore ensued, as was usual with Diana, although her main (laughing) concern was her 'ghastly' voice.

20 Of *Poor, Dear Brendan: The Quest for Brendan Bracken* (Hutchinson, 1974), by Andrew Boyle, reviewed for *Books and Bookmen* in 1974.

21 This snippet appeared in a coolly entertaining diary – like a superior contemporary newspaper column – written by Diana for *The European* (1953–9), the monthly publication that she edited for her husband Sir Oswald Mosley. Although the point of the magazine was its political content, written anonymously by Mosley, the diary was infinitely more readable.

22 In a letter to Nancy, 8 November 1949.

23 As Diana wrote to Mosley's biographer Robert Skidelsky, a friend of her son Max: 'you no more have to learn that [sex] than how to eat a Mars bar… '

PART I

1 Nancy translated Madame de Lafayette's *La Princesse de Clèves* – her favourite novel – for the Mosleys' publishing house, Euphorion Books, in 1950, and the same year had a huge West End hit with her version of André Roussin's play *La Petite Hutte.* Also for Euphorion, Diana translated Balzac: *La Duchesse de Langeais* and *Le Curé de Tours.* But her most successful venture was the 1978 translation of *For the Record*, the autobiography of the racing driver Niki Lauda (a friend of her son Max, a prominent figure in motor sport who later became president of the Fédération Internationale de l'Automobile).

2 Accounts of the Mitford–Fuld marriage in *The Times* hint at a very strange tale. After the Berlin wedding, at which Max Reinhardt performed, the new Mrs Mitford – said to be the richest girl in Germany – was presented at court and briefly seen at every London party. That same year, however, the marriage was declared null and void in Germany, and Jack Mitford issued a libel action over his wife's allegations of 'unnatural conduct'. The mind instantly leaps to sexual deviancy although, at a court action in 1923, designed to establish whether the declaration of nullity was valid in Britain, it transpired that Marie had accused her husband of being 'addicted to masculine indolence'. He meanwhile counter-attacked with claims of adultery. It

is unsurprising that Jack thereafter dedicated himself to the jolly life of a man about town and did not remarry. Aged seventy-seven, in 1963, he became the 4th Lord Redesdale (succeeding his brother Bertram, who had inherited from David in 1958), but died within the year.

3 This information comes from *The Mitford Girls.* Mary S. Lovell writes in her own endnotes that Blanche Hozier was said to have confided the 'truth' about Clementine's parentage to her friend Lady Londonderry.

4 From a review of *Friends Apart* by Philip Toynbee, published in *The European*, 1954.

5 Her granddaughter, Madeau Stewart, became a producer at the BBC and interviewed Nancy for the radio in 1970. An excerpt from their lovely chat was played in *Nancy Mitford – A Portrait by her Sisters.* Nancy conjured her image of heaven, which would hold the sounds of *The Lost Chord* and 'an occasional nightingale… I look forward greatly.'

6 Nancy wrote to Diana in March 1931, saying that George Bowles had offered this opinion to Sydney, although he also expressed the hope that the book would sell.

7 Nancy said this in an interview, given in 1966, for the ABC Television programme *Tempo.*

8 In *Don't Tell Alfred.* The house in question is the fabulous Montdore residence that features in *Love in a Cold Climate* (from where Lady Montdore pities the poor people who have to live in Chelsea).

9 From the essay 'Mothering the Mitfords', published in *The Sunday Times* in 1962, and reprinted in the collection *The Water Beetle* (also 1962) under the title 'Blor'.

10 This remark was made in the 1966 interview for *Tempo.*

11 David's stance was backed by Lord Moyne, whose son Bryan Guinness married Diana Mitford in 1928. The ending of that marriage, just four years later, had been strongly opposed by David and Moyne; nevertheless by 1937 they were both of the view that divorce should be made easier.

12 In *Nancy Mitford – A Portrait by her Sisters.* Those were not Pamela's exact words – rather an approximation from a deeply amused Deborah – but certainly that was her meaning.

13 As recalled in *Counting My Chickens* (Long Barn Books, 2001).

14 The lucrative gold mine, which ultimately proved to be the second largest in the Americas, was that of Harry Oakes. Later knighted, he moved to the Bahamas for tax purposes and became a friend of the then Governor, the Duke of Windsor. Oakes was murdered in 1943; the crime was never solved.

15 From 'Blor'.

16 Specifically in a letter dated 26 October 1976. Jessica, with admirable honesty, cited Deborah's extreme prettiness as the probable reason.

17 In 1965, Jessica wrote to Nancy that Pamela, who had noticed how rich both her sisters had become from their literary careers, was planning a book.

18 Diana described her sister thus to the author in 2001.

19 Deborah's account of her schooling comes from *Wait for Me!* (John Murray, 2010).

20 By Mary S. Lovell, who writes that Unity would, in adulthood, say this to her friends.

21 From a review of the reissued *Nancy Mitford: A Memoir* by Harold Acton, *Daily Mail*, 2001.

22 *The Sunday Times*, 1997.

23 From the interview in 1966 for the ABC Television programme *Tempo*.

24 The Parents' National Educational Union was a respected organization that conducted education by correspondence.

25 Miss Hussey was interviewed for *Unity Mitford: A Quest* by David Pryce-Jones (Weidenfeld & Nicolson, 1976).

26 Nancy is heard speaking these words, in a tone of the utmost generous sincerity, in the 1980 television programme *Nancy Mitford – A Portrait by her Sisters*.

27 In conversation with the author in 2001.

28 From Anne de Courcy's *Diana Mosley* (Chatto & Windus, 2003).

29 *The Honourable Rebel*, a 1977 television programme about Jessica.

30 Jessica to Nancy, 16 November 1971.

31 *The Times*, 26 April 1945.

32 Tom's bisexuality (in adult life) was alleged in a lurid book entitled *Hitler's Valkyrie: The Uncensored Biography of Unity Mitford* by David R. L. Litchfield (The History Press, 2014). It was also claimed that Unity had had ritualized sex with stormtroopers on a bed draped with swastika flags, that she staged orgies for Hitler and – with Diana's encouragement – slept with Sir Oswald Mosley. Evidence for all this was scant, to say the least. It may have been true, however, that Unity had an affair with Almasy. *The House of Mitford*, by Jonathan and Catherine Guinness (Hutchinson, 1984), suggests that some members of her family believed that there was a brief liaison between them. Charlotte Mosley, the daughter-in-law of Diana who edited *Letters Between Six Sisters* (Fourth Estate, 2007), states in the book that the affair definitely happened. This is convincing, although in *Unity*

Mitford: A Quest most of the interviewees who knew Unity in Germany took the view that she and Almasy were merely friends.

33 Mrs Rattenbury was acquitted but her lover, George Stoner, was convicted and sentenced to death. Mrs Rattenbury then killed herself; subsequently Stoner was reprieved.

34 From *Unity Mitford: A Quest* by David Pryce-Jones.

35 From *Beloved Infidel* by Sheilah Graham (Cassell, 1933).

36 In conversation with the author.

37 From *Wait for Me!*

38 The word used by David was actually 'suar' – Tamil for 'pig' – which he had picked up during his time in what was then Ceylon. His daughters transmuted this into 'sewer'. As Sydney remarked, it was hard to tell which term was the more offensive.

39 Deborah described this childhood habit in *Wait for Me!* She also mentioned that her close friend, the distinguished travel writer Patrick Leigh Fermor, had done the same thing.

40 From a letter to his friend Henry Yorke (the novelist Henry Green), September 1929 (*The Letters of Evelyn Waugh*, ed. Mark Amory, Weidenfeld & Nicolson, 1980).

41 The ABC Television interview broadcast in 1966.

42 In a 1946 radio talk for the BBC programme *Women's Magazine*.

43 *The Sunday Times*, 1997.

44 Boothby, a successful and self-publicizing politician, who became a life peer in 1958 and lived a couple of doors away from Lord Lucan on a corner of Eaton Square, married twice and was said to have fathered three illegitimate children. He was, however, openly bisexual and campaigned for the legalization of homosexuality. At Oxford he was exclusively gay and known as 'The Palladium' (in reference to the 'twice-nightly' shows then staged at the theatre). In 1963 he began an affair with an East End cat burglar who introduced him to Ronnie Kray, also bisexual, who with his twin brother Reggie was the foremost gangster of the period (and in 1968 sentenced to life imprisonment). Subsequently it emerged that Kray had supplied Boothby with young men in return for personal favours.

45 Quoted in *Unity Mitford: A Quest* by David Pryce-Jones.

46 In conversation with the author.

47 Howard killed himself in 1958, aged fifty-three, after the death of his lover.

48 From *A Little Learning* (Chapman & Hall, 1964), the first volume of Waugh's unfinished autobiography. Nancy wrote to say that she loved

the book – 'of course' – and that Jessica, who by that time was a highly successful author, had received an offer of '1000 (or a million) dollars' to review it in America.

49 From 1933 onwards Bryan wrote nine published novels, six children's books, two plays and three volumes of memoirs. His poetry was also published.

50 From *Rules of the Game: Memoirs of Sir Oswald Mosley and Family* by Nicholas Mosley (Secker & Warburg, 1982).

PART II

1 In an interview for *Unity Mitford: A Quest* by David Pryce-Jones. A gifted designer, Lancaster was best known for the *Daily Express* cartoons in which he fondly mocked a society woman named Maudie Littlehampton. Lancaster, a friend of Nancy's, provided the illustrations for *Noblesse Oblige* and for her collection of essays, *The Water Beetle*, about which Evelyn Waugh cattily remarked: 'I wish they had not had those coarse drawings.'

2 From a letter to Diana dated 9 March 1966, a month before Waugh's death.

3 In conversation with the author.

4 From *Unity Mitford: A Quest*.

5 In 1983, Diana wrote to Deborah that she had seen Bryan by chance in the House of Lords. When she called his name, he went over, kissed her and said: 'Which of you is it?'

6 Nancy to Betjeman, 14 June 1969.

7 These quotations are taken from 'Lytton Strachey and Carrington', one of the pen portraits in *Loved Ones* (Sidgwick & Jackson, 1985). Other subjects, wonderfully evoked by Diana, included Evelyn Waugh and Gerald Berners.

8 In an interview with *The Times*, 6 October 1967.

9 Diana wrote a lethal review of *Old Men Forget: The Autobiography of Duff Cooper* (1953) in *The European*. Later, in a letter to Deborah, she would suggest that Cooper's venomous outburst was partly provoked by the fact that his wife was having an affair with Mosley at the time.

10 From 'Less than Zero' on the album *My Aim is True* (1977). Costello later wrote that he conceived the song 'after seeing the despicable Oswald Mosley being interviewed on BBC television. The former

leader of the British Union of Fascists seemed unrepentant about his poisonous actions of the 1930s. The song was more of a slandering fantasy than a reasoned argument.'

11 Mosley had a good relationship with Benito Mussolini, and in April 1933 was invited to appear with the Italian leader on the balcony of the Palazzo Venezia in Rome. He always denied that Mussolini gave him money. A report in *The Times* (13 November 1936), for example, had Mosley firmly refuting the allegation that he received foreign subsidies, as claimed in the House of Commons by the then Home Secretary, Sir John Simon ('We demand that Sir John Simon produces his evidence in support of this statement'). Italian records, however, prove that the Home Secretary's information was correct. In her biography of Diana, Anne de Courcy writes that Mussolini subsidized British fascism between 1933 and 1935.

12 From *Beyond the Pale* by Nicholas Mosley (Secker & Warburg, 1983).

13 Ibid.

14 Review in *Books and Bookmen*, 1975, of *The Impact of Hitler: British Politics and British Policy 1933–1940* by M. Cowling.

15 The description comes from Elsie Corrigan, the maid at Mosley's country house, Savehay; she is quoted by Anne de Courcy in *Diana Mosley.*

16 An interesting reference to British fascism comes in Agatha Christie's 1940 novel *One, Two, Buckle My Shoe.* A young man, suspected of an attempted shooting, is described to Hercule Poirot by his girlfriend as 'one of those Imperial Shirts, you know – they march with banners and have a ridiculous salute'. The organizers of this movement, she suggests, 'just work up these poor young men – quite harmless ones like Frank – until they think they are doing something wonderful and patriotic'.

17 Dietrich Eckart's 'Bolshevism from Moses to Lenin' (1925).

18 James wrote this in his capacity as peerless television critic for *The Observer*, reviewing a 1976 episode of the BBC Television programme *Tonight*, in which Sir Oswald Mosley and David Pryce-Jones discussed the latter's new biography of Unity.

19 In *Nancy Mitford – A Portrait by her Sisters.*

20 From a 1978 review in *Books and Bookmen* of *Longford: A Biographical Portrait* by Mary Craig. In 1936, Lord Longford – then Frank Pakenham – had attended an infamous Mosley meeting in Oxford, where he was badly hurt (in his own account, 'someone stamped on my kidneys') and where Mosley's followers attacked hecklers with

'steel chairs and bicycle belts'. Diana, who was not unfriendly towards Longford, calmly questioned this version of events ('What is a bicycle belt?') and dismissed the disputatious undergraduates in the audience – who had sought to break up the meeting – as 'sillies'.

21 In his *Nancy Mitford: A Memoir* (Hamish Hamilton, 1975).

22 Quoted in *Unity Mitford: A Quest* by David Pryce-Jones.

23 From an unpublished manuscript, held with Jessica's papers in the Rare Books and MSS Department of Ohio State University.

24 By David Pryce-Jones in *Unity Mitford: A Quest*. Pryce-Jones found a copy of this novel, autographed and dated by Unity, and understandably thought it significant. Mary S. Lovell, on the other hand, regards Unity's choice of reading at this stage as incidental rather than formative.

25 According to Diana, in conversation with the author, none of Nancy's brothers-in-law liked her. 'Derek Jackson really hated her. And Kit – well.' (Although Mosley was known as Tom, Diana used the name Kit to differentiate him from her brother.) Diana did not mention Nancy's relationship with Andrew Devonshire, although the pair definitely quarrelled in 1967. As for Esmond Romilly: 'Of course [he] didn't like anyone, that's different.'

26 Weenie's son, Timothy Bailey, was quoted in *Unity Mitford: A Quest*: 'I took Aunt Sydney and Debo and Tom to one of Mosley's last big rallies in London.' This may be taken to refer to the major event at Earl's Court in 1939, which Tom certainly attended, but when Diana mentioned the rally in a letter to Deborah she made no allusion to her sister's presence (nor was there a sense that Deborah had ever been at *any* rally).

27 From *Nancy Mitford – A Portrait by her Sisters*.

28 In conversation with the author.

29 From *Prophesying Peace: Diaries 1944–45* (Chatto & Windus, 1977).

30 *The Times*, 26 April 1945.

31 In *Unity Mitford: A Quest*.

32 From Clive James's 1976 *Observer* review of *Tonight*.

33 Said by the porter of the fictional Oxford college, Shrewsbury, in Dorothy L. Sayers's *Gaudy Night*.

34 Quoted in *Unity Mitford: A Quest*.

35 Ibid.

36 Throughout most of the Second World War, Joyce broadcast an English-language radio programme, entitled *Germany Calling*, to audiences in Britain and the US. A vehicle for Nazi propaganda, and

widely known to be such, the programme was designed to sap the morale of the Allied war effort. It acquired a large audience, as it frequently gave the only available news from behind enemy lines. The 'Lord Haw-Haw' nickname referred to Joyce's bizarre, almost absurdly upper-class accent, and was designed to make him a figure of fun rather than danger. Joyce, who was American-born and raised in Ireland, became a naturalized German citizen. Nevertheless he was convicted of treason at the Old Bailey – on the grounds that he had begun broadcasting while in possession of a British passport – and was hanged in January 1946.

37 Noël Coward's intensely patriotic play, first produced in 1931, was filmed two years later. Its subject matter includes the British struggle against Germany in the First World War.

38 Diana made this point very firmly – and convincingly – in a 1975 review in *Books and Bookmen* of *Eva and Adolf* by G. Infield.

39 This was stated in a 2007 Channel 4 television documentary, *Hitler's British Girl*. The information came from the investigative reporter Martin Bright, who five years earlier had published an article in *The Observer*, suggesting that Unity's suicide attempt may have been faked in order to prevent her being questioned, as a possible traitor, on her return to Britain from Germany in 1940. Bright based his thesis upon newly declassified documents including the diary of the wartime head of MI5, Guy Liddell, who wrote: 'We had no evidence to support the press allegations that she was in a serious state of health and it might well be that she was brought in on a stretcher in order to avoid publicity and unpleasantness to her family.' In a subsequent article Bright made it clear that Liddell had been mistaken, and that Unity's injuries were genuine.

In December 2007, in a further article about Unity, Bright wrote in the *New Statesman* that he had been contacted by a woman whose aunt had run a maternity hospital in Oxford during the war, where (according to the informant's family) Unity had a baby that was given up for adoption. The father was said to be Hitler. Bright viewed the story with scepticism, although he spoke to an elderly woman who suggested that Unity *had* attended the hospital, albeit for treatment for a nervous breakdown; this claim was roundly refuted by Deborah. Further research by Channel 4 found a very large number of birth registrations relating to the hospital. Unsurprisingly, none bore the name 'Mitford'.

40 Cited in *Hitler's Table Talk*, ed. Hugh Trevor-Roper (Weidenfeld & Nicolson, 1953).

41 As quoted by Clive James in his 1976 *Observer* review of the television programme *Tonight*.
42 Jessica to Deborah, 26 October 1976.
43 Mary S. Lovell suggests this convincingly in *The Mitford Girls*.
44 From *A Fine Old Conflict* (Michael Joseph, 1977).
45 This particular calculation, based on intensive research but inevitably an approximation, was cited by Timothy Snyder in *The New York Review of Books*, 27 January 2011.
46 To Evelyn Waugh, 24 May 1960.
47 Letter dated 26 October 1976.
48 *Daily Telegraph*, 25 March 1960.
49 In the 1966 ABC Television programme, *Tempo*.
50 In an essay entitled 'Hitler's England: What if Germany had invaded Britain in May 1940?', published in *Virtual History: Alternatives and Counterfactuals*, ed. Niall Ferguson (Picador, 1997).
51 From *Wait for Me!*
52 As described in *Beyond Nab End* (Little, Brown, 2003) by William Woodruff, who lodged in East London in the 1930s. His landlady, he wrote, 'would have had to burn the house down' to defeat the bugs.
53 *The Times*, 31 March 1960.
54 In *Friends Apart* (MacGibbon & Kee, 1954).
55 Quoted in *Unity Mitford: A Quest*.
56 As described by David Pryce-Jones, ibid.
57 Ibid.

PART III

1 A desert-explorer and aviator, László (or Teddy) Almasy was the figure upon whom Michael Ondaatje loosely based the protagonist of his 1992 novel *The English Patient* (later an Oscar-winning film).
2 She expressed this view in a sad, alarmed letter to Violet Hammersley, 7 January 1940.
3 See p. 356, note 39.
4 In the 1966 interview for *Tempo*.
5 Quoted in *Unity Mitford: A Quest*.
6 Again, this was written to Violet Hammersley, 10 February 1940.
7 Diana said this to Mary S. Lovell in 2000; it is quoted in *The Mitford Girls*.
8 A reference to the Norwegian fascist politician Vidkun Quisling,

whose name has become synonymous with the concept of collaboration. Backed by the Nazis, he seized power in 1940 at the time of the German invasion of Norway. Between 1942 and 1945 he led a puppet government of the kind that Pétain headed in Vichy France, and that Mosley was suspected of wishing to lead in Britain. He was executed in late 1945.

9 A Tory minister, John Moore-Brabazon, was obliged to resign that year for saying that a struggle between Germany and Russia would have 'suited us'. Quite a lot of people agreed with him, nonetheless. As Andrew Roberts writes in the essay 'Hitler's England' in *Virtual History* (ed. Ferguson): 'It was the same stance as Henry Kissinger took during the Iran–Iraq War: "A pity they both can't lose".'

10 Said to *The Times*, 6 October 1967.

11 Part of Diana's evidence to the Advisory Committee that met on 2 October 1940, led by Norman Birkett KC (later a judge at the Nuremberg Trials). The committee was set up by the Home Office to establish whether those held under Regulation 18b should be released or kept in detention.

12 The letter was reproduced in Diana's diary for *The European*. Sydney had been responding coldly to a 'Comment' piece in *The Observer*, which stated that wartime political prisoners, such as Mosley, had been treated with admirable restraint in Britain.

13 From Andrew Roberts's essay 'Hitler's England' in *Virtual History* (ed. Ferguson).

14 From the 1975 review in *Books and Bookmen* of M. Cowling's *The Impact of Hitler*.

15 Bryan said this to Selina Hastings – Nancy's biographer – in reference to the meeting with Diana in 1983, when she hailed him in the House of Lords and he asked: 'Which of you is it?' Much mirth ensued, but it is interesting that Bryan, then aged seventy-eight, was still so aware of Diana's effect upon his emotions.

16 In a 1978 review in *Books and Bookmen* of *The Goebbels Diaries*, ed. Hugh Trevor-Roper.

17 In a 1969 review in *Books and Bookmen* of *Political Violence and Public Order* by Robert Benewick.

18 Martin Rynja, in the Editor's Note to *The Pursuit of Laughter* (Gibson Square, 2009).

19 In a letter dated 23 November 2000.

20 In a 1955 review in *The European* of *Against the Law* by Peter Wildeblood.

21 From the diary written for *The European*.

22 Ibid.
23 From *Diana Mosley* by Jan Dalley (Faber and Faber, 2000).
24 In conversation with the author, 2001.
25 In conversation with the author.
26 In *A Fine Old Conflict.*
27 In her 1966 television interview, Nancy said that David himself would write 'Occupation: Honourable'.
28 From *Hons and Rebels.*
29 Constancia's nickname was given before she was even born: when Jessica was pregnant, the vigorous movements of the baby led her friend, Virginia Durr, to joke that it was the kicking of the Democratic Donkey (symbol of the US Democratic Party). Jessica called her unborn baby 'the Donk' and the name – or its variant 'Dinky' – stuck.
30 From a series of interviews, given in 1988–9 to Robert Larsen, for the Berkeley Oral History Project of the Berkeley Historical Society.
31 Letter dated 28 June 1943.
32 From the interviews given to the Berkeley Historical Society.
33 Diana told this story in *Nancy Mitford – A Portrait by her Sisters.*
34 This description made its way into *The Pursuit of Love.*
35 Sir Joseph Paxton, who designed the Crystal Palace in London, had been made head gardener at Chatsworth by the 6th Duke of Devonshire in 1826.
36 Quoted in *Unity Mitford: A Quest.*
37 Ibid.
38 The three sisters wrote a letter to *The Times*, published 18 November 1976, in reference to David Pryce-Jones's book, 'which we do not accept as a true picture of her or of our family. We hold letters from a number of people quoted in the book saying that they have been misquoted. Some of these letters were supplied to the publisher before publication, but to little avail.'
39 To Deborah, 17 August 1976.
40 From a 1954 review in *The European* of *The Second World War*, vol. VI: *Triumph and Tragedy* by Winston Churchill. Diana states in the article that, owing to the war, the number of people living under Communism increased from 170 million to 770 million.
41 Letter dated 27 March 1944.

PART IV

1 Thus Nancy wrote to Diana in 1962, in reference to *Curzon: The End of an Epoch*, a life of Mosley's ex-father-in-law (by Leonard Mosley), published two years previously.
2 In conversation with the author.
3 In his autobiography *Formula One and Beyond* (Simon & Schuster, 2015), Max Mosley wrote of an apparent ambivalence in his father's political views, something that could properly be understood only by reading Sir Oswald's books. In an interview promoting the book, given in June 2015 to the BBC's Radio 5-Live, he stated that his father had abandoned fascism as it had been proved not to work.
4 In conversation with the author.
5 In a 1951 portrait for the 'Book of the Month Club News'.
6 Used in conversation with the author.
7 This too arose in conversation with the author: one of Diana's friends – a man in his eighties who had also known Nancy – came to tea and hissed the remark when Diana (who was extremely deaf) turned away to draw back a curtain.
8 In conversation with the author.
9 In conversation with the author.
10 In conversation with the author.
11 Letter dated 17 August 1980.
12 Deborah to Jessica, 8 July 1973.
13 Letter dated 11 January 1949.
14 To Evelyn Waugh, 24 May 1960.
15 To Deborah, 21 March 1976.
16 During the 1976 debate with David Pryce-Jones on BBC Television's *Tonight*.
17 In conversation with the author.
18 In the 1988–9 interviews for the Berkeley Historical Society.
19 Nancy wrote to Evelyn Waugh (2 September 1955) that Jessica's children had been told that Andrew Devonshire made his money by selling slaves. Deborah's alleged comment was: 'But if we had any slaves we wouldn't *sell* them for anything.' One would suspect typical Nancy exaggeration, were it not for the fact that the children had believed that they should bow to their grandmother, Sydney (see p. 306).
20 In the *Manchester Guardian*, Taylor wrote that Nancy had transported the Mitford family to the court of Versailles. This is generally regarded

as a great *aperçu* but in fact has only the air of being one; it is clear that Taylor brought his preconceptions to *Pompadour.* Beneath her gleaming smiles Nancy was hurt by his review, and wrote to the *Guardian* to alert them to an incorrect quotation within it, although she was also at pains to remain gracious: 'Please don't answer, or bother Mr. Taylor again. I suppose what I minded was getting such a beating from the M. Guardian which is the only English paper I ever see. However such beatings are always deserved and should be taken without complaint.'

21 Nancy was parodying the first words of the monologue of Don Diègue in Pierre Corneille's *Le Cid.*
22 See p. 354, note 20.
23 *My Life* (Nelson, 1968).

AFTERWARDS

1 From *Wait for Me!*
2 In conversation with Deborah Ross, the *Independent*, 12 November 2001.

SELECT BIBLIOGRAPHY

Harold Acton, *Memoir of Nancy Mitford,* Hamish Hamilton 1975.

Mark Amory, editor, *The Letters of Evelyn Waugh,* Weidenfeld & Nicolson 1980.

Jan Dalley, *Diana Mosley,* Faber and Faber 2000.

Anne de Courcy, *Diana Mosley,* Chatto & Windus 2003.

Deborah Devonshire, *Wait For Me!* John Murray 2010.

Counting My Chickens, Long Barn Books 2001.

Niall Ferguson, editor, *Virtual History: Alternatives and Counterfactuals,* Picador 1997.

Jonathan and Catherine Guinness, *The House of Mitford,* Hutchinson 1984.

Selina Hastings, *Nancy Mitford,* Hamish Hamilton 1985.

Bevis Hillier, *Young Betjeman,* John Murray 1988.

Betjeman: The Bonus of Laughter, John Murray 2004.

James Lees-Milne, *Another Self,* Hamish Hamilton 1970.

Ancestral Voices, John Murray 1975.

Ancient as the Hills, John Murray 1997.

Deep Romantic Chasm, John Murray 2000.

Mary S. Lovell, *The Mitford Girls,* Little Brown 2001.

Jessica Mitford, *Hons and Rebels,* Victor Gollancz 1960.

A Fine Old Conflict, Michael Joseph 1977.

Nancy Mitford, *Highland Fling,* Thornton Butterworth 1931.

Christmas Pudding, Thornton Butterworth 1932.

Wigs on the Green, Thornton Butterworth 1935.

Pigeon Pie, Hamish Hamilton 1940.

The Pursuit of Love, Hamish Hamilton 1945.

Love in a Cold Climate, Hamish Hamilton 1949.

The Blessing, Hamish Hamilton 1951.
Madame de Pompadour, Hamish Hamilton 1954.
Noblesse Oblige, Hamish Hamilton 1956.
Don't Tell Alfred, Hamish Hamilton 1960.
The Water Beetle, Hamish Hamilton 1962.
Charlotte Mosley, editor, *A Talent to Annoy: Essays, Journalism and Reviews by Nancy Mitford*, Hamish Hamilton 1986.
Love from Nancy: The Letters of Nancy Mitford, Hodder and Stoughton 1993.
Letters of Nancy Mitford and Evelyn Waugh, Hodder and Stoughton 1996.
The Mitfords: Letters Between Six Sisters, Fourth Estate 2007.
Diana Mosley, *A Life of Contrasts*, Hamish Hamilton 1977.
Loved Ones, Sidgwick & Jackson 1980.
Nicholas Mosley, *The Rules of the Game*, Secker & Warburg 1982.
Beyond the Pale, Secker & Warburg 1983.
Sir Oswald Mosley, *My Life*, Nelson 1970.
David Pryce-Jones, *Unity Mitford: A Quest*, Weidenfeld & Nicolson 1976.
Martin Pugh, *We Danced All Night: A Social History of Britain Between the Wars*, The Bodley Head 2008.
Martin Rynja, editor, *The Pursuit of Laughter – Diana Mosley*, Gibson Square 2009.

ACKNOWLEDGEMENTS

This analysis of the Mitford 'phenomenon' is immensely indebted to several books that have been written about the sisters. In particular I must acknowledge four brilliant biographies: Mary S. Lovell's *The Mitford Girls,* David Pryce-Jones's *Unity Mitford: A Quest*, Selina Hastings's *Nancy Mitford* and Anne de Courcy's *Diana Mosley.* I am hugely indebted to Charlotte Mosley, editor of the glorious Mitford correspondence, without which this book could not have been written. I should also like to acknowledge *The Pursuit of Laughter,* edited by Martin Rynja, a fascinating collection of the writings of Diana Mosley.

I remain grateful to Diana Mosley and Deborah Devonshire, to whom I spoke when they were the last surviving Mitford girls. These were encounters that I shall always treasure. It was also a great pleasure to meet Diana's son, the late Alexander Mosley.

My thanks to Rogers, Coleridge and White, which handles the estates of Nancy Mitford and Deborah Devonshire; I am deeply grateful to Gill Coleridge and Rosie Price, who could not have been more helpful in dealing with my request for permissions.

I give my heartfelt thanks to Anthony Cheetham, who asked me to write this book; to all at Head of Zeus, especially Richard Milbank, Georgina Blackwell and Claire Nozières; and to my wonderful agent, Georgina Capel.

Lastly I extend gratitude to those who have generously granted permission for the use of copyright material, as follows:

The Estates of Nancy Mitford and Deborah Devonshire, for quotations from Nancy's novels, journalism and letters.

The Estate of Deborah Devonshire, for quotations from Deborah's writings.

Charlotte Mosley and the Estate of Diana Mosley, for quotations from Diana's journalism and letters, together with letters from Lady Redesdale.

Benjamin D. Weber, agent for Jessica Mitford Heirs, for quotations from Jessica's writings.

The Hon. Rosaleen Mulji for quotations from letters written by her father, Bryan Guinness.

Hannah Goodman and the Orion Publishing Group, for quotations from *Unity Mitford: A Quest, The Letters of Evelyn Waugh* and *Hons and Rebels.*

Jeanine Castello-Lin and Tonya Staros, Co-Presidents of the Berkeley Historical Society, for quotations from interviews with Robert Treuhaft conducted by Robert Larson.

David Higham Associates, for quotations from the writings of James Lee-Milne.

Attempts have been made to obtain permission for all the material used in this book. I apologize for any unforeseen omissions, and very much hope that any copyright holder will contact my publisher in order that these may be rectified in future editions.

INDEX

PICTURE ACKNOWLEDGEMENTS

Page 1: Lord and Lady Redesdale (© *Devonshire Collection, Chatsworth. Reproduced with kind permission by Chatsworth Settlement Trustees*); Bertie Mitford (*Mary Evans Picture Library*); Thomas Bowles (*Beresford/Getty Images*)

Pages 2–3: Nancy (© *National Portrait Gallery*); Pamela (© *National Portrait Gallery*); Diana (*Popperfoto/Getty Images*); Unity (*Illustrated London News Ltd/Mary Evans Picture Library*); Jessica (*Illustrated London News Ltd/Mary Evans Picture Library*); Deborah (© *National Portrait Gallery*)

Page 4: Batsford Park (© *foto-zone/Alamy*); Asthall Manor (*Country Life Picture Library*)

Page 5: Swinbrook House (*Tim Graham/Getty Images*); Unity and Jessica (*Getty Images/Evening Standard*)

Page 6: Bryan Guinness and Diana (*Illustrated London News Ltd/Mary Evans Picture Library*); Diana and Nancy (*Illustrated London News Ltd/Mary Evans Picture Library*)

Page 7: Nancy on the cover of *The Tatler* (*Illustrated London News Ltd/Mary Evans Picture Library*)

Page 8: Oswald Mosley (*Daily Herald Archive; Mary Evans Picture Library*); Unity in Munich (*Mary Evans/Sueddeutsche Zeitung Photo*)

Page 9: Deborah at a point-to-point (*Central Press/Getty Images*); Unity in 1938 (*Keystone/Hulton Archive/Getty Images*)

Page 10: *Partout* article (*Roger-Viollet/Topfoto*); Unity returns to Britain (*Fred Ramage/Stringer/Getty Images*)

Page 11: Esmond Romilly and Jessica (*Keystone/Hulton Archive/Getty Images*)

Page 12: Deborah on her wedding day (*Keystone/Hulton Archive/Getty Images*)

Page 13: Diana and Oswald Mosley under house arrest (*Popperfoto/Getty Images*); Unity's cottage (*Laura Thompson*)
Page 14: Nancy in Paris (*Philippe Le Tellier/Paris Match/Getty Images*)
Page 15: Deborah in 1954 (*Evening Standard/Hulton Archive/Getty Images*); Robert Treuhaft and Jessica (*Jon Brenneis/The LIFE Images Collection/Getty Images*)
Page 16: Swinbrook churchyard (*Laura Thompson*); The Mitford children (*Illustrated London News Ltd/Bridgeman Images*)